Political Parties and Democracy

Endorsements for *Political Parties and Democracy*
(See back cover for additional endorsements)

"This monumental work consists of five volumes with 46 chapters each devoted to the parties of a different nation. Many of the party systems included in the volumes are studied here for the first time in a systematic way with unprecedented levels of knowledge and competence by authors who are native to the respective countries. The chapters are not limited to summary descriptions of the systems they study, but present extremely interesting and original insights. This is crucial for the usefulness and scientific relevance of the chapters dedicated to the more established American, European and, in general, Western democracies' party systems, whose authors manage to present novel views of extensively researched subject areas. Saying that with this work Kay Lawson has set new standards for editorship in the field of political science would be an obvious understatement. *Political Parties and Democracy* is the result of an impressive project that will greatly benefit the scientific community. I am sure that the five volumes it has produced will become fundamental references for the field of political party studies and will take a very prominent place in every party expert's library."

Luciano Bardi
Professor of Political Science, University of Pisa

"This welcome and remarkable collection of original essays covers assessments of political parties in an unusually broad range of countries. Taking into account the critical importance of parties for the operation of democracy, juxtaposed with their weaknesses both as democratic organizations and as agents of state democracy, results in clear and honest assessments of the state of parties today. Bickerton on Canada and Dwyre on the U.S. represent this well-reasoned approach with the confidence that comes from a thorough understanding of their own country's situation."

Mildred A. Schwartz
Professor Emerita at University of Illinois and Visiting Scholar,
New York University

"These volumes provide a valuable in-depth and up-to-date analysis of the state of political parties across five continents, written by country experts, and will be an important source for scholars interested in the comparative study of political parties."

Lars Svåsand
Professor of Comparative Politics, University of Bergen, Norway

"Kay Lawson's *Political Parties and Democracy* is a tremendous success in giving readers the most recent information and insights about political parties around the globe. The set includes not only excellent contributions on the party systems that exemplify strong democratic regimes like the United States and the United Kingdom, but careful insights on volatile party systems in newer democracies such as Poland, and on systems still transitioning to democratic rule in places as diverse as Kenya and Morocco. The universal challenges to parties as linkage mechanisms in the early 20th century are everywhere apparent."

Robin Kolodny
Associate Professor of Political Science, Temple University

Political Parties and Democracy

Five Volumes
Kay Lawson, General Editor

Volume I: The Americas
Kay Lawson and Jorge Lanzaro, Volume Editors

Volume II: Europe
Kay Lawson, Volume Editor

Volume III: Post-Soviet and Asian Political Parties
Baogang He, Anatoly Kulik, and Kay Lawson,
Volume Editors

Volume IV: Africa and Oceania
Luc Sindjoun, Marian Simms, and Kay Lawson,
Volume Editors

Volume V: The Arab World
Saad Eddin Ibrahim and Kay Lawson, Volume Editors

Political Parties in Context
Kay Lawson, Series Editor

Political Parties and Democracy

General Editor, Kay Lawson

Volume III: Post-Soviet and Asian Political Parties

BAOGANG HE, ANATOLY KULIK, AND
KAY LAWSON,
VOLUME EDITORS

Political Parties in Context
Kay Lawson, Series Editor

 PRAEGER

AN IMPRINT OF ABC-CLIO, LLC
Santa Barbara, California • Denver, Colorado • Oxford, England

Library of Congress Cataloging-in-Publication Data

Political parties and democracy / Kay Lawson, set editor.
    p. cm.—(Political parties in context series)
    Includes bibliographical references and index.
    ISBN 978-0-275-98706-0 (hard copy : alk. paper)—ISBN 978-0-313-08349-5 (ebook)—ISBN 978-0-313-38314-4 (vol. 1 hard copy)—ISBN 978-0-313-38315-1 (vol. 1 ebook)—ISBN 978-0-313-38316-8 (vol. 2 hard copy)—ISBN 978-0-313-38317-5 (vol. 2 ebook)—ISBN 978-0-313-38060-0 (vol. 3 hard copy)—ISBN 978-0-313-38061-7 (vol. 3 ebook)—ISBN 978-0-313-35302-4 (vol. 4 hard copy)—ISBN 978-0-313-35303-1 (vol. 4 ebook)—ISBN 978-0-275-97082-6 (vol. 5 hard copy)—ISBN 978-0-313-08295-5 (vol. 5 ebook) 1. Political parties. 2. Democracy. I. Lawson, Kay.
    JF2051.P5678 2010
    324.2—dc22   2009047965

ISBN: 978-0-275-98706-0 (set)
EISBN: 978-0-313-08349-5 (set)

14 13 12 11 10   1 2 3 4 5

This book is also available on the World Wide Web as an eBook.
Visit www.abc-clio.com for details.

Praeger
An Imprint of ABC-CLIO, LLC

ABC-CLIO, LLC
130 Cremona Drive, P.O. Box 1911
Santa Barbara, California 93116-1911

This book is printed on acid-free paper ∞

Manufactured in the United States of America

Contents

Political Parties and Democracy: Three Stages of Power

Kay Lawson

Political Parties and Democracy consists of five volumes with 46 chapters, each devoted to the parties of a different nation. The first volume is dedicated to the Americas: Canada and the United States for North America, and Argentina, Bolivia, Brazil, Chile, Mexico, Peru, and Uruguay for Central and South America. Volume II is on European parties: Denmark, France, Germany, Italy, Norway, Spain, and the United Kingdom in the West, and the Czech Republic, Hungary, and Poland in the East. Volume III begins with four chapters on the parties of the post-Soviet nations of Georgia, Moldova, Russia, and Ukraine and continues with the parties of five Asian nations: China, India, Japan, Malaysia, and South Korea. Parties in Africa and Oceania are the subject of Volume IV: Cameroon, Kenya, Namibia, Nigeria, and South Africa, followed by Australia, Fiji, New Zealand, Samoa, and the Solomon Islands. Finally, Volume V is devoted first and foremost to the Arab world, beginning with the parties of Algeria, Egypt, Lebanon, Mauritania, and Morocco and continuing with the parties of two neighboring states in which Arab politics play an important role: Israel and Turkey. All authors are themselves indigenous to the nation they write about. Indigenous[1] co-editors, whose essays introduce each section, have helped recruit the authors and guide the development of their chapters; final editing has been my responsibility as general editor, and the final volume concludes with my Conclusion to the Set.

The purpose of each chapter is to examine the relationship between political parties and democracy, providing the necessary historical, socio-economic, and institutional context as well as the details of contemporary political tensions between the two. To understand this relationship requires a serious effort to understand as well the basic nature of the state. That nature shapes the work of the parties. Whatever mission they give themselves, it is control of the state that they seek. Without that power, programs are mere words on paper or in cyberspace.

Parties are expected to provide the key building blocks of democracy by forming a strong link between citizens and the state. It is a challenge fledging parties commonly accept, because promising to establish a government in keeping with the will of the people is the best way to achieve adequate support and wrest power away from nondemocratic leadership. Even today's most democratic and established parties trace their roots to that primeval calculation and the struggle it entails. Many of the parties studied here are still trapped in that early stage.

Some of the parties formed to wage the battle for democracy have accepted defeat, at least for now, and live on only in puppet-like roles that permit them to share the perquisites but not the substance of power. Others have only recently formed organizations strong enough to have led the way forward from dictatorship and are still working out the new relationship. They came to power waving the banners of democracy, but they are not necessarily bound—or able—to obey its precepts once in power. In some cases, the move to democratic governance has been short-lived and military, religious, or ethnic autocracy has retaken control.

Still other parties, such as the ones scholars in the West have studied hardest and longest, have thrived for many years as more or less genuine agencies of democracy, but are now gradually but perceptibly moving forward to a third stage of power. Serious links to the populace no longer seem to be necessary, as the central organization becomes expert at using the tools of political marketing and the victorious party leaders adopt policies that satisfy their most powerful supporters. Moving steadily away from participatory linkage, parties tend to maintain a degree of responsive linkage, but the answer to the question of to whom they are responsive is not necessarily a reassuringly democratic one.

In short, the development of political parties over the past century is the story of three stages in the pursuit of power: liberation, democratization, and dedemocratization. In every volume of *Political Parties and Democracy* the reader will find parties at all three stages. Sometimes the story of liberation will be part of the recent history that must be understood; in other chapters the unfinished quest for freedom is the only story that can yet be told. Sometimes the tale of post-liberation democratization is very much "a work in progress" (and perhaps a dubious one). Sometimes dedemocratization takes the form of accepting failure under impossible circumstances after the first joys of liberation have been tasted, and sometimes it is a more deliberate effort to escape the bounds of what still hungry leaders consider a too successful democratization. Understanding parties—and their relationship with democracy—means understanding the stage of power their leadership has reached.

Is democracy always dependent on parties, or are there other agencies capable of forcing governments to act on behalf of the entire demos? Perhaps mass movements working via the Internet can be used to hasten liberation, fine tune democratization, and even to forestall dedemocratization. Possibly in the future such movements will not only help the parties take control of the state, but then tame them to live in comfortable league with democracy, offering party leaders sufficient rewards for staying in power democratically and followers better designed instruments for reasonable but effective participation.

However, party democracy, cybertized, is still no more than an interesting dream, and one that goes well beyond the purview of these studies. What one can find in *Political Parties and Democracy* is the actual state of the play of the game.

PART I

Post-Soviet Parties

Introduction to *Political Parties and Democracy: Part I: Post-Soviet Parties*

Anatoly Kulik

The attempts undertaken by Mikhail Gorbachev to democratize the Soviet Union in the mid-1980s to early 1990s undermined the power of the Communist Party of the Soviet Union (CPSU). In March 1990 an amendment to the Constitution deprived the CPSU of its dominant position in the state and society, and in October 1990, Gorbachev signed a law that allowed emerging parties to register, thus opening the way for them to enter institutionalized politics.

By that time the relaxation of censorship was contributing to the awakening of suppressed nationalist and anti-Russian feelings throughout the USSR and a new aspiration for national sovereignty, beginning in the Baltics, but soon extending to Georgia, Ukraine, and the other Soviet republics as well. The failed coup d'état launched in August 1991 by the hardliners in the Soviet leadership to remove Gorbachev from power and prevent the signing of the new union treaty brought about the final collapse of the Soviet Union. All the former Soviet republics declared their independence, including Ukraine, Moldova, Georgia, and Russia itself. Gorbachev was urged to resign on December 25, and the Soviet Union was formally dissolved the next day.

This day marked the beginning of the post-Soviet political history of newly independent states (NIS). All of them acclaimed the decay of the Soviet Union as a birth of "national revival" and declared themselves at once to be democratic, social, law-based states, where human rights and freedoms were guaranteed by constitutions, and political parties were accepted as the indispensable attributes of their political systems.

The emergence of the NIS was enthusiastically perceived by Western politicians and promoters of democracy as a component part of the "third wave" of democracy.

However, what the NIS had achieved was not yet democracy, but simply liberation from the control of the Kremlin. At the same time most of the former national elites managed to preserve and even to reinforce their own positions. The denunciation of the Soviet past in favor of declared democracy was evidently the only option to legitimize their coming to power. But as Thomas Carothers argues, "the core impulses and interests of power holders—such as locking in access to power and resources as quickly as possible—ran directly contrary to what democracy building would have required."[1]

The reasons for such a development can be found in the Soviet institutional and structural legacy, a legacy that meant the trajectory of post-Soviet political transformation toward democratic consolidation would be far from linear. Furthermore, the diversity of political, economic, and social conditions, ethnoterritorial conflicts, and the geopolitical location of former Soviet republics, as well as differences within ruling elites, created many differences in the paths followed in the era of post-Soviet evolution and many discrepancies in political development from republic to republic.

In the analytic framework of the transition paradigm, political parties are assumed to be the main contributor to democratic consolidation through strengthening links between the political elite and society, deepening the political participation of the population and ensuring the democratic accountability of government. Now that a rather considerable time has elapsed since the emergence of the NIS, we are able to look at the role parties have played and are playing in political transformation, and especially at the relationships between parties and democratic governance in these countries. The purpose of this section of Volume III of *Political Parties and Democracy* is to present contemporary scholarship on parties and democracy in Georgia, Moldova, Russia, and Ukraine—four NIS in the western (some would say European or, for Russia, Euro-Asian) part of post-Soviet space. Whereas the Baltic States have become members of the European Union since 2004 and their parties are evolving in the mainstream of European politics, political processes in the part of post-Soviet space treated here may be said to be both more complicated and less researched. Our work here continues that began in 2005 in *Political Parties in Post-Soviet Space: Russia, Belarus, Ukraine, Moldova and the Baltics* in the Praeger series "Political Parties in Context" under the general editorship of Kay Lawson.[2]

The authors of these four country chapters are established political scientists affiliated with reputable academic or nonpartisan research institutions, all citizens and residents of their respective nations. They are thus included observers of political development in the countries they are writing about (as are all the authors in the five volumes of *Political Parties and Democracy*). The advantage of such a position is that they can notice and interpret details, hidden causes, and relationships that are often beyond the capacities of an outside observer. They all try to offer an impartial interpretation of development under discussion. If some of the contributors' personal judgments do not coincide, they nonetheless are in agreement in their shared desire to see their countries become democratic.

Democracy is one of the most complicated, permanently changing, and constantly debated concepts. However, its multidimensionality gives contributors to this volume the opportunity to take different dimensions of democracy as their own starting points in studying the relationship between parties and democracy in their own country. At the same time, when addressing a particular painful problem in the development of democracy in one country, the contributors are able to place their discussions in context—that is, in the holistic framework of a single national setting—and thereby interpret properly the meaning of every event. Thus although it may be that the introduction of the proportional system of voting in Ukraine ensured the preservation of political competition, in the Russian setting that same system was initiated and effectively employed by a powerful leadership to accomplish the transition to a fully noncompetitive quasi-party system.

The author of the chapter on the political parties of Georgia, George Tarkhan-Mouravi, codirector of the Institute of the Social Policy, has chosen the concept of freedom of association to guide his work. He concludes that democracy in Georgia still fails to ensure fair political competition, protect the supremacy of law, provide effective distribution of power between different branches of governance, or establish a clear line between the ruling party and either the state or business. He notes that mass movements and "botanical revolutions" such as in Georgia tend to reinvigorate the same authoritarianism against which they were directed. The current state of affairs within the political parties creates a "democracy" that demonstrates that all the democratic institutions may be in place, but that so far they have very little democratic content.

The author of the Moldova chapter, Igor Botan, executive director of the Association of Participatory Democracy, emphasizes institutionalization of freedom as one of the crucial dimensions of democracy. As he mentions, most Moldovan citizens have received freedom and the independence of the state as a gift and, having no democratic experience, have not actually known what to do with them. With social and material conditions dramatically worsening and interethnic tensions on the rise, they simply began to miss the lost paradise of "preindependence." Democratization actually consisted in borrowing formal democratic institutions assisted by international bodies such as the Council of

Europe and the Organization for Security and Co-operation in Europe. However, these institutions were filled with domestic content and had no immediate effect beyond building "imitative" democracy. Nevertheless, parties have played an important role in the evolution of Moldovan democracy, opposing more than once attempts by authorities to consolidate their power by following the example of Russia. The Moldovan democracy is not a clear emanation of conscious activity, but rather a phenomenon produced by the competition of parties unable to take control over the whole authority or control it for a limited term as stipulated in the constitution.

In the chapter on Russian parties, Anatoly Kulik, senior research fellow of the Institute of Scientific Information in Social Sciences, Russian Academy of Sciences, emphasizes the fundamental importance of public political competition and takes it as a point of departure. It is argued there that after Russia achieved sovereignty and adopted its new constitution in 1993 the entire process of shaping parties by the ruling regime aimed at converting them into an instrument that would secure its own survival and self-reproduction. Not having faced the resistance of the feeble and dissociated civic society, the authoritarian-bureaucratic regime transformed parties into a tool that blocked all possibility of open political competition. However, the intended ambitious goals of authoritarian modernization of Russia to which the political rights of the citizens and the free competition of political parties were sacrificed have not been approached, but have rather moved farther away. The closed nature of the political system with its omnipotent bureaucracy turned feckless when faced with new challenges.

Andrey A. Meleshevych, Dean of the School of Law, National University of Kyiv-Mohyla Academy (Ukraine), stresses the question of accountability of rulers to citizens in Ukraine. He is rather more optimistic than the other contributors regarding the prospects for parties to play a meaningful role in the process of democratization. Drawing from Schumpeter's definition of democracy as a competitive struggle of elites for the people's vote, Meleshevych argues that the Orange Revolution made its important contribution to the process of institutionalizing and legitimizing free and fair elections in Ukraine as the exclusive mechanism for obtaining state power. Redistribution of political powers from the office of the president to parliament and the prime minister has strengthened the role of political parties in government formation and enhances the accountability of party members of a ruling coalition. However, these developments do not mean that Ukraine has established a highly institutionalized party system. A never-ending stalemate between branches of government, lack of stable electoral bases, the strong charismatic nature of parties and personal animosity between party leaders, and deeply rooted suspicions among party elites prevent parties from reaching a compromise and developing coherent and effective policies even in the cases of national emergencies. These are just some of the factors that undermine the legitimacy of political parties in Ukrainian society. In a public opinion poll in December 2008, 80% of respondents said they mistrust political parties as an institution and less than 1% had complete trust in them. Greater visibility of parties, and, as a result, their greater accountability, seems to cause widespread and long-lasting distrust. The sooner parties learn this lesson and change their behavior accordingly, the quicker they will gain credibility among the electorate and the greater the chance that democracy will survive in Ukraine.

Although the contributors to this volume have chosen different aspects of democracy to start with, all of them draw attention to the impact of political competition. As Meleshevych observes, competing parties tend to watch one another carefully, on the alert that a rival will not misuse state "administrative" resources for electoral purposes and thereby upset the balance of powers. Where political elites have managed to preserve political competition opposing authoritarian tendencies, as in Moldova and Ukraine, prospects for democratic development remain alive.

This assumption is confirmed with the most recent data of the Economist Intelligence Unit's Index of Democracy 2008. Ukraine and Moldova are classified as "flawed democracies" and placed 53rd and 62nd, respectively, whereas Georgia and Russia are tagged as "hybrid regimes" and given 104th and 107th place, respectively, in the list of 167 countries that are covered.[3]

As can be seen from the following chapters, parties in this part of the world are playing different roles in fostering or impeding democratic development depending on the particular interplay of numerous endogenous and exogenous factors of the national setting.

Among such differences we find geopolitical contradictions between Russia and the Euro-Atlantic communities in bordering countries. The politics of promoting democracy, practiced by the Euro-Atlantic communities in these countries, accompanied by NATO's expansion to the border of Russia, is judged by Russia's leadership as anti-Russian. Claiming these countries to be a zone of its national interests, Russia's government is trying to support pro-Russian parties and to thereby counter the pro-western outlook, which is perceived as anti-Russian. This confrontation became evident during the Orange Revolution in Ukraine when Russia was trying to support Viktor Yanukovich in his struggle for the presidency, whereas Euro-Atlantic communities vigorously promoted pro-western Viktor Yushchenko.[4]

It seems that parties per se are far from being irrefutably agents of democratization in the NIS. They are rather structures borrowed from Western democratic settings that national elites adapted to suit their own struggles for power. Their activities may bring about either democratic consolidation or reconsolidation of authoritarian regimes. Clearly the most efficient methodological approach in investigating links between parties and democracy is to take them as variables depending on the variety of external and internal factors within the holistic, institutional, and structural framework of their own nations. Broad generalizations based on statistical averages or correlations may be suggestive but are unlikely ever to do a satisfactory job of fully explaining what role parties play in any actual nation.

The chapters that follow tell a great deal about complicated interrelationships among parties, elites, common people, and leaders in political processes that are being shaped by particular national settings weighed down by the Soviet legacy and the personal qualities of contemporary leaders.

These few introductory words do not aim to do justice to the ideas presented by contributors in the individual country chapters. Rather it is an invitation for readers to a deliberative perusal.

CHAPTER 1

The Stumbling Gait of Pluralist Democracy and Political Parties in Georgia

George Tarkhan-Mouravi

INTRODUCTION

The majority of the contemporary political parties in Georgia are relatively newly created and still immature, despite the claims of some to a certain historical ancestry. The oldest of the movements active today emerged in the 1970s as dissident groups, united by the aims of opposing the communist ideology and protecting national unity and cultural identity of Georgians.

The heritage of the Soviet past in the form of underdeveloped democratic institutions and political culture, along with the scars caused by civil wars and ethnoterritorial conflicts, still continues to haunt political processes and party building, narrowing the space for political discourse. The legacy of the decades of totalitarian rule does not wane quickly. Democracy in Georgia still fails to draw a line between the state and the ruling party, to enjoy fair political competition among different parties, effective distribution of power between different branches of governance, and the supremacy of law. Against the background of extremely complex and tumultuous years of the past two decades, Georgia's political parties demonstrate some general patterns characteristic for post-Soviet societies: lack of clear ideology, values, vision, or strategy; excessive role of leaders' personalities; heightened degree of political opportunism and populism; and lack of internal democracy. Development of mature, efficient political parties remains the key to functional and sustainable democratic governance in Georgia.

POLITICAL STRUGGLE AND PARTIES IN GEORGIA'S MODERN HISTORY

The modern political history of Georgia began when, early in the 19th century, Georgia was incorporated into the vast Russian Empire. Frequent mishandling of sensitive issues and local traditions by the Russian administration caused uprisings throughout the 19th century, but with the appointment of the first viceroy in the Caucasus, Mikhail Vorontsov (1845–1854),[1] Georgia began to integrate more rapidly into the Russian political fabric. At the same time, a nationalist political movement emerged, headed by the prominent poet and public figure Ilia Chavchavadze and aimed at protecting the cultural identity of Georgians and achieving greater autonomy.[2] The 1860s were also marked by the emancipation of the serfs in Georgia. Notwithstanding significant resistance from the local nobility, on October 13, 1864, Russian emperor Alexander II signed the decree abolishing serfdom in Tiflis *gubernia*, three years later than in central Russia. Subsequently, peasants were also freed in the rest of Georgia, in a rather painful process that led to further social stratification and economic difficulties, as both liberated peasants and the petty nobility were left with reduced income base, while the bourgeoisie was getting richer.

Rapid social change created a particularly favorable environment for the development of socialist ideas.[3] The first Marxist group, Mesami Dasi, was created in 1892. Seven years later the Tiflis committee of the All-Russian Social Democratic Labor Party was formed, dominated by a Menshevik, legalist wing led by Noe Jordania. Georgian Mensheviks, who gained popularity especially during the 1905 revolution, started to play an important role at the all-Russian level. In Georgia as elsewhere, Mensheviks were fervently opposed by Bolsheviks, among whom Iosif Jughashvili (Stalin) gradually acquired significant influence.

When, in November 1917, the Bolsheviks seized power in Petrograd, leading political forces in the Transcaucasus responded by creating an executive body, the Transcaucasian Commissariat. The Commissariat, headed by a Georgian Menshevik Eugeni Gegechkori, initially intended to keep its function only until the All-Russian Constituent Assembly would be convened in Petrograd. However, after the Bolsheviks dissolved the latter on January 6, 1918, a regional legislature—the Seim—was created in February 1918 out of the already elected deputies of the Constituent Assembly. The leading role was played by Georgian Mensheviks (32 members out of 125), Armenian Dashnaks (27) and Azeri Musavatists (30), as well as Esers (Socialist-Revolutionaries, 19), with just a few Bolsheviks (4). The remaining 12 seats were held by representatives of smaller political groups (4, Menshevik "Humetists"; 3, Socialist-Federalists; 3, Bloc of Russia's Muslim Socialists;

2, Constitutional Democrats [Kadets]).[4] The speaker of the Seim was Georgian Menshevik Nikolay Chkheidze.

An independent Transcaucasian Democratic Federative Republic (TDFR) was proclaimed by the Seim on April 22, 1918. Another Georgian Menshevik—Akaki Chkhenkeli—became the head of the executive provisional government. However, soon disagreements between Armenians, Azeris, and Georgians put an end to the federation. On May 26, the Georgian Democratic Republic declared its independence. A few days later, in June 1918, the Georgian Soviet was dissolved and Menshevik leader Noe Jordania became the chairman of the government, which lasted less than three years.[5]

During 1920, the geopolitical situation changed dramatically as civil war in Russia came to an end. Russia signed a peace treaty with Georgia on May 7, 1920, which appeared to be just a tactical move. On February 16, 1921, a Revolutionary Committee was formed by the Bolsheviks in Georgia, and a few days later Russia's Red Army entered Georgia. On May 21, Georgia's new Bolshevik government signed a treaty with the Russian Soviet Federative Socialist Republic, and Georgia became a Soviet Socialist Republic, subsequently a constituent part of the Transcaucasian Federation.[6]

Most of the leading Mensheviks who remained in the country were arrested in January 1922. A Menshevik congress was held in August 1923, and under strong pressure delegates decided to disband the party. Though officially dismissed, the Menshevik Party shifted to clandestine operation and started preparing an anticommunist revolt. Five main opposition parties joined the Mensheviks in their anti-Bolshevik stance, creating in the beginning of May 1922 the Committee for Georgia's Independence.

Uprisings in Guria, Kakheti, and Svaneti in 1922–1923 were brutally suppressed. In February 1923, the Extraordinary Commission (CheKa, Chrezvychaynaya Kommissia) arrested and shot leading conspirators. Nevertheless, a rebellion started on August 28, 1924, but its initial success was short-lived and followed by widespread and bloody executions.

During the last half of the 1920s, the political atmosphere temporarily eased. Repressions in Georgia increased again after 1931, when Lavrenti Beria became First Secretary of the Transcaucasian Committee of the Communist Party. On December 5, 1936, the new (Stalin) Constitution was adopted in Moscow. The Transcaucasian Federation was dissolved, and Georgia became a "sovereign" Union Republic.

On June 22, 1941, Germany invaded the Soviet Union. Shortly after the Soviet army achieved its first military successes, Stalin ordered the deportation of entire peoples for alleged treason. In late 1944, some 90,000 Muslims from southern Georgian Meskheti province were accused of pro-Turkish sentiments and deported overnight to Central Asia.[7]

Georgian emigration concentrated mostly in Germany and France. The rise of Nazi Germany gave Georgian exiles an opportunity to pay back the Soviets, and some of them joined the Fascist movement. A Georgian Fascist Front was formed, the nucleus of which consisted of a nationalist organization named Tetri Giorgi.

After the end of World War II, Stalin became weary of Beria's control over Transcaucasus and decided to restrict his powers there.[8] However, Stalin's death in March 1953 changed the distribution of power in Kremlin. Georgian leadership was immediately reshuffled by Beria, now the leading political figure. However, he soon fell victim to a conspiracy himself.

At a closed session of the 20th Congress of the Communist Party of the Soviet Union, held on February 25, 1956, Nikita Khrushchev devoted his speech to uncovering the crimes of Stalin and his "cult of personality." Many Georgians, however, were unhappy with the sudden criticism of the iconic figure of Stalin, an ethnic Georgian; in March 1956, students celebrating the anniversary of Stalin's birth were brutally dispersed, causing numerous casualties.

The period of the 1960s was not rich with spectacular events, but it was important for the formation of new mass consciousness. Vasili Mzhavanadze's uninterrupted 19-year rule (1953–1972) as First Secretary of the Communist Party of Georgia (CPG) was characterized by an extensive parallel economy and criminalization of the society, but also by the growth of nationalist sentiments among intelligentsia. In 1972, then republican Minister of Internal Affairs Eduard Shevardnadze succeeded Mzhavanadze as the leader of the CPG as a result of complex intrigue.

The new dissident movement started in Georgia in the early 1970s with the dissemination of *samizdat* literature and calls for defending national identity, cultural, and natural heritage, but also democratic and liberal values. In April 1977, a young philologist dissident Zviad Gamsakhurdia was arrested and accused of anti-Soviet activities. A recording of Gamsakhurdia's recantation was broadcast on television, representing an important victory for the Secret Service and a temporary reverse for emerging Georgian dissent.

After a new Soviet constitution was adopted in October 1977, the Supreme Soviet of Georgia considered a draft republican constitution; in contrast to the Constitution of 1937, however, Georgian was declared to no longer be the state language. Reacting to the demonstration of protest during the parliamentary session of April 14, 1978, Shevardnadze contacted central authorities and obtained permission from the Kremlin to reamend the Constitution. In 1982, Leonid Brezhnev died in Moscow. After two brief periods of rule by Yuri Andropov and Konstantin Chernenko, the dramatic era of final metamorphosis started in the Soviet Union that directly influenced Georgia's political fate.

PARTIES DURING PERESTROIKA AND THE FIRST YEARS OF INDEPENDENCE

With the ascent to power in 1985 of the new Soviet leader Mikhail Gorbachev, the first steps of his policies of glasnost and perestroika brought immediate changes to the distribution of power in Georgia. In early July 1985, Shevardnadze was appointed Soviet minister of foreign affairs and his former deputy, Jumber Patiashvili, became First Secretary of the CPG.

Dissident and liberal ideas became combined with those of nationalism in the following years, leading to the emergence of political movements in Georgia.[9] Zviad Gamsakhurdia, a political outsider since his recantation and the founder of Saint Ilia the Righteous Society, gradually gained unprecedented popularity, due to his skillful populism, overtly anticommunist rhetoric, and nationalist slogans. Other leading opposition movements included the Ilia Chavchavadze Society, National-Democratic Party, the Georgia's National Independence Party, the Liberal-Democratic Party, the Union of Georgia's Traditionalists, and the Popular Front.

Dangerous tensions emerged as nationalism was considered a growing threat by ethnic minorities. Abkhazia and Ossetia linked their hopes to support from Moscow and demanded their incorporation into the Russian Federation. At the end of March and the beginning of April 1989, a number of demonstrations took place in Tbilisi, initially directed against Abkhazian secessionism, but later extended to general demands for Georgian independence. On April 9, Soviet armed forces were used to violently disperse protesters, as a result of which some 20 people died. Nationalist passions intensified, and in mid-1989 there were new, violent interethnic clashes in Sukhumi, with many casualties.

Many actions of communist leaders aimed at discrediting dissent further radicalized the national movement, already fully dominated by Gamsakhurdia and his allies. In the situation of a deep crisis of the mass consciousness, caused by the rapid disintegration of the familiar patterns of everyday life and aggravated by the violence of April 1989, it was the most radical nationalist and anticommunist slogans that were able to garner public support.[10] Elections to the Supreme Soviet of Georgia took place in October–November 1990 and brought victory to the Round Table-Free Georgia bloc led by Gamsakhurdia, which obtained 64% of the votes cast, while the CPG took only 29%. Interestingly, communists would subsequently support Gamsakhurdia and the parliamentary majority in most cases.

Many leading intellectual and public figures such as renowned philosopher Merab Mamardashvili joined the so-called National Congress that held alternative elections in September 1990 and criticized Gamsakhurdia's policies.

The Georgian Supreme Soviet declared the country's independence on April 9, and thereby Georgia became one of the first republics to secede from the Soviet Union. A few weeks later, on May 26, 1991, Gamsakhurdia became the elected president of Georgia, winning 86.5% of the votes cast.

Although Gamsakhurdia initially secured the overwhelming support of the ethnic Georgian population, his nationalist rhetoric alienated him from both non-Georgians and the intelligentsia. His lack of administrative skills, authoritarian tendencies, and haphazard personnel policies created enemies even among those who had been friends, such as former Prime Minister Tengiz Sigua and Minister of Defense Tengiz Kitovani. He also lost support of his former allies, such as the National-Democratic Party under Gia Chanturia, Popular Front leader Nodar Natadze, or the Party of National Independence under Irakli Tsereteli. Gamsakhurdia's economic policies were even less successful, and the country gradually moved toward financial catastrophe.

Anti-Gamsakhurdia sentiments mounted after violence was used to disperse a protest demonstration by the now opposition National Democratic Party. The government gradually lost control of the military, and mass arrests of members of the much feared Mkhedrioni militia, led by Jaba Ioseliani, only prolonged the crisis.

Georgia sent observers to a meeting held in Almaty, Kazakhstan, on December 21, 1991, at which the leaders of 11 former republics of the Soviet Union agreed to form the Commonwealth of Independent States (CIS). Georgia, however, refused to join the new structure. The same day, the Georgian opposition and the paramilitary led by Sigua and Kitovani began concentrating tanks and other weaponry, received or purchased from the Russian army, in the center of Tbilisi. On December 22, armed conflict began. Ioseliani was released from prison, and Mkhedrioni joined forces with Kitovani's troops. On January 2, 1992, Gamsakhurdia was declared deposed by the opposition and fled the country.[11]

The Military Council was formed to replace the government, headed by Kitovani and Ioseliani, with Sigua acting as premier. Existing political parties lost an opportunity to get directly involved in the democratic process, although in the situation of the weak state some of them would control paramilitary groups (Merab Kostava Society, National-Democratic Party, Popular Front) and exert significant influence.

The Military Council encountered great difficulties in managing the country, while Gamsakhurdia's supporters—Zviadists—organized armed resistance in western Georgia. In an attempt to increase the legitimacy of the regime, former Soviet Minister of Foreign Affairs Eduard Shevardnadze was invited from Moscow as chairman of the State Council, a structure created in March 1992 to replace the Military Council in legislative and executive matters. In October 1992, he was elected chairman of the new Supreme Council and the head of state.[12] However, the real power was still held by the military leadership, while the country's integrity was threatened by civil war and separatist conflicts in former autonomous entities of South Ossetia and Abkhazia. Gamsakhurdia launched an offensive in September 1993 when Georgian forces were defeated by Abkhazian units supported by the Russian army and by north Caucasia volunteers. To prevent the final partition of Georgia, in October 1993, Shevardnadze was forced to accept the assistance of Russian troops and commit Georgia to entering the CIS. As a result, in early November Gamsakhurdia and his supporters fled to the mountains, and Gamsakhurdia died shortly afterward under mysterious circumstances.

As a sign that Georgia was once again under Moscow's clout, on February 3, 1994, Georgia and Russia signed a 10-year Treaty on Friendship, Good-Neighborliness and Co-operation. One year later, a further agreement was signed that provided for the establishment of four Russian military bases in Georgia. Russia's dominant role in the region was acknowledged, although neither treaty was ever ratified. But nothing was said about party development throughout this time.

POLITICAL PARTIES UNDER SHEVARDNADZE: 1994–2004

Although initially Shevardnadze assumed only the formal leadership position, the situation soon changed.[13] An experienced statesman skilled in political intrigue, Shevardnadze gradually outsmarted his opponents and strengthened his grip on power. He was also able to break the international isolation of Georgia. In the meantime, the economy had also started to grow after a long hiatus, boosted by the introduction of the national currency, the lari, and by stability. The party of power—Citizens' Union of Georgia (CUG)—was organized by the former leader of the Georgia's Green Party, Zurab Zhvania, the political apprentice and partner of Shevardnadze.

On August 24, 1995, the Supreme Council adopted Georgia's new constitution, providing for a strong executive presidency and a 235-seat unicameral parliament. Five days later, Shevardnadze survived an assassination attempt and used this opportunity finally to take the government under firm control. In early October Minister of State Security Igor Giorgadze was named the principal instigator of the plot, and he escaped to Russia. Later, in May 1996, Ioseliani was convicted of complicity in the assassination attempt and imprisoned.

On November 5, 1995, Shevardnadze won 75% of the votes cast in a presidential election.[14] His candidacy was supported by the autocratic leader of Ajara autonomy, Aslan Abashidze, as well as others. CUG secured a relative majority in the parliament, taking 91 seats of the 235. Members of parliament were elected by a mixed voting system, 150 based on national party lists with a 5% threshold and 85 by the first-past-the-post (plurality vote) system. Two other parties that were able to overcome the threshold and get into the parliament were the National-Democratic Party and the Union of Georgia's Revival, led by Abashidze (31 and 25 seats, respectively). Other seats were taken through plurality vote by independent MPs or several representatives of other smaller parties. The elections of 1995 legitimized Shevardnadze's leadership, while political groups supporting Gamsakhurdia were marginalized. The latter denounced Shevardnadze's election as illegitimate and retained influence in some regions such as Samegrelo, Gamsakhurdia's homeland.

Having assumed full control, Shevardnadze attempted a new reorientation toward the West.[15] A new government was announced in December 1995, with Nikoloz Lekishvili appointed minister of state, a post that replaced that of prime minister. Along with political stabilization, an economic revival began, with the annual rate of growth over 10% annually in 1996–1997, and the society began to feel confident of the future. Public opinion surveys would reveal this optimism as well as a reliance on market and democratic reforms exceeding by far those among other CIS countries.[16]

However, the economic crisis of 1998 in Russia had dire consequences for Georgia's fragile economy, causing growth to decelerate to a virtual standstill. Against the background of heightened expectations, frustration came, and this was also reflected in the attitudes toward different political parties. From this perspective, particularly interesting was the local election held on November 15, 1998,[17] which brought significant success to two leftist parties—the Labor Party led by Shalva Natelashvili and the Socialist Party headed by Vakhtang Rcheulishvili. However, the success of the leftist parties was relatively short-lived and by the next parliamentary elections, held October 31, 1999, only three parties appeared capable of overcoming the increased 7% threshold in the proportional vote: CUG received 42% of the votes, securing 130 of the 235 seats, Abashidze's Union for Georgia's Revival received 26%; and the bloc Industrialists' Union of Georgia received 7%. This was followed by another victory on April 9, 2000, when Eduard Shevardnadze was once more elected president of Georgia for a five-year period, winning with about 80% of the votes.

Notwithstanding the successful reelection, Shevardnadze's popularity declined significantly after 2000, as did that of the ruling party, the CUG.[18] In the ruling party, divisions increased between the older generation of former communist functionaries and the younger and more energetic "reformist" wing led by the parliamentary speaker Zurab Zhvania. The reformists aimed at liberalizing economy, fighting corruption, increasing the role of the parliament of political parties, strengthening pro-Western orientation, and radically reforming the judiciary system.

Although Zhvania could not decide whether to break his alliance with his political mentor, he started to rally his supporters within CUG. One more apprentice of Shevardnadze, the young Minister of Justice Mikhail Saakashvili, resigned and started energetically creating his National Movement, trying to attract the CUG members dissatisfied with raging corruption in the government and nationalistic followers of the late Gamsakhurdia.

During the winter of 2001–2002, the confrontation between Shevardnadze and his former junior partners became more strained. Severe crises in both the government and the governing political party were followed by significant changes to all branches of power. Continuous mass protests during the autumn of 2001, with demands to deal with rampant corruption and the resignation of the government, led to the resignation of the powerful interior minister on the condition that at the same time Speaker of the Parliament Zhvania would also leave and be replaced by at that time a less conspicuous figure, Nino Burjanadze. As a result, President Shevardnadze decided to resign from the CUG chairmanship, intending to stay above party politics. He also reshuffled the rest of the government, removing a number of reformists, and finally dismissed the entire cabinet at the beginning of November 2001.

Zhvania was still trying to take control of the CUG, but having failed in this, he gave open support to the opposition and began to build a new party, the United Democrats' Union. However, his irresolution and delay in moving to the opposition, as well as his lack of charismatic qualities, prevented him from gaining wide popularity. The traditional opposition, still lacking both unity and popularity, was again opportunistically closing ranks around Abashidze. Ongoing protests had already served to demonstrate the CUG's dramatic loss of support. Now, the first testing ground for the strengthening opposition became the local elections of June 2002. Overall, despite numerous electoral violations, the elections demonstrated a shift in public sympathy. Significant success was achieved by the New Rights, led by young businessmen previously close to Shevardnadze, Levan Gachechiladze, and David Gamkrelidze. Basically pro-business and pro-American, the New Rights have attracted significant private funding and have been able to field candidates all over the country. As a result, they received more than two-thirds of local votes. The populist, leftist Georgian Labor Party chaired by Shalva Natelashvili was also quite successful, as were other reformist descendents of the CUG, led by Saakashvili and Zhvania, the more radical nationalist National Movement, and the more moderate centrist United Democrats, behind them. Laborites won the majority in the Tbilisi City Council, followed by the National Movement, while CUG experienced a humiliating defeat, gathering summarily just below 2 percent of the overall local vote. Having struck a deal with the Laborites, Saakashvili was elected the chair of the Tbilisi

City Council, acquiring thus a powerful post for further assault. It should be noted that while Laborites demonstrated leftist populism, speaking of free education, health care, and other public goods, most of the other parties were unable to present any consistent and comprehensive party programs. Whether pro-business parties such as Industrialists and the New Right, liberals such as Republicans, or more leftist ones like CUG, they declared support for democratization, free market, and integration into the West, but would not go into details how to achieve this. Therefore, the electorate was actually choosing on the basis of vague hopes, personal attractiveness of the leadership, or an individual's past record.

In June 2002, Minister of State Avtandil Jorbenadze, appointed in December 2001, was elected chairman of the embattled CUG. The parliamentary and presidential elections, scheduled to take place in November 2003 and in 2005, respectively, posed a clear challenge to the opportunistic, corrupt government of the aging Shevardnadze, whose term was due to end approximately 18 months after the legislative elections. However, the ruling elite was unwilling to cede power without struggle, putting into use all available resources and political tricks.

Throughout 2002–2003, preparations for the legislative elections increasingly influenced the political climate of Georgia. CUG, under the leadership of Jorbenadze, began to consolidate support, becoming the core of the new political bloc. For a New Georgia, which attempted to use administrative leverage to unite opportunistic opposition elements that had lost popularity lately, such as the Socialist Party and the National Democratic Party. Major political battles were over voting arrangements, such as the composition of the Central Electoral Commission and the creation of voter lists, controlled by the government appointees.

As the space for democratic practices and access to media was rather limited, the incumbent government appeared unwilling to compromise, and opposition adhered to street protests. In early June 2003, the main opposition parties, in an attempt to pressurize the government, organized political rallies on electoral issues, while student associations mounted antigovernment actions under the slogan "*Kmara*" (enough), formed along the model of the Serbian uprising in 2000, reputedly with international support (e.g., from the prominent U.S. philanthropist George Soros), at which demands were made for Shevardnadze's resignation. Meanwhile, the popular parliament speaker Nino Burjanadze appealed to the U.S. government to ensure that free and fair elections took place.

The parliamentary elections were important as they would determine who would succeed Shevardnadze. Among the leading candidates were the increasingly popular parliamentary speaker Nino Burjanadze and the pro-Western, energetic, and charismatic Mikhail Saakashvili, but also Labor candidate Shalva Natelashvili, supported by the poorer layers of society lured by his leftist populism. Their personalities and organizational skills were much more important than the political agendas of their respective parties.

As November elections drew closer, it became evident that the government was using all of the administrative resources at its disposal to stay in power. CUG had created a hodgepodge coalition of political groupings around itself, but the opposition was also actively preparing, and both Saakashvili and Zhvania were working hard. The former was focusing on boosting his personal popularity but also negotiating clandestinely with the police and the army. They well understood that the eventual retirement of Shevardnadze demanded caution and cooperation with the most probable future leaders. Zhvania, in his turn, persuaded Burjanadze to join forces (creating a coalition Burjanadze-Democrats) and therefore improved the rating of his party by riding on her popularity. Thus, Burjanadze acquired an institutional basis for her political activity. The parliamentary elections of November 2003 were supposed to be the last rehearsal for the opposition, still not sufficiently popular to win.

PARTY POLITICS AFTER THE ROSE REVOLUTION

The parliamentary elections held on November 2, 2003, represented a test of the willingness of the country's government to proceed further in the process of democratic transition. International pressure was formidable, demanding that the elections be held fairly, with an unending sequence of high-profile political visitors reiterating this demand. When the parliamentary elections finally took place on November 2, 2003, it became evident that notwithstanding numerous warnings coming both from the international community and the internal opposition, the actual vote was marred by irregularities and violations. The Central Electoral Commission did not present the results until November 20. Allegedly, this time was used to negotiate with the opposition and adjust the results. The final distribution of votes appeared quite different from both the results of the parallel count by an independent NGO and the exit polls conducted by an external polling company (Table 1.1).[19]

Even if one assumes the correctness of the parallel count or the exit poll results, the National Movement and the Burjanadze-Democrats were not able to garner jointly more than 40% of votes. Thus, if elections were conducted fairly, the new opposition would be unable to get the clear majority in Parliament. However, the elections were now universally perceived to have been fraudulent, and the opposition, led by the triumvirate of Saakashvili, Burjanadze, and Zhvania, was well prepared for such an outcome. They worked to transform the frustration

Table 1.1 Disputed Results of the November 2003 Parliamentary Elections

Party/Bloc	Official results (%)	Parallel count (%)	Exit poll (%)
For New Georgia (coalition led by CUG)	21.32	18.91	17.79
Union of Democratic Revival	18.84	8.13	8.55
Saakashvili—National Movement	18.08	26.26	28.69
Laborites	12.04	17.36	17.66
Burjanadze—Democrats	8.79	10.15	10.48
New Rights	7.35	7.90	8.28

Source: Hans Dieset. Georgia: Parliamentary Elections of November 2003. Norwegian Centre for Human Rights/NORDEM Report 07/2004, as well as numerous media reports.

that electoral malpractice had created, together with the general dissatisfaction with the state of affairs in the country and with endemic government corruption, into mass demonstrations (later named the Rose Revolution) that ultimately led to the resignation of President Shevardnadze on November 23, 2003.

As Gene Sharp points out, the opposition leaders conducted a modern, politically aware, coup, involving and invoking international media in their activities.[20] It was notable that, from the very beginning of the uprising, the West, and the United States in particular, explicitly demonstrated its dissatisfaction with the incumbent leadership and supported the opposition. On November 23, 2003, the first act of the political drama ended with Shevardnadze's letter of resignation, as the triumvirate of the young leaders came to power amid popular jubilation.[21]

Burjanadze, as the parliamentary speaker, temporarily became acting president. On January 4, 2004, the election (with more than 96% of the votes cast) of the young new President Mikheil Saakashvili took place. In February, the post of prime minister was restored, Zhvania taking this post. Parliamentary elections were held on March 28, 2004 (controversially, only those seats determined by proportional representation were contested, while those who had been elected through plurality vote retained their seats), although observers reported an increase in procedural violations in comparison with the presidential election. The National Movement, the United Democrats, who had joined forces, together with their coalition partners—the Republican Party led by David Berdzenishvili, and the Conservatives, headed by Zviad Dzidziguri—won the majority of the party-list votes (67.3%), while only one other political force, the Rightist Opposition (a coalition of the New Rights Party and Industry Will Save Georgia), was able to pass the 7% threshold (with 7.5% of the party-list vote). CUG appeared to be totally demoralized, and while 19 of its members had taken their seats through the plurality vote in November 2003, the party itself was soon dissolved. Other members of parliament elected earlier by the plurality vote included 10 deputies from the National Movement, 7 Burjanadze-Democrats, 6 New Rights, 4 Industry Saves Georgia, 6 Democratic Revival, and 2 Laborites. Twenty-one independents from Abashidze's Democratic Revival refused to participate in these elections.

Subsequently, dramatic events took place in Ajara autonomy, where the Adjaran leader had armed his militia and vowed to fend off any attempt by the central government to curb his regime. However, amid mass demonstrations in Batumi, soldiers in Abashidze's militia began to lay down their arms and to join the demonstrators. On May 5, Abashidze agreed to resign, following a meeting with the Russian envoy Igor Ivanov, who had also been involved in Shevardnadze's resignation. The exit of the Ajarian autocrat advanced Saakashvili's position by creating the first step toward restoring Georgia's territorial integrity. The central authority also regained control over much-needed tax funds from the strategic border crossing with Turkey and the Batumi cargo port.

New elections in Ajara followed on June 20, 2004. Recent events had reshuffled the political landscape, as the Union for Democratic Revival dissolved itself. Now the National Movement, registered under the name of Saakashvili–Victorious Ajara, dominated the campaign. Having used administrative resource and Saakashvili's popularity, it secured 28 of the 30 parliamentary seats, while the Republican Party that stood separately won only the remaining two seats. The failure prompted Republican leadership to accuse the National Movement of manipulating the vote and to withdraw from the ruling coalition. Subsequently, legislative changes largely reduced Ajara's autonomy to a pure formality.

However, further developments in the country were not as successful. An attempt to repeat the same approach as in Ajara,[22] this time in South Ossetia in August 2004, led to the loss of human life and obvious failure, demonstrating the deficiency and incompetence in strategic planning as well as the lack of team spirit within the government. Significant public support for the new government provided favorable conditions for decisive reforms and a more unwavering pro-Western political orientation. However, the ensuing progress was not without some dramatic developments. On February 3, 2005, Prime Minister Zhvania died in suspicious circumstances. Five days later, President Saakashvili nominated Zurab Noghaideli, a former minister of finance, as Zhvania's successor. However, the change of leadership did not remedy the fundamental lack of team spirit, coordination, or shared reform strategy within the government.

Significant achievements were nevertheless observed in economic and fiscal reform. Georgia's economy received a strong impetus from the construction of the Baku-Tbilisi-Ceyhan crude oil pipeline, which came on line in late May 2006. Later, the south Caucasus gas pipeline started operations in January 2007, bringing in significant direct and indirect benefits. Greater international assistance, improved taxation, and cash coming from the accelerated privatization allowed the government to pay all pension and salary arrears. However, the level of poverty in the country did not change much, involving more than half the population. At the same time, there was little prospect of restoring sovereignty over Abkhazia and South Ossetia, and though some improvement was evident, dissatisfaction grew. By the spring of 2005, the popular rating of Saakashvili and the National Movement started to fall. Still, Georgia's leadership had garnered much international assistance, and the visit to Tbilisi in May 2005 by U.S. President G. W. Bush was evidence of strong Western support, whether it was caused by the active military participation of Georgian troops in Iraq and Afghanistan, geopolitical considerations, or Georgia's democratic credentials (Bush hailed Georgia in his speech as a "beacon of Democracy").

The new government focused on stabilizing the economy, eliminating corruption, and bringing order to the budget. The first phase of stabilization yielded impressive results. Despite an economic blockade established by Russia, the Georgian economy grew by 9.4% in 2006 and above 10% in 2007. Foreign direct investment increased dramatically. Simplified tax legislation, introduced in 2004, and improved tax collection brought a sharp increase in budget revenues. The government started addressing long-standing issues in the energy sector. There were other notable achievements in social policies, with improved social protection for vulnerable groups.

However, there were also some difficulties associated with the underdeveloped democratic and civic culture and with the dangerous domination of a single political power. So, although the law protecting freedom of speech in Georgia was considered strong, journalists and opposition groups claimed that legislation had not increased security for journalists. Authorities allegedly pressurized local media and used indirect measures to influence the content of published or broadcast material. Owing to a weak economic base and a small market, media outlets depended on subsidies linked to various economic and political interests, and media operating outside the capital appeared especially vulnerable.

Particularly disturbing were still frequent human rights abuses and the lack of civil control over military and law-enforcement bodies. Public outcry following the murder in January 2006 of a young banker, Sandro Girgvliani, by high-ranking police officers led to a high-profile court case and demands for the resignation of Minister of Internal Affairs Ivane

Merabishvili. Equally disturbing was the excessive brutality with which riots in Tbilisi prisons were suppressed in "special operations," which left many inmates dead or injured. The judiciary continued to be the weakest link in the chain, its powers radically eroded by the constitutional amendments of 2004. The Constitutional Court was moved from Tbilisi to Batumi and totally lost its relevance.

The downsizing of the armed forces advocated in the late 1990s by the International Security Advisory Board of Western advisers was reversed in contradiction to previous claims that Georgia needed small and efficient armed forces able to work with NATO troops. The legal limit for the number of troops also increased from 23,000 in January 2006 to 37,000 in July 2008, with the actual number of troops being 29,000. Rapid growth in the military budget also continued, until finally on July 15, 2008, Parliament approved an amendment to the 2008 state budget that envisaged the increase of the total funding of the Ministry of Defense to 1.395 billion lari ($1 billion).

The Parliament, dominated by the National Movement, routinely approved all legislative initiatives of the executive. The frustrated opposition announced on April 7, 2006, that it would boycott parliamentary sessions in an attempt to boost its influence in national politics, but this appeared ineffective. The opposition was further disconcerted by President Saakashvili's unexpected decision to bring forward the date of local elections, scheduled for December 2006, to October 6 with less than six weeks' notice. The highly unpopular reversal of their own previous demands made by the National Movement (while in opposition) for the direct election of local government officials had revived political debate over Saakashvili's commitment to democratic reform. Additional controversy surrounded the restructuring of the Central Election Committee to include members with ties to the incumbent government. Five candidates contested the Tbilisi mayoralty on October 6, 2006, including the incumbent mayor Giorgi Ugulava. The National Movement received 77.1% of the votes cast throughout the country, and won 34 of the 37 seats in the Tbilisi City Council, ensuring that Ugulava would be reelected to the post.

In October 2006, President Saakashvili announced the submission of a proposal to Parliament that the next presidential election be held simultaneously with legislative elections in 2008, some eight months in advance of its due date. This was perceived as an attempt to manipulate the election's outcome through synergy, as the personal popularity of President Saakashvili was still much higher than that of his party. However, by autumn of 2007, no political opposition was strong enough to challenge the full political dominance of the governing elite. As a result, the only politician to challenge Saakashvili's popularity was the former Defense and Interior Minister Irakli Okruashvili, known previously for his "hawkish" policies.

Okruashvili was arrested on charges of corruption in September 2007, shortly after having announced the formation of a new party, the Movement for United Georgia, and after having publicly accused Saakashvili of involvement in corruption and criminal conspiracies. Soon after, following his recantation and withdrawal of accusations, Okruashvili was released on bail and allegedly allowed to leave for Germany, where he reiterated his previous accusations. This scandal fell on the fertile ground of widespread public dissatisfaction and eventually led to the mass protests of October–November 2007. An additional factor was related to the billionaire and co-owner of the most popular television channel Imedi, Badri Patarkatsishvili, who supported some of the oppositional parties, while Imedi played a leading role in rallying protests.

Okruashvili's arrest and repentance shocked the society, as well as emboldened the opposition, which now saw an opportunity to confront authorities. Mass protests brought thousands to the streets demanding Okruashvili's release and the reform of the presidential system. As the focus of demands shifted to a general antigovernment attitude, manifestations held on November 2 brought more than 50,000 protesters, many coming from provinces. Ten opposition parties established a coordinating council that proposed joint demands to the government, mainly focused on a call for holding early elections.

By November 7, manifestations had already lost much of their popularity, as the demands were hardly appealing to the public. At that point the government made a fatal decision to disperse the gathered people by force. This turned into highly violent actions by police using tear gas, water canons, rubber bullets, and batons against basically peaceful protesters. Many protesters were taken to hospitals and scores were arrested. Imedi offices were taken over by police and vandalized, with much of its equipment deliberately smashed. Emergency rule was announced for the entire country. Saakashvili, following the already overused pattern, increased anti-Russian rhetoric, and some opposition leaders were accused of collaborating with the Russian intelligence services.

Violent action against peaceful protesters caused both a public outcry and international criticism. As a result, the government appeared to be cornered. In a few days the president made a smart compromise: presidential elections were promised for January 5, 2008, occurring in less than two months. This would hardly give the opposition any opportunity to prepare well. Elections would be accompanied by a plebiscite that would determine the timing of the parliamentary elections. The state of emergency was lifted on November 16, and the majority of those arrested during the turmoil were released. On November 22, the Georgian Parliament endorsed the appointment of a new prime minister, the successful young banker Lado Gurgenidze. In accordance with the constitution, Saakashvili stood down as president ahead of the elections, while Parliament Speaker Nino Burjanadze became acting president as of November 25.

A significant part of the opposition agreed to field a joint candidate for the forthcoming presidential elections, former leader of the New Rights Party Levan Gachechiladze. Gachechiladze was quite popular among younger voters but was looked at with suspicion by many western decision makers due to his lack of political experience and some confusing statements he had made about his political agenda, as well as some vulgar wording he had used. Financial support was provided by Patarkatsishvili before scandalous tapes revealed he had planned postelections violence, discrediting him as a possible political ally. A few weeks later, Patarkatsishvili's health suddenly deteriorated and he died in London.

Both international and local observers have noted numerous preelectoral violations, such as unfair use of mass media and using "administrative resources" (promises or actual increases of salaries for teachers, higher pensions, distribution of various types of vouchers, the employment program, etc.) to secure public support. With significant delay after the disputed elections on January 5, Saakashvili was announced to have won the election in the first round by 53.38%, even though he lost in the capital—Tbilisi, where Gachechiladze took the majority of the votes (overall Gachechiladze was reported to have taken 25.66%).

The opposition declared the elections had been rigged and Saakashvili's presidency was illegitimate. However, international support strengthened Saakashvili's standing, while his tactical skills helped him in organizing parliamentary elections, held on May 21, 2008, with much greater success. Before that, Saakashvili reshuffled the government in an attempt to create the impression he was ready to meet the demands of the opposition and the public, bringing into the government some new faces of professionals who were formally not affiliated with the ruling party. However, the opposition dismissed these "cosmetic" changes, as the most unacceptable figures in the government, such as the notorious Minister of the Interior Merabishvili, retained their positions.

Parliamentary elections of May 21, 2008, demonstrated one more electoral success of the ruling party led by Saakashvili, which garnered 59.18% of the proportional vote, and even greater domination in the plurality vote. As a result, 119 deputy seats in the 150-seat Parliament of Georgia were taken by the members of the United National Movement. Five parties were admitted to the Parliament. The opposition, other than a small and freshly created Christian-Democratic Movement (8.66% of vote), headed by Giorgi Targamadze and a few other elected MPs considered by the opposition as collaborationists, refused to accept the MPs' mandates, accusing the government of yet another rigged election.

As a result of political processes after November 2007, Georgia got a virtually single-party parliament fully controlled by the executive power, a weak and corrupt judiciary, and an electronic media controlled by the incumbent government.[23] Also, since property rights remained insecure and justice arbitrary, there continued to be grounds for serious concern over the direction of reform. After initial unconditional support from the West, more voices started criticizing the quality of democracy in Georgia and the authoritarian tendencies of its leadership. The culmination of these tendencies found their ultimate realization before and during the "strange five-day war" in early August 2008.

In a fatal move, just before midnight on August 8, 2008, provoked by the heavy exchange of fire by artillery and rockets from the Ossetian side targeting Georgian villages, Georgian troops started to advance toward the breakaway capital Tskhinvali, claiming to "restore the constitutional order" in the region. The next morning, a well-prepared Russian army attacked Georgian positions. Russian military aircraft entered the Georgian airspace, bombing Georgian positions, including military and civilian targets outside South Ossetia. After several days of heavy fighting and losses on both sides, Russia's overwhelming power and domination in the air squeezed Georgian troops out of their positions. The Russian army took control not only of South Ossetia, but proceeded much further beyond its borders.

On August 12, French President Nicolas Sarkozy flew to Moscow. Under pressure, Russian President Dmitry Medvedev agreed to sign a six-point ceasefire agreement that provided for the withdrawal of all troops to their positions as of August 7, an end to military actions, and free access for humanitarian aid. Notwithstanding the agreement, Russian military action continued, although at a reduced scale. On August 26, Russia officially recognized the sovereignty of South Ossetia and Abkhazia, a move quickly condemned by much of the international community. Three days later the Georgian government broke off diplomatic relations with Russia.

The August developments in Georgia came as a shock to much of the world, bringing it to the brink of a new cold war. However, the greatest shock was experienced by the Georgian society itself. In the best case, simply misguided by a wrong assessment of U.S. and Russian commitments in the Caucasus, and in the worst case, due to incompetence, political infantilism, or neglect, the Georgian leadership apparently regarded the situation in South Ossetia as a window of opportunity for reconquering the region by force. In spite of warnings from the West and evident Russian military preparedness for invading Georgia, the totally unprepared Georgian leadership risked an unequal war and suffered a decisive defeat, loss of more territories, and massive human casualties.[24]

Now the leadership, responsible for the error of starting military action in South Ossetia, could expect to hear demands for its resignation during the fall 2008, and the plans for its integration into NATO remained uncertain, as did its relations with Russia and its secessionist provinces—Abkhazia and South Ossetia. Russia's aggressive actions caused mobilization of mass support for Saakashvili, whose rule the Russian leadership was willing to bring down. Once the external danger was reduced, the Georgian citizens could be expected to reconsider their support for the national leaders and reflect on the reasons for and the consequences of what had happened. Intensified visits of leading Georgian politicians to Washington, D.C., and other western capitals increased criticism from former Saakashvili's allies, such as Burjanadze, and may also be an indication that the future of Georgia's leadership is uncertain. Unless the opposition is again outsmarted by Saakashvili, there is little doubt that Georgia may again experience political struggle, possibly leading to a change in leadership and bringing other politicians to the fore, a move that would probably be cautiously supported by the West.

CONCLUSION: KEY FACTORS IN THE RELATIONSHIP BETWEEN PARTIES AND DEMOCRACY IN GEORGIA

The specific trajectory of Georgia's political life has had a direct influence on how political parties have developed, although the situation may be essentially not too different from other postcommunist transitional societies.

Party building and political participation in Georgia[25] are still, after all the difficult years since independence, following the *nomenclatura* (or *komsomol*, taking into account the young age of many politicians) model, but with a naïve version of liberal democracy mixed with nationalism replacing communist ideology. This is particularly visible if one pays attention to the strong centralization and bureaucratization of the most politically successful parties, the decisive authority of their leaders, the demagogical and populist rhetoric employed, the disunion between words and deeds, and the lack of internal democracy within the party structure.

The first opposition parties of the perestroika period (1985–1990), apart from a few movements with socialist orientation, generally aimed at the achievement of state sovereignty in Georgia and removing the communist ideological legacy, with rather vague support for Western political models. Nationalism appeared as the most competitive alternative to the communist ideology, since nationalist parties were in opposition to communist totalitarianism, and the latent conflict of their vision with democratic values was not yet evident. These parties would overtly speak of human rights, protection of the environment and cultural identity, respect for the western values of democracy, and interethnic relations, but while all this was implicitly critical of the Soviet reality, still these topics were not too dangerous from the viewpoint of the regime, but rather relatively safe. At the same time, preoccupation with the environment as the safest area of discontent was rather pragmatic, as there was in fact no deep concern for the environment among the leaders or the people. It was simply a handy and safe political tool—as demonstrated by the subsequent disrespect for environmental issues as soon as the former opposition came to power.

With the weakening and the downfall of the Soviet regime, the political scenery in Georgia represented a rather diversified and multicolored spectrum of political parties. The decades of monopoly of a single party came to an end, and all politically active individuals moved quickly to another extreme. Initially, there was a feeling that almost anyone with some ambition could launch a party and become a politician, but of course the majority of these parties, counted in scores, were rather irrelevant for the political process, although their plurality was symptomatic.[26]

The ruling regime became extremely unpopular in Georgia, particularly in the wake of the bloodshed of April 9, 1989. Thereafter, an anticommunist stance became one of the basic characteristics of the more popular parties. And in the situation of mass confusion and ideological vacuum, it appeared that the most radically nationalist and anticommunist leader with strong charisma and tactical skills, Zviad Gamsakhurdia, would become the most popular politician and that his Round Table-Free Georgia coalition could easily win elections and come to power. Although Gamsakhurdia stayed in power for only a short period of time, being replaced in a coup during the winter of 1991–1992, he demonstrated the same tendencies as another charismatic leader, Saakashvili, tendencies that are in fact characteristic for the majority of post-communist leaders: demagogy and populism, a mixture of nationalist and democratic rhetoric, intolerance toward and attempts to suppress opposition, lack of a long-term vision for the country, unstable political personality, authoritarianism, and voluntarism.

In general, such characteristics of the leaders of the ruling parties make one think that this pattern is the most competitive one in a transitional political arena, when a party comes to power by replacing the previous unpopular regime. Somewhat different was Shevardnadze's party—Citizens' Union of Georgia—which was created (basically, by Zurab Zhvania) while Shevardnadze at least formally was already in power, and therefore its ideology was to a lesser extent based on the criticism of the preceding regime (even though it was in some ways an alternative to Gamsakhurdia's Round Table) and was based instead on the promises of stability and a bright future. Furthermore, from the very start it relied on a powerful party bureaucratic apparatus designed to control elections and the legislature. Nonetheless, as if to demonstrate some kind of equifinality principle, all ruling parties and their leaders appear to share the same patterns of conduct and existence, even though the personal style of a weathered Communist functionary like Shevardnadze (at least during his first years in power: 1994–1998) was very different from either Gamsakhurdia or Saakashvili. The Soviet legacy of a one-party system continues to have direct implications for the functioning of strong political parties in Georgia that do not essentially represent any distinct social layers, values, or group interests. The membership of the parties in power, but also of some lesser parties, is dependent on the pragmatism, skills, and ambitions of individuals rather than any political program or value system, often not even formulated explicitly and clearly. As a result, when a party comes to power it attracts all career seekers and grows in power, leading to political dominance. But as soon as this party loses power, it immediately disappears (as happened with Shevardnadze's CUG, or Abashidze's Democratic Revival, but also essentially to Gamsakhurdia's Round Table, which completely dispersed).

As the ruling party comes to power through populist promises and public enthusiasm, which it is often unable to meet, it tries, as happened after the Rose Revolution, to concentrate more power and quell opposition, simply to survive and preserve its dominance. On the one hand, the National Movement under Saakashvili fully controls the Parliament and the government, and its grip is strong. On the other hand, its personnel policy is based on party or personal loyalty and therefore the government that is formed lacks talented cadre, professional competence, and team spirit. As the number of reliable and loyal figures is scarce, the same people rotate between ministries and the parliament, while some professionals whom one would expect would be invited soon instead become victims of party intrigues and leave.

Until recently, opposition parties had very little chance of coming into power and somehow got used to playing a secondary role in politics. The majority of these parties were also organized around one or several political leaders and substituted the continuous criticism of the government (or one another) for any serious political agenda. The leadership of the leading opposition parties tends to be permanent, as it is the leaders who form the parties. Even if it is obvious that these leaders may become a liability rather than an asset for a party, rotation rarely happens, as leaders also prefer to stay in their positions even if this reduces the party's chances for success, while the lack of intraparty democracy weakens the possibilities for change.

New parties still form from time to time, most often by spinoffs from the ruling party or by politicians moving into opposition from some key government positions. This was how some important political parties were founded, including Saakashvili's National Movement,

Gamkrelidze/Gachechiladze's New Rights, or Zhvania's United Democrats, and more recently Salome Zurabishvili's Georgia's Way and Irakli Okruashvili's Movement for United Georgia. Just recently former Parliament Speaker Nino Burjanadze launched a wave of criticism against her former ally Saakashvili and announced she was founding a new party. Most of these parties are formed only as instruments for bringing their leaders back into power or keeping them occupied.

One more type of party, as already described above, is the pseudoopposition party. Often, such parties are founded just before an election, and their role is obvious: to demonstrate political pluralism, take votes from more disobedient opposition parties, and support the government on issues that matter. One example of such a party is the newly set up Christian-Democratic Party, led by Giorgi Targamadze, which unexpectedly gained sufficient votes to be able to enter Parliament, while other opposition parties boycotted it due to the allegedly rigged parliamentary elections of 2008.

As the Georgian legislation prohibits the creation of political parties on ethnic or regional basis, there are also a number of such ethnic parties that are refused registration but still have significant support locally. Such was the case of Javakh and Virq parties in the Armenian-populated districts of Akhalkalaki and Ninotsminda, in the Samtskhe-Javaklheti region. Excluding ethnic parties from legal political arenas obliges Armenian politicians to ally formally with the ruling (or an opposition) party in order to start a political career, but it is hardly an effective way of enhancing public participation in minority populated areas, as it radicalizes other political groups unwilling to compromise (e.g., New Javakh in the same area).

In some cases political parties still represent particular social layers. Labor, characterized by leftist populism, has support among the poorer population in some rural areas, and the New Rights and the Industrialists are supported by businessmen. Similarly, the Republican Party mainly appeals to the more educated and moderate social electorate. However, as these group interests are not well structured and the respective parties are unable to offer clear and attractive political agenda, ideology plays a relatively limited role in current opposition politics: the main vector of political struggle is simply opposing and weakening the ruling party.

Nevertheless, it is these parties (other than the ruling National Movement) that are capable of addressing the needs and aspirations of certain social groups or layers to some extent that played a prominent role until recently. However, the events during the autumn of 2007, followed by the August war of 2008, have significantly changed the agenda, and once again the political clout of any opposition party depends rather on the mode of its criticism or action against, or cooperation with, the incumbent government.

Recent political developments in Georgia thus once again demonstrated the difficulties of postcommunist transition in the complex geopolitical environment. Formally existing democratic institutions may lead to formal or virtual (or facade) democracy, even in the absence of any communist ideology. Even if the system is hailed for various reasons by international democracy watchdogs of democratic states, as was the case of Georgia after the Rose Revolution, it may bring to power elites who are not necessarily democratic or effective but who tend to slip to authoritarianism or remain authoritarian. In such states, developing in accordance with the "dominant power paradigm,"[27] the ruling party is often based not on ideology, values, or vision but on the personality of a leader and power greed or career pragmatism. Furthermore, it is not separated either from the state or from business; any functional and independent judicial power is basically absent, and the executive branch has overwhelmingly strong prerogatives, with the legislature serving most of the time as merely a rubber-stamping institution; high-level corruption is unavoidably strong, and much of the economy is devoted either to specific visions of a leader (fountains and merry-go-rounds in the case of Georgia) or to creating a state-controlled pseudo-liberal system serving certain group interests based on loyalty rather than effectiveness.

At the same time, based on the Georgian experience, it is possible to say that paths of authoritarianism in post-Soviet space do not depend much on such issues as affluence of resources (as in the case of the "oil wealth curse" of Azerbaijan), religion, or ethnicity. Much more important are such factors as explicit pro-Western orientation, existence of an educated urbanized middle class, and the tradition of political struggle.

In fact, as viewed by the presidency, opposition parties in Georgia are becoming irrelevant and considered as just an unavoidable evil that the leadership is obliged to tolerate in order to demonstrate the democratic facade and remain acceptable for the international community, due to the globalization of democratic values that nowadays every authoritarian rule swears to adhere to. There are, however, several ways of dealing with opposition: the most radical opposition is either deprived of any real possibility of winning seats in the legislature (through manipulation of elections, loss of public funding, or sometimes direct intimidation) or access to (electronic) media, thereby unable to publicize their criticism of the ruling elite or offer their own agenda; or, finally, by creating alternative pseudo-opposition with better access to the legislature and media, which voices mild criticism of the government and disagrees with it on minor points, but basically supports it in all important matters.

Extreme populism, manipulation through controlled mass media (which, for example has astonishingly presented the events of August

2008 as a victory for the Georgian state), conspiracy theory, nationalist rhetoric, and enemy images all serve to maintain internal domination within the national political scene; the liberal and democratic Volapük, speaking of national interests, external enemies, or even human rights, may be just a trick to pursue some internal or specific goals that may cheat some of the willing believers of democratic mythology in the world ("Georgia—the beacon of Democracy"). Mass movements and "botanical revolutions" such as in Georgia tend to reinvigorate the same authoritarianism against which they were directed, leading to public frustration and disappointment in democracy and western values, plus a degree of political passivity that may again explode, leading to a new revolution.

However, an authoritarian regime is much more unpredictable and dangerous than democratic ones are. Its stability is frequently illusionary, as are its democratic credentials. Even softer authoritarian regimes can easily make controversial political or military decisions that may be fatal, as there are no functional mechanisms of parliamentary or judiciary control, no constraints on strong party coalitions, no effective feedback mechanisms, while public opinion can be manipulated through controlled mass media. Authoritarian leaders may ignore the necessity of consulting partners or allies, neglect a nation's international commitments, lose contact with reality, and become unable to assess possible risks linked to their actions realistically. The blunders of Saakashvili during August–September of 2008—whether due to incompetence and political myopia or to deliberately neglecting the basic interests of his nation in order to either follow voluntarism and often irrational decisions, or to serve some group interests of his close entourage—are clear illustrations of such a situation.

When the nation-state is still the most effective structure in a situation of emergency, and international organizations such as the United Nations remain indecisive, slow, and ineffective, nationalism and the imagery of a dangerous external enemy is most likely to be the unifying ideology and the best way of mobilizing support for a society. National politics influenced by internal power struggles still remains the driving force in Georgia's political developments.

The prolonged crisis of the 1990s and the mass dissatisfaction with politicians and politics in general, as most were convinced that the political elites were profoundly corrupt and immoral, has led initially to general political passivity prior to the explosion of public anger, as happened in November 2003 and again in November 2007. There is a certain cycle according to which these two trends show themselves: disappointment and passivity replaced by mass protests and demand for change.

Prolonged frustration, a political culture rooted in the Soviet past, and inadequate democratic skills among the population, coupled with weak political parties that lack internal democracy or clear-cut ideology, have created a situation in Georgia where either charismatic, populist, or adventurous leaders may come to power on the wave of public discontent; or, alternatively, a spin-off of the ruling party will bring to power the former functionary of the previous regime. This means that the current state of affairs within the political parties, their lack of vision of internal democracy and of clearly set values, creates a virtual democracy that demonstrates all the democratic institutions in place but little democratic content. This means that democratic or para-democratic procedures such as elections may serve the resurgence to power of authoritarian or antidemocratic forces and persons, as has happened repeatedly throughout the world.

However, the current situation may also bring the Georgian society and political forces to reflect on mistakes made and possibly mean more flexibility and democracy. Or, alternatively, it may bring to the fore another radical, nationalist elite or prompt the government to start another adventure that may help rally the population behind it. In any case, it is clear that the winter of 2008–2009 was a period of bifurcation. It may yet bring more maturity to Georgian society and to Georgian parties—or it may plunge Georgia into yet another cycle of authoritarianism and political degradation.

EPILOGUE

At present writing, Georgia is once again in limbo. There is a deadlock in the country since the events of April 9, 2008, when the political opposition brought tens of thousands of protesters to the streets, demanding the resignation of President Saakashvili, accusing him of initiating and losing the disastrous war of August 2008, of authoritarianism, voluntarism, and unpredictability. While the dissatisfaction with Saakashvili is on the rise, there is no obvious mechanism by which he could be replaced. Along the familiar lines, numerous opposition parties appear unable to suggest any unity on issues other than the president's resignation and seem to lack any consistent strategy or a universally appealing leadership. On the other hand, even if the incumbent government wins this round, stabilization is hardly in sight. Therefore, Georgia seems to be bound to experience another prolonged period of instability and tension, aggravated by external factors and pressures.

CHAPTER 2

Political Parties and Democratization of the Republic of Moldova

Igor Botan

INTRODUCTION

The role of political parties in the democratization process of the Republic of Moldova may be easier to understand if we consider democracy to be the institutionalization of freedom. Most Moldovan citizens have received the freedom and independence of the Republic of Moldova, declared in August 1991, as a gift. Although the Republic of Moldova experienced a "national revival" like other Soviet republics, its agenda was somehow synchronized with internal political struggles within the Moscow communist elite. In consequence, most Moldovan citizens did not actually know what to do with the gifted freedom. A supportive political culture, the capacity to start up and administer one's own business, the opportunity to protect one's own interests and rights in an open competition, and so forth were all so far from possible that contemplating them could generate nothing but frustration. Thus, with social and material conditions dramatically worsening and interethnic tensions on the rise, most Moldovan citizens simply began to miss the lost paradise of preindependence.

After the collapse of the Soviet Union and declaration of independence of the Republic of Moldova, the democratization process—the institutionalization of freedom—actually consisted in borrowing forms of state organization, protection of citizen rights, self-organization of civic, nongovernmental institutions, and other trappings of democracy from others. In this regard, the Republic of Moldova was aided by international institutions such as the Council of Europe and the

Organization for Security and Co-operation in Europe (OSCE). The economic life of the Republic of Moldova was restructured with the support of international financial organizations, such as the World Bank and the International Monetary Fund. However, such an institutionalization of freedom on Moldovan land could have no immediate effect beyond building a kind of shop-window democracy[1] or imitative democracy.[2] Modern western institutional forms were filled with domestic Moldovan contents. The notions of shop-window democracy or imitative democracy became accepted, being widely used by sociologists and political researchers from neighboring countries Romania and Russia, which had and continue to have the greatest influence on developments in the Republic of Moldova. These large notions suggest the expectation that the maturing Moldovan democracy will be distorted for a certain period; eventually able to go forward to genuine democracy—or not. In this context, the experience of Central European and Baltic countries, on the one hand, and of the Commonwealth of Independent States (CIS), on the other hand, is important for developments in the Republic of Moldova. Thus, Central European and Baltic countries quickly developed from the imitative to the genuine democracy in the western meaning of the term. It is well known that positive developments in Central European countries were influenced most by promises to be accepted into the European Union, a body built on definite values and standards. On the other hand, 12 of 15 former Soviet republics, including the Republic of Moldova, created the CIS in December 1991 in an effort to attenuate the negative effects of centrifugal forces after the collapse of the Soviet Union. The CIS lacked standards and values to encourage the passage from the imitative to the genuine democracy. On the contrary, imitative democracies in certain CIS members have turned into authoritarian states.

Moldova has now joined the countries with the highest democracy index[3] in the CIS, coming after Ukraine and Georgia. However, the Republic of Moldova is special. Its electorate has never participated in revolutions; it has never been offered a referendum on Moldova independence or adoption of the constitution or other important documents for the fate of society and the democratic development of the country. Only representatives of parliamentary parties voted for important documents on such matters. It seems that Moldovan political parties, especially while they are in opposition, do not believe that the Moldovan electorate is very discerning, an opinion well balanced by the contempt in which that electorate holds the parties, rating them as one of the least trusted (about 15% to 20%) among all public and private institutions.

Given these facts, it is not surprising to learn that Moldovan political parties have played an important role in the democratic evolution of the country, opposing more than once the attempts by authorities to consolidate their power, following the example of the Russian Federation and Ukraine. In the first case, Russia had institutionalized its freedom by adopting a new constitution in 1993, leaving much room for building the state power vertically and for a controlled democracy. In the case of Ukraine, democratization has been about the consolidation of vertical power after the modification of the constitution in 2000.

Although Moldovan political parties have constantly and successfully resisted the introduction of a presidential regime and successfully called for a semiparliamentary regime with a quite even checks and balances system, the Republic of Moldova could not avoid building a vertical power structure. This happened because the Moldovan electorate awarded in 2001 the absolute victory to the Party of Communists of the Republic of Moldova (PCRM) in the freest and most democratic elections ever held in Moldova. This victory was used by PCRM to promote its image as the first communist party in the world that gained an absolute victory in free and fair elections, not through revolutions and coups d'état, as has happened across the world. However, since the PCRM has not had any other experience than that of rigid and vertical organization of state power, shortly after its electoral victory it started to construct such a power structure even within a semiparliamentary constitutional regime.

Furthermore, the behavior and perceptions of the Moldovan electorate have encouraged the domination of certain parties on the political scene. There is a Moldovan particularity here that makes the application of modern classifications of parties to the Moldova's case irrelevant. Instead, an analysis of the evolution of parties according to their place on the political scene, from left to right, explains their essence pretty well, despite the fact that main political parties in Moldova no longer represent the interests of specific social classes or castes. The representation of all important political parties in local public administration bodies is generally uniform in terms of the levels of education and occupational backgrounds of local elected officials. In this respect, the profits gained by the most powerful parties represented in public administration bodies are irrelevant for understanding political cleavages in the Republic of Moldova, and the social status of representatives of political parties, as determined by education and occupation, does not underlie claims to represent certain social castes. Entrepreneurs are the most active social segment in political terms, being represented in approximately one-fourth of the district/municipal councils, coming from small- and medium-sized businesses and working as the heads of limited societies, stock societies, and individual enterprises. However, the curious fact is that the share of entrepreneurs representing the ruling PCRM is higher than that coming from the liberal parties. Still, there are clear signals that business interests join politics to protect themselves against pressures rather than because they realize their role in society. As it turns out, politics itself is the best business in the Republic of Moldova. As the Republic of Moldova is an imitative democracy, its parties are in many respects similar to those found in western democracies.[4]

This chapter will explain the evolution of Moldovan democratization by following the party system through the key stages of its development. First, however, I begin with a discussion of key particularities of the Moldovan electorate. Next, I examine the recent political history of Moldovan parties, looking at the impact of those particularities on parties of the left, right, and center and pointing out how the nation's political history has followed an alternating cycle of change and stabilization, which I divide into four periods: romantic, pragmatic, pseudo-restoration, and finally an emergent national consensus. The third section reviews the impact of legislation on the parties and elections. In the conclusion I assess the meaning of these developments for Moldovan democratization.

PARTICULARITIES OF THE MOLDOVAN ELECTORATE

Like most voters everywhere, the behavior of Moldovan electors is based on fundamental values and traditions. They prefer to vote for political parties ingrained in the domestic "political field" or for new parties that provide the perspective of "change." The experience of the past 20 years of transition has shown that only parties capable of appearing to fit in the political niches evoked by traditional typologies of the right, left, and center will enjoy electoral success. Although such a pattern is not unusual in East European countries, in Moldova it is shaped by several particular factors.

First, the Republic of Moldova is a preponderantly rural country, being also called "the village of Europe," since it is the only European country in which the size of the rural population is higher than that of the urban population—53% to 47%. Perhaps it is not surprising that the most rural country in Europe is also the poorest one, although the preponderant rural nature of the country is not the only cause of poverty. The Moldovan intelligentsia, which should have a certain influence on the electoral behavior by articulating the national aspirations, is strongly rooted in the past, viewed differently by different groups of intellectuals, who accordingly have different views of the future of Moldova. Despite the presence of many distinctive personalities, those who became intellectuals during Soviet times are now unable to provide a synthesis of traditions because of the lack of strong links between cultural strata and statehood forms. The same may be noted for political and administrative elites. The conservatism and inertia in assimilating new sociopolitical and economic practices are so serious that the most active people choose to leave the country and look for higher salaries or better lives abroad, rather than try to improve the situation at home. In consequence, approximately one-third of the employable population and one-fourth of the people entitled to vote live abroad. This is the most active part of the population, most educated, and most able to adjust to new conditions. They scarcely participate in elections by virtue of the fact that they are abroad and could cast their ballots only at 15 to 20 diplomatic representations with limited capacities. Therefore, only about 10,000, or a mere one-fiftieth of the nearly half a million Moldovan nationals who are abroad, cast their ballots.[5]

Second, the Republic of Moldova is actually the only country in Europe where an identity crisis on the dimensions of Moldovans versus Romanians is a decisive factor in polarizing attitudes of political forces. The question of the link between the two nations on the basis of ethnic identity has been constantly speculated about during electoral campaigns since the 1994 parliamentary elections. In this regard, ethnolinguistic and historic discussions are often deliberately substituted for serious debates between parties on socioeconomic and political topics. Such discussions have a maximum propagandistic impact, as they appeal to citizens' emotions. It is noteworthy that shortly after the Republic of Moldova became independent, local intellectuals stood mainly for the pro-Romania position, since the rural population was pro-Moldova, whereas national minorities, which comprised approximately 35% of population in the early 1990s and were preponderantly concentrated in main cities, were and are Russian speaking and pro-Russia.

Third, the ideological experiment in the Soviet period related to the "confiscation" of faith in God and "the Last Judgment," replacing it with belief in the "bright future" and the "paradise on earth" within a communist society, had a stronger impact in a preponderantly rural region like Moldova than in urbanized countries and regions where values are less based on religion. The only systems of values Moldovans shared throughout centuries were Christian values, for approximately a millennium, and then communist values during the period 1940–1990. The communists not only guaranteed a certain minimal standard of living but also addressed the needs of the pro-Russian segment of the Moldovan Orthodox Church (about 90% of the parishioners), as opposed to the pro-Romanian segment (about 10%). Other modern political parties whose names indicate their doctrinaire preference do not attract ordinary Moldovan voters to whom the ideas of liberalism, social democracy, conservatism, and so forth, say almost nothing; their appeal is limited to a very narrow segment of party elites, researchers, and students, and perhaps some groups of supporters. For others, the need for identity (Moldovan versus Romanian) and social protection is more important.

The most important fact here is that the freedom and independence of the Republic of Moldova have become key conquests in very specific circumstances—after a long period of "confiscation of God" and immediately after the collapse of communism. This generated frustration and a lack of guidelines for most of the population on the one hand, and a true "paradise" for ambitious populist politicians on the other hand. In such cases, the lack of guidelines is usually remedied through calls for returning to traditional national values, the traditions and faith of ancestors, and so forth, which encouraged the ascension of nationalism in the late 1980s and early 1990s during the collapse of the Soviet Union. To build a new society during the transition years, it was required to choose attractive and modern social models, which could only be the western ones. The popular attitude toward public and civil institutions after 20 years of transition is informative to understand how successful the "institutionalization of freedom" in Moldova was. In this regard, the church is the most trusted institution,[6] enjoying approximately 70% to 80% confidence, followed by local public administration with 35% to 45%, central administrative institutions with 25% to 35%, justice with 25% to 30%, while civil society institutions enjoy 15% to 30%. Thus Moldovan citizens trust traditional institutions more than those that have emerged during democratization. It is worth noting that trade unions and political parties, key institutions in articulating the daily interests of citizens, have the lowest confidence rating, at 20% and 15%, respectively.

For this reason, it is not accidental that main right-wing and left-wing political parties have established very close relations with religious institutions. Thus, the PCRM has a very special relationship with the Metropolitan Church of Moldova under the jurisdiction of the Russian patriarchy. At the same time, the Christian Democratic People's Party (PPCD) was the key promoter in registering the Metropolitan Church of Bessarabia[7] under the jurisdiction of the Romanian patriarchy. In this respect, there is a clear correlation between the PCRM rating and the percentage of parishioners of the Moldovan Metropolitan Church estimated at 80% to 90% out of all Orthodox Christians, while other Orthodox Christians are parishioners of the Metropolitan Church of Bessarabia.

Fourth, the question of property law is also important. Moldovans experienced serious injustice twice in the span of 50 years. In the 1940s, private property was nationalized and the majority of former owners were deported. A reverse but unfair process took place in the 1990s, when public property was privatized, mainly by the former communist nomenclature, and people did not own anything. The way authorities have behaved regarding property has fueled the nihilist attitude toward property and business, and none of the political parties that focused on property, drawing on the support of small and medium business and putting forward other goals that would essentially further the modernization and reformation of the country, enjoyed electoral victory. However, these issues were also included in the agenda of the main political parties.

In general, the electoral conduct of Moldovan electors is predictable enough. Electoral preferences change little from one electoral cycle to another, if the socioeconomic situation is relatively stable. The electoral behavior is also predictable if the socioeconomic situation worsens dramatically, in which case the voters punish ruling parties by a protest vote and choose parties that ruled the country when their material condition was better. So far, Moldovan voters have been slow to offer much support to new political forces, which are not embedded in the Moldovan political field. However, after 20 years of a multiparty system, there are trends indicating possible changes may be forthcoming.

THE IMPACT OF THE ELECTORATE'S PARTICULARITIES ON THE PARTIES

The preferences and behavior of the Moldovan electorate have influenced the rating of political parties and their electoral success. Consequently, parties that send clear messages to voters, evoking older and newer traditions and answering calls to return to national values and social protection, have enjoyed electoral success. In the past 200 years, the territory of the Republic of Moldova was consecutively part of the Russian Empire, the Kingdom of Romania, and the Soviet Union; segments of the Moldovan electorate have followed political parties that have expressed doubts about Moldova's capacity to survive independently and have preferred either to go back to the Russian orbit or to join Romania, although others have argued for independence. These attitudes are clearly reflected in the ironic remark that Moldova does not have political but "geopolitical parties."[8] It is true that left-wing parties are usually pro-Russia or pro-CIS; right-wing parties are pro-Romania or pro-West; and centrist parties are pro-Moldova, promoting the independence of the Republic of Moldova and arguing for a "multivector" foreign policy.

Appeals based on doctrinaire preferences have not had a serious impact on Moldovan voters, although doctrinaire affinities are important for consolidating party elites. However, in general Moldovans rely on the nation's western partners—the European Union, international financial and democratic institutions—for advice on solving problems and how to modernize, rather than on doctrinaire perceptions. Western partners were chosen by all sides largely because CIS partners had little or nothing to propose. As a result, the political programs of pro-European parties and pro-CIS parties are actually very much alike, with few exceptions. Differences can be found only in the structure and style of documents.

In fact, any ruling party of any political color in Moldova would have to do the same thing, i.e., implement minimum sociopolitical and economic standards by using the best ways and methods recommended by international partners. In this regard, no one is surprised that the PCRM declared the "liberal revolution" in April 2007, no matter how paradoxical that may have seemed. On the other hand, for electoral reasons, namely to hold a dominant position in one of the three segments of the political spectrum (right, center, left), the parties often evoke a certain tradition or seek to be regarded as "promoters of change," no matter whether "change" is a step forward in the modernization or a backward move toward the "lost paradise." In general, the ruling parties try to ensure minimum socioeconomic stability in order to maintain their standing.

At the moment, after 20 years of multipartyism and political races, former right-wing and left-wing antagonist parties are both "slipping" to the center. This phenomenon is suppressing borders and diffusing traditional "political niches." Consequently, the most educated electorate remains confused, and a reshaping of the political spectrum is required. It is possible this will be realized in the forthcoming 2009 parliamentary elections (see the epilogue to this chapter for an update). Meanwhile, there are interesting differences from left to right to center.

Left-Wing Segment of the Political Spectrum

This segment was initially occupied by two parties emerging from the Interfront (International Front—the Socialist Party of Moldova [PSM]) and the Unitatea-Edinstvo (United Moldovan and Russian Movement), which created an electoral bloc in the 1994 parliamentary elections, gaining 24 of 104 seats. Once the PCRM was registered in April 1994, it quickly eliminated the two above-mentioned parties from political life. This phenomenon can be partly explained by the domination of the communist ideology in the nearly 50 years of Soviet rule. The majority of citizens had a predictable reaction to the difficulties of transition in the 1990s and were eager to retrieve the "lost paradise." The wish of the majority of the electorate to see left-wing forces ruling their country was noticed at the first parliamentary elections after Moldova's independence, when the former communist party was prohibited. People massively voted for the main temporary substitute of communists—the Democratic Agrarian Party of Moldova (PDAM) and the Electoral Bloc of Socialist Party and Movement Unitatea-Edinstvo. Once the PCRM was legalized, citizens reconfirmed their option, bringing the PCRM to an absolute victory in February 2001 in the freest and fairest election ever held in Moldova, promising to restore socialism, keep building communism, and participate in "building a federation of former Soviet republics on voluntary and updated bases."[9]

However, the PCRM started "slipping" toward the center only half a year after coming to power. In this respect, the PCRM repeated the fate of many western "antisystem" parties, which upon gaining authority make themselves comfortable and join the system, becoming its most fervent protectors. In order to retain power, the PCRM gave up basic principles of the Marxist-Leninist doctrine it claimed to share. In fact, the PCRM policies aimed to revise the results of reforms launched by former governments.

In the ideological area, the PCRM progressed from the Marxist-Leninist doctrine to promoting the idea of "postindustrialism" in only seven years of rule. It is curious that in the new western typology,[10] parties promoting postindustrialism are regarded as extremely right. These parties usually have strict structuring based on traditions and a leader whose directives cannot be discussed or contested, and the PCRM is a case in point. It did not follow the promised ideological precepts in eight years of rule, choosing instead to meet current necessities of the people and their own interests by pragmatic measures.

PCRM leaders have surprisingly become key promoters of orthodox Christianity. Under their auspices, the "Holy Fire" from Jerusalem is brought every year on Easter Eve; churches are being renovated, and new ones are being founded. However, the PCRM does not give up communist rhetoric and rites, which are constantly practiced to keep the electoral support of the most disadvantaged social categories. In the economic area, after declaring the "liberal revolution" in April 2007, in 2008 the PCRM government made public one of the most impressive lists of facilities to be privatized. New privatization plans of the PCRM government together with privatization programs for 1995–1996 and 1997–1998 elaborated under the auspices of PDAM (a "substitute" and political ally of the PCRM) in reality exceeds the privatizations operated by the so-called democrats. Thus, the communists and their allies proved to be the most important adepts of privatization in the Republic of Moldova. At the same time, the modernization and "slipping" toward center of the PCRM motivated several left-wing parties during the PCRM rule to try enlarging their electoral basis at the expense of PCRM, accusing it of not being an authentic communist party and of having changed its pro-Russia option into pro-West. But efforts of the Socialist Party of Moldova, Party of Socialists of Moldova Patria-Rodina, Social-Political Republican Movement Ravnopravie, Labor Union Patria-Rodina, and Movement of Moldovan gastarbeiters from Moscow Patria-Moldova to compete with the PCRM on the left-wing segment have failed. Most recently the Movement of Russia's Friends in Moldova worked hard to set up a civic platform that would consolidate the pro-Russia electorate against the PCRM. This movement was led by Vasily Tarlev, a former prime minister and key character of the PCRM ruling team during 2001–2008. After resigning in March 2008,

Tarlev has displayed his own political ambitions and the PCRM is now presumably more alert to the danger of finding other left-wing parties and movements eager to "seize" its electorate.

Right-Wing Segment of the Political Spectrum

After the perestroika period, the right-wing segment of the political spectrum has been dominated by parties promoting the ideas of the People's Front of Moldova (FPM)—the first and largest alternative to the communist party. For this reason, the Christian Democratic People's Party (PPCD) has constantly had an influential position as the FPM successor on the right-wing part of the political scale.

Although the FPM had a speedy ascension lasting approximately three years (1988–1991), its efficiency and influence started declining when its leaders had to show flexibility and administrative skills. In addition, the FPM leaders were not prepared to replace the heroic and confrontational rhetoric adequate while contesting the communist domination with a suitable rhetoric and behavior for holding state authority. A series of factors, such as external political-military pressure and the need to smooth away ethnolinguistic and socioeconomic conflicts and solve the people's problems of daily life, led to the reemergence of the only holders of administrative capacities—former nomenclatura— behind various democratic screens. Undoubtedly the above-mentioned problems proved to be difficult and boring for the FPM intellectuals installed on a heroic platform of making history and creating national revival, and so the former nomenclatura who remained set in the administrative cobweb did not face any difficulty in taking over authority from the FPM representatives in 1993.

When the reorganized former nomenclatura were recalled to regain authority at the first free and pluralist elections in 1994, the FPM experienced a continuous splitting process that went through several rounds. After the 1994 parliamentary elections, two massive fragments of the FPM—the Christian Democratic People's Front (FPCD) or the PPCD since 1999, and the Congress of Intellectuals (CI), which turned into the Party of Democratic Forces (PFD)—as well as some "pieces" of the former FPM started competing for an electoral segment that had shrunk to approximately 20% to 25%. Only the PPCD has survived to the present time, tenaciously cultivating its identity mythology and the role of promoter and builder of the country's independence. In fact, no other political party has been able to influence continuously the socioeconomic developments of the nation, or demonstrate a ceaseless "institutional memory" (despite the many former FPM personalities present within other political parties).

One other particularity of the PPCD is that it has been in a continuous acute conflict with its political opponents, including those relatively close to it on the political spectrum. The party had to respond to assaults from the right and the left in the second half of the 1990s. On the one hand, the PPCD was accused of promoting radical approaches and attitudes that rejected potential partners and voters. In this regard, the former FPM partners of PPCD accused it of "behaving like a boy in politics" because it did not know how to maintain cooperation with the PDAM, a party gathering the former heads of kolkhozes (Soviet collective farms), which supported the FPM in the late 1980s and early 1990s. On the other hand, the party (and its predecessor the FPM) was unlike all other national revival movements working for independence in the post-Soviet countries in that its final program goal was to join Romania. When accused of extremism during electoral campaigns on this account, it responded with virulence to its opponents, labeling them as "false friends" or "corrupt." Furthermore, a declared but failed goal like seeking union with Romania gives rise to conflicts among its supporters and promoters and an eagerness to determine who could be blamed for the impossibility of reaching the desired goal. In these circumstances, the rating of the PPCD has fallen to approximately 8% to 10% during several electoral cycles. Other parties emerging from the FPM, except for the PFD, which had a rating of approximately 10% before its definitive fall in 2001, could not surpass a rating of 2% to 3%.

After getting a very modest score of 7.5% in the 1994 parliamentary elections, the PPCD leaders repeatedly tried to get rid of clichés and stereotypes, be they self-created or labels imposed by others. The party decided not to participate in the 1995 local elections, justifying that decision by saying the new law on local public administration was undemocratic, but in fact it needed a break to reconsider its positions and regain its place in politics. For this purpose, the PPCD had surprisingly supported President Mircea Snegur in the 1996 presidential elections, though he was the main villain in PPCD pamphlets in 1991–1995 for seeking wider presidential authority and signing the Alma-Ata Agreement establishing the CIS. Then in the 1998 parliamentary elections the PPCD was part of the Democratic Convention of Moldova (CDM), which built on the party of former president Mircea Snegur to create the Party of Rebirth and Conciliation of Moldova (PRCM). These actions suggest that since 1996 the PPCD has been trying to connect itself to administrative resources such as cars, phone communications, and state television and radio stations for campaign purposes, resources that ensure a priori a gain of about 10% to 15% of the vote. Thus despite the fact that President Snegur was the political enemy of PPCD, the party nonetheless agreed to support his reelection in order to transform him into an ally and consequently to gain the resources that would enable it to reenter political life and give itself a more contemporary image in public opinion.

After the 1998 parliamentary elections, the PPCD participated in building the parliamentary majority called Alliance for Democracy and Reforms (ADR).[11] Only the PPCD among the four ADR constituents had in its statute-based goals a clause on union with Romania. The PFD as a political force emerging from FPM did not have such a clear goal, while two other parties, the PRCM and the Bloc for a Democratic and Prosperous Moldova (BMDP), have emerged from the PDAM, known as an antiunionist party. In order to participate in governing as part of such a coalition, the PPCD leaders had to clarify that the union with Romania was a dream of the PPCD, and anybody can dream, but the party will act in compliance with existing realities, as the union could only be achieved through a referendum, with a majority of the population accepting it.[12]

This public explanation did not diminish the suspicions of ADR partners that the PPCD was a unionist (i.e., a movement seeking union with Romania) and hence an antistate party. During the governmental crisis in February–March 1999, the ADR representatives refused to offer the PPCD the required offices in the government, alleging its "antistate" character. The latter action was probably used as an additional excuse by the PPCD to justify its withdrawal from ADR and launch a campaign to accuse the ADR members of corruption.

Once again the PPCD faced the need to change its image. For this purpose, the party adopted a new statute and program at its Fourth Congress in December 1999, eliminating clauses on union with Romania and transforming the PPCD from a "front" into a "party." This way, the PPCD was "Europeanized" to make it possible for it to join the Christian Democrat International. After the 2001 parliamentary elections, the PPCD was the only right-wing party represented in Parliament, and antagonisms between the PPCD and PCRM in 2001–2005 polarized much of the political spectrum, a situation giving the advantage to the Democratic Moldova Bloc (BMD) in the 2005 parliamentary elections. The BMD succeeded because it was represented by a conglomeration of social democratic, social liberal, and liberal parties united around the Alliance Moldova Noastra (Our Moldova) (AMN). Since the PPCD was willing to set up a biparty system in the Republic of Moldova, the PPCD perceived the AMN success as a threat, just as the PDF had been a threat in the second half of the 1990s. Considering that the AMN-PCRM relations were as antagonistic as those of the PPCD-PCRM, despite the different reasons of such an antagonism, the PPCD had an alternative— either to compete with the AMN for being considered the most "anti-communist" party or to become a partner of the PCRM that needed support to reelect the chief of state.

Under the influence of external forces, which urged the necessity of maintaining the political stability of the country, the PPCD set aside antagonisms and supported the reelection of the PCRM leader Vladimir

Voronin as head of state in the 2005 presidential elections (just as it had supported Mircea Snegur in 1996).[13]

PPCD behavior over the years has revealed that the party always seeks either to be the unique opposition force or to cooperate with the ruling party. In 1996, it justified its decision to ally with Snegur on the grounds that that leader had changed his "pro-Moldova" visions in 1995, proposing a referendum to modify Article 13 of the constitution and replace "Moldovan language" with "Romanian language." The PPCD-PCRM "consensus" in 2005 was reached after the PCRM replaced the strategic goal of joining the Russia-Belarus Union with the goal of joining the European Union.

After such changes in the PPCD attitudes, many local observers forecast the party's withdrawal from the political scene, but despite its low percentage of support (now approximately 10%), the party manages to convince its voters that it has the right goals: After all, ruling parties deny their own goals to embrace those of the PPCD. In such circumstances PPCD leaders argued that there is no need to oppose PCRM anymore as it pushes Moldova in the correct direction—closer to European Union. In their turn, those who accused PPCD of treachery because of cooperation with PCRM argue that it is absurd to trust in the sincerity of a communist party.

By virtue of this history, PPCD activity is among the most contested in Moldovan politics. The PPCD shift to the center and its cooperation with its former greatest political enemy, the PCRM, after the 2005 parliamentary elections has caused three liberal parties—the Liberal Party (PL), the Liberal Democratic Party of Moldova (PLDM), and the National Liberal Party (PNL)—to contest the PPCD positions on the center-right segment, accusing it of "betrayal." The PPCD replies by displaying its accomplishments in the battle for the country's independence (anyone seeking to undermine the PPCD positions would actually commit a "sacrilege") and by insisting on the skills it has acquired over the past 20 years in fighting the corruption of the other opposition parties of the center right.

The Centrist Segment of the Political Spectrum

The centrist part of the political scene is usually controlled by parties that may be called "emanations of authority," meaning parties created with administrative support by influential political groups, which ruled the country. The PDAM, supporting agricultural interests and created by the parliamentary group Viata Satului (Country Life) in October 1991, was the first such party after the Republic of Moldova became independent. Besides being legislators, the majority of Viata Satului members were heads of kolkhozes (collective farms), sovhozes (state farms), and other agroindustrial enterprises and were thus known as the "rural nomenclatura." Viata Satului members were quite careful to prepare what they called a "centrist" political platform for taking over power, claiming to provide a compromise aimed at getting rid of the "radical-isms" of both the FPM and the Interfront. The PDAM influence increased rapidly after the party was created. In the beginning, after the February–March 1990 parliamentary elections, the Viata Satului parliamentary group consisted of 60 of 380 members of Parliament. Before the early parliamentary elections in February 1994, the party had already run key offices in the state leadership. In particular, the informal PDAM leader held the office of prime minister, while the president of the country and chair of parliament supported the party, although they were not party members. The common centrist position and nomenclatura past no doubt made the three highest-ranking char-acters feel comfortable under the political shelter of the PDAM. This guaranteed an extraordinary administrative support for the PDAM that ensured it the absolute majority in Parliament—56 of 104 seats.

Unexpectedly, however, the breakup of PDAM came faster than its ascension. Just one year after gaining the absolute majority in Parlia-ment, the party began to split up and the process ended by putting the party entirely out of political life after the 1998 parliamentary elec-tions. The "centrist" ideology was inefficient against the ambitions of the three leaders, all competing for the office of president. However, the PDAM did not disappear altogether. Two former groups of the party gave rise to another two parties, which may be described as "emanations of authority" like PDAM. Thus, the PRCM was created in 1995 by former president Mircea Snegur together with a group of for-mer PDAM parliamentarians who decided to follow him. The second party—the Movement for a Democratic and Prosperous Moldova (MMDP)—was created in February 1997 by a group of former PDAM parliamentarians in order to ensure parliamentary support to newly elected President Petru Lucinschi, former chair of parliament. The MDPM turned into the Democratic Party of Moldova (DPM) in 2000.

The AMN is another "emanation of authority." It has origins in the Alliance of Independents of the Republic of Moldova (AIRM) that became a true "emanation of local authority," especially in the capital of the country, Chisinau. This is because Chisinau's share in the econ-omy of the country is 60% to 70% and Chisinau voters constitute approximately 25% of the total; electorate. The AIRM emerged as the will of the "politically unaffiliated" representatives of the local admin-istration to oppose the expansion of the PCRM power at the local level. This new "output of local authority" managed to become an alternative center for the strengthening of opposition forces.

A distinct particularity of parties that are "emanations of authority" is that they were, or still are, led by former highest-ranking officials: the chief of state, speakers, prime ministers, and the mayor of Chisinau.

An additional advantage held by these parties is that they always have the possibility of gaining the golden share of power, a possibility reserved for centrist parties in a two-and-a-half-party system. Although the party system in Moldova is not stable and no clear classic party system is observed, the centrist forces are able to change the balance in favor of either the right- or left-wing forces when the two are relatively evenly matched. This happened after the 1998 parliamentary elections, when the BMDP swayed toward the creation of the ADR. Although the absolute PCRM majority in Parliament starting in 2001 deprived centrist parties of this advantage, there are clear signs that the role of centrist parties will be important once again after the 2009 parliamentary elections.

The big problem of "emanation of authority" parties is how to keep themselves afloat when they have to pass from governance into opposition. It is normal for their period of governance not to last for more than one parliamentary legislature. Once in opposition, these parties become "normal parties" and their survival depends on their ability to take advantage of the state administrative resources while governing and create large networks of influential persons in various administrative structures or other bodies, around which the party's territorial branches are set and developed.

So far, two "emanation of authority" parties have survived and have opposition factions in the Parliament of the Republic of Moldova— PDM and AMN—the former being placed on the center left and the latter on the center right. Although centrist "emanation of authority" parties seem to be concerned about maintaining some political groups in power, in fact they play a positive role in mitigating conflicts between the political right and left, calling for a golden middle way and the avoidance of extremes.

In general, political developments in the Republic of Moldova can be said to have gone through four distinct periods as it swung back and forth between change and stabilization. The first period may be called romantic, taking place as the country gained independence and affirmed its symbols; the second, pragmatic, when the freedom gained in the romantic period was institutionalized by adopting a new constitution and the massive privatization process got under way; the third, which I name pseudo-restoration, began when the communist PCRM took power, making unkeepable promises to rebuild socialism and communism on the basis of Marxist-Leninist theory and to re-create the Soviet Union on new principles; and finally there is the period of national consensus, in which former confirmed political enemies PCRM and PPCD, on the one hand, and other opposition parties, on the other hand, have pledged to promote the process of integrating Moldova in Europe, an initiative that may yet have a chance to become a national goal, consolidating the society and focusing party competition around a single question: Which of them is most capable of bringing the country into the European Union quickly and efficiently?

Perhaps the time of transition will be completed as society passes into a new normality and the amplitude of change possible begins to oscillate around equilibrium, rather than seesawing between radical change and stagnation. The Moldovan political class has been looking for such a point of equilibrium for the past 15 years, trying to find the so-called national idea. Since the influence of external factors has a bigger impact on the political stability of Moldova than her internal capacities to oppose them, the identification of that national idea has proved to be a very difficult exercise. So far the Moldovan political class has failed to agree on a series of key problems: how to settle the Transdniestrian conflict, now internationalized with the participation of Russia, Ukraine, European Union, the United States, and the OSCE; how to deal with the opportunities and challenges following the European Union and NATO enlargements, which reached the borders of the Republic of Moldova; how to treat the question of European integration and presence in CIS structures; what to do about commercial challenges after Russian embargoes on Moldovan exports and the dramatic rise in the price of fuel; how to determine and address the impact of the Russian-Georgian war on regional security; and how to gauge prospects for settling the Transdniestrian conflict and reintegrate the country.

It is a formidable list. However, a national consensus on European integration was reached in the Republic of Moldova after several electoral cycles, and this consensus of political parties is a positive step, promising the possibility of all pursuing a common course.

THE IMPACT OF LEGISLATION ON PARTIES AND ELECTIONS ON THE MOLDOVAN MULTIPARTY SYSTEM

Given the fact that the multiparty system in the Republic of Moldova began as a race of national movements, the development of that system does not run counter to the approach of Georges Lavau, who says that party systems are the results of social and historic processes,[14] and to a smaller extent, of electoral systems. National movements were particularly likely to invoke historic arguments and aspirations to adjust sociopolitical processes to the "historic truth." The problem is that the various forms of "historic truth" promoted by various parties run counter to one another, giving birth to social tensions, separatist movements, and socioeconomic degradation. In such circumstances the most powerful political force that manages to take control of Parliament will impose its visions, adopting laws and regulations governing the parties' activity and electoral processes, as suits its purposes.

The Impact of Legislation on Parties

The first law on parties and other sociopolitical organizations, adopted by Parliament on September 17, 1991, was very permissive and contained ample and easy-to-respect regulations regarding the registration of parties and sociopolitical organizations: It required 300 signatures and respect for some formal procedures. The law did not stipulate any essential difference between political parties and movements, accepting all those who were willing to participate in politics. It described both types of organizations as "voluntary associations of citizens established on the basis of a community of interests, ideals and goals to jointly meet the political willingness of a part of population by legally gaining the state authority and exercising it."[15] The law explained political leagues, fronts, unions, and movements as sociopolitical organizations. The registration of membership was mandatory for all parties and sociopolitical organizations.

The above-mentioned norms were effective until 1998, when the number of parties exceeded 60 due to the easy registration procedure. The 1994 and 1998 parliamentary elections proved that only four parties and blocs were capable of achieving the 4% electoral threshold. Another approximately 10 to 15 parties and electoral blocs, which participated in elections, failed the electoral threshold but gathered about 20% of the votes. Almost half of the registered parties could not participate in elections, not having met the single necessary condition of registering lists of candidates with the Central Election Commission. Therefore, the law on parties was modified in September 1998, making it more difficult to register a party. All existing parties were obliged to register again, while new parties were registered only if they had at least 5,000 members from at least half of the administrative-territorial units, with no fewer than 150 members in each of them. In fact, the new regulations obstructed the new registration of regional parties, raising discontent particularly among political forces in the autonomous Gagauz-Yeri region.

The ruling PCRM introduced new amendments to the law on parties in 2002, obliging parties to report and register again every year, in order to demonstrate that the number of members did not decrease below 5,000 persons. Under the influence of protests by parties and pressures by European institutions, the authorities had to give up and reintroduce the previous norms.

In December 2007 the parliament adopted a new law on parties to regulate the funding of parliamentary parties for those that reach the 6% electoral threshold or have at least 5% of all seats in regional local councils. For this purpose, 0.2% of the state budget is now allocated to fund parties proportionately to the number of seats in parliament and regional councils. This clause will enter into force after the spring 2009 parliamentary elections. These regulations aim to make it more difficult for small parties in comparison with stronger parties and thus to "clear up" the political spectrum. Estimations based on results of the last elections and findings of surveys say that only 7 of the 28 registered parties are now capable of entering parliament. However, only five of the seven parties are likely to be able to make use of their chances in the next election.

Impact of Legislation on Elections

The development of the party system in Moldova was greatly influenced by the absolutely proportional electoral system, which was constantly used in four electoral cycles starting in 1994. The introduction of the proportional system was preceded by the February–March 1990 elections to the Supreme Soviet of Moldavian Soviet Socialist Republic held on an alternative basis for the first time after approximately 50 years. The proportional system replaced the majority system in a situation after the 1990 elections where many lawmakers had left the political structures that promoted them, arguing that they alone represented the people, not the parties. Thus the inefficient functioning of the parliament caused by the division of the corps of parliamentarians was partly due to the majority electoral system.

The new law was adopted before the early parliamentary elections in February 1994. It stipulated the organization of legislative elections on the basis of the "limited proportional system," namely on the basis of closed lists of candidates in electoral constituencies with more mandates, which should correspond to regional administrative-territorial units. Since the administrative-territorial organization on the basis of large regions was unfinished, building electoral constituencies in compliance with the new law on elections was impossible. Even more, it was impossible to build electoral constituencies and commissions in the districts controlled by the separatist Transdniestrian regime. In such circumstances, the parliament decided to reenforce the law on elections, replacing the limited proportional electoral system with an absolutely proportional one, with the whole country now a single electoral constituency.

The deputy mandates were distributed only among parties that garnered more than 4% of the votes, according to the d'Hondt method, which encourages big parties. The electoral threshold was not effective for independent candidates who could enter parliament only if the votes they won were part of the decreasing number of series composed after the D'Hondt method. None of the independent candidates won the necessary votes to enter parliament in the 1994 legislative elections, as well as those that followed. In addition, the parties that did not pass the 4% electoral threshold nevertheless won 18% of the votes. Such votes qualified as "lost" ballots and were distributed proportionately among the four parties that passed the threshold. A new Electoral Code was drafted and adopted in 1997, unifying all electoral norms and procedures and stipulating the creation of a Central Election Commission with a six-year mandate for its members. The Electoral Code maintained the absolutely proportional electoral system for parliamentary elections. The 4% electoral threshold was now introduced for independent candidates as well. The president of those times, Petru Licinschi, did not appreciate the Electoral Code, insisting on the necessity to reintroduce the majority electoral system or at least to adopt a "parallel" system according to the German model. However, parliamentary factions sought an absolutely proportional electoral system with a 4% electoral threshold for all electoral competitors, including independent candidates.

The next substantial changes in the Electoral Code were introduced in March 2000 when the electoral threshold was raised to 6% for parties and reduced for independent candidates to 3%. The changes clearly targeted small parties, which could not reach the 4% electoral threshold. In consequence, two former parliamentary parties—PRCM and the DPM, which initiated and supported those changes—in effect disadvantaged themselves as they failed to gain the number of votes needed to pass the new threshold at the 2001 parliamentary elections (the PRCM lacked only 0.1% to pass the threshold). Their failure helped account for the fact that the majority communist faction was able to gain the constitutional majority (71 of the 101 seats), and thus the change to 6% had a very serious impact on political life and the multiparty system.

The trend to raise obstacles in the way of "small" parties had a logical evolution in 2002, when the ruling PCRM supported the initiative by its number one political rival, the PPCD, raising the electoral threshold for electoral blocs. Now blocs consisting of two parties had to win more than 9%, while those comprised of three or more parties had to reach at least 12% of the votes to gain seats in parliament. Of course, this action targeted possible preelectoral coalitions, which could compete with well-known political forces—the PCRM as ruling party and its number one political rival PPCD. In fact, it was an attempt to impose a two party system, an attempt that failed because the PCRM vote was approximately fivefold higher than that of the PPCD. In addition, the possibility of building electoral blocs allowed another political force, the BMD, to find a place between the PCRM and PPCD by garnering a vote higher than the PPCD.

An opposite trend in the evolution of the situation was observed after the 2005 parliamentary elections. At the demand of opposition parliamentary parties, which accepted a partnership with the PCRM on the basis of the newfound national consensus on seeking membership in the European Union, parliamentary working commissions were formed to revise many legislative acts of Moldova in line with recommendations by the Venice Commission of the Council of Europe. The Electoral Code was part of the list of revised laws. Under the new Electoral Code, the Central Election Commission had nine members, one appointed by the country's president, one by the government, and seven by the parliament (including five members of opposition factions, according to their number of seats). Another important change was to bring back the 4% electoral threshold for parties and sociopolitical organizations participating in elections. The electoral threshold for all preelectoral blocs was unified and established at the level of 8%. Without testing the impact of the last modifications, the PCRM parliamentary majority partly supported by the PPCD faction modified the Electoral Code again in April 2008, making the conditions for entering the parliament yet more difficult. In particular, the electoral threshold was again set at the level of 6%, electoral blocs were prohibited, and holders of dual citizenship were restricted from running for the parliament.

In this context, it is worth mentioning that surveys reveal that the majority of respondents (53%) call for a majority electoral system, while another 30% support the proportional electoral system.

CONCLUSIONS

The multiparty system in the Republic of Moldova has become an indispensable element of the shop-window democracy. The shortcomings of Moldovan democracy are a direct consequence of the country's political culture as manifested during transition. Nevertheless, the role of political parties in Moldova has generally been a positive one in the past 20 years. The parties' greatest contribution to democratization was its resistance to the establishment of a presidential system in Moldova, calling constantly for a checks and balances system.

Still, although one can admit that the main Moldovan political parties were committed to democratization, Moldovan democracy is not a clear emanation of conscious activity of parties, but rather a collateral phenomenon of the party competition to dominate the political scene. In a sense, Moldovan political parties are acting like the invisible hand of Adam Smith's economic theory—each party seeks its own interests and the defeat of the others. No one can say that the effects of this partisan "invisible hand" are entirely negative, although some regulation is needed beyond the regulatory norms imposed by international organizations.

Indeed, democracy has emerged from political competition among parties that were unable to take absolute control of the state or control it for a limited term as stipulated in the Constitution. The semipresidential constitutional system (1994–2000) and semiparliamentary system (from 2000 on) have produced a multiparty system, and this has been a positive factor for democratization of the Republic of Moldova. External factors have strongly influenced the behavior of the Moldovan political class. In order to articulate the interests of a small country, dependent on international support, the Moldovan political class had to consider the conditionality of external economic and political support by reforming the economy and internal democratic institutions. In this respect, the external influence was generally positive. It is not unimportant that in recent years Moldova has received direct grants from the European Union and the United States that account for up to 7% of its annual budget. The promotion and observance of democratic reforms and standards are conditions for receiving such grants. For a small, poor country, without even the transportation capacities of Georgia or Ukraine, those grants and political support are very serious and no Moldovan political force in power can afford to ignore the imposed norms of behavior. International influence is extremely important in the democratization of Moldova.

The national consensus on European integration indicates the maturation of the Moldovan political class and its new capacity to reach compromises. But once the national consensus was reached, the pivot of ideological and "geopolitical" competition between main parties was demolished. The parties do not compete as to which of them could bring Moldova closer to European Union membership. This situation gives rise to new risks related to the cartelization of parties. (The consensus between PCRM and PPCD could be seen as an example of cartel agreement.) Recently, the first signs of such a development were very clearly observed. In addition, the "de-ideologization" of competition between parties leaves room for the penetration of large donors into the political scene. The risk of this phenomenon cannot yet be estimated, but it is not negligible given the quality of the Moldovan political culture. Whether the unseen hand of party competition will continue to guide Moldova's "imitative democracy" along the path of serious democratization remains to be seen.

EPILOGUE

On April 5, 2009, parliamentary elections were held in Moldova. Turnout was 57.5% and the distribution of votes was as follows: PCRM—49.48%; PL—13.13%; Liberal Democratic Party of Moldova (LDPM)—12.43%; "Our Moldova" Alliance (OMA)—9.77%. Other parties and independent candidates were unable to pass the electoral threshold of 6%. Accordingly, PCRM obtained 60 mandates, PL and PLDM obtained 15 mandates each, and AMN obtained 11 mandates. Thus, although the PCRM gained a great advance over its showing in 2007 (34% of the national vote), it still lacked the 61 seats necessary to be able to elect the new president of the country without the help of the opposition parties. However, the leaders of the three liberal opposition parties had declared in advance that they would never vote for a communist candidate for that office.

Immediately after the results were announced, a hastily formed anticommunist group, representing several Moldovan politically nonaffiliated NGOs, sent out a call over the Internet for a "funeral of democracy" ceremony, and on April 6 several thousand young people attended the meeting in Central Square in Chisinau. The manifestation was peaceful, but it inspired leaders of the opposition to call for further protests. The LDPM organized a protest meeting on April 7 and other opposition leaders joined in signing a statement asking the Central Electoral Commission to suspend the aggregation of election results, as a result of numerous violations.

However, the LDPM and the other two liberal parties that passed the electoral threshold proved to be unprepared for large mass protests and were unable to keep control of the vast crowd that turned out for the second day of protest. Young people gathered in Central Square in Chisinau demanded that the elections be annulled and new ones organized. They divided into two groups, one peacefully remaining in the square and the other staging protests in front of the presidential and parliament buildings. The latter protests soon degenerated into violence, with altercations between police and protesters taking place. Serious damage was done to the government buildings, and the government accused the opposition leaders of preparing a coup d'état. The situation was complicated by fear of the impact of the global financial and economic crises on a politically weakened Moldova and questions as to the involvement of Russia and Romania in the events. Even when calm was restored, the events had clearly deepened Moldova's traditional cleavages—urban versus rural, youth versus older citizens, pro-Romanian versus pro-Russian versus pro-independence. Outgoing President Vladimir Voronin accepted the proposition of the plenary session of the communist party that he become the chair of parliament. In this way the center of power was moved from the presidency to the parliament. A search began for a new president, one who would be obedient to Voronin and dependent on him, as well as somehow satisfy the expectations of the opposition regarding changing procedures to be used in naming persons to that office. Under these circumstances, the prospects for Moldovan political parties to serve as effective agencies of democratic linkage can only be seen as seriously impaired.

CHAPTER 3

Are the Parties of the Russian "Sovereign Democracy" Sustaining Democratic Governance?

Anatoly Kulik

INTRODUCTION

More than half a century ago, E. E. Schattschneider stated that "political parties created democracy and modern democracy is unthinkable save in terms of parties."[1] Since then, his assertion has become an axiom. Despite the dramatic alteration in recent decades in the relationship between the changing nature of political parties and the changing meaning of democracy, as well as the rather wide antiparty criticism, parties are generally accepted as a necessary and desirable institution for representative democratic governance. The fact that they have played a major role in the institutionalization of democratic government underlines the widely shared belief that strong political parties are essential to competitive democratic politics, particularly in emerging democracies.

Just after being elected to the presidency in March 2000, Vladimir Putin declared in his first address to the Federal Assembly of the Russian Federation that Russia needs competitive politics and political parties enjoying public support and a stable reputation to provide a link between power and people in democratic society.[2]

Eight years later he handed over to his chosen successor Dmitry Medvedev the defragmented multiparty system wherein four "strong" parties occupied all 450 places in the State Duma, the lower chamber of the federal legislative body. The "strongest" among them, United Russia (Yedinaya Rossiya) claims to have more than 1.5 million members.

According to the supposed relationship between parties and democracy, one could expect that with the consolidation of its political parties, Russia will now advance, entrenching democratic changes in governance. However, many political scientists and observers, both in Russia and elsewhere, have noted instead a growing authoritarian tendency in political development. Experts at Freedom House even contend that from 1999 to 2008 Russia has moved backward on every nations-in-transition (NIT) indicator of democracy and has become the leading antidemocratic force in its region.[3]

To examine this paradox of failing democracy while parties are getting stronger, I will trace the evolution of political parties throughout the nation after the declaration of Russia's sovereignty and analyze their main functions in the current political regime, self-labeled as a "sovereign democracy."

Given the crucial importance of political competition for democratic governance, I take the open competition of parties as a point of departure in my reasoning. I will show that after Russia gained sovereignty and adopted its new constitution in 1993, the entire process of shaping parties to fit the sovereign democracy was aimed at transforming them into a tool that would in fact secure the survival and self-reproduction of a monarchical regime of governance. In the absence of any resistance from a feeble and dissociated civic society, the ruling regime converted parties from institutions, providing arenas for free political competition into a mechanism that blocked all competition. This is the crucial distinction between genuine democracy and "sovereign democracy." In keeping with the general strategy of authoritarian bureaucratic modernization of Russia, the multiparty system was incorporated into the vertical framework of power created by Putin and has become its appendage. Parties have had no other options: They have had to agree to this "only game in town" imposed by the Kremlin or disappear.

Besides performing the function of decorating the state with a facade of democracy, Russian parties are also expected to control the power ambitions of administrative and business elites at all levels. Depending entirely on the presidential administration, party factions in the Duma are now nothing more than a rubber stamp for decisions made by the closed circle at the top of power.

In the conclusion, I argue that the ambitious goals of authoritarian modernization of Russia to which the political rights of citizens and competition of political parties were sacrificed have not been reached but have on the contrary moved farther away. Moreover, it becomes ever more evident that these goals, as well as sustained economic development and enduring social stability, cannot be achieved within the limits of the present bureaucratic paradigm, a structure that has proved to be not only ineffective, but possibly counterproductive. Even if it were to give up this paradigm in favor of genuine political contestation, the Kremlin would still face a serious deficiency of actors who could create such a transformation. Reformers in the Kremlin have remained without support from either the bureaucracy seeking its own private interests or from the politically apathetic population. These are the main challenges in the foreseeable future.[4]

DEMOCRACY AND PARTY COMPETITION

Representative democratic governance is accepted and widely practiced all over the world. Despite the fundamental transformation in its institutions and processes that have taken place in the past quarter century, there is no doubt regarding its overall institutional framework, wherein political parties continue to play an important, perhaps even increasingly important, role.[5]

The indispensability of political parties in representative democratic governance arises from the fact that there is no better social institution to set about the business of recruiting leaders, structuring electoral choice, and organizing government. They remain the main mechanisms capable of putting into motion the entire procedure of democratic governance and securing regular legitimate turnover in office and change of government policies. Representative government, universal suffrage, and political parties compose the main pillars of democratic governance. It is the parties that connect the first two in the political process.

The "third wave" of democratization entirely changed the political landscape of the world in the last quarter of the 20th century. With the fall of communism and the breakup of the Soviet Union in 1991, 15 post-Soviet republics, Russia among them, joined the great tide of countries moving away from dictatorial rule and declared democracy as a primary goal in the transformation of their political systems.

The phenomenon of the third wave called into being the teleological "transition paradigm" that a priori considered all these countries as transitioning to democracy despite many variations in patterns of political change and underlying "structural" conditions such as political history, institutional legacies, and sociocultural traditions. It was a paradigm inspired by belief in the determinative importance of establishing regular elections that would broaden and deepen political participation and the democratic accountability of the state to its citizens.

Yet already by the early 2000s, it was becoming evident that of the nearly 100 countries considered as transitional, only a relatively small number were clearly en route to becoming successful, well-functioning democracies or at least making some progress in that direction.[6] Although the majority of these nations have taken on the main formal attributes of democratic governance, including a democratic constitution, political parties in government and opposition, and regular elections, and thus have met the terms of the Schumpeterian minimalist theory of democracy, only a few have become relatively well-functioning democracies. And Russia does not fall even within the 100: In the category of "hybrid regimes" in the Economist Intelligence Unit's Index of Democracy for 2007, Russia was listed as 102 of 167.[7]

The failure of the transition paradigm shows clearly that political institutions associated with democracy are irrelevant if they are only superficially institutionalized. What makes institutions of representative democratic governance work, and what is lacking in the minimalist conception of democracy? Evidently, one of the answers might be party competition.

As Schattschneider said, "The parties created democracy, or perhaps more accurately, modern democracy is a byproduct of party competition."[8] The centrality of institutionalized party competition for democratic governance was stressed later by Seymour Martin Lipset in his attempt to present his own minimalist conception of democracy.[9] Robert Dahl believed that despite the vast variety of democratic institutions, the presence of competition in a political system is sufficient to qualify it as democratic.[10] In this view it is not elections and parties as such that move a nation toward democracy, but rather free party contestation. Just as competition in the economy helps prevent one business from gaining monopolistic control over the market, so free political competition is likely to prevent one single person or group of people from gaining monopolistic control over state power. To understand why democracy is failing even as parties grow stronger in Russia, we need to look more closely at the development of multiparty competition in the post-Soviet period.

THE PATH-DEPENDENT TRAJECTORY OF MULTIPARTY SYSTEM DEVELOPMENT

On June 12, 1990, the Russian Soviet Socialist Republic (RSSR) was one of the first republics to declare its sovereignty within the Soviet Union and thereby opened the way to the breakdown of the Soviet Union. The Declaration of State Sovereignty proclaimed Russia a democratic law-governed state with separation of powers, and shortly thereafter Russia adopted a law legitimizing *mnogopartijnost*—a multiparty system. In August 1991, during the attempted coup d'état, the first freely elected Russian president, Boris Yeltsin, banned activities of the Communist Party of the Soviet Union in Russia and confiscated its huge property, thus eliminating the strongest possible challenger to his own regime.

At that time the newly emerging parties were not entitled to nominate candidates and campaign for them in the party's name, despite formal legalization. Even if a campaigning candidate adhered to a party, he had to present a personal "program." Among the 1,032 People's Deputies of

Russia in January 1993, only 195 declared their party affiliation. Lacking legal instruments permitting them to influence politics, parties performed only two functions—facilitating the self-actualization of political entrepreneurs and intraelite communication.

The foundation of the current model of mnogopartijnost was laid by both the Constitution of the Russian Federation adopted on December 12, 1993, and by Yeltsin's stipulation by decree that half of the 450 seats in the newly established State Duma were to be elected on the federal party-list system of proportional representation (PR).

The election campaign of 1993 started with the appearance of the presidential decree of September 21, 1993, dissolving the Congress of the People Deputies—the supreme body of state power—and the then Supreme Council of the Russian Federation. The decree was issued at the peak of the collision between the president and the legislative body on the matters of national political and economic development, as well as the distribution of power and assets between the two branches of government. At the same time, the decree announced elections for the State Duma, the new Russian parliament, in an effort to renew that body and eliminate rebellious deputies calling for the drafting of a new Russian constitution. The Supreme Council and the head of the Constitutional Court judged this move as an unlawful seizure of power, and the political collision evolved into a direct clash. In the state of emergency imposed by Yeltsin, armed troops obedient to him took the building of the Supreme Council by storm and broke down the resistance of its defenders.

The new parliament was to be inaugurated under a new constitution. The applicable law at that time, "On referendum of the RSSR" from October 16, 1990, required that questions concerning amendments of the constitution must be decided by an all-Russian referendum, and power to hold a referendum was given to the Congress of the People's Deputies or to the Supreme Council. In defiance of that law, as well of the acting Constitution, on October 15, 1993, Yeltsin issued a decree, "About the National Vote on the Draft of the Constitution of the Russian Federation." The law "On Referendum of the RSSR" also required that decisions concerning constitutional change must be adopted by the majority of registered voters. However, Yeltsin's decree stipulated that the constitution should be adopted by a simple majority of votes. The voting on the constitution was set for the same time as the election for the members of the new parliament. Thus, Yeltsin was resolutely seeking to prevent any possible fiasco likely to disturb his plans. The draft of the constitution was published on November 10, 1993, one month before the national voting. The short time span, as well as the postcollision situation in the country, did not allow for popular discussion. According to official data, the national voting turnout was 54.3%, and 57.6% of those who did vote approved the new constitution.[11]

Twenty-four regional governments of the federation rejected the draft, and in 17 the turnout was insufficient for valid voting. All ballot papers were destroyed soon afterward, and the vote on constitution returns, as well as the election to the State Duma results, were nowhere published in their entirety, thus calling into question their credibility.

The state of emergency was cancelled on October 10 after the active phase of collision ended, but a presidential decree issued on October 19, 1993, nevertheless banned the participation of those parties, public organizations, and movements that had backed the Supreme Council in its confrontation with the president, on the pretext that this was necessary to ensure state and public security during the election campaign.

A national constitution defines the fundamental political principles and establishes the structure, procedures, powers, and duties of a government. Whereas many of the constitutions adopted after World War II and after the collapse of communist regimes in southern and Eastern Europe acknowledge the relevance of parties and free competition for democracy, the Russian constitution has very little to say about their role in governance: "Political plurality and a multiparty system shall be recognized in the Russian Federation."[12] One of the main goals pursued by Yeltsin in holding the national vote on the new constitution was to redistribute powers in favor of the president, not to ensure party government via a strong parliament.

The constitution guaranteed Yeltsin's victory over the people's deputies on the principle of "winner-takes-all." After the Constitutional Assembly had reconciled different disagreements and presented its draft, Yeltsin inserted new provisions that actually reproduced the traditional pattern of Russian political systems, wherein power is concentrated in the hands of a dominant ruler.[13] In this model the president has became the head of the state with wide-ranging yet quite loosely defined powers; he is separated from all branches of government and is set above all political and legal institutions.[14] The system of checks and balances is severely one-sided and does nothing but secure his domination. He is practically unaccountable to any representative institution.

The new constitution made a starting point in laying out the trajectory for multiparty system development. It significantly reduced the powers of parliament, the institution that is the vital arena for party participation in democratic governance. Parties in the Duma exercise a minimal effect on formation of the executive branch: Federal ministers are appointed and dismissed by the president; the Duma approves nomination of a prime minister under the threat of dissolution by the president; parties have almost no powers enabling them to oversee and influence the executive branch. The Duma's power to issue a vote of no-confidence in the government appointed by the president must be exercised under the threat of likely dissolution.[15]

Since the parties in the Duma have no power to form the government and keep a check on its activity, they cannot perform their primary functions in representative democratic governance, providing for turnover in government and alteration of its policy when the government loses popular credibility among the voters. A party's victory in an election does not bestow upon it even the theoretical possibility of putting its program into practice. Party programs thus have only minor value in electoral competition.

Hence, at the very emergence of the current multiparty system, parties were trapped in a vicious circle. Not having real powers in governance they cannot mobilize partisans, and without active support of citizens they cannot expect to play a substantive role in politics. At the same time, achieving parliamentary status is a crucial factor of party survival: It opens access to resources of government—administrative, financial, informational, and others—that cannot be obtained otherwise. The essence of the multiparty system established in 1993 might be interpreted as follows: The president has given parties attractive parliamentary privileges but has not shared any real power with them.

This situation foredooms parties seeking parliamentary status to dispirited conformity to the wishes of a presidential administration, which holds in check regional authorities, mass media, law enforcement practice, financial currents, and resources distribution. Having a good relationship with the presidential administration is much more important for the well-being of a party than having a good relationship with its own constituency. Even for the Communist Party of the Russian Federation (CPRF) and for the Liberal Democratic Party of Russia (LDPR), ostentatious opposition to government serves more as electoral symbolism, reinforcing the party's "brand name," than as designation of its real position in the national political spectrum.[16] Thus it is not surprising that the Duma has never ventured to vote no-confidence in government, not even in 1995 when the CPRF and its allies controlled nearly half the votes. The self-preservation instinct of MPs in the majority always takes precedence. The risk of losing political comfort and the privileges of the parliamentary status have always prevented members from crossing the dangerous line.

Being unable to participate in governance, parties in the Duma perform instead as political entrepreneurs pursuing their own goals within the terms of the game. When ideological stimuli for party membership fade, demands for identity and solidarity give way to an expectation of material benefits, and party MPs became nothing more than well-disciplined "yes" men.

Furthermore, the proximity of parliamentary parties to the real center of decision making makes them easy targets for corrupt practice when government actively intervenes in business. Parliamentary parties, no less than the bureaucrats in public administration, seek to increase personal and corporate well-being. The central newspaper Izvestiya, referring to the chair of the Duma's Commission on Corruption, affirmed that the majority of the laws passing through the Duma were biased. Lawmaking has become an MP's consistent and perhaps most reliable source of income for his personal budget and that of his party.[17] Members of parliament themselves have acknowledged that the interests of the business oligarchy[18] are of second priority after those of the Kremlin in the lawmaking process.[19] Vyacheslav Nikonov, a prominent Russian political analyst and president of the Politika Foundation, has noticed the degradation of ideology, the growing pragmatism of the Duma, the commercialization of lawmaking, and the transformation of the Duma into an arena for bargaining among different lobbies' interests, increasing its servility in regard to power.[20] Tatyana Zaslavskaya, one of Russia's leading sociologists, has also commented on the significant pull back from democracy after 1993, just after the multiparty system was institutionalized as an element of the Russian political system.[21] And yet despite the flourishing corruption, a law on lobbying that presumably would have curbed that tendency, first introduced in 1995, has never been adopted by the parliament.

The constituting election of 1993 aimed to restore the faltering legitimacy of Yeltsin's regime and, at the same time, to ensure there would be a manageable majority in the new parliament. From the very beginning Yeltsin sought to get control over the new multiparty system by reducing party competition, and overt opposition was eliminated from electoral participation. During his tenure as prime minister, Yegor Gaidar also headed the pro-presidential electoral bloc Russia's Choice, which included eight other members of the cabinet. The acting deputy minister, together with another three leading members of the cabinet, created another pro-presidential electoral association—the Party of Russian Unity and Concord (PRES). To be registered for the ballot, a public association (a party, an organization, or a movement) or a bloc of such associations had to gather 100,000 or more signatures in a very short time. For most aspirants this was difficult without the support of federal or regional authorities. Of the 35 contenders, the Central Election Commission (CEC) admitted only 13, and only 8 eventually overcame the 5% threshold established by presidential decree. Party leaders decided on the order of the names on the list and thus on the chances of nominees to receive MP mandates.

Four parties were among the winners in 1993: the Liberal-Democratic Party of Russia, CPRF, the Agrarian Party of Russia (APR), and the Democratic Party of Russia (DPR)—whereas the other four—namely, Russia's Choice; the political movement Women of Russia; Bloc Yabloko (Apple), and PRES—were electoral groupings assembled just before the elections (Table 3.1).

Once in the Duma, parties adopted a procedural mechanism of legislation that made themselves the main players and pushed to the

Table 3.1 Results of Parties That Won Elections to the State Duma, December 12, 1993

	Votes (%)		Seats		
	List	SMD	List	SMD	Total (%)
Valid votes (% of electorate)	50.6	50.6			
Invalid votes (% of electorate)	3.7	4.0			
Total votes (% of electorate)	54.3	54.6			
Liberal Democratic Party	21.4	2.7	59.0	5.0	14.3
Russia's Choice	14.5	6.3	40.0	30.0	15.6
Communist Party	11.6	3.2	32.0	16.0	10.7
Women of Russia	7.6	0.5	21.0	2.0	5.1
Agrarian Party of Russia	7.4	5.0	21.0	12.0	7.3
Yabloko	7.3	3.2	20.0	3.0	5.1
Russian Unity and Concord	6.3	2.5	18.0	1.0	4.2
Democratic Party of Russia	5.1	1.9	14.0	1.0	3.3
Movement for Democratic Reforms	3.8	1.9	0.0	4.0	0.9
Civic Union	1.8	2.7	0.0	1.0	0.2
Future of Russia	1.2	0.7	0.0	1.0	0.2
Cedar	0.7	0.5	0.0	0.0	0.0
Dignity and Charity	0.7	0.8	0.0	2.0	0.4
Independents	—	45.2	—	146.0	32.5
Against all	3.9	14.8	—	—	—
Others	0.0	0.7	0.0	0.0	0.0
Invalid ballots	6.8	7.4			
Total	100	100	225	224*	100

*One seat left vacant in Chechnya

Source: Adopted from Russia Votes—a joint project of Centre for the Study of Public Policy, University of Aberdeen and the Levada Center (formerly VCIOM). http://www.russiavotes.org/

background independent members of parliament elected from single-mandate districts.

Despite these discouraging signs, throughout the 1990s many scholars and political observers charged the debility of parties in Russian politics to immaturity and kept faith that they would mature with time and become a driving force in the country to democratic governance. This expectation that so-called proto-parties would inevitably develop into full-grown substantive political actors was the key article of faith in the above mentioned "transition paradigm."

However, by the end of the decade, the truth was becoming clear. Usually the second electoral cycle is associated with consolidation of the new political regime. For analysts of the Moscow Carnegie Center, the second regular election to the Duma in 1999 and the presidential election of 2000 accomplished a transition from a "soviet decorative democracy to [a] Russian manipulative and decorative one."[22]

THE "TUNING" OF THE MULTIPARTY SYSTEM UNDER VLADIMIR PUTIN

Political crisis, exacerbated by the economic crisis and debt default in August 1998, led to the weakening of Kremlin control over political developments. The regional bureaucracy began to join the governors' blocs Fatherland and All Russia, which in August 1999 merged under the popular politician Evgenii Primakov, a presumed candidate for the office of president. One of the key points of his political program supported the redistribution of power, namely, the transition from a presidential to a presidential-parliamentary republic.

Yeltsin, who sought to preserve the general line of his policy after retirement, reacted to that threat by appointing Vladimir Putin, the director of the FSB (Federal Security Service), to the head of the government. Putin's resolute antiterrorist actions in response to the Chechen invasion in Dagestan and a number of explosions that killed numerous victims in some of Russia's cities including Moscow quickly brought him growing popularity. The visible comparison of this young and determined politician to the infirm and discredited Yeltsin also worked in Putin's favor. Still, in September, the chosen successor trailed all other presidential contenders in the polls.

Nearly two months before the election, the presidential administration created its own stakeholder in the run for the Duma, the interregional movement Unity/Bear (Medved) led by the minister for emergency situations and civil defense. The Unity movement was assembled from several minor political groupings, not one of which had a chance of winning more than 1% of the total votes if competing separately. Putin publicly articulated his support for Unity, and the bloc fully profited from this publicity. Its rating rose along with the

growth of Putin's reputation. The election campaign of Unity was neither programmatic nor ideological, its main mottoes being "Strong
State" and "Struggle Against Corruption and Criminality," and its
most sound raison d'être being "We are the party of Putin."

Thus in the campaign of 1999, the Kremlin was no longer wrestling
for power with the traditional communists, but with another clan of the
same state bureaucracy. Since there were no ideological divergences
between the two rivals, the main factors of electoral success became
access to administrative resources and black PR technologies. The
Kremlin's attack frequently overstepped the bounds of acceptable practice.[23] Possessing large financial resources and the backing of the presidential administration, as well as the media support of the two
dominant federal television channels (ORT and RTR) controlled by the
Kremlin, Unity won against Fatherland All Russia (OVR). Under the
rigid pressure of the Kremlin, most regional heads changed their support from OVR to Unity.

Both political and business elites fully accepted the Kremlin's victory
in the election. Many politicians and political groupings, including
those who struggled against Unity in the recent elections, sought to
adhere to it now. Regional leaders also hurried to demonstrate their
loyalty to the Kremlin by creating local branches of Unity in their
regions.

The Kremlin had restored control over the fragmented political elite
on the eve of the presidential election. Access to state-owned mass
media, particularly television channels, was blocked for Putin's rare
opponents in the election campaign.[24] Three months later, Putin won
election in the first round with 52.9% of the votes. A prominent Russian
political observer, Lilia Shevtsova, characterized the new political
regime as "authoritarian-bureaucratic."[25]

From this moment, the policy of the Kremlin regarding parties
became much more consistent, goal-oriented, and vigorous. Its content
was determined by Putin's general approach to securing political stability in the country and promoting the modernization of Russia. Not
relying on the institutions of social self-organization, Putin, just like all
previous reformers in Russia's history, chose the authoritarian model.
He staked his fortunes on the upper layer of federal administration, a
team of top managers of the "Closed Joint Stock Corporation Russia,"
as labeled by some media observers. He gathered his close confidants
around and appointed them to top positions in public administration.
Many of the ministers, deputy ministers, governors, and other office-
holders came from existing power structures, mainly from security
agencies.[26] In his first address to the Federal Assembly of the Russian
Federation 2000, Putin declared: "Self-motivated and responsible agencies of the federal executive branch should serve as a motor of our politics. The foundation of their powers [is] the constitutional duty to

secure stability of the vertical, national mandate endowed to the president in democratic election, [in pursuit of an] integrated strategy of domestic and foreign policy."[27] To make real this intention, a hierarchic power structure was constructed from the top down, and all powers in policy making, including wide-ranging control over resources, as well as over political competition, were concentrated in the presidential administration. This monarchial model of governance is a direct opposite of the polyarchical model introduced by Robert A. Dahl.[28] Justifying this model, Putin referred to the underdevelopment of the political system and civil society in Russia, as well as the lack of a "truly multiparty system."[29]

Putin's interpretation of the Russian policy of western countries has played a significant role in his choice of the monarchial model. He perceives that policy as unequal, unfriendly, and ignorant of the national interests of Russia. He has judged the policy of Euro-Atlantic communities promoting democracy in former soviet republics, accompanied by NATO expansion to the border of Russia, as anti-Russia and threatening to its security.[30]

To facilitate the creation of this form of governance, federal districts with plenipotentiary representatives of the president were created in 2000; governors were no longer elected but were appointed by the president, who could now dismiss them on his discretion on the reason of "loss of credibility." There was a serious change in the policy of intergovernmental fiscal relations that made regions considerably more dependent on the federal administration. All these efforts evidenced the shift from federal to centralized unitary state governance. "The Case of Mikhail Khodorkovsky," the founder of the Russian biggest oil company UKOS who was stripped of his possessions and imprisoned, told business interests in 2003 where they stood in the new system of relations with power. A close group of high-ranking officials from the presidential administration and federal government took positions as top executives on boards of big corporations on a part-time basis and as early as 2006 began to keep a close check on businesses that, in combination, produce above 40% of gross domestic product (GDP).[31]

The presidential administration tried to construct a corporatist regime with the purpose of exerting control over the entire social and economic life of Russia. The regime incorporates all interest groups— federal and regional bureaucracy, political and business elites, mass media, trade unions, and emerging structures of civil societies—into the vertical power construction and makes them its appendages. The party system constitutes one of the agents of this regime, licensed by the Kremlin in exchange for compliance. In this model of governance, parties have been assigned not only the decorative function of being an attribute of "democratic transition," but a no less important instrumental task as well.

Thus the tuning of the party system has included the regulation of party activities through public law, alteration of the electoral system, as well as law enforcement practices that ensure that administrative resources serve as ultima ratio in determining the winners in electoral competition.[32] In combination, these practices have aimed at transforming the party system into an effective tool for manipulating democracy, one that allows the presidential administration to bring under control political competition of business and administrative elites at the federal and regional levels.

Political Parties Law of 2001

Continuing in this vein, the On Political Parties law of 2001 converted a multiparty system into an "only certain parties system" with a unified structure. It reduced the number of parties appearing on the ballot by establishing hard to meet organizational criteria for registration with the Ministry of Justice, including at least 10,000 members and regional branches with a minimum of 100 members each in at least 45 of the country's then 89 regions, and no fewer than 50 members in each of the remaining branches. In these terms, creation of a new party without approval and support of presidential administration became practically impossible.

In addition, this law disallowed regional and interregional parties and imposed a ban on creation of political parties on a professional, racial, national, or religious basis: Parties must not be formed on the basis of social cleavages, as has been common in the genesis of party democracies in western Europe.[33]

The prohibition of regional parties that have served as a tool of influence for regional political elites has abated their impact in politics. Now, to take part in elections and to get seats in legislatures of different levels, regional politicians have to join one or another federal party that has regional branches in more than half the subjects of the Russian Federation (45 or more), blend into the crowd, and accept the decisions of the party caucus in Moscow.

At the same time, the law has made parties the only category of public associations eligible to nominate candidates in elections to the State Dumas and to the regional legislative (representative) bodies of state power.[34] From 2007 on, parties became the only category recognized as electoral associations in both national and regional elections, meaning that since then they have had a monopoly on legislative power at the state and regional levels, whereas heretofore a public organization or a social movement was able to take part in elections as electoral associations.

At the same time, however, this reform complicated the registration of parties, hardened administrative control over them, and made parties financially dependent on the federal administration. Strengthening the instrumental role of parties in politics while simultaneously reinforcing control over them has furnished the administration with an additional lever of power over legislation on all levels.

Changes in Electoral Law

Elections are the main mechanism of turnover in government, and party competition concentrates on them. A nation's electoral system is a codified corpus of legal acts that establishes the rules of administering elections, defining winners, and serving as a powerful institutional factor shaping parties. At the same time, an electoral system is much more vulnerable to manipulation than many other political institutions. The weaker the mechanisms of self-organization and self-regulation of a society are, the more it is vulnerable to such manipulation. While constitutional change is usually a rather difficult and complicated procedure, requiring overcoming high judicial barriers, electoral laws may often be adopted by a simple majority of votes in the parliament. This is the case in Russia where the parliament is under the control of the presidential administration.

The reform of the party system was supplemented by amendments in 13 federal laws relevant to the electoral system, the most important of which (for our purposes here) were the laws "On Basic Guarantees of Electoral Rights and the Right of Citizens of the RF [Russian Federation] to Participate in a Referendum" and "On the Election of Deputies of the State Duma of the Federal Assembly of the RF." Beginning with the first election in 1993, Russia has had a mixed electoral system on the federal level: half of the 450 seats in the State Duma are elected on the federal party-list system of PR, and the other half in single mandate districts where the winner was determined by a simple plurality of votes. The subject regions of the RF each had their own electoral systems, but the most common system was one in which all deputies were elected in single mandate districts. The most important provisions in the new laws added new controls on political competition:

- not less than half of the deputy mandates in elections to the legislative (representative) bodies in the subject regions of the RF must now be distributed among the lists of candidates nominated by political parties (i.e., federal parties);
- lists of candidates nominated by political parties would henceforth be registered without collection of voter signatures and payment of an electoral deposit, provided the federal lists of these political parties gained seats in the most recent elections to the Duma;
- the minimally required number of votes received by the list of candidates of a party in the federal electoral district to be included in the distribution of

deputy seats is now 7% (an increase from 5%), thus diminishing the chances of most competitors. The number of candidates to be chosen by the party leadership has been increased, thereby strengthening the power of party caucus. Candidates nominated by political parties in the election of the president of the RF are granted essentially more free airtime and free print space than nonpartisan candidates.[35]

Summing up all these innovations in election legislation, President Putin declared in his address to the Federal Assembly of RF in 2003: "We have improved the electoral system. We now have the conditions we need for the development of a real civil society, and also for the establishment of genuinely strong political parties."[36]

By that time, many political groupings, including those who in the past pretended to play "party of power" and those who bitterly struggled against Unity in the recent election, OVR among them, merged into Unity, which now took the name United Russia. "We are going to build a mass party as a pillar that the president can lean on," declared the then head of the General Council of the party.[37]

The 2003 Election

By the election of 2003, changes had been made that permitted administrative campaign resources to be almost entirely employed in favor of Unity. In the early 2000s, vigorous efforts were taken to restore control over mass media, particularly over television, the medium that plays such a decisive role in the political socialization of voters. During 2001–2002, two of the most influential media tycoons who had taken anti-Kremlin stances were deprived of their television channels and other media resources and forced out of the country. Soon afterward, 80% of the mass media, according to the former ombudsman Oleg Mironov, came under the control of federal or local authorities.[38]

Thus by the beginning of the electoral campaign all federal television channels and large print media were either controlled by the Kremlin or unreservedly loyal to it. Notwithstanding that the law forbids persons who hold state offices to use the advantages of their official position or status for election of any list of candidates or to conduct election propaganda in the mass media, Putin publicly expressed his support for United Russia: he attended its preelection congress and overtly supported the party a week before voting. Three national state-owned television channels devoted considerable time to United Russia and its nominees, to the detriment of other competitors. Furthermore, the information given was always positive or at least neutral, whereas information on the CPRF, the closest rival of United Russia, was mostly negative. The state-owned national radio broadcasting system and print media behaved likewise.[39]

As a matter of fact, there is now no public space left where different viewpoints can critically engage with one another. It is not surprising that "Reporters Without Borders" put Russia at 144st place, between Yemen and Tunisia, in the World Press Freedom Index 2007 of 169 countries, where a ranking of first signifies "most free."[40]

United Russia won 37.6% of the votes in the PR part of the mixed system of deputy seats distribution retained for this election. Nevertheless, according to the Hare method of calculation set by electoral law, this resulted in 120 seats—more than half the number of seats distributed in the PR part. With 102 seats obtained from single member districts the total number of United Russia's seats in the Duma reached 222 of 450. Only four party lists overcame the 5% threshold (the threshold was raised to 7% after the election of 2007).

Concentration of Power over Parties after the 2003 Election

The chair of United Russia and the leader of its faction, Boris Gryzlov, the former minister of the interior, became speaker of the Duma. Both vice speakers and five of the eight speakers are members of the faction. The party controls all of the committees.

In 2003, in his annual address to the Federal Assembly of the RF, Putin declared: "I have already said that I support the general policy to strengthen the role of parties in public life. And taking into account the results of the upcoming elections to the State Duma, I think it will be possible to form a professional, effective government, supported by a parliamentary majority."[41] His words were taken by the party leadership as a promise to form a party cabinet, but even though the results exceeded all expectations of the Kremlin, this did not happen. Despite the absolute domination in the Duma of his "party of power," Putin did not venture to share real powers with it, evidently not relying on the security of the created construction.

Continuing to Increase Control over the Parties: 2004–2005

The level of control exercised by United Russia permits the government to pass federal constitutional laws and even constitutional amendments without paying any attention to the wishes of the other parties. The federal constitutional law "On Referendum of the RF," 2004, consisting of 93 articles and more than 200 pages of text, was adopted by the Duma within 23 days, with no careful consideration. Another no less important law on revocation of election of governors took only about a month to pass.[42]

Incumbent parties in the Duma, entrenched within the state and employing its resources in order to guarantee their own survival, did not hesitate to support the efforts of the presidential administration to exclude all outsiders from political competition. In December 2004, they initiated an amendment to the law that increased the membership requirements for registration with the Ministry of Justice fivefold, to 50,000 members, requiring as well branches of at least 500 members in each of 45 regions and no fewer than 250 members in the remaining branches.[43] The goal, publicly avowed, was to prevent the creation of new parties and close down the majority of those existing. The law also now obliges regional branches of parties to submit lists of members at the registration, making the members of oppositional parties vulnerable to harassment by the authorities.

In the spring of 2005 the Duma passed a new election law according to which all 450 deputies will be elected in the federal electoral district in proportion to the number of votes cast for the federal lists of candidates. Nomination of candidates will be carried out by political parties that are entitled to participate in the elections. It is worth noting that at the time this law was passed parties were at a new low in public opinion, with only 17% expressing trust in them.[44] This provision allowed the administration to carry out more efficient control over elections and avoid unpleasant surprises that might take place in some single member district voting.

Increasing the Power of United Russia

United Russia now numbers over 1.5 million members in 53,740 primary cells all over the country, and it is the largest party in the country. It has become, unquestionably, the party of the government and is highly centralized, having adopted a change in its charter in 2005 that requires that all nominees for positions of speakers and leaders of the party faction in regional legislatures, as well as nominees to the Council of Federation, be endorsed by the Presidium of the General Council.[45]

As of September 2008, over half of all Russians, 57%, believed United Russia to be the only strong party, and 68% of its partisans were convinced that no multiparty system exists in Russia.[46] United Russia is also the wealthiest party. According to its financial report for 2006, party income amounts to 1.5 billion rubles (US$56 million), although where the money comes from is never made clear.

Created by bureaucracy, United Russia is a party of "nomenclatura," similar to some extent to the Communist Party of the Soviet Union, a conveyer of power pretending to play a central role in political system. The old Soviet cliché "Party and Government" is now appearing in the rhetoric of its functionaries, who tend to perceive the comparison with the Communist Party of the Soviet Union as a compliment.

In keeping with the emergence of the party as the party of nomenclatura, more and more governors now join its ranks. In 2003, United

Russia numbered 30 governors, but by May 2007, this number had grown to 73 of the total 85.[47]

The party tries to avoid any ideological positioning in the political spectrum. In autumn 2006, United Russia declared itself the "party of sovereign democracy." Having named Putin the leader of the nation and pretending to serve his "pillar," the party committed itself to performing whatever he recommends.[48] If Putin says to double the GDP, or launch "national projects," or solve the "demography problem," or anything else, no matter what, the party program incorporates the new idea. Later, with the turnover in presidential office in 2008, the party changed its mottos to "In Medvedev, Putin, We Trust!" and "People! Medvedev! Putin! Together [We] Win!"

Creating a Pseudo Opposition on the Left

However, despite the apparent absolute loyalty of United Russia, the Kremlin apparently does not believe in the reliability of its newly created party system and has recently turned back to a failed plan of Yeltsin, who tried in 1995 to construct a system of two obedient dominant parties—the "left and right hands of power"—intended to occupy the main part of electoral space and edge out other competitors. The then prime minister was charged to head the "right" party; the then speaker of the Duma, the "left."[49]

Although Yeltsin failed, today the Kremlin again feels the need for a party that can gain enough votes on the left to weaken the CPRF but will not make problems for the government. This function has been entrusted to Fair Russia, headed by the speaker of the Federation Council, Sergei Mironov.

In March 2006, Vladislav Surkov, the deputy head of the presidential administration and the president's aide, as well as the assumed author of most party initiatives of Kremlin, declared publically at a meeting with the functionary of the Russian Party of Life that the country needs a "second big party," a "second leg to lean upon when the first falls asleep and makes the system unstable. . . . Nevertheless, for a long time the political process will evolve around one larger party and namely 'United Russia' must remain this party."[50] Six months later Fair Russia: Motherland/Pensioners/Life was formed as a merger of Rodina, Russian Party of Life, and Russian Pensioners' Party under Sergei Mironov. Not long before this event, Putin met with the leaders of these parties. In 2007, two other parties—People's Party and Socialist United Party of Russia—officially merged into Fair Russia.

Fair Russia is now the second-best financed party in the Russian party system. In 2006, the party took in 166 million rubles (nearly US$6 million) with over 141 million rubles (nearly US$5.2 million) coming from the donations of corporate bodies.[51] In the 2007 election, the new party obtained 38 seats at the Duma, mainly at the expense of the LDPR. Later on, other minor parties—Green Party, Party of Constitutional Democrats, Party of Social Justice, and Party of Entrepreneurship Development among them—merged into Fair Russia as the best way to survive in the hardening political climate.

While Fair Russia seeks to challenge United Russia, it has nonetheless strongly supported Putin and has been criticized as being an opposition party in name only. In December 2007, the party Central Council unanimously voted to support the candidacy of Dmitry Medvedev in the 2008 presidential election.

Continuing to Increase Control over the Parties: 2006–2007

In 2006–2007, the Duma adopted new acts fostering party and electoral reforms. The entire period between the third and the fourth electoral cycles has been judged by experts as further reduction of the political rights of citizens and of political competition, limiting the ability of small parties to compete for parliamentary seats through cancellation of electoral blocks; stiffening requirements for all parties; moving to an entirely PR system for elections to the Duma with the threshold pushed up to 7%; cancellation of nonpartisan public control over elections; cancellation of the turnout minimum required for election validation, as well as cancellation of the option "against all" in the ballot to free authorities from the troubles regarding formal legitimacy of elections; and, last but not least, numerous restrictions on the conduct of federal referenda and canceling direct election of governors.[52] Banning unwanted candidates and parties from the election process and the wide-scale use of "administrative resources" to ensure that victory goes to the chosen few have become the main tendencies in law enforcement practice.

As a result of eliminating any public political competition, Putin became the only significant actor in Russian politics, enjoying people's trust and credibility. A considerable part of the population who cannot find representation and advocacy of their interests in parties seeks the paternalism of the state as personalized in the figure of the president. These sentiments are actively fed by Putin himself as he regularly communicates, on camera, with ordinary people, hears some petitions of citizens, and immediately decides on their vital problems: supplying water, gas, or heat to a particular village; granting citizenship to a particular serviceman of the Russian Armed Forces in Tajikistan; augmenting the amount of the pension of a particular veteran of the Great Patriotic War; improving the housing conditions of a particular family; and so forth. Given that television serves as the main source of information for 90% of population,[53] it is quite natural that any structures of government, as well as parties, are perceived as irrelevant. As of May

2007, the president enjoyed full or partial confidence of 88% of the population, whereas the score of the Duma and the Federation Council was only 27%.[54]

The Duma election of 2007 was held in a new format: all 450 deputies were elected by a system of proportional representation (Table 3.2). With the electoral cycle 2007–2008, the Russian party system has met its 17th anniversary entirely incorporated within the regime of power as its obedient agent. Even two long-standing opposition forces—communists and liberal democrats—have fully complied with the imposed rules of the game to preserve their presence in the Duma.

The most notable initiative of the Kremlin in 2003 was the voluntary dissolution of right-wing political losers: the Union of Right Forces, Civic Strength, and the Democratic Party of Russia, merging into Right Cause. Leaders of the new supposed opposition party do not even try to conceal their organization's Kremlin origins. This effort to cover the denuded right flank of decorative party democracy provides the last brushstroke to the picture of Russia's multiparty system. Recent suggestions made by Dmitry Medvedev, Putin's successor in the office of president, that parties gaining 5% to 7% of the vote should be allotted one or two seats in the Duma and that the number of members required for a party to register should gradually be lowered from 50,000 to 40,000 or 45,000 can be seen as mere cosmetic touches on a system that maintains the whole process of legislation under the top leadership's control; such touches will not change the essence of established mnogopartijnost.

Table 3.2 Final Result of the Duma Election, December 2, 2007

	Votes	*%*	*Seats*	*%*
Electorate	109,145,517			
Valid votes	68,777,136	63.01		
Invalid votes	759,929	0.70		
Total votes	69,537,065	63.71		
United Russia	44,714,241	64.30	315	70.0
Communist Party	8,046,886	11.57	57	12.7
Liberal Democrats	5,660,823	8.14	40	8.9
Fair Russia	5,383,639	7.74	38	8.4
Agrarian Party	1,600,234	2.30	0	—
Yabloko	1,108,985	1.59	0	—
Civic Strength	733,604	1.05	0	—
Union of Right Forces	669,444	0.96	0	—
Patriots of Russia	615,417	0.89	0	—
Party of Social Fairness	154,083	0.22	0	—
Democratic Party of Russia	89,780	0.13	0	—

Source: Russia Votes, http://www.russiavotes.org/

PUTIN'S LEGACY: SOVEREIGN DEMOCRACY

Freedom House has registered in Russia a striking decline from 1999 to 2008 "in the openness and independence of institutions that could be paving the way for more transparent and accountable governance."[55] Certainly the parties are not performing that function. The chief editor of the informational and analytical weekly Partinform, a journal long devoted to reporting on the activities of parties, factions, and electoral groupings in Russia, titled his last review of party life "The Sunset of the Second Party System." He announced the cancellation of the weekly, caused, he said, by the shrinking and transformation of party space and the falling off of interest in the "activities of structures that have no impact on political decision making on the national level."[56]

In sum, Putin has worked steadfastly to eliminate any and all competition in governance, imposing rules that guarantee the preservation and reproduction of the regime he has shaped. In his system the fight between parties is as similar to real political competition as a puppet show is to a real wrestling match. The outcome is predictable and hardly depends on the voters' will.

After the collapse of the communist regime in Russia, party democracy was the only option succeeding authority could offer to society that would justify its coming to power and claim of legitimacy. The enthusiasm of western promoters of democracy and the expectations of the new regime that this would in turn lead to financial help and international recognition contributed to this decision. However, as it turned out most of the former ruling elite, with the exception of a few most odious figures at the top, managed not only to preserve, but even to reinforce their own positions.[57] As Thomas Karosers argues, "The core impulses and interests of powerholders—such as locking in access to . . . power and resources as quickly as possible—ran directly contrary to what democracy building would have required."[58] The Russian transition to democratic institutions, including a multiparty system and political contestation, was based on the adoption of formal institutions borrowed from western democracies that morphed in the course of naturalization into simulacrums deprived of the substance of the originals. Artificially created entities that the law constitutes as parties are denied the functions parties enjoy in democratic governance. In the post-Soviet national setting, parties have turned into a tool for blocking competition. As stated by Schattschneider, "As a matter of fact, the condition of the parties is the best possible evidence of the nature of any regime."[59]

Any regime is as authoritarian as society is compliant and apathetic. The multiparty system in Russia has been constructed in an era when civil society was dissociated and deinstitutionalized after the lengthy and devastating rule of the communist regime. Therefore, the post-Soviet successor regime met no significant resistance from society while shaping a party system that fits its interests.

Surkov, the author of a work on the notorious conception of "sovereign democracy" presented to the public as a national ideology, justifies concentration of power and all resources in the hands of the president.[60] He contends that "Democracy in our country is partially 'like all others,' but partially—somewhat—particular. Just like models of successful democracies in America, Europe, and Asia that are universal and similar to each other, but at the same time, unique."[61] However, despite some apparent resemblance of the Russian mnogopartijnost to party systems in successful democracies, its function in "sovereign democracy" is just the reverse: to prevent a turnover in government through free and fair election. Surkov emphasizes that the concept of sovereign democracy "interprets the course of the President." He declares further that it "conforms best to the basis of Russian political culture."

Sovereign Democracy versus the Representation of Cleavages

S. M. Lipset was convinced that "Parties in new electoral democracies will be inherently unstable unless they become linked to deep-rooted sources of cleavage, as parties in the older, institutionalized western democracies have been."[62]

Party systems in successful western democracies evolved entrenched in systems of social and political cleavages based on regional, religious, ethnic, or professional distinctions of citizens and, therefore, became mechanisms for reconciling heterogeneous social interests and intergroup conflicts. However, one of the key principles of multipartyism in the Russian "sovereign democracy" is that political parties created "on a professional, racial, national, regional or regional basis" are forbidden.[63] Surkov is happy with this ban and alleges that it contributes to the ability of mnogopartijnost to integrate Russian voters with different views and beliefs around common values. But in fact "sovereign democracy" ignores problems of legitimating and institutionalizing cleavages, the only realistic way to integrate a society. If parties are forbidden to represent cleavages and the social and political interests supporting them, then what and whose interests are they representing in current politics? The Russian approach to society integration is likely, at best, to edge social conflicts out of the public space and into the sphere of Byzantine politics, contributing to the growth of corruption and organized crime, and thereby destabilizing society. Instead of public party contestation, there is a covert struggle of different corporate-bureaucratic clans for redistribution of property and power. And in the worst case scenario it will stimulate overt coercion, as is happening today in the northern Caucasian regions of Russia.

Sovereign democracy evolves in the direction of strengthening the ever growing presidential vertical administrative apparatus and building up defense and law enforcement agencies as the only remedy for solving the numerous painful problems of society. Putin has justified his regime of a soft "enlightened" authoritarianism with underdevelopment of the political system and civil society in Russia and the lack of a truly multiparty system as well. However, his policy is actually aimed at suppressing any real democratic development. It is not surprising that 43% of Russians believe that current parties do more harm than good to Russia. The opposite viewpoint is shared by only 23% of respondents; the rest found it difficult to answer.[64]

PROSPECTS FOR PARTIES IN "SOVEREIGN DEMOCRACY"

The system of sovereign democracy has proved to be rather stable when the demand for stability and order among the public has been high (after the tumultuous years of Yeltsin's rule in the 1990s). As president, Putin has enjoyed great popularity as a "powerful hand" capable of ensuring order and stability in the country, and incomes from the exportation of oil and gas have been steadily growing. However, the durability of this model of governance is uncertain, especially now when the country is being hit with the global economy crisis and prices of raw products are falling.

Any model of governance has its own limits of efficiency. When the political regime of the Soviet Union exhausted its capacity and lost its contest with western democracies in the late 1980s, the then leader Mikhail Gorbachev realized that reform was possible only by creating mechanisms for the free representation of the interests and demands of different classes and social groups. He did not manage to create such mechanisms, and this failure brought about the collapse of the state, as well as of his personal political fortunes.

Putin sought to restore Russia as a prospering and respected great power. Given that his mentality was shaped in a particular professional milieu, it is not surprising that he has chosen a monocentrist authoritarian-bureaucratic model of governance to secure political stability and fight corruption, enhance the effectiveness of public administration, provide transition to an innovative economy and high-technology industry, fight poverty, and, eventually, make Russia competitive in the global world. Political competition was sacrificed for these ambitious goals. His choice was not deliberately antidemocratic; it was rather a pragmatic technocratic decision aimed to replace the "bad governance" of the country he inherited from Yeltsin with a "good" one. According to him, inefficient government was the main cause of the deep and enduring economic crisis and imposing order in governmental agencies was the key mission to accomplish.

However, it seems fair to say that the authoritarian-bureaucratic model of governance that contributed to some extent to overcoming the chaos and destabilization of society caused by the collapse of the Soviet Union is now past its peak of efficiency.

The administrative reform initiated by Putin to fight corruption in government, reduce the administrative apparatus by 10% to 15% and enhance its efficiency has failed and has in fact contributed to the blossoming of corruption.[65] According to official data, under Putin's rule the number of bureaucrats has increased by 200,000—mostly in federal agencies—double the number in Yeltsin's time.[66] Corruption has increased along with the growth of bureaucracy—the Ministry of the Interior measures the damage to national economy from corruption as 40 billion rubles (nearly US$1.5 billion), whereas some foreign experts judge it at US$20 billion. The organization Transparency International found the level of corruption in 2008 to be at its highest over the past 8 years.[67] Analyst Andrei Pionkovsky also considers the present situation as "the highest and culminating stage of bandit capitalism in Russia," given that the businessmen, the politicians, and the bureaucrats are in fact the same people.[68]

According to Worldwide Governance Indicators for 1996–2007, released by the World Bank Institute, none of the indicators of quality of governance for Russia—voice and accountability, political stability and absence of violence, government effectiveness, regulatory quality, rule of law, control of corruption—changed greatly from 1998 to 2007 but remain at the same point on the negative side of the −2.5 to +2.5 scale. The value accorded Russia in the Index of Political Stability and Absence of Violence in 2007 did not improve compared to 1998—the year of the second Chechen war.[69]

Prominent Russian researcher Nataliya Rimashevskaya asserts that at the 7% economy growth rate the scale of poverty in the country does not diminish. Despite a total increase in income, the lowest 10% of population gets 40-fold less than the highest 10%.[70] In November 2007, 77% of those polled believed that the gap between the rich and the poor over the past eight years of Putin's presidency had increased and only 2% believed it had decreased.[71]

Furthermore, growth of income from selling oil and other raw material resources has not influenced the development of human capital. The Human Development Indices for Russia gives the country a rank of 73 of 177 countries on the basis of data from 2006, a drop of 16 places in only four years.[72]

President Dmitry Medvedev has acknowledged the importance of the development of information technology and implementation of electronic government for economic growth, an upsurge of research and development, and enhancement of the efficiency of public administration, but has publicly stated that almost no progress has been made in this area.[73] He has also admitted that up to now there have been practically no improvements in the high tech sphere.[74] The 2008 World Competitiveness Yearbook of IMD (a global business school) ranked Russia 47th in the list of 55 countries, a drop of four places since the previous year.[75]

Thus, in spite of the extremely favorable situation in raw materials markets, proclaimed goals were not achieved or even approached. It becomes evident that even if this model could provide growth of GDP, the other goals of effective "good governance" and sustained social stability, as well as economic and technological development, are hardly attainable in the framework of this bureaucratic paradigm and will require genuinely competitive party democracy. The social stability achieved due to high prices on oil and gas may well fade away as the country drifts into global economic crisis.

Those at the top of the vast post-Soviet bureaucracy have learned how to simulate reforms while damping or distorting any initiatives that might threaten its well-being and will never be reformed by the bureaucrats themselves. As Oksana Gaman-Golutvina has asserted, the Russian administrative apparatus is unlike the Weberian model of rational bureaucracy. It features closeness, conservatism, low executive discipline, very high levels of corruption, and servility to persons, but not the rule of law.[76]

As Putin's successor in the presidency, Dmitry Medvedev faces a difficult choice—whether to endure the inefficiency of governance, large-scale corruption, the growing gap between government and public, and the low competitiveness of the country as the inevitable costs of maintaining a sovereign democracy, or to attempt to change the vector of political development in favor of public political competition and genuine parties for the sake of the enduring national interests of Russia.

Not long before taking office Medvedev, speaking as first vice premier of the RF at the Economic Forum in Davos (January 2007), declared: "Today, we are creating new institutions that are based on the fundamental principles of full-blooded democracy: Democracy—without additional unnecessary definitions—efficient democracy on the foundation of market economy, rule of law, and accountability of authority to the society."[77] At present he is in a position to embody his vision of democracy in political decisions. After all, establishment of democratic institutions has always been an answer of elites to social demand for development, a pragmatic choice aimed at solving vital needs of society. With all its limitations, democracy is the best way to guard against wrong decisions, corruptibility, and other common defects of nondemocratic governance.

However, even if it decides in favor of a genuine party democracy, the Kremlin will still face the lack of genuine parties to compete for government, given the total sterilization of the public political space. The existing multiparty system has no stimuli for self-evolution and has amassed such a bulk of inertial resistance that any transformation seems unlikely. Moreover, there are no actors to play the key roles in party democracy beyond those in the puppet mnogopartijnost. Answering the question "Can people like you influence government decisions in the country now?" in October 2007, 72% said "Definitely no" or "No," rather than "Yes," whereas 3% said "Definitely yes," 21% said "Somewhat," and the rest were uncertain.[78]

In any case, there are no enthusiasts of political participation amid the general public, nor amid elites. Mikhail Afanas'ev has investigated the views and capacities of prosperous, well-educated, and informed persons who enjoy a rather good standard of living and are not associated with the regime, somewhat analogous to the western middle class. This group was assumed to be most interested in transparent and plain rules of game, law and order, and fair public political competition in party democracy. However, his study demonstrated that while declaring commitment to democratic change, these people lack the required civic capacity for self-organization and enduring collective action for promoting their political interests, as well as a sufficient level of interpersonal trust. Consumerism and rugged individualism impede them from participating in politics.[79] Thus, power in Russia can rely neither on bureaucracy nor on society to bring about desperately needed change. What, then, does the future hold for Russia?

CONCLUSION

The public opinion research organization Levada Center asked people in 2007, whether Russia is a democracy. The results are presented in Table 3.3.

Yurii Pivovarov contends that throughout its entire history, power in Russia has been based not on the law, but on coercion, and that this has not changed today.[80] If he is right, speculations on when and how political parties will serve democracy in Russia are perhaps irrelevant.

Table 3.3 Russian Opinion Survey Results, 2007

Do you think Russia at present has become a democratic country? If not, how long will it take for a lasting, effective democracy to be established in Russia?	February 2004 (%)	October 2007 (%)
Russia has already become a democratic country	10	16
No, it'll take about 5 years	9	7
No, it'll take about 10–20 years	23	17
No, it'll take about 20–50 years	13	13
No, it'll take over 50 years	8	10
It'll never happen	18	16
Difficult to answer	20	21

Source: Russian Public Opinion—2007. Levada Center, 2008. http://www.levada.ru/eng/

SUPPLEMENTARY BIBLIOGRAPHY: RELEVANT WORLDWIDE WEB RESOURCES IN ENGLISH

The Constitution of the Russian Federation, adopted December 12, 1993. http://www.kremlin.ru/eng/articles/ConstMain.shtml

Central Election Commission of the Russian Federation. Site includes election and referendum legislation, data on elections and referendum in the Russian Federation, data on participation of political parties in federal elections, bulletin of the CEC of Russia, journal about elections, and other information. http://www.cikrf.ru/eng/

Russia Votes: a joint project of the Centre for the Study of Public Policy, University Strathclyde and VCIOM Analytic Agency. http://www.russiavotes.org/

Russian Public Opinion—2007, Moscow: Levada Center, 2008. The eighth issue of the yearbook, Public Opinion, summarizes results of the public opinion surveys mostly in tabulations and charts. The yearbook contains the indices of trends in public sentiment, attitudes, evaluations, and interests concerning different aspects of everyday life; processes in the sociopolitical and socioeconomic spheres, events in the life in Russia and in the world. Among the issues covered in the yearbook are politics and political structure, government institutions, parties and the state, Duma elections, freedom of speech, human rights, and others. http://www.levada.ru/eng/

President of Russia—events, speeches, etc. http://www.kremlin.ru/eng/

CHAPTER 4

Political Parties in Ukraine: Learning Democratic Accountability?

Andrey A. Meleshevych

DEMOCRACY, ACCOUNTABILITY, COMPETITION

Democracy is one of those key social science concepts that lacks a universally accepted definition. A number of excellent studies have been devoted to the discussion of different meanings of democracy and its defining elements. Many authors adopt the mainstream minimal definition of democracy in western democratic theory: a system of government characterized by majority rule, political equality under the law, and the protection of individual rights. Although not in disagreement with these three important pillars of democracy, this chapter employs a somewhat more detailed definition: "[M]odern political democracy is a system of governance in which rulers are held accountable for their actions in the public realm by citizens, acting indirectly through the competition and cooperation of their elected representatives."[1] This definition, suggested by two recognized experts in comparative democratization, is well suited for a current discussion of the relationship between political parties and democracy in a transitional society such as Ukraine.

Along with other essential characteristics of democracy, Schmitter and Karl's definition emphasizes two principal aspects: political accountability of rulers and the competition among citizens' representatives. Are these two elements redundant? Is it not true that "the mere holding of regular and honestly conducted elections in which all adult citizens are equally eligible to participate provides 'the' most reliable and effective mechanism through which citizens can hold their rulers accountable?"[2] The answer is far from simple. In a nation with highly institutionalized, easily identifiable, and stable political parties and a party system, it may be unnecessary to distinguish political account-ability as a separate element of democracy. As a result of free and fair elections, voters select among usually well-known alternatives, for example, political parties or individual candidates, rewarding or pun-ishing elites currently in government depending on their performance in office and the voters' personal preferences. Due to easy identifiability of electoral participants among voters, political accountability of the rulers and competitive elections go hand in hand.

Transitional countries, these great zones of uncertainty, offer a very differ-ent scenario. Many states that undergo a transition from authoritarian rule are termed "electoral democracies," meaning that they meet some minimal standards of conducting free and fair elections.[3] At the same time, national legislatures that are comprised of numerous nonaffiliated parliamentarians and representatives of marginal political organizations; "technical" cabi-nets, which are formed and operate irrespective of electoral results and the composition of the parliament; loose and unstable electoral coalitions, hast-ily formed on the eve of elections; a constantly changing list of electoral par-ticipants; and high levels of "deep" electoral volatility all destroy the idea of political accountability of rulers in many transitional nations. As the case of Ukraine will demonstrate, sufficiently honest elections and political accountability are not necessarily connected to each other.

The second element of the definition of democracy adopted in this chapter deals with the competition among public representatives. Although representatives of citizens may compete in the public sphere in different ways in a democratic society, a free and fair electoral con-test is the single most important, though insufficient, defining charac-teristic of democracy.[4]

This chapter's purpose is twofold. First, it provides a brief analysis of the main political parties and other electoral contestants in inde-pendent Ukraine: basic facts about their history, electoral performance, ideology (or lack thereof), the role of charisma, social and regional bases, as well as the electoral system(s), relations between the presi-dency, prime minister, and the legislature, and so forth. Second, the chapter discusses the relationship between political parties and democ-racy in post-1991 Ukraine. Particular attention is paid to the impact that Ukrainian political parties have on establishing the political account-ability of rulers and the institutionalization of free and fair elections in the nation.

POLITICAL PARTIES IN UKRAINE

Ukraine gained its independence from the former Soviet Union on August 24, 1991, when the national parliament adopted the Act of the

Declaration of Independence of Ukraine. The Declaration of Independence was overwhelmingly approved by referendum on December 1, 1991. More than 90% of voters in all 27 administrative-territorial units of Ukraine voted in favor of national independence. Article 1 of the new constitution adopted on June 28, 1996, established Ukraine as "a sovereign and independent, democratic, social, law-based state."

Ukraine consists of 24 *oblasts*, the Crimean Autonomous Republic, and two cities with special status: Kyiv and Sevastopol in Crimea. The main waterway in Ukraine, the Dnieper River, splits the country into the Right Bank to the west and Left Bank to the east. This geographic division transfers into historical, cultural, regional, language, and religious cleavages.

The eastern part of Ukraine is more populated, more industrialized, and more affluent than the rest of the country. For example, more than one-sixth of the Ukrainian electorate nationwide dwells in two easternmost oblasts—Donetsk and Luhans'k. Eastern Ukraine is home to most of the Russian minority, which comprises about 17% of the population nationwide. Historically, eastern oblasts of Ukraine and Crimea have been the most russified and sovietized due to the geographic and cultural proximity of Russia and the heavy industrialization of coal, steel, and chemical spheres in the Soviet period that required extensive immigration to these territories from Russia proper. The Russian language and the pro-Russian Eastern Orthodoxy (Moscow Patriarchate) dominate the Left Bank.

The Growing Crimean Tatar Population in Crimea Practices Islam

The Right Bank was subjected to the Russian Empire and Soviet domination for a shorter period of time than the Left Bank. Thus, Galicia, or the three westernmost oblasts, L'viv, Ivano-Frankivs'k, and Ternopil', was added to the Soviet Union shortly before the Soviet Union entered World War II and became the critical center of the national revival in the early 1990s. The Ukrainian language dominates western Ukraine and is widely spoken in the Right Bank. The pro-independence Greek Catholic (Uniate) and Orthodox (Kyiv Patriarchate) churches coexist here with the Moscow Patriarchate of the Eastern Orthodoxy.

Since independence, Ukraine has held five cycles of elections to the national legislature, the Rada: in 1994, 1998, 2002, 2006, and the snap elections in 2007, as well as five presidential electoral contests. The first president of independent Ukraine elected in December 1991 was Leonid Kravchuk. He was succeeded by Leonid Kuchma, who was first elected in 1994 and then reelected to his post in 1999. Since all these electoral cycles corresponded to minimal criteria of free and fair elections, Ukraine was recognized as an electoral democracy according to the Freedom House standards. The fourth cycle of electoral contest for the presidential post between pro-establishment nominee Viktor Yanu-kovych and oppositional candidate Viktor Yushchenko led to the events that became known as the Orange Revolution.

The Orange Revolution

The definition of democracy used here traces its roots to Joseph Schumpeter's classical work *Capitalism, Socialism, and Democracy.* Schumpeter defined democracy as a competitive struggle of elites for the people's vote.[5] In such a system, a populace has essentially only one political right—periodic change of its rulers in free and fair elections. If one set of political elites abandons open competition for power and instead distorts electoral results in favor of its candidate(s), then voters are deprived of their main democratic function, and the democracy ceases to be a democracy. In the second round of the 2004 presidential elections in Ukraine, the incumbent power establishment resorted to electoral falsifications in favor of its presidential candidate, subsequently bringing about the Orange Revolution.

It is difficult to overestimate the significance of the Orange Revolution for Ukrainian democratic development. In November–December 2004, millions of Ukrainian citizens took part in a peaceful protest against the massive electoral fraud of the 2004 presidential elections. The rerun of the second round of voting, which was held under tight supervision of domestic and international observers, proved that the previous round had been falsified. The opposition candidate, Viktor Yushchenko, claimed an electoral victory. On January 13, 2005, the European Parliament adopted a resolution on the results of the Ukrainian elections that stated: "Ukrainian society has strongly manifested its commitment to democracy, the rule of law and other values, which are the basis of the European Union."[6] Beginning in 2006, Ukraine moved to the category of "free" nations in the Freedom House's annual survey of political rights and civil liberties in the world.[7]

Along with other legacies of the Orange Revolution, this event has contributed to the further development of the Ukrainian party system in several instrumental ways. First, the Orange Revolution made its important contribution to the process of institutionalizing and legitimizing free and fair elections in Ukraine as the exclusive mechanism for obtaining state power. Political elites of different shades came one crucial step closer to the realization that electoral fraud might be too costly a risk for aspiring politicians on their way to the political Olympus. Second, as a part of the constitutional compromise among the members of the Orange coalition (Electoral Coalition Our Ukraine, Yuliya Tymoshenko Bloc, and the Socialist Party of Ukraine) at the peak of the revolution, the Ukrainian Parliament passed a bill transferring important political powers from the office of the president to the parliament and the prime minister, thus strengthening the role of political parties in the government formation.

A combination of these factors—an emphasis on free and fair elections as an exclusive means of gaining parliamentary representation and government formation, and the transfer of some powers from the president to the parliament, along with the introduction of the new electoral system and the formation of the whole composition of the national parliament based on proportional representation—boosted the role of political parties and gave them an additional powerful incentive to assert their unique political niche in the society. A new institutional framework conducive to the development of political parties was in place.

Electoral System

For her five parliamentary elections since 1991, Ukraine has used three different electoral systems, making a gradual transition from the absolute majority runoff model to a proportional representation formula. The first postindependence elections to the Rada were held in 1994 under the Law on Elections of People's Deputies of Ukraine adopted by the national legislature on November 10, 1993. The law preserved an old Soviet electoral formula: 450 members of the Rada were elected in single-member districts according to the double ballot majoritarian system, which is commonly used these days only in the world of authoritarian states.[8] The 1993 Law on Elections was explicitly biased against political parties; it openly diminished their electoral function and hindered the process of their development. For example, it was much easier for representatives of the informal party of power and nonaffiliated candidates to get nominated, registered, and consequently win an electoral race than for members of political parties to do so.[9] It came as no surprise that elections produced an amorphous parliament where almost two-thirds of elected members of parliament did not belong to any party.

On October 22, 1997, the national legislature changed the electoral system used for the elections to the Rada. The parliament was formed according to a mixed majority/proportional representation system with a 4% electoral threshold: 225 MPs were chosen by a party-list vote in one countrywide electoral district, and the remaining 225 people's deputies were elected in single-member constituencies according to a simple plurality formula. Two cycles of regularly scheduled elections in 1998 and 2002 were held under the mixed voting system.

Two subsequent parliamentary contests—regular elections in 2006 and snap elections in 2007—were conducted according to the proportional representation model. On March 25, 2004, the Rada passed a new version of the Law on Elections of People's Deputies of Ukraine, which establishes that all 450 people's deputies are to be chosen on the basis of the proportional representation formula in one statewide multimember electoral constituency. The electoral threshold was decreased to 3%.

Executive-Legislative Arrangements

Ukraine is one of many postcommunist Eastern European countries that have adopted a mixed presidential-parliamentary model of government. However, the balance of powers between the president, prime minister, and parliament has not been uniform throughout the 17 years of Ukrainian sovereignty; it has shifted back and forth depending on the strength and ambitions of the main political actors. For a limited time at the dawn of independent statehood under President Leonid Kravchuk the Ukrainian system of government was leaning toward parliamentarianism. After his election in 1994, President Leonid Kuchma continuously interpreted his constitutional powers in an expansionist way and developed a model that resembled a "presidential-parliamentary" form of government featuring "the primacy of the president, plus the dependence of the cabinet on parliament."[10] Although unlike his counterparts in neighboring Russia and Belarus, Vladimir Putin and Aleksandr Lukashenko, Kuchma never succeeded in establishing "presidentialism with the 'cover' of a presidential prime minister,"[11] and some elements of super presidentialism became evident in the Ukrainian political system by the end of Kuchma's second term in office.

On December 8, 2004, at the peak of the Orange Revolution, the Rada passed numerous amendments to the 1996 Constitution that considerably altered the balance of powers between the three main institutions: the Rada, the cabinet, and the president. The system, which in the Ukrainian political discourse is called "parliamentary-presidential," features: (1) the cabinet, which is formed on the basis of an established parliamentary coalition and depends on parliamentary confidence; and (2) the popularly elected president, who has the right to disband the parliament and possesses the exclusive power to nominate the minister of defense, the minister of foreign affairs, and the head of the security service.

Main Political Parties

There were 162 political parties officially registered in Ukraine as of February 2009.[12] Almost every month the Ukrainian Ministry of Justice records a new political party. On the eve of the registration deadline before regularly scheduled elections, the number of new parties grows like mushrooms after a rain.[13] For example, in just two days in March

2005, the Ministry of Justice registered 12 new political parties. The overwhelming majority of Ukrainian parties and their leaders never emerge from obscurity to become known to the public and are not able to perform the most important function of political parties in a democracy—participation in the electoral process.

This chapter will focus only on those parties in post-1991 Ukraine that have successfully competed in more than one cycle of parliamentary elections, have been represented in the Rada of at least two convocations, and have played a significant role in the government or the opposition. The list of such parties is still lengthy: Communist Party of Ukraine, Socialist Party of Ukraine, Rukh, Electoral Coalition "Our Ukraine" ("Our Ukraine-People's Self-Defense" in 2007), Electoral Coalition "For United Ukraine," Party of Regions, Yuliya Tymoshenko Bloc, and Volodymyr Lytvyn Bloc.

The Communist Party of Ukraine

The Communist Party of Ukraine (CPU) traces its roots back to the party with the same name, which functioned as a branch of the Communist Party of the Soviet Union (CPSU) in the territory of Soviet Ukraine. Article 6 of the USSR Constitution and the identical corresponding article of the Constitution of the Ukrainian Soviet Socialist Republic gave the CPSU and its republican branch a monopoly of power and established it as the only lawful political party in the Soviet Union—"the leading and guiding force of Soviet society and the nucleus of its political system." The influence of the CPSU/CPU has considerably decreased since Article 6 was altered in 1990, paving the way for the establishment of a multiparty system in the Soviet Union. On August 30, 1991, several days after the CPU officially supported the failed anti-Gorbachev coup, the Ukrainian legislature banned this organization.

The process of the party's revival started immediately after it was outlawed and continued through two stages. During the first stage, members of the banned CPU formed two clones of the outlawed party: the Socialist Party of Ukraine in October 1991 and the Peasant Party of Ukraine (SelPU) in January 1992. The leader of the communist majority in the Rada Oleksander Moroz became the chairman of the Socialist Party of Ukraine. The second step was taken in June 1993 when the CPU held the so-called Restoration Congress, which elected Petro Symonenko as the party leader. Symonenko continued to serve as the party head despite a massive decline of party support and dismal performance in the 2006 parliamentary elections. In October 1993, the CPU has been registered at the Ministry of Justice.

The newly restored party quickly became an influential player in Ukrainian politics. In fact, the CPU is the only party in the independent

Ukraine that has participated in all five cycles of elections for the national legislature under the same name and has been represented continuously in the Rada of all five convocations. The CPU gained the largest share of the national vote in the 1994 and 1998 elections and consequently formed the largest faction in the Rada (Table 4.1). In the founding elections, held under the absolute majority formula, the CPU received 14.85% of all votes in the first round in the spring of 1994. This is an impressive result considering that 64.5% of the elected members of parliament were nonaffiliated, and Rukh, the second largest party, obtained almost two and a half times fewer votes than the CPU.

The CPU candidates also took part in all presidential elections in Ukraine. The 1999 presidential election was perhaps the closest when the party approached regaining political power in the nation. The party candidate, Petro Symonenko, reached the second round where he obtained 37.8% of the national vote, winning 10 oblasts in central and eastern Ukraine, losing, however, to the incumbent president Leonid Kuchma (56.25% of the vote).

An expected and rapid downfall of the CPU came in 2006 when the ambitious Party of Regions put forth a massive effort to target the traditional electorate of the communists. In the electoral contest held that year, the CPU was able to gain only 3.66% of the national vote in comparison to 19.98% in the previous electoral cycle, barely clearing the 3% electoral threshold. Although the CPU performed somewhat better in the 2007 snap elections (5.39% of the vote), its future looks rather bleak. An intense competition with the Party of Regions for the essentially identical electoral base, a lack of sufficient financial support from private sources, an inability to attract young voters, and the shrinkage of politically active ideological supporters among the older generation due to natural causes are all likely to contribute to the further decrease of the party's strength and influence.

Most of the communist supporters inhabit eastern and southern parts of Ukraine. For example, in the 2007 elections to the Rada, the CPU gained 9.1% of the vote in the Kherson oblast, 8.5% in Luhans'k, and 8.3% in the Kharkiv and in the Zaporizhzhya oblasts. Conversely, the party has meager support in western Ukraine—in the Ivano-Frankivs'k, Ternopil', and L'viv oblasts the CPU received 0.7%, 0.8%, and 1.0% respectively.

Many scholars of Ukrainian politics argue that the CPU is among few ideological parties in Ukraine, if indeed it is not the only one. In point of fact, the party has changed little from the Soviet times and adheres to major postulates of the communist ideology. However, a signing of the coalition agreement in 2006 with the Party of Regions, which represents big business and consistent support provided by the communists to Party of Regions, challenges this assertion. Although Ukrainian politics quite often produces strange bedfellows, an instance

Table 4.1 Selected Results of the Postindependence Parliamentary Elections in Ukraine (%)

Party	1994 SMD	1998	2002 MMD	2006	2007
Communist Party of Ukraine	14.85	24.65	19.98	3.66	5.39
Rukh	5.96	9.40	—	—	—
Socialist Party of Ukraine[1]	3.80	8.56	6.87	5.69	2.86
People's Democratic Party	—	5.01	—	0.49	0.34
Electoral Coalition For United Ukraine	—	—	11.77	—	—
Electoral Coalition Our Ukraine	—	—	23.57	13.95	14.15
Yuliya Tymoshenko Bloc	—	—	7.26	22.29	30.71
Party of Regions	—	—	—	32.14	34.37
Lytvyn Bloc	—	—	—	2.44	3.96

Notes: SMD, single-member district; MMD, multi-member district.
[1]The Electoral Coalition of SPU and SelPU in 1998.

Source: For 1994: Author's calculations based on data from the International Foundation for Electoral Systems, Archive of Ukrainian Elections: Full Election Results, Elections to the Verkhovna Rada of Ukraine, 1994. For 1998, 2002, 2006, 2007: The Central Election Commission of Ukraine (http://www.cvk.gov.ua/).

of the "ideological" communist party, the supposed champion of the working class, creating a governmental coalition with and backing its political antithesis, is very unusual in world history.

The Socialist Party of Ukraine

The idea of creating a new left party emerged several days after the old CPU was outlawed in August 1991. The Socialist Party of Ukraine (SPU) was conceived by its future leader Oleksander Moroz as the successor of the banned CPU and as "the heir of Lenin's Communist Party."[14] However, when the CPU was re-created in 1993, causing a mass withdrawal of the SPU members in favor of the CPU, the socialists decided against merging with the communists. The reappearance of the more powerful CPU "on the Ukrainian political scene demanded that the socialists change their tactics: the SPU started to move slowly from the left towards the center. At the fifth SPU Congress (October 1994), it was said that unlike the orthodox communists, the socialists do not intend to cling to ideological dogmas that are no longer topical."[15] In 2003, the SPU joined the Socialist International, an international association of the world's socialist and social democratic political parties, with a status of "a consultative party."

Another principal difference between the two major parties on the left is their views toward the disintegration of the Soviet Union and the declaration of independence by Ukraine. Unlike the revived CPU, which considered itself an integral part of the CPSU and called for a restoration of the Soviet Union,[16] the leadership of the SPU supported both Ukrainian independence and the separation of the Ukrainian left from the Soviet Communist Party. These ideological and national dissimilarities helped the SPU to find its own electorate and claim its distinct niche on the national political scene: the party appealed to the left and center-left nationally conscious voters.

The SPU participated in all five cycles of postindependence elections to the Rada and until 2007 has been represented in the national legislature. Geographically, the SPU draws most of its support from the central part of Ukraine—Poltava, Vynnytsya, Cherkassy, Chernihiv, Sumy, Khmel'nyts'ky oblasts among others.

The fate of the SPU is inextricably linked to one person—its founder and continuous leader Oleksander Moroz, whose "moral authority and charisma" is perhaps the main asset of the party.[17] Moroz not only founded the SPU and preserved it after the reestablishment of the CPU, he also shaped party ideology and is the undisputed center of power within the organization. Ironically, Moroz became the cause of the party downfall when after the 2006 elections he and his party abruptly switched sides, splitting from the Orange coalition and forming an alliance with their rivals—the Party of Regions and CPU (see the section "Learning Accountability?" below).

Rukh

By many counts the People's Movement of Ukraine, or Rukh ("movement" in Ukrainian), is the political organization that has made the most significant contribution to the creation and development of independent Ukrainian statehood.[18] Along with its nemesis the CPU, Rukh is one of only two parties that has participated in all parliamentary elections in sovereign Ukraine and has been continuously represented in all five convocations of the Rada. The Founding Congress of Rukh took place in September 1990. It was conceived as an all-inclusive organization that comprised numerous political and cultural groups and individuals that challenged the monopoly of power by the communist party. Although Rukh was not allowed to nominate candidates in the 1990 elections to the Supreme Soviet of Ukraine, 125 people's deputies affiliated with this organization were elected to the national legislature. Rukh members were instrumental in drafting both founding documents that led to national independence: the Proclamation on the State Sovereignty of Ukraine and the Act of the Declaration of Independence. V'yacheslav Chornovil, one of the Rukh leaders, took part in the presidential race held in December 1991. He finished second, gaining 23.3% of the national vote and losing to Leonid Kravchuk (38.3%) who became the first democratically elected president of independent Ukraine.

In early 1993, Rukh completed the process of transition from a loose "people's front" to a political party. V'yacheslav Chornovil was elected as the party head. The new party was registered at the Ministry of Justice on February 1, 1993. In the 1994 and 1998 parliamentary elections, Rukh came in second after the CPU (see Table 4.1). Similar to its major rival at the time, Rukh's electoral strength across the territory of Ukraine has been far from uniform. The geographic pattern of Rukh's electorate base is diametrically opposite to that of the communists. For many years western Ukraine has been the stronghold of this party; it has the weakest electoral support in the easternmost oblasts.

Throughout its history Rukh has experienced several major splits that have not served to strengthen it. The first split occurred shortly after Rukh became a party in 1993. A group of prominent functionaries split from this organization over the issue of whether Rukh should support President Kravchuk and his policies. The second major in-party division, from which Rukh has never recovered, took place in February 1999 shortly before the death of V'yacheslav Chornovil. Yuriy Kostenko and some 30 members of the Rada elected from Rukh split from the party, accusing its leadership of authoritarianism and forming an alternative organization—the Ukrainian People's Rukh, which was later renamed the Ukrainian People's Party (UPP) and registered in December 1999.

In 1998, Rukh was the only center-right party that was able to gain parliamentary representation. Realizing that a proliferation of national-democratic forces hurt their electoral performance, both Rukh and UPP along with several other like-minded political organizations initiated the formation of a broad electoral coalition. This bloc, Our Ukraine, was created shortly before the 2002 Rada elections. Since then both parties have been leading forces in this coalition.[19]

People's Movement of Ukraine is a center-right party that claims that it "adheres to a national democratic platform, supports a conservative ideology, based on the principles of national statehood and European democratic values," as well as supports "the development of private entrepreneurship, . . . the cultural revival of Ukrainian society, of the Ukrainian people's national identity," and integration into the European Union and NATO.[20] Rukh became the first Ukrainian party to be granted the status of "an observer member" in the European People's Party.

The Electoral Coalition Our Ukraine

The name Our Ukraine refers to two different though somewhat overlapping political organizations: an electoral coalition Our Ukraine (Our Ukraine-People's Self-Defense in 2007) and a political party People's Union Our Ukraine. The electoral coalition Our Ukraine was first created on the eve of the 2002 elections with the purpose of uniting center-right national-democratic forces around the emerging leader and future president, Viktor Yushchenko. This niche in the national political arena has always been overcrowded with many small and largely insignificant organizations, and since the death of Chornovil, it has lacked a well-recognized and popular leader. The emergence of Yushchenko as someone who would be able to unite national-democratic forces was an important factor behind the formation of this electoral bloc. In 2002, the coalition Our Ukraine consisted of three fairly influential parties, Rukh, UPP, and Party Reforms and Order, and seven marginal political groupings. The attempt to bring many small parties under one cover was successful. Our Ukraine won elections by gaining 23.57% of the vote and bypassing the second-placed communists (19.98%) with a comfortable margin.

In the 2006 and 2007 elections to the Rada, the coalition Our Ukraine has remained a loose bloc of a somewhat different combination of like-minded political parties (six parties in 2006 and nine in 2007), which claimed their allegiance to President Yushchenko. At the end of both parliamentary electoral cycles the coalition Our Ukraine finished third after the Party of Regions and Yuliya Tymoshenko bloc (see Table 4.1).

The political party People's Union Our Ukraine (NSNU) was created in late 2004 to early 2005 and was registered at the Ministry of Justice in March 2005. Unlike most other Ukrainian parties, which are considered "political projects" of regional clans, groups of elites, or individual politicians, the origin of NSNU mirrors Angelo Panebianco's mixed model of organizational development, which combines territorial penetration (the "center" guides the development of the "periphery") and territorial diffusion (spontaneous construction of local party organizations which are later integrated into a national structure).[21] The party came into existence as a combined effort of pro-Yushchenko political elite in the center and local grassroots movements to support his presidential bid during the 2004–2005 presidential elections and the Orange Revolution.

Naturally, from the moment of its creation, NSNU became a de facto and then also de jure active and consistent constituent part of the electoral coalition Our Ukraine. The unconditional and strong support of President Yushchenko differentiates this political party from its coalition partners who otherwise have mainly similar ideological positions in domestic and foreign spheres, as well as the same geographic support base. Like its coalition partner Rukh, NSNU is also "an observer member" of the European People's Party.

The Electoral Coalition For United Ukraine

Although the electoral coalition For United Ukraine participated only in the 2002 parliamentary elections, it well deserves mentioning in our discussion of Ukrainian political parties. The bloc was established in December 2001 and brought together five mainly regional-based parties of power including the Party of Regions (PR), the Party of Industrialists and Entrepreneurs of Ukraine (PPPU), People's Democratic Party (NDP), Labor Ukraine, and the Agrarian Party of Ukraine (APU). Facing a threat of unification of national-democratic forces around Viktor Yushchenko, five constituent members of the bloc who had a previous record of conflict and animosity among themselves were compelled to join forces. The main objective of the coalition For United Ukraine was to provide support to the incumbent president Leonid Kuchma and his political establishment and secure access to power resources for the leaders of party members of this alliance. Volodymyr Lytvyn, who served as head of the presidential administration at the time, was selected to lead the electoral list of the coalition.

Electoral performance of the coalition For United Ukraine fell below expectations: it received 11.77% of the national vote and finished third after Our Ukraine and the CPU. The Donetsk oblast granted For United Ukraine almost a third of all votes received by the alliance. Unsurprisingly, the three westernmost oblasts and the city of Kyiv gave this electoral bloc the smallest share of the vote in comparison to other regions nationwide.

Typical for parties of power, For United Ukraine lacked any clearly defined ideology. It portrayed itself as a pragmatic organization that would be positioned in the political center between the left and national-democratic forces.

The unity of the coalition For United Ukraine proved to be short-lived; it started disintegrating soon after the elections. The fate of the five member parties of the alliance turned out to be very different: three parties ceased to exist either de jure or de facto, the APU managed to get elected to the Rada in 2007 under a new name and leadership, and the PR has become the major player in Ukrainian politics today.

The Party of Regions

The Party of Regional Revival of Ukraine (PRVU) was founded in October 1997. In the 1998 elections, the party gained less than 1% of the vote nationwide, taking 19th place out of 30 participants. In November 2000, PRVU merged with four other marginal organizations and in March 2001 adopted its current name—the PR. Mykola Azarov, who served as the chief of the State Tax Administration at the time, was elected as the party head. The process of party building has since intensified. A regionally based group representing mainly Donetsk oblast became the dominant force within the party.

In the 2002 elections to the Rada, the PR participated as part of the For United Ukraine bloc. PR proved to be the most successful part of this coalition. Donetsk oblast, the principal regional base of PR, gave For United Ukraine almost a third of all votes received by this electoral alliance nationwide. This achievement allowed the PR to nominate Viktor Yanukovych, who had served as the governor of Donetsk oblast, to the post of the prime minister of Ukraine. Other parties of power, including Labor Ukraine (influential at the time because it represented the Dnipropetrovs'k clan, powerful from Soviet times) and the Kyiv-based Socialist-Democratic Party of Ukraine (United), reluctantly had to accept this nomination. Yanukovych was appointed prime minister for the first time in December 2002.

Yanukovych is a very controversial and divisive figure in Ukrainian politics. On the one hand, there is no doubt that after his election as the head of the PR in April 2003, he became an undisputed leader of this political organization. Some experts argue that as many as 80% of those who cast votes for PR voted for Viktor Yanukovych personally.[22] Before the 2006 elections, electoral technologists affiliated with this politician suggested forming the Viktor Yanukovych Electoral Coalition and argued that this "personal" bloc should participate in the parliamentary elections instead of the PR.[23] On the other hand, a great number of Ukrainian voters find Yanukovych absolutely unacceptable for the top post in the Ukrainian political hierarchy for a simple reason: In his youth, Yanukovych was twice sentenced for criminal offences and served two prison terms. He acknowledged these facts in his own autobiography submitted to the national legislature in November 2002 before his appointment as the head of government.[24]

Both in the 2006 and 2007 elections to the Rada, the PR was victorious, gaining approximately one-third of the national vote. As expected, the party achieved a landslide triumph in its powerhouse, the Donbas region, gaining 73.63% of the vote in 2006 and 72.05% a year later in the Donetsk oblast, and 74.33% and 73.53% respectively, in the Luhans'k oblast. Overall, in both elections PR came first in 10 of 27 territorial-administrative units located in the eastern and southern parts of the country.

It is a challenging task to describe the ideology of the PR. Similar to other parties of power that cannot afford to have a well-defined ideology, PR positions itself as a "centrist" political organization, which "does not fit traditional left and right ideologies."[25] In addition to its "political pragmatism" and "centrism," the PR advocates economic liberalism and political and economic decentralization within the country. The party also champions the interests of the regions; expansion of trade with fellow World Trade Organization members; adoption of an enhanced trade agreement with the European Union; and close political and economic relations with the Russian Federation. In every election the party raises and capitalizes on issues widely popular among its electorate, such as the introduction of the Russian language as the second official language in Ukraine and the anti-NATO campaign. A lack of understandable and cohesive ideology prevents this political organization from establishing partnership relations with European political parties. Accordingly, representatives of the PR in the Parliamentary Assembly of the Council of Europe (PACE) are split between the leftist socialist and the "conservative/centre-right" European democrat groups.[26]

The Bloc of Yuliya Tymoshenko and the Bat'kivshchyna Party

Writing about political parties formed and led by charismatic leaders, Angelo Panebianco states: "Weberian theory implies that the leader founds the party, proposes its ideological goals, and selects its social base by himself. . . . A total overlap of the leader's image and party identity is the sine qua non of charismatic power."[27] With one exception, this definition is a good description of a political organization discussed in this section: The charismatic leader of the Bloc of Yuliya Tymoshenko (BYuT) is a woman.

Like many electoral coalitions, BYuT was established in December 2001, several months before the 2002 elections to the Rada. The four constituent members were the center-right Sobor and Ukrainian Republican Party (URP; soon merged with Sobor), the Ukrainian Social-Democratic Party (USDP), and Batkivshchyna, with no recognizable ideological leaning. The Ukrainian Republican Party, created by a group of Soviet political prisoners and dissidents, was the first political party officially registered by the Ukrainian Ministry of Justice in November 1990. The All-Ukrainian Union Batkivshchyna was founded by Tymoshenko and her supporters in 1999. BYuT gained 7.26% of the national vote in 2002.

BYuT played an instrumental role during the 2004–2005 presidential election, throwing its support behind Viktor Yushchenko. Along with the future president, Tymoshenko became the symbolic "princess" of the Orange Revolution. Tymoshenko's visibility and decisiveness contributed to her name recognition and recruited many new sympathizers among Ukrainian voters. Nevertheless, BYuT's performance and outcomes in the 2006 and 2007 parliamentary elections came as a surprise to many observers.[28] In 2006, BYuT finished second, gaining 22.29% of the vote and bypassing Our Ukraine by a wide margin, although trailing the PR by 10%. A year later, BYuT delivered another surprise; it greatly increased its support nationwide, obtaining 30.71% and narrowing its difference with PR to 3.66%. In addition to winning 16 administrative-territorial units in the nation, the BYuT gained ground in all traditionally "unfriendly" territories. For example, in 2007 BYuT obtained 23.06% of the vote in the Kherson oblast (17.43% in 2006 and 4.33% in 2002); Dnipropetrovs'k oblast—20.93%, 15.03%, and 4.32% respectively; Kharkiv oblast—16.36%, 12.68%, and 1.85%, etc.

Since the moment of their creation, both Batkivshchyna and BYuT lacked a coherent ideology. Until recently Batkivshchyna was an essentially nonideological charismatic party. At different times, BYuT included center-right (URP), center-left (USDP), and liberal (Reforms and Order) parties. A telling example is the affiliation of BYuT members with political groups in the Parliamentary Assembly of the Council of Europe. Until the 2007 parliamentary elections, BYuT had six representatives at PACE. Three of them were affiliated with the Alliance of Liberals and Democrats, two with the Socialist Group, and one with the European Democrat Group.

The absence of an ideology recognizable in Europe prevented BYuT from establishing meaningful relations with European political parties both at the national and supranational levels. In May 2006, soon after the Rada elections, Yuliya Tymoshenko said: "We shall become a member of an international union of parties. We will be looking at the Socialist International because this is the most significant union of parties."[29] Unexpectedly, however, a year later BYuT "changed its orientation." In September 2007, president of the European People's Party (EPP) Wilfried Martens, addressing the BYuT Congress in Kyiv, invited Batkivshchyna to join the EPP as an observer. The vote taken right after Martens's speech was unanimous.[30] In 2008, Batkivshchyna joined the EPP as an observer party.

The Bloc of Lytvyn and the People's Party

The APU, which was formed in 1996 and was a part of the For United Ukraine Coalition in 2002, received a second life in 2004 when Volodymyr Lytvyn, the leader of this electoral bloc and the speaker of the Rada at the time, joined this party and was almost simultaneously elected its head. Afterward, the party was renamed several times, first to the People's Agrarian Party of Ukraine, and then simply to the People's Party. To capitalize on Lytvyn's name recognition, the People's Party participated in both 2006 and 2007 elections to the Rada as the People's Bloc of Lytvyn. In 2006, the bloc failed to clear a 3% electoral threshold. A year later the Bloc of Lytvyn was successful in obtaining 3.96% of the national vote and gaining parliamentary representation. Except for Donetsk and the three westernmost oblasts, the Bloc of Lytvyn has relatively uniform support across Ukraine. The ideology of the People's Party is not clear. This is an organization that (1) adopted a name similar to the alliance of European center-right political parties and on its official Web site compares itself with the EPP,[31] (2) declares its adherence to the doctrine of "people's centrism" in its electoral campaigns, and (3) calls for a creation of the united center-left alliance in Ukraine.[32]

PARTIES AND DEMOCRACY IN UKRAINE

The second section of this chapter investigates the relationship between political parties and democratic consolidation in post-Soviet Ukraine. Among the topics analyzed are the impact of different types of parties of power on political accountability and competitive elections, the role of parties in the cabinet formation, and party proliferation and *apparentement* as a roadblock to accountability. In conclusion, the chapter discusses several cases in which voters have taught lessons in democratic accountability to political actors who did not live up to their expectations.

Parties of Power and Democracy

Many publications on the topic of political parties in the post-Soviet context refer to the concept of "parties of power." A party of power may be defined as "a political bloc that (1) has a deideological, pragmatic, and centrist nature; (2) is created (i.e., founded or utilized) by and acts in the interests of the executive branch of government; (3) relies on state and other 'administrative' resources available to representatives of the executive managers to achieve its goals including participation in elections; and (4) bases its electoral participation on a strong personality-centered factor."[33] In many former Soviet republics including Ukraine, parties of power have evolved from informal blocs of nonaffiliated politicians to formal political organizations.

After the breakup of the Soviet Union, the former Communist *nomenklatura* (i.e., appointees to the senior positions in the Soviet Union that required a prior approval by the CPSU) tried to retain its grasp on power both in the center and in regions. These "pragmatically oriented and deideologized upper level circles of the old nomenklatura, representatives of the state apparatus, mass media, managers of traditional sectors of industry and agriculture"[34] formed the first variety of the party of power, its informal type. This stratum of political elite that was united by nothing other than their desire to maintain their power had to adjust to a new game in town—competitive elections. Mobilization of state and other "administrative" resources available to them proved to be sufficient to run many successful electoral races to legislative bodies. There was no need for a formal organization, party affiliation, or ideology to win a legislative seat. Two factors—devolution of political power and the majoritarian electoral formula—were instrumental in bringing about the informal party of power. In the Rada, these politicians would form different types of "centrist" parliamentary factions, providing support to any existing government at the time. The 1994 elections produced 64.5% of nonaffiliated deputies, most of whom represented the informal party of power. Although in the 1998 and 2002 elections a proportion of independent MPs elected in single-member district constituencies decreased, it still remained significant—45.3% and 32.0% respectively.

The formation of formal parties of power followed the introduction of the proportional representation electoral system in Ukraine. Power holders had to compete in elections held under a new voting formula. Suddenly, aspiring nonaffiliated deideologized politicians turned to political parties; they realized that the use of a party's "powers, resources, and institutional forms would increase their prospects for winning desired outcomes."[35] The NDP, led by Prime Minister Valeriy Pustovoytenko at the time, became the first formal party of power in Ukraine. Although the party received only 5.01% of the national vote in the 1998 elections, the ranks of its parliamentary faction swelled thanks to representatives of the informal party of power elected in the majoritarian constituencies. Following the example of NDP, many regional clans in Ukraine formed their own parties of power: "regional elite clans, hiding under the name of political parties, are transforming their regions into their own electoral patrimonies."[36] For example, in the 2002 elections six parties of power—For United Ukraine, consisting of five parties and the Social-Democratic Party of Ukraine (United)— gained representation in the Rada. The process of transformation of the informal party of power into the formal one was completed with the changing of the mixed electoral system in favor of proportional representation in 2006. Party affiliation has become the principal vehicle for aspiring politicians to gain access to power.

Both variations of parties of power are detrimental for democratic transitions. Indeed, an institutionalized "competitive multi-party system cannot emerge within a system of parties of power, which unbalances the electoral game in favor of a single party or a set of political parties that thrive on the spoils of the state."[37] The informal party of power, consisting of nonaffiliated and disjunct representatives of ruling elites who rely on state resources for electoral purposes, hurts both political accountability and fair electoral competition. The transformation of an informal party of power to a formal one enhances the significance of political parties in a society and advances their electoral visibility and accountability. However, when a country features a political organization or a set of organizations that abuse (misuse, manipulate) state and other "administrative" resources and uses their ruling status to maintain a grip on power at the expense of other competitors, the concept of free and fair elections remains grossly violated.

Unlike its Russian counterpart, the Ukrainian power establishment never succeeded in institutionalizing one single formal party of power. Until the 2004–2005 presidential elections, a number of such organizations, including three major regionally based parties of power (Labor Ukraine—Dnipropetrovs'k oblast, the PR—Donetsk oblast, and the Social-Democratic Party of Ukraine United [SDPU]—Kyiv region), competed among themselves as well as with the political opposition. Labor Ukraine and SDPU (U) ceased to exist for all practical purposes after they were removed from power. The PR has a significant representation in the central organs of power and dominates local governments in eastern and southern Ukraine.

Although four years after the Orange Revolution three main rivals—Our Ukraine, BYuT, and PR—all retain to a different extent some features of parties of power, none of them corresponds fully to the definition suggested above. The disappearance of "genuine" parties of power, which were able to massively violate the principles of democratic competitive elections, was one of the reasons that allowed Ukraine to move up to the category of "free" nations in the Freedom House ratings since 2006. The introduction of the traditional European "party government" model recently became another democratic innovation in Ukraine.

Political Parties and Cabinet Formation

A distinct feature of any democracy is the linkage between electoral outcomes and the formation of the top echelons of the executive branch. In democratic nations with parliamentary and mixed presidential-parliamentary systems, the party or a coalition of parties victorious on the basis of electoral results forms the cabinet. The ultimate goals of most parties that compete in elections are access to political power in the nation and formation of party government where "decisions are made by elected party officials or by those under their control . . . officials are recruited and held accountable through party."[38] In a country with a highly institutionalized party system, a party affiliation is a primary criterion of recruiting politicians to top executive positions. Some exceptions, such as the early years of the French Fifth Republic when President Charles de Gaulle tried to minimize the role of political parties by paying scant attention to party membership when naming his ministers, do not essentially change the overall picture.

A regular appointment of nonaffiliated "professionals" to the top positions in the executive branch of government without a prior endorsement by political parties is a characteristic of a weak party system and individual parties. The establishment of "a technical cabinet" or "a government of experts" that does not depend on electoral outcomes to the national parliament, challenges a fundamental characteristic of a democracy—majority rule. "Technocratization of the cabinet hinders the democratic principles of inclusion and contestation, distances the government even further from the legislature, and cramps parliamentary responsibility,"[39] impeding the political accountability of the ruling elites.

Due to the weakness of Ukrainian political parties, party identification was not a factor for government formation in Ukraine for 11 years after it gained independence. Although the profiles of the 10 different cabinets that existed between 1991 and 2002 were somewhat different—they comprised representatives of the old communist nomenklatura, the industrial and agricultural lobby, technocrats, politicians personally loyal to the president, and an insignificant number of reformists—none of these governments were composed on the basis of electoral outcomes and the party identification of its ministers. In November 2002, five parties of power formed a coalitional party-based cabinet led by Viktor Yanukovych, setting up a precedent in Ukrainian politics. However, the significance of this "party" government should not be overestimated since it represented little more than a situational alliance of nonideological regional parties of power that set aside their quarrels to prevent the largest political force in the nation at the time, the Our Ukraine coalition, from gaining access to the government.

After the constitutional reform was passed during the Orange Revolution, the fundamental principles of government formation in Ukraine have changed cardinally. Party affiliation has become the determining factor for recruitment into the cabinet. All four post-2004 cabinets (Tymoshenko-1, Yekhanurov, Yanukovych-2, Tymoshenko-2) were formed strictly along partisan lines by parties that established a governing coalition in the national legislature. Although a great proportion of the cabinet members were recruited from the Rada, in those cases when a nonaffiliated minister joined a government, he or she was selected by a party member of the ruling coalition within its quota. A political profile of these cabinets demonstrates that diverse political forces in Ukraine adopted a traditional European model of party government, which establishes party monopoly of cabinet recruitment. At present, Ukrainian political parties have succeeded in claiming their exclusive political niches in the society. In addition to the electoral function, the governing function extends accountability of party members of a ruling coalition "for policy creation and implementation beyond one man or the narrow interests of his cronies."[40] However, the party government model does not necessarily mean the acceptance of political parties by the general public. Many factors, including the party-based government's failure to fulfill successfully the governing function, the incapacity of oppositional parties to play the role of "constructive opposition," and a bitter stalemate between party elites and their inability to reach compromise, contribute to the negative attitudes toward these organizations among the general populace and their delegitimization in the public eyes.

With several exceptions prime ministers in post-1991 Ukraine have resisted being overshadowed by the presidential power and have attempted to play an independent role on the national-political scene. The 2004 constitutional reform, which strengthened powers of the prime minister at the expense of the presidency, intensified a political standoff between two institutions. Deep personal distrust between President Yushchenko and prime ministers Yanukovych and Tymoshenko, combined with these leaders' excessive ambitions, has created an environment of perpetual political crisis in post-Orange Ukraine. For the most part, political parties unconditionally supported their leaders. This stalemate demonstrated the lack of a tradition of consociational democracy in Ukrainian politics and a failure of national elites to reach a compromise, even in cases of emergency that affected the whole country such as the natural gas issue with Russia and the financial crisis in 2008–2009. It should come as no surprise that in a public opinion poll conducted by the well-respected Razumkov Center in December 2008, 80% said that they mistrust political parties as an institution and less than 1% had complete trust in them.[41] In the same poll, an unprecedented 85.4% believed that the country is moving in the wrong direction.[42]

Roadblocks to Accountability: Proliferation and Apparentement

As strange as it may sound, the Ukrainian system of political parties is undergoing the process of further proliferation and consolidation simultaneously, with both currents affecting the political accountability of electoral participants. Although the effective number of electoral contestants in Ukraine is constantly decreasing with every electoral cycle (Table 4.2), it still remains rather high in comparison to many other democratic nations.[43] Moreover, since the Ukrainian electoral legislation allows political parties to file joint electoral lists, or *apparentements*, the number of political parties in Ukraine is, in fact, significantly higher than the number of electoral contestants. Realizing that they are not able to compete successfully in parliamentary elections on their own, many political parties are forced to create electoral blocs and submit joint lists. Regardless of whether party members of an electoral alliance form separate factions in the Rada after elections or stay together, apparentement hurts political accountability. Thus, the five parties that established the coalition For United Ukraine in 2002 set up four separate factions in the Rada. Initially, these parties, along with three other parliamentary factions comprising representatives of an informal party of power signed a governmental coalitional agreement. However, this alliance proved to be short-lived. Eventually, several factions stopped supporting the Yanukovich-1 government and the PPPU went as far as backing Viktor Yushchenko and the Orange Revolution.

Even in those cases when an electoral bloc remains a single faction in the Rada after elections, political accountability is still an issue due to (1) volatility and fluidity of electoral coalitions, and (2) a lack of a common position among alliance members on many important subjects. The coalition Our Ukraine is a good illustration. In 2002, this alliance consisted of 10 political organizations. By the 2006 elections, seven parties including two major coalitional members (UPP and Reforms and

Table 4.2 Effective Number of Electoral Contestants in the MMD in Post-independence Elections in Ukraine

Year	Percentage
1998	10.75
2002	7.46
2006	5.65
2007	4.22

Note: MMD, multi-member districts.
Source: Author's calculations based on data from the Central Election Commission of Ukraine (http://www.cvk.gov.ua/).

Order) quit the electoral bloc. Instead, three new parties including the PPPU joined Our Ukraine. A year later, the coalition Our Ukraine experienced another major overhaul; it lost two of its former members (for example, the leaders of the PPPU joined the list of the Party of Regions) and admitted five new parties.[44] The alliance also adopted a new name: Our Ukraine–People's Self-Defense. On some important issues, the party members of the coalition did not have a unified position. For instance, during the conflict between President Yushchenko and Prime Minister Tymoshenko in 2008–2009, People's Self-Defense and Rukh supported Tymoshenko, the NSNU took a staunch pro-presidential stand, while several other alliance members took a wait-and-see position. In December 2008, Our Ukraine–People's Self-Defense split over the issue of supporting the new governing coalition comprised of BYuT, Lytvn Bloc, and Our Ukraine–People's Self-Defense. A significant number of MPs elected on the ticket of this electoral alliance did not sign a new coalition agreement.

Unlike Our Ukraine, the PR adopted a diametrically different approach to apparentements. After being a part of an electoral coalition in 2002, the strengthened PR declined propositions from like-minded organizations to join any electoral coalition. Beginning with the 2006 elections to the Rada, the PR competed under its own name, absorbing smaller political parties. The electoral list of the PR submitted for the 2007 elections included leaders of many marginal political parties coopted by the PR: Iryna Bogoslovs'ka (Party "Viche," number 4 on the PR electoral list), Nestor Shufrych (SDPU-U, number 5), Hennadiy Vasyliev (Party Derzhava, number 17), Yuriy Boiko (Republican Party, number 49), Anatoliy Kinakh (PPPU, number 53), Valeriy Konovaluk (Labor Ukraine, number 84). Neophytes were advised to quit their membership in the parties that they led and join the PR. Overall, more than 20 leaders of these parties who ran on the list of the PR in 2007 became members of the PR shortly before or after parliamentary elections. Taking into account the charismatic nature of the leadership of many of these parties, the "beheading" of these organizations meant their de jure or de facto removal from the national political scene. Indeed, during 2007–2008, the Republican Party and Labor Ukraine decided in favor of merging with the PR. No other party whose leaders switched their allegiance to the PR participated in the 2007 elections to the Rada on their own or as a part of any electoral bloc.

There can be no doubt that the absorption of small political parties by the PR helps to consolidate the national party system and leads to less electoral volatility and party fluidity. Whatever its reasons, the PR's refusal to enter electoral coalitions and share responsibility with other political organizations makes this party both more recognizable and potentially more accountable among the electorate.

Learning Accountability?

A disappearance of the informal party of power, institutionalization of party monopoly on top political appointments in the executive branch, competitive elections, as well as structuring of political competition nationwide in general along party lines have all contributed to greater visibility and identifiability of political parties in Ukraine. Both political organizations and individual politicians have been forced to learn lessons of political accountability—their future and status on the national political scene depend on their credibility and trust among the voters.

The Socialist Party of Ukraine became the first major Ukrainian political party to be punished by its electorate and given a bitter lesson in democratic accountability in action. After the 2006 elections, three main parties behind the Orange Revolution, Our Ukraine, BYuT, and the SPU, gained the majority of seats in the national legislature. The SPU, which campaigned under the slogans of the Orange Revolution and drew its main electoral support from nationally conscious center-left voters in the central part of Ukraine, received 5.69% of the national vote. It was widely expected that these three organizations that had together obtained 243 seats in the Rada would form a coalitional government. However, the SPU unexpectedly split from two other Orange parties and signed an alliance agreement with its former adversaries—the PR and the CPU. Our Ukraine and BYuT went to the opposition; Oleksander Moroz was elected the speaker of the parliament.

This change of political partners had dire consequences for the Socialists. The party has split—many prominent party functionaries and rank-and-file members quit the SPU. In addition, the voters did not forgive what many of them believed was the betrayal of their mandate on the part of Moroz and his party. In the 2007 snap elections, the SPU lost ground in its traditional powerbase in central Ukraine. Thus, in 2006 the party obtained 14.69% of the vote in the Vynnytsya, 12.87% in Chernihiv, 12.74% in Poltava, 10.55% in Sumy, and 9.21% in Khmel'-nyts'ky oblasts. A year later, the results were strikingly different: 2.53%, 2.93%, 2.98%, 1.96%, and 1.72%, respectively. On the contrary, in 2007 the SPU improved in the overwhelmingly "anti-Orange" Donetsk oblast, which gave almost a third of all votes received by the party nationwide. However, an improved performance in the Donetsk region did not help the party to clear the electoral threshold. For the first time in independent Ukraine, the socialists failed to gain parliamentary representation. It remains to be seen if the SPU will be able to restore its influence in Ukrainian politics.

In comparison to the 2006 parliamentary elections, a year later the PR fared better in 24 of 27 administrative territorial units of Ukraine. The region where the PR had missed the largest share of the vote in 2007 was Kharkiv oblast. In 2006, the PR gained 765,901 votes or

51.70% in this region. The next year the party obtained 659,324 votes (49.61%), losing over 106,000 supporters. In 2007, the PR lost votes in 9 of 11 electoral constituencies that comprise Kharkiv oblast. However, it was the second largest city in Ukraine, Kharkiv, that demonstrated the largest decline of the PR vote, giving the PR almost 60,000 fewer votes in 2007. For example, in 2006, 51.01% of voters in Electoral District 174 and 52.43% in Electoral District 175 (both districts are located in the city of Kharkiv) voted for the PR. In 2007, these numbers dropped to 45.74% and 47.61% respectively.

Many experts link the weaker performance of the PR in the 2007 elections in Kharkiv to the mayor of this city, Mykhailo Dobkin, and his cronies.[45] Dobkin was nominated to this post by the PR and was supported personally by its leader, Viktor Yanukovych. Within one year after his election in March 2006, Dobkin and his team became the center of numerous corruption scandals, which seriously tarnished the image of the PR and its leader among the electorate in Kharkiv. As a result, many former supporters of the PR either stayed home on Election Day or voted for other parties. Although the PR leadership expressed its dissatisfaction with Mayor Dobkin and the performance of his team, he still remains at his post as the present volume goes in print.

Not only are political parties and their leaders compelled to learn lessons of political accountability, but individual members of the Ukrainian parliament have also been held responsible for their actions. In June 2006, a member of the PR Oleh Kalashnikov attacked two journalists from the STB television station, threatening them, inflicting an injury on one of them, and forcefully taking a tape from a cameraman. The incident caused a mass outcry among Ukrainian journalists who asked Yanukovych to expel Kalashnikov from the PR and its parliamentary faction. The reaction of the party leadership was mixed: although Kalashnikov was not expelled from the PR or from the party faction in the Rada, his name was not included on the party list for the 2007 elections.

A list of the times when Ukrainian political parties, their leaders, and individual parliamentarians were held publicly accountable for their behavior is still a short one and the record of outcomes is mixed. However, it does exist. The Orange Revolution and other examples demonstrate how whole parties and individual politicians were penalized by the public for actions that were deemed inappropriate. The sooner the parties stop neglecting the factor of democratic accountability, the more trust and credibility they are likely to have among the electorate and this, in turn, will affect their electoral performance.

CONCLUSIONS

The Soviet Constitution established a monopoly of the Communist Party on political power in the Soviet Union. Even after Mikhail

Gorbachev launched his perestroika and glasnost reforms, the hard-line Brezhnevite leadership of the Communist Party of Ukraine actively discouraged the creation of alternative political organizations that challenged its power on the territory of Ukraine. Thus when first emerging as an independent nation at the time of the breakup of the former Soviet Union, Ukraine had neither a competitive party system nor "genuine" political parties except for the CPU. Traditional unique niches that political parties occupy in democratic societies—their electoral and governing functions—were filled in other ways, mostly by nonparty officials. The informal party of power, vague and fluid groupings (alignments) of independent politicians who occupied a great share of the seats in the national legislature, and "technical" cabinets formed outside of party channels lessened the political accountability of the ruling circles—one of the fundamental characteristics of a democratic society.

Andrew Wilson and Sarah Birch state that "Parties change over time, and they change most rapidly in newly competitive states."[46] Ukraine is a good illustration of this process. In the 17 years that have passed since the country proclaimed its independence, Ukraine has established an institutional framework that has allowed political parties to assert their proper place in the national political system, at least on the surface. The fourth cycle of presidential elections and the Orange Revolution in late 2004 to early 2005 became a crucial step toward institutionalizing fairly competitive and honest elections as the exclusive mechanism of obtaining political power in the nation. This demonstrated to political elites of all shades that electoral fraud is unlikely to be tolerated. Along with the transfer of some important powers from the presidency to the parliament and the cabinet, and the introduction of the proportional representation system for the election of the complete composition of the Rada, it made Ukrainian parties the main political actors in the country. In fact, parties became key agents of political recruitment: They are principal "gate-keepers" in the process of selection of candidates for the Rada and the cabinet, which since 2002 are formed by a party coalition on the basis of electoral outcomes.

It is only recently that the informal party of power was removed from the political scene by organized political parties. Main parties, some of which still retain elements of parties of power, carefully watch one another to ensure that their competitors do not misuse state "administrative" resources for electoral purposes to upset artificially the balance of powers between the parties. The winner of this party rivalry is a relatively free and fair competitive electoral process, which is perhaps the single most important characteristic of democracy.

Today, major Ukrainian parties are no longer "virtual." They are visible and recognizable elements of the national political life; politics in Ukraine is structured mainly along the party lines. Main political parties are in control of the electoral and governing social niches—two unique functions of parties in a democracy. Increased identifiability of political parties in Ukrainian society makes them more accountable for their activities than in the not-so-distant past.

However, these developments do not mean that Ukraine has established a highly institutionalized party system. Whether they like it or not, Ukrainian political parties have to stand the test of democratic accountability. So far they have failed this test by failing to win the "hearts and minds" of ordinary citizens. Although parties have never been popular in Ukrainian society, in December 2008 the proportion of those who distrusted these institutions approached 80%. A never-ending stalemate between branches of government, lack of stable electoral bases, the strong charismatic nature of parties, and personal animosity between party leaders, and deeply rooted suspicions among party elites prevent parties from reaching a compromise and developing coherent and effective policies even in the cases of national emergencies. These are just some of the many factors that undermine the legitimacy of political parties in Ukrainian society.

The institutional framework that allows parties to claim their unique niche on the national political scene has not transferred to stronger trust in them among the general population. On the contrary, greater visibility of parties, and, as a result, their greater accountability, seems to cause the opposite effect. A widespread and long-lasting distrust for political parties as institutions presents a challenge for a democratic society. It breeds a sense of frustration in foundations of democracy and eventually may delegitimize competitive elections as the exclusive mechanism of government formation among the general public. Democratic accountability delivers bitter lessons to Ukrainian political parties. The sooner that parties start learning these lessons, the more credibility they will have among the national electorate and the greater chance democracy will have to survive in Ukraine.

EPILOGUE

On February 7, 2010, Viktor Yanukovich was elected president of Ukraine, defeating both Victor Yuschenko and Yulia Tymoshenko (the latter in a runoff). He has stressed Ukraine's commitment to European values while maintaining the importance of its historic, cultural, and economic ties to Russia.

PART II

Asian Parties

Introduction to *Political Parties and Democracy: Part II: Asian Parties*

Baogang He

Since 1974, the third wave of democratization has engulfed southern Europe and Latin America, swept through Asia, and decimated dictatorship in the Soviet bloc.[1] At the beginning of the 1980s, of the 26 main political regimes in Asia, only six were more or less democratic: Japan, India, Sri Lanka, Malaysia, Singapore, and Papua New Guinea. Nine were either military dictatorships or regimes controlled by a civilian leadership beholden to the military: Pakistan, Bangladesh, Afghanistan, Burma, Thailand, Indonesia, Taiwan, the Philippines, and South Korea. Five were royal autocratic or colonial regimes: Brunei, Bhutan, the Maldives, Nepal, and Hong Kong; and six were communist party mobilization regimes: China, North Korea, Mongolia, Vietnam, Laos, and Kampuchea (or Cambodia). In the 1990s, 9 of the 20 authoritarian regimes featured on this list had started on the road to democracy: Pakistan, Bangladesh, Nepal, the Philippines, Thailand, Indonesia, Taiwan, South Korea, and Mongolia.

Historically, however, a number of Asian democracies have been characterized by one-party domination. In Japan, the hegemony of the Liberal Democratic Party (LDP), which had ruled since 1955, was not disturbed until 1993. In India, the Congress Party (also known as the Indian National Congress) won seven of the first eight elections between 1952 and 1984 (1977 being the exception).[2] In the 1980s, this created a perception that democracy in Asia—even where it did arise—was not competitive in any meaningful sense. Political power tended to be concentrated in the hands of a single, overwhelmingly dominant party that was liable to electoral defeat only in theory.

Today, however, one-party domination seems to be in decline throughout Asia. Golkar (Partai Golongan Karya, Federation of Functional Groups) and the Kuomintang (KMT) are a shadow of their former selves. In Malaysia, grassroots support for the opposition Pan-Malaysian Islamic Party (PAS) has increased substantially, threatening the United Malays National Organization's (UMNO) hegemony for the first time. Both Korea and Taiwan have moved progressively toward the entrenchment and extension of democracy. Competition between government and opposition has intensified, and independent judiciaries have been formed in both states. Admittedly, the Chinese Communist Party (CCP) in China, People's Action Party (PAP) in Singapore, and the Communist Party of Vietnam (CPV) have all bucked this trend by reinforcing their dominance in recent years.

This section of Volume III of *Political Parties and Democracy* focuses on the role that political parties play in enhancing or inhibiting democracy in China, India, Japan, Malaysia, and South Korea. These five countries have been selected not only because of the significance of their respective transitions to democracy, but also because of their size, geographic distribution, and sharply contrasting developmental histories. This introduction will briefly review the existing literature on political parties and democracy in Asia and the contributions each of our chapters makes to the topic, and then offer a fuller treatment of four particular topics covered by all of them.

Both the party system and democracy in Asia have been explored at length in various edited volumes. Harunhiro Fukui introduced the political parties of 82 countries across Southeast, East and South Asia, the Pacific Islands, and Australasia in 1985.[3] In 1998, two volumes edited by Wolfgang Sachsenroder and Ulrike E. Frings provided an introduction to, and analysis of, the party system, major political parties, and the prospects of democracy in a number of East and Southeast Asian countries, including Brunei, Burma, Cambodia, Indonesia, Malaysia, Philippines, Singapore, Thailand, Vietnam, China, Japan, Korea, and Taiwan.[4] *Party Politics in East Asia: Citizens, Election, and Democratic Development*, edited by Russell J. Dalton, Doh Chull Shin, and Yun-Han Chu, published in 2008, explored the relationship between partisanship and popular support for the democratic process, using cross-national survey data to examine the institutional structures of party systems and voting preferences across East Asia.[5]

There are also numerous book chapters and journal articles available, some of which address the specific question of whether there is a distinctive Asian model of democracy.[6] Y. M. Kim describes what he takes to be "Asian-style" democracy and critically evaluates the arguments in its favor. He finds that a clearly distinguishable and convincing model of East Asian democracy has yet to emerge.[7] Through an examination of electoral systems, political parties, and parliaments in the Asia Pacific region, Benjamin Reilly similarly attempts to identify an Asian model of electoral democracy. He also suggests that, in a number of East Asian countries, political institutions have been reformed with the aim of reducing the number, and thus increasing the size, of political parties. As a result, a more majoritarian variant of democracy is taking shape, and in some cases, a two-party system is emerging.[8]

Much research has also been devoted to the institutionalization of political parties—widely assumed to be essential to a functioning democracy. Hans Stockton takes concepts and measures of institutionalization used in the study of Latin America and applies them to the cases of South Korea and Taiwan. He identifies a curvilinear relationship between institutionalization and consolidation.[9] In a similar vein, A. Ufen, comparing the Philippines, Thailand, and Indonesia, considers whether there is a positive correlation between the degree of party and party-system institutionalization and the avoidance of democratic breakdown, and is skeptical of any causal relation.[10]

Each of the following chapters contributes to this literature. They offer up-to-date case studies of the party system in five major countries across Asia, with particular emphasis on the prospects of democracy in each country. In "China's Step toward Democratization: Intraparty Democracy," Baogang He points out that although the CCP does not allow external challenges to its rule, there is a growing level of democracy within the party structure. In "Political Parties and Democracy in India," M. V. Rajeev Gowda and E. Sridharan provide a thorough discussion of the main political parties in India and discuss the growing strength of ethnonationalist and regional parties. In "Fledgling Two-Party Democracy in Japan: No Strong Partisans and a Fragmented State Bureaucracy," Takashi Inoguchi offers a chronological overview of the evolution of the Japanese party system and discusses whether Japanese political parties facilitate or impede democratic politics. Edmund Terence Gomez provides a brief history of the Malaysian political system and its main parties in "The Politics of Ethnicity: Authoritarianism, Development, and Social Change in Malaysia," before appraising the role of these parties in aiding or hindering democracy. He suggests that the results of the most recent elections reveal a desire for the deepening of democracy and nonracialized government. Hoon Jaung tracks the transition from majoritarian democracy to consensual democracy in his chapter on South Korea, noting that behind this shift is a change of focus, from governability to representativeness. Needless to say, a fuller appreciation of the richness and complexity of the party systems in the countries discussed will require a close reading of each chapter. To facilitate comparison of the five cases, I group together the main characteristics of each with respect to four broadly defined themes: (1) origins and development, (2) levels of competitiveness and the number of effective parties, (3) patterns of democratization, and (4) representation of ethnic divisions. As above, the chapters are taken in the order they appear in the book (alphabetical by nation).

ORIGINS AND DEVELOPMENT

The CCP, founded in 1921, gained control of all of mainland China, its military forces, and governmental organizations following the civil war against the nationalist KMT party, and swiftly established a single-party state. The CCP has justified its absolute rule and intolerance of opposition by appealing to the chaos and civil war that marked the republican period (1912–1928), when competitive multiparty politics were part of the Chinese political landscape.[11] Today, the CCP boasts 74 million members (more than 5% of the Chinese population), making it the largest political party in the world.[12]

After leading the struggle for independence from the British, the secular Indian National Congress dominated Indian politics in the following decades, ruling the country for 49 of the past 61 years. The Congress competes against a large number of opposition parties, including Hindu nationalist parties (such as Bharatiya Janata Party [BJP]), communist parties (such as the Communist Party of India [CPI]), lower caste populist/agrarian parties (such as the Janata Dal and its offshoots), and a whole host of ethnoregional parties (including Dravida Munnetra Kazhagam [DMK] and the All India Anna Dravida Munnetra Kazhagam [AIADMK] of Tamil Nadu). In 2004, 6 national parties, 36 state parties, and 173 registered parties contested the elections. Although the Indian National Congress has been the historically dominant force, the popularity of ethnonationalist and regional parties is undeniably on the rise. Since 1989, the Congress plurality fell from 39.6% to as low as 26%. Gowda and Sridharan explain that "this decline was due to parts of the Congress base going over to regional, agrarian-populist, lower caste–based parties that reaped the benefits of identity politics and popular mobilization from below." It is little surprise, then, that while the popularity of the Congress has declined, the Hindu nationalist BJP party has increased its vote share from only 11% in 1989, to 25% in 1998, and still maintained 22% in 2004.

Further, the popularity of single-state–based regional parties has increased to the point that the combined vote shares of the Congress and BJP was less than 50% in 1996, 1999, and 2004. Consequently, no party is now in a position to win government without entering into a coalition with other parties. Coalition politics has become the norm and is only further reinforced by the first-past-the-post electoral system, which encourages coalition building to aggregate votes. Today it is common for the ruling coalition to be comprised of a multitude of parties. In 1996, a nine-party United Front (UF) minority coalition was formed. This was replaced in 1998 by an 11-party BJP-led minority government. And in 2004, the nine-party Congress-led United Progressive Alliance (UPA) formed a minority coalition government.

Japan's first political party was founded in 1874. The formation of the first cabinet soon followed. However, the emperor retained sovereign authority and supreme command, and in 1940 all political parties were dissolved. The party system would not reemerge until after World War II, when the American occupation force reduced the role of the emperor to a symbolic one and transformed Japan into a liberal, parliamentary democracy.[13] The country would quickly evolve into a two-party system, pitting the conservative LDP against the Japanese Socialist Party (JSP). By the mid-1950s, however, the JSP would begin to break up into smaller parties, marking the beginning of a multiparty system and one in which the LDP grew increasingly dominant, to the point that compromise with opposition parties ceased to be a political necessity.[14] Some commentators have described this, perhaps more accurately, as a "one and a half party" system, rather than a multiparty system. The LDP occupied just over 50% of the seats, while the JSP and the Japanese Communist Party occupied 30% combined, making them something of a permanent opposition to the predominant LDP. In the 1990s, however, the LDP itself began to splinter and weaken, bringing an end to its dominance and ushering in the current phase of "coalition government system."[15]

In Malaysia the first democratic elections were held in 1955. The Alliance coalition and its successor, the Barisan Nasional (National Front), have maintained control of the government ever since. The Alliance coalition was comprised of three ethnically based parties. The largest component party—the Malay-based UMNO—joined with the Chinese-based Malaysian Chinese Association (MCA) in 1952, and two years later the Malaysian Indian Congress (MIC) entered the fold. In the first democratic elections, the Alliance captured all but one of the 52 contested parliamentary seats.

Following World War II, the British returned to Malaysia and proposed a Malaysian union scheme, which would place all of the nine Malay states under one government and guarantee equal citizenship regardless of race. The scheme was widely perceived as an attempt by the British to abolish the Malaysian Sultanate, and the notion of equal citizenship aroused much opposition. In May 1946, an assortment of Malay associations and political organizations came together to form the UMNO, whose purpose was to resist the implementation of the Malaysian union. The other original member of the Alliance, the MCA, was formed after the relationship between the British and the Malaysian Communist Party broke down. The MCA was created to take the place of the latter in dealings with the British. It included wealthy

Chinese businessmen and professionals who saw political involvement as a way of protecting their economic interests. Finally, the MIC was formed in 1946 after the visiting Indian prime minister Jawaharlal Nehru encouraged local Indians to remain in Malaysia. The MIC became the third party of the Alliance in 1954, securing for the Alliance the support of the Indian working class.

In the 1960s, popular support for the Alliance declined, while opposition parties grew stronger. In the 1969 election, only 48.5% of the vote went to the Alliance—enough to retain control of the government, albeit with a severely diminished majority. Mounting tensions and growing instability in the country erupted into race riots in the early 1970s. Shortly thereafter, the members of the Alliance were regrouped into an enlarged coalition that included numerous other parties. This new coalition—the Barisan Nasional—would supplant the Alliance, but the UMNO would retain its hegemony. In the 1995 general election, Barisan Nasional contested 192 seats; 103 of these were allocated to the UMNO, 35 to the MCA, and only 10 to Gerakan, one of the larger parties to join the coalition in the 1970s.

South Korea is characterized by fluid party politics. Splits within and mergers between political parties have been common occurrences since democratization. Furthermore, since the parties are "generally leader-oriented rather than program-oriented," it is very common for members to switch from one political party to another.[16] Despite each party claiming to represent the nation as a whole, the parties have strong regional support bases, and regional voting patterns are salient. The conservative, right-leaning Grand National Party (GNP) is currently in government. This party was formed by a merger between the New Korea Party (NKP)—formerly the Democratic Liberal Party, which was formed by a merger of the three major parties of the preceding military dictatorship period—and the Democratic Party (DP) in 1997. A countless number of opposition parties have drifted in and out of existence on a regular basis since the country's democratic turn.

LEVELS OF PARTY COMPETITIVENESS AND EFFECTIVENESS IN THE FIVE NATIONS

Apart from the lack of multiparty competition in China, parties have openly contested political power by way of democratic elections in each of the other countries under consideration. India stands out in particular, with power alternating between Congress-led and BJP-led coalitions in recent times. Moreover, the Indian communist party was able to win around 10% of the votes in recent elections—enough to gain control over a small number of states. In Japan, the two major parties in the 1920s to 1930s were reduced to one and half from 1955 to 1993. Whether Japan will retreat in the direction of a two-party system is a question that is likely to arouse great interest. The expanding support base of the PAS suggests that a two-party system may be in store for Malaysia in the not-too-distant future, and South Korea has certainly already taken steps along this route.

Competitiveness and effectiveness are related, but of course not the same. Parties may compete with little or no effect on governance, and it is useful to consider as well how many parties are actually effective—that is, how many have a real possibility of occupying government roles or determining electoral and/or policy outcomes. Needless to say, in China there is only one effective party: the CCP. In addition to the UMNO, the parties that make up Malaysia's Pakatan Rakyat (People's Alliance)—and in particular the PAS—can also be considered effective. The electoral performance of the Pakatan Rakyat in 2008 saw it occupy 37% of seats in the Federal Parliament. According to Steven I. Wilkinson, the effective number of parties in Malaysia is 5.2.[17] In Japan, the most accurate account of the effective number of parties was "one and a half" in the 1950s and 1960s according to Inoguchi, though this may not be so for too much longer. Nevertheless, Benjamin Reilly offers a different calculation. For him the effective number of parties in Japan was 3.7 during the postwar period, and has been 2.4 since 1994.[18] The effective number of parties in Korea has remained relatively steady, hovering at around 3.0. Meanwhile, the effective number of parties in India has increased steadily over the years. The effective number of parties by votes/seats was: 4.80/4.35, 5.10/3.70, 7.11/5.83, 6.91/5.28, 6.74/5.87, and 7.6/6.5 in 1989, 1991, 1996, 1998, 1999, and 2004, respectively. In contrast, in the eight general elections between 1952 and 1984, the effective number of parties by seats exceeded three only once (3.16 in 1967) and the effective number of parties by votes exceeded five only once (5.19 in 1967).[19] This has enhanced representation for smaller interests and identities, as has the rise of regional parties, given that "it is easier in regional parties for local level leaders to access their party leaders and to influence their decision making."

PATTERNS OF DEMOCRACY/DEMOCRATIZATION

Similar patterns of democratization are apparent when we focus directly on the theme of the set of studies in which this volume appears. China, the first case, offers a few surprises, inasmuch as how intolerant it may be of external challenges to its authority: the CCP does allow—indeed promotes—a significant level of competition and democracy within the party. The CCP's constitution stipulates that decisions on major issues must be made through consultation and discussion, where the majority's will prevails over that of the minority. Intraparty elections are held in which the votes of all party members are weighted equally, and party operations are subject to a host of checks and balances.

Moreover, intraparty democracy in China is gradually being deepened. At an annual party congress in Ya'An in 2003, all major party leaders were subjected to evaluation by party representatives, 40% of whom were nonelite, ordinary members. A dismissal process was initiated against any leader who failed to gain a confidence vote of over 70%. In 2008, the party arranged for a survey of some 80,000 citizens, with the intention of gauging their satisfaction with the performance of the cadres. The results of the survey are expected to have a significant impact on future appointments and promotions. And in July 2008, a new regulation was introduced that provides all party members with sufficient funding to exercise their right to contribute to the formulation of policies (by carrying out investigations, for instance). Having said this, Chinese intraparty democracy remains limited in various respects. There are no guarantees of gender equality, no democratic control of party funding, and no primary elections to decide on the candidates for office. Such limits are typically justified by the need to ensure cohesion and prevent factionalism.

The CCP has also taken positive steps to shed its status as the "vanguard of the working class" and to become more representative of all sectors of Chinese society. In February 2000, Jiang Zemin proposed the concept of the "Three Representatives": the notion that the CCP should represent the "most advanced mode of production, the most advanced culture, and the interests of the majority of the population." The proposal was formally adopted in the 16th party congress. Most significantly, this has led the CCP to recruit more members from the new private entrepreneurial class, which forms a large part of the most advanced mode of production.[20] Thus the CCP is being transformed from a representative of the working class and peasantry to a representative of all social classes.

Gowda and Sridharan, following Kanchan Chandra, describe India as a "patronage democracy" in which the relationship between the party and the voter is "clientelistic": Politicians work to provide their (often ethnically defined) "clients" with private goods, such as the federal allocation of resources, and public jobs and services, in return for votes.[21] Furthermore, democracy within the political parties has declined. A large number of the parties are becoming dynastic—led and controlled by families that crowd out competition for party leadership through their control over resources and their "brand appeal." Gowda and Sridharan state that "Leaders disagreeing with the family that runs the party typically have only exit and not voice as their option." In this respect, the evolution of Indian democracy is in direct contrast to the development of Chinese democracy, where interparty democracy remains nonexistent, but intraparty democracy is improving.

Japan is a full-fledged competitive liberal democracy. Japan's 1946 Constitution guarantees a wide range of rights and liberties, including freedom of expression, the right to property and a fair trial, the right of assembly and association, and the right to form a political party. Further, the major political parties have grown increasingly representative. The LDP was originally seen as the party of the rural population, but its support base has shifted to urban centers and the "new middle class" as well. Likewise, following the drastic decline in union membership, the support base of the Japan Socialist Party shifted away from unionists. Large numbers of nonunion members are now also represented by the Democratic Party of Japan (DJP). In addition to this, appealing directly to the needs and wants of ordinary citizens has become the norm in Japanese politics, whereas previously political parties tended to make interest-based appeals to business and bureaucratic sectors.

Malaysia can be described as a semidemocracy in which UMNO is still dominant while opposition parties are able to gain seats and even control a few state governments through elections. Elections are being held on a regular basis but political freedoms are often compromised.

South Korean democracy has likewise deepened over time. Originally a majoritarian democracy where the proliferation of parties was held in check, a series of reforms between 2002 and 2004 have transformed South Korea into a highly representative, consensual democracy. One such reform was the decentralization of the nomination system. Party members and advocates now have a greater say in the selection of candidates for office. This has helped all parties improve their ideological representation of their supporters. A second significant reform was the easing of entry conditions for new parties. Previously, new parties were required to win a minimum of 5% of the vote to gain any seats. This was lowered to 3% in 2002, leading to the inclusion of parties that would previously have been ruled out, such as the Party for Advanced Korea (PAK). The PAK won two list-seats with its 3.8% of the vote—a proportion that would have failed to return a single seat prior to the reforms. Consequently, South Korean democracy has become significantly more representative and inclusive.

THE PARTY, ETHNICITY, AND THE STRUCTURE OF THE STATE

A final consideration here is the difference among the parties with respect to the representation of ethnicity and how federal or quasi-federal state structures facilitate that form of representation. In contrast to most western countries, where the party represents a part or section of society, the CCP sees itself as being equivalent to the Chinese nation. It reaches out and attempts to unify ethnic groups into a cohesive unit and represents all of its people collectively. Similarly, in India, the Indian National

Congress promotes a culturally and linguistically diverse notion of Indian nationhood and "remains broadly acceptable to all members of the population." However, the rise of coalition politics in India has led to what Gowda and Sridharan refer to as the "ethnification" of political parties, some of which represent only specific ethnic or religious groups, many of them harboring ideological agendas that are explicitly or implicitly hostile to the interests of other groups. The BJP, for instance, would prefer to see India transformed from a secular democracy to a "Hindu Rashtra" or Hindu polity and supports the construction of a temple for Rama—an incarnation of Lord Vishnu—on the site of the Babri Mosque, which was destroyed by Hindu nationalists in 1992. In Malaysia, the Barisan Nasional (BN) is comprised of, and represents, members of all of the country's main ethnicities. However, it is important to point out that BN is seen as "a multiracial coalition of parties instead of a single multiracial party."[22] And within the BN, the Malay-based UMNO remains dominant, regularly invoking its ethnicity to justify its position and portraying challenges and criticisms as evidence of communal agitation.

Each of the countries discussed also displays federalist elements. In some cases, the federal arrangements serve to accommodate a plurality of social classes and ethnoreligious communities. The most apparent example of successful federalism in Asia is found in India, where the federal system has given previously marginalized groups access to political power and given regional elites the chance to influence policy making at the national level.[23] Malaysian federalism, on the other hand, is organized along territorial lines. This has caused the disorganization of social minorities as well as prevented secessionist movements from forming.[24] Here, federalism is "designed and managed so as to scramble and blunt ethnic differences."[25] China, although not formally federal, has been described by some as a de facto federalism. Hong Kong enjoys significant autonomy in terms of monetary policy and external economic relations, and the workings of market capitalism are providing a number of seaboard provinces with the economic base for greater political independence. Finally, Japan, while formally unitary, has a "centuries old tradition of decentralization and quasi-federalism."[26] Between the 16th and 19th centuries, Japan afforded autonomy to some 300 of its domains. In some sense this has survived in the form of highly autonomous bureaucratic agencies within government. Furthermore, Japan's attempts to increase representation of marginalized groups are precipitating the loosening of the unitary, centralized state.[27]

In sum, political parties have become an entrenched, permanent feature of Asian politics. The parties vying for power are as complex as they are diverse, defying clear-cut classification and simplistic generalizations. The same can be said for the democratic institutions in which the political parties operate; the varieties of democracy across Asia are many. Multiparty cooperation under the leadership of the CCP, rather than multiparty competition, characterizes the unique form of "democracy" rapidly taking root in China. In this connection China is swimming against the current. In each of the four remaining countries discussed here, the political arena is becoming increasingly competitive, and a general shift in the direction of two-party systems seems to be taking place.

I would like to thank Nenad Dobos for his research assistance.

CHAPTER 5

China's Step toward Democratization: Intraparty Democracy

Baogang He

BACKGROUND AND AIMS

To understand the Chinese Communist Party (CCP) is to hold a key to the "secret garden" of Chinese politics. One cannot completely grasp developments in Chinese politics without first grasping the role of the CCP in China.

The CCP is one of the oldest and certainly the largest political party in the world. It is also the wealthiest, with the politburo and central organization claiming control of 42 major corporations. As the most powerful organization in the nation, it has full command over all government and military services. The CCP has been enjoying increasingly more absolute power than before, but this growth in absolute power is accompanied by widespread ideas and experiments of intraparty democracy. There has been a progressive push to promote internal party democracy and generate innovative solutions.

The CCP's intraparty democracy must be understood in light of the two specific contemporary challenges facing the CCP today. The first challenge lies in unifying, managing, and controlling 74 million party members (equivalent to the population of a middle-sized country). The second challenge is its ability to provide basic living standards and social services for a population of 1.3 billion and to maintain a double-digit growth rate; in other words, the ability to govern, to maintain the unity of the nation-state, and to achieve its political legitimacy. Beijing relies on a unified CCP organization across and above all classes and ethnicities, implementing order from the top down to village, factory, street, and school and reaching out into all four corners of the country. Through this comprehensive and omnipresent organization, the CCP is able to unify all political forces in China and maintain stability and political order. It does not allow or tolerate any opposition party to compete for power; and it forbids the formation of any alliance between workers and peasants, between intellectuals and outside organizations, or between any social organizations and religious bodies. Clearly, such a monopoly of political power brings with it a risk of corruption and potential decay, as the party is well aware. It is in an effort to avoid these problems while maintaining absolute power that the CCP has introduced a measure of intraparty democracy.

The new emphasis on intraparty democracy has been "inspired by CCP assessment of the causes of collapse of the Soviet Communist Party in the Soviet Union [CPSU]."[1] The demise of the CPSU in 1991 was particularly alarming for CCP officials in Beijing. Their analysis persuaded them that the mechanisms of self-destruction, or the processes of disintegration of a powerful party, are found at all levels. The bottom-up process is the collapse of local organizations. The centrifugal process is the use of party organizations by ethnic groups for their independence or the dismantlement of party branches in the peripheral republican states. The top-down process is the split of the core organization at the center. For the CCP, the challenge was how to prevent the three processes from occurring.[2] In 2002, at the 16th National Congress of the Communist Party of China, intraparty democracy was confirmed as fundamental to the future survival of the CCP. Reform of the party's leadership and rules of governance was considered a foremost priority. On the agenda was the improvement of existing election and monitoring institutions and the protection and expansion of the right of party members to access information and participate in political processes. These reforms were regarded as essential to make the party more democratic and to make party democracy more concrete, responsive, and meaningful.

There are comparative precedents in history. The Communist Party in Hungary introduced intraparty democracy, the South African Communist Party managed to transform itself into a democratic party, and the Swedish Social Democracy Party, which ruled Sweden from the 1930s through the 1980s, revitalized itself to regain political power from the 1990s until today.

This chapter will develop a revisionist view of the CCP. In doing so, it provides an examination of the ideas of intraparty democracy, grassroots changes in elections, political party representation, and the Permanent System of Party Representatives (PSPR). It calls for a new way of thinking about the unthinkable—about the prospect of intraparty democracy in China and the possibility that this in turn may lead to the greater democratization of China itself.

THE MAIN CHARACTERISTICS OF THE CHINESE POLITICAL SYSTEM

The CCP was founded on July 1, 1921, in Shanghai, China. After 28 years of struggle, the CCP in 1949 became the ruling party of China and founded the People's Republic of China. Almost 70 years later, China is still ruled by the CCP, which has enjoyed complete dominance and control over the military forces and governmental organizations. In a unitary system, it is the responsibility of central leaders to appoint and regulate local leaders, and in China the central leaders are the leaders of the CCP. China's political system differs from that of a competitive multiparty or biparty system. China adheres to a multiparty cooperation system whereby political consultation takes place with and among other parties but under the leadership of the CCP. This system is the product of a Marxist-Leninist tradition, integrated with both authoritarian Chinese tradition and China's own experience of revolution. It is justified, in the eyes of the party, by the history of the republican period when the multiparty competition system led to civil wars and chaos in the 1920s.[3]

China's Constitution reinforces the hegemonic position of the CCP. Although democratic parties are encouraged to participate in government affairs, they must ultimately remain under the leadership of the CCP.[4] These efforts aim to strengthen the leadership of the CCP, maintain the stability of the country, push forward political reform, and open China to the outside world.

The CCP holds all senior positions within China and continues to dominate national and local politics. In a western democracy, a political party's power is measured by the number of votes it receives in an election or the number of seats it holds in a parliament. However, in China the CCP's power is measured by the size of the party's membership and by the politburo's ability to command and control the government and the party. The party controls formal state organizations and selects the candidates for the appointment of top state's leaders. Because members of the State Council are concurrently members of the CCP Central Committee, and because all policies adopted by the State Council must be approved by the CCP, the party's leadership is instrumental in formulating the very governmental policies that it must oversee. The State Council is at the top of the state's organization. The premier is its chairman. The State Council's membership is composed of the premier, who acts as its head, vice premiers, state councillors (who are mostly former vice premiers or elder leaders on their way out), and ministers. All ministries, commissions, special agencies, and centrally administered banks report to the State Council. In theory, it is responsible to the National People's Congress (whose delegates are elected by lower-level people's congresses) and its Standing Committee.

The Definition of Party and Intraparty Democracy

The concept of party in China differs considerably from that in the liberal tradition. The main differences between the two concepts are highlighted in Table 5.1. Different concepts of party stem from different understandings of democracy. If we apply a liberal framework, then it is clear that a genuine Chinese democracy cannot coexist with the domination of the CCP. As Bruce Dickson argues, "If the country [China] does become democratic, it will be essentially at the expense of the CCP."[5] If, however, we take these different conceptions seriously, it is possible to envision the Chinese idea of intraparty democracy, and this in turn may lead us to appreciate the possibility of plural paths toward nationwide democracy—including a Chinese way.

To understand any new development of the party and the idea of intraparty it is important to question whether our thinking and assumptions about the party in general are problematic in understanding China's party. In particular, we should be aware of the limits in applying a liberal definition of party to China. The notion of Chinese intraparty democracy is quite different from that of intraparty democracy in liberal democracies.[6]

Intraparty democracy has taken on a variety of forms, in different historical periods, at different levels, in many aspects, and through multiple channels.[7] The Chinese understanding of intraparty democracy falls under five main principles. First, intraparty democracy is seen as enhancing political rights—an institution whereby all party members can participate in party affairs directly or indirectly on an equal basis. Second, all party members are equal and enjoy the rights provided by the party constitution. Even the party secretary and other members in the same party committee should be equal, and the principle of one member, one vote should be implemented in intraparty elections. Third, the existence of elections forms a key principle of intraparty democracy. In some constituencies multiple candidate elections replace single candidate elections for party congress delegates. In some places elections for village party secretary, township party secretary, and even county party secretary are permitted and carried out. It is further suggested that the party's General Secretary should be elected by the Central Committee or even by the party congress, which in turn should become the most important body in determining crucial issues. Fourth, a combination of electoral and nonelectoral representation is needed in an intraparty democracy. Fifth, the introduction of checks and balances for certain government and party operations is also a key aspect of the CCP's attempt to embrace intraparty democracy. It is proposed that power should be divided into party committees, executive committees, and party discipline inspection commissions, with each being independently responsible to party congresses.[8] Essential to intraparty democracy is the idea of three divisions

Table 5.1 Comparing Two Concepts of Party

Chinese concept of party	*Liberal concept of party*
Party (*dang*) is a collective concept excluding private interest. Party is for the promotion of collective and public interests such as community and nation-state beyond private ones.	Individualism is the foundation of party. Individuals form parties to advance their private individual interests.
The party is or represents the whole, the Chinese Communist Party (CCP) represents all peoples in China and is equivalent to the Chinese nation. The concept of party does not contain the idea that part becomes a party.	The origin of the modern party system has developed from "parts" (section of society) to party. Party is "part," not "whole"; no single party can claim "the whole," therefore a multiple party system is needed.
Because party is and represents the whole on a collective basis, factions within the party are denied in terms of moral principles, unity, and solidarity. In real party life, factions do exist but the party suppresses them.	Because party is "part" or "faction" on an individual basis, factions within a party are allowed to articulate the interests of different parts.
CCP monopolizes political power in the name of providing national security, unity, and social control. This is a link between one party domination and denial of liberal democracy.	Multiple parties compete for political power through elections. This is a link between party and democracy.
Dissent is an enemy of party; and discipline is a key to maintain the unity of the party.	Disagreement produces modern party; Dissent is a virtue of party politics.
The party believes that plural parties will lead to disintegration.	Plural parties are able to establish and maintain one polity through constitution and consensus.

of powers within the party, as first proposed by Liao Ganlong and now endorsed and advocated by Wang Guixiong from the central party school. According to this proposal, legislative power should lie in the party representative to congress; executive power should be exercised by the Central Committee; and the judicial power should belong to the party disciplinary committee and the monitoring committee from the party congress. It is argued that such a system would be a unifying force able to keep different powers under the party leadership, with the source of all powers coming from the party congress. Although the proposal is not endorsed by the central leaders openly and completely, the experiment with empowering the party representatives has been conducted in Ya'An and other places, as will be discussed later.

Chinese understanding of internal party democracy shares with international advocates of intraparty democracy a stress on the principles of participation and inclusiveness, accountability and transparency, and representation. The Chinese idea of intraparty democracy, however, does not emphasize gender equality, fair primary elections that produce a party list of candidates, or democratic control of party funding. The U.S. style of primary elections is viewed as a system bound to create division and factions within the party, and excessive intraparty democracy is seen as weakening discipline and solidarity. Therefore, from the perspective of the CCP, internal party democracy must be limited to such a degree that it will not weaken the unity of the party. There is a tradeoff between discipline and competitiveness.

The CCP's model of intraparty democracy also does not include party factionalism. Some suggest that the CCP should learn from the Liberal Democratic Party in Japan, where party pluralism contains one party plus factions, or parties within the party. However, it remains unlikely that the Chinese model of intraparty democracy would legitimize internal factions within the party. This is largely because Chinese intraparty democracy is oriented toward collective solidarity rather than individual liberty. It aims to maintain one party rule rather than to create a multiparty system. It wants to maintain the rule of law, but only under the leadership of the CCP. It aims to improve the party's congress system, not to adopt referenda or general elections. It stresses the importance of a checking and monitoring role for journalists rather than absolute freedom of press. Thus although the outside world's expectation may be that as China adopts democratic reform the CCP will be forced to end its dictatorship, this normative assumption is in sharp contrast to the CCP's expectation that "Beijing's major goal is to perpetuate the CCP's ruling legitimacy by developing intra-party democracy."[9]

Historical Development of Intraparty Democracy

Although there is a new sense of urgency now, many of the ideas and practices of intraparty democracy have existed in China since the birth of the CCP in 1921. As demonstrated in Table 5.2, contemporary intraparty democracy has been a piecemeal process, dating back to historical roots. Although there were a variety of approaches to intraparty democracy in different historical periods, most of them were situational responses to the specific issue at particular times.

MEMBERS' PARTICIPATION IN INTERNAL PARTY POLITICS

Once again, the purpose of intraparty democracy in China is to realize the CCP's general program, and its point of departure is to guide, protect, and promote initiatives. Thus its approach to the role of party members is to encourage them to have the courage to explore new things and to dare to tell the truth. This aspect of intraparty democracy is to be implemented at all levels from the party Central Committee to every party branch, from the decision making of leading organs to the participation in policy discussions at party meetings or on party newspapers and magazines, and from internal party elections to the appraisal and supervision of leading cadres. In order to promote

Table 5.2 The Development of the Chinese Communist Party's (CCP) Intraparty Democracy, Congress by Congress

First, 1921	The party constitution adopted the Soviet form of intraparty democracy, designed to include, represent, and organize workers, farmers, and soldiers.
Second, 1922	Majority rule is adopted in all party meetings.
Third, 1923	Kuomintang-CCP cooperation established to deal with two party cooperation and competition.
Fourth, 1925	Rotation of party branch chairman suggested in the party constitution.
Fifth, 1927	The party's guiding principle of democratic centralism explicitly put forward for the first time.
Sixth, 1928	Importance of each individual party member to the process of democratic life emphasized.
Seventh, 1945	The rights and duties of each individual party member are defined, providing a foundation for individuals to exercise their rights.
Eighth, 1956	Establishment of the permanent system of party's representatives at province and county levels.
Eleventh, the third plenary, 1978	After the Cultural Revolution,[1] democratic practices were reintroduced into the party. This required all major decisions to be based on scientific, democratic, and deliberative discussion. The "one person one vote" rule was also implemented.
Twelfth, 1982	The requirement for cadres such as democratic leadership was introduced, undermining the paternalist culture.
Thirteenth, 1987	The procedure of nomination and semicompetitive elections was explicitly specified.
Sixteenth, 2002	General Party Secretary Jiang Zemin declared that intraparty democracy is the life of the CCP; without it, the party is likely to collapse.

[1]The Cultural Revolution (1996–1976) was a campaign against "liberal bourgeoisie" elements and a continuing struggle for revolution. It led, however, to widescale social, political, and economic violence and chaos. It revealed the weaknesses and shortcomings of the Chinese Communist system and discredited Mao Zedong's ideal of "proletarian democracy." The tragedy of the Cultural Revolution resulted in or, more precisely, was a prelude to the democratic movements in contemporary China.

intraparty democracy, the party aims to safeguard the democratic rights of party members and party organizations at various levels.

In the experiment in Ya'An in 2003, party representatives were granted five basic rights—the right to election; the right to discuss major policies; the right to evaluate party leaders; the right to monitor; and the right to propose a motion. As few as 10 permanent party representatives were able to put forward a motion in the party congress. The relevant party or government organization must answer an inquiry made by any permanent party representative within 3 to 6 months. Moreover, in exercising these rights, party representatives are protected by state laws and the party's disciplinary committee. The party secretaries have no right to remove arbitrarily party representatives.

At the 17th Party Congress, party members were praised as providing the "subjectivity" of intraparty democracy. In recognition of this, the central party organization in July 2008 introduced a new regulation providing for the full protection of the rights of party representatives. In particular, it provided party members with sufficient funding to exercise the right to contribute to the formulation of major policies such as carrying out an investigation. It also provided party representatives with the right to attend committee meetings and evaluate the performance of committee members. Nevertheless, the question of how much the regulation will be implemented fully or partially remains to be seen.

DECISION-MAKING PROCESS: COLLECTIVE LEADERSHIP

According to the party's constitution, collective leadership is the main decision-making procedure. All major matters relating to principles and policies, all issues concerning overall interests, all issues in connection with recommendation, appointment, and removal, as well as rewards and punishment of cadres in important positions should be determined collectively by central or local party committees. Decisions on major issues should be made through deliberation, consultation, and discussion and by vote according to the principle of minority being subordinate to majority. No individual has the right to change collectively made decisions. Individuals and the minority are allowed to reserve their different opinions but must obey the decisions unconditionally and implement them actively.

Although Mao Zedong may have praised the principle of collective leadership, his actions and leadership style were paternalistic, absolute, and arbitrary. Learning from the mistakes of Mao Zedong, in 1987 Deng Xiaoping actively enforced the principle of collective leadership. This principle was further supported by Marshall Ye Jingying who reintroduced democratic life among the circle of top leaders in the party.[10] Leadership styles are crucial. Mao adopted a chairman system in which the chairman was entitled to make the final decision. This system strengthened Mao's absolute power and weakened the institutional mechanism against tyranny. After the Cultural Revolution, the chairman system was abolished and replaced with the General Secretary system in which the General Secretary convenes the meetings of the Politburo and its Standing Committee and presides over the Secretariat's work, and the CCP Secretariat carries out the CCP's daily work under the direction of the Politburo and its Standing Committee. The power of the General Secretary thus is limited by the party's Secretariat and by members of the Politburo and the Standing Committee of the Politburo.[11]

"Three Representatives"

Political parties around the world are experiencing a loss of connection with community. Although the CCP is not an exception to this rule, it has worked hard to address the issue of representation. In an attempt to safeguard its legitimacy, the CCP has been supportive of nonelectoral forms of representation. The introduction of the "three representatives" concept has been particularly significant in maximizing inclusiveness and representation.

In February 2000 in Guangdong, Jiang Zemin proposed the concept of "three representatives" (*san ge dai biao*), that is, the CCP represents the "most advanced mode of production, the most advanced culture, and the interests of the majority of the population." He recognized that the CCP had to reposition itself to be representative of the whole nation instead of just being the vanguard of the working class. Given that the new private entrepreneur class forms a large part of "the most advanced mode of production," he proposed that the party should recruit more members from this new class. The proposal was adopted in the 16th Party Congress, marking a significant change in the nature of the CCP and radically transforming it from being representative of the working class and peasants to being representative of all social classes including the new entrepreneur class. Now in Ya'An, the party branch in each village is required to recruit between two and five private entrepreneurs into the party each year. At the same time, the party branch is obliged to help party members become richer through supporting his or her business.

It should be noted that while the concept of three representatives aims to further increase the percentage of the private entrepreneur class in the party so as to enlarge the social basis of the CCP, it cannot be understood as adding only the representation of the new rich class. Jiang's emphasis on the CCP's representation of the interests of the majority of the population can be seen as an attempt to rebuild the party as a "national party" (*minzu dang*). This seems to return to Song Ping's earlier call in 1990 for nationalizing the CCP into an "all-people party" (*quanmin dang*).[12] Of course there is an internal contradiction between the interests of people such as workers and the interests of the rich, but it is precisely this contradiction that justifies the party's intervention and its role of coordination in dealing with the conflict of interests.

The idea and practice of the three representatives concept aim to go beyond the division of social classes. The Chinese official concept of the party does not contain the idea of representing diverse interests through a plural party system (see Table 5.1). It is unlikely that China will replicate a European model of multiple parties backed by conflicting social classes. The CCP endeavors to deal with class conflicts through the means of technocracy—capitalists sharing power with technocrats—and the three representatives. At the same time the party adopts tough measures to suppress any political group that aims to mobilize social classes. In addition, the Chinese idea of party does not imply sharing power and the turnover of power between two parties. It can claim its legitimacy as long as it maintains control. It justifies one-party domination in terms of economic growth, that is, one-party domination provides the stability and the environment that rapid economic development needs.

The Election of the Village Party Secretary

Before village elections China had a monopower structure in which party secretaries were in command. Since the introduction of elections, a dual power structure has emerged; that is, villages have two seats of power: the power of village party secretaries and the power of elected village heads (Table 5.3).

Village elections create or widen the conflict between village party secretaries and elected village heads. The contest for the locus of power comes from two sources. According to the principle of party organization, the party secretary should be at the core of leadership in a village. However, in the spirit of the governance of law, the village head, rather than the party secretary, should be in that top position. An elected village leader claims to have more authority than that of the party secretary because he or she is elected. Consequently, the elected village head constitutes a challenge to the power of the secretary, and rivalry and power struggles have followed.

Although village elections contribute to the dual power structure, a close examination reveals that the fundamental source is the domination of the CCP. From a comparative perspective, village elections did not create such dual power structures in Taiwan, Indonesia, Malaysia, and India. It was the CCP's refusal to withdraw its power from villages that created the problem. If the CCP had not established its branches at the village level, the village elections alone would not have created the

Table 5.3 Dual Power Structure in Villages

	The nature of power	The source of power	Methods	Authoritative recognition
Village party organization	Political organization	Party's constitution	Leaders are appointed by above, but now increasingly elected.	Appointed and confirmed from above
Village committee	Mass and autonomous organization	Village organic law	Elected	Confirmed by villagers and competitive election

dual power structure. The dual power structure is the product of the Chinese political system in which the CCP attempts to maintain its domination while introducing village elections to solve the governance crisis in rural China.

In order to reduce the tension between elected village committees and the village party branch, the central government has encouraged and pushed the village party secretary to win the position through elections. The aims were to gain democratic legitimacy for village party secretaries and to overcome the phenomenon of the "older party" or "kinship party," that is, a village party organization dominated by the old or by one kinship group.

Party elections aim to enhance the popular legitimacy of the secretaries in order to prevent the erosion of absolute party control. If the local party resists democracy, and if its survival depends on institutional guarantees and protections from above and immunity from democratic pressure from below, the party will undergo further decay and lose its relevance. On July 14, 2002, the Central Party and State Council issued an important document, number 14, which guarantees the right of villagers to nominate representatives or candidates, forbids the practice of appointment for party members who run for village elections, and requires the nomination of candidates by villagers. More significantly, it recommends that all those who want to be village party secretaries must first stand for the village elections; and these who fail to gain popular support will automatically lose the candidature for village party secretaries. Document 14 also recommends that elected party secretaries should hold the position of village heads. The party has discovered elections to be a new solution that "may [reconcile] the requirements of village self-government and the survival of the

Party."[13] There are three types of party elections and their basic features are summarized in Table 5.4.

Since 2002, 4,124 village party secretaries have been elected as village chiefs, increasing from 4.27% in 2002 to 16.73% in Jianxi in 2003.[14] In Jintan county, Jiangsu Province, 92% of the village party secretaries were elected as village chiefs, and 47.6% in Baoying county in 2004.[15] In Qionghai city, Hainan Province, 86.7% of village party secretaries were elected as village heads in 2004–2005.[16] In Shandong, 91.9% of 81,988 village party organizations adopted the "*liantuiyixuan*" method.

Table 5.4 Three Models of Party Election

	Shanxi model	*Guangdong and Hubei model*	*Shandong and Zhejiang model*
Method	Villages will elect village committee first, then elect party secretary.	Two elections emerged. Village committee elections produce the village chief who automatically becomes party secretary.	Two nominations and one election method (*liantuiyixuan*), that is, candidates are nominated by both party members and nonparty members, but elected only by party members.
Result	The result is likely to produce dual power in the village power structure, increase power conflicts, but it will help to form checks and balances of power.	The result gives rise to a power monopoly in village power structure, merging the party branch and the village committee, thus preventing power conflict, but not effectively forming checks and balances.	Results in maintaining dual power structure in village, but strengthens the authority of village party secretaries who still lack legitimacy as they are not elected by all villagers.
Restriction	There is no restriction on nonparty members running for the village committee election.	It is likely to restrict nonparty members from running in the merged election.	The restriction of nonparty members is not an issue as it is merely an intraparty election.

There were 5,384 village party secretaries elected through public speech making and secret vote ballot by village party members in 2005.[17] In Linhai, Zhejiang, those who failed to get more than 50% of the villagers' vote could not be a candidate for the village party secretary.

If village party secretaries are confirmed by election, it is assumed that they enjoy popular support. On this basis, the central government also recommended the Yijiantiao policy, that is, one person serves as both village party secretary and village chief. This turns two power organizations—elected village committee and village party branch—into one. It aims to prevent "two tigers in a village" and assumes that a single power center is best in a village power structure. The merged model is a deliberate attempt to strengthen the party branch and to overcome the problems arising from conflict between the party secretary and the village chief. It also aims to reduce the number of village cadres and reduce expenses. In Linan county, all the village heads were party branch leaders in 1994. In Weihai city, Shandong Province, 71.8% of elected village chiefs from 2,679 villages were also party secretaries in 1998.[18]

Spread of Township Party Secretary Elections

In the past, party members have elected party committee members only. Only a high-level party organization could decide who would be town party secretary and deputy secretary. In 2003 Xindu district, near Chendu, carried out an experiment to set up a procedure to decide the township party committee profile: The position of who will be township party secretary is now directly decided by party members' votes. This experiment is far more important than direct election of township heads in the existing political system. Direct township elections can elect township government heads but do not impinge upon the township party secretary who is ultimately the number one person in the town. The township party election addresses this fundamental question by introducing a further election.

The election of the township party secretary was held in Mulan town, Xindu district, on December 4, 2003. An electoral college comprised of 243 delegations from town cadres, village party representatives, village heads, representatives from enterprises, deputies of the local people's congress, and members of democratic parties listened to public speeches made by 11 preliminary candidates and cast their votes for two final candidates. On December 7, a general party member meeting attended by 639 party members was convened, and they elected the town party secretary.[19] This experiment was repeated in all other 11 townships where all party secretaries were elected by direct party assembly in March 2005 in Xindu district.

On May 28, 2008, in Guiyang city, 20 candidates running for five county party secretary positions gave public speeches and were questioned by a panel of experts. The appointment of the party secretaries was decided by the vote of the Standing Committee members of Guiyang. Table 5.5 lists the party secretary elections at the township level and above.

China's Communist Party Congress has also used contested elections to select candidates for the Central Committee, the policy-making body from which top leaders are chosen. The 13th Party Congress in October 1987 was the first in which the delegates were elected by secret ballot, and the first in which the slate of candidates for the Central Committee was actually larger, 5% more candidates than the number of seats in the Central Committee.[20] In 1992, there were more candidates than seats for the committee, which had some 170 members.[21]

The voting procedures were found to have several flaws. First, only an electoral college decided the final candidate in Xindu's experiment. Second, elections were a controlled participatory process. A small "leading group" of the party organization controlled each step and took all necessary measures to minimize uncertainty. They were able to use the party disciplinary mechanism to ask candidates to withdraw or turn out for elections.

Table 5.5 Summary of Party Secretary Elections at Township Level or Above

Date	Location	Types of elections
October 2002–January 2003	Yichang City, Hubei	Party secretaries and government leaders
October 2002	Ya'an City, Sichuan	Party members elect deputies to country party congress
December 4–7, 2003	Mulan Town, Xindu, Chendu	Township party secretary
February 2003–2004	Shuyang, Suyu counties, Jiangsu	Party secretaries and government leaders
August 31, 2004	Jintan County, Jiangsu	Party members elect township party committee
2005	Sichuan	787 towns and townships party secretaries were voted through *gongtui gongxuan*
May 28, 2008	Guiyang	5 county party secretaries elected

Source: This expands the table originally developed by Dong Lisheng with the author's updated data. Dong Lisheng, "Direct Township Elections in China: Latest Developments and Prospects," *Journal of Contemporary China* 15, no. 48 (2006): 507.

Permanent System of Party Representatives

A rejuvenation of the party requires empowering party representatives. Party democracy needs its own parliament, just as national democracy is dependent on a national parliament. The Permanent System of Party Representatives (PSPR) is the parliament of the party where party representatives, similar to MPs in western systems, engage in deliberation and debate on major policies.

In the past, party representatives were restricted from engaging in policy formation after their attendance in meetings. In the PSPR, however, there are permanent positions for the period of the party congress, "permanent" in the sense that party representatives exercise daily rights and powers. The PSPR was originally suggested by Mao Zedong and proposed by Deng Xiaoping in 1956. In the 13th Party Congress, Zhao Ziyang's team proposed that a PSPR be established. In 1988, the central party organization approved 12 experimental sites for trying out the idea, among them Jiaojiang and Shaoxing. Before the 16th Party Congress, 7 of 12 sites stopped their experiments. The system was improved in Ya'an, however, in August 2002.

In the past, party congresses were held every five years, and party representatives elected party committee members who in turn elected party secretaries. Now party congresses are held every year. In Ya'An party representatives hold quarterly meetings each year. In the past, the Party Representative Congress was a consulting body, but now it is a decision-making institution and the source of final authority.[22]

In the past, party representative election was only a formality. However, in Yinjin county, Ya'An city, party representatives were competitively elected in 2003. Among the 5,800 party members, 736 (that is 12.7% of party membership) participated in running for election, 241 were decided as final candidates, and 166 were elected as party representatives in August 2003. During the election process, 17 party leaders at the township level lost their positions.

Several initiatives were taken so that a Party Representative Congress can be held more frequently and more efficiently. The size of the constituency of each party representative was reduced so that one representative is able to make close contact with, and represent, about 100 party members; the standing committee and the alternate member system were abolished to make the Party Representative Congress a decision-making body. Ya'An has also set up a new institution for party representatives called the Party Representative Liaison Office.

Over the past 20 years, experiments were carried out in 17 cities of Meishan and Zhigong in Sichuang; in the Baoan district of Shengzhen, Huizhou city, Yangdong county in Guangzhou, Chengbei district in Nanning city, and Yichang city. Following these experiments, the central party committee decided in July 2008 that the PSPR be implemented nationally.[23] This lays a firm foundation for the vote system in which all major policies are decided by a vote cast by party representatives.

There are, however, some problems with the PSPR. First, this is a bureaucratic expansion of the party, illustrated by the fact that five staff members for a representative office were added in Ya'An. Additionally, there is a representatives' monitoring committee that checks the disciplinary committee. Second, there is uncertainty about the relationship between the Party Representative Congress and the People's Congress. In taking over the role of People's Congress, the Party Representative Congress will be held first, followed by the People's Congress, which is supposed to endorse the decisions made by the Party Representative Congress.

DEMOCRATIC EVALUATION

In 2003 in Ya'An city, at an annual party congress, all major leaders were evaluated by party representatives, 40% of whom had to be ordinary members. Crucially, if any leader does not gain a confidence vote of over 70%, a dismissal process will begin automatically against him or her. In practice, with a first no-confidence vote a leader is given a warning and opportunity to improve his or her work within one year. Dismissal only occurs after a second no-confidence vote.

Ordinary citizens are involved in democratic evaluation. In July 2008, the central party organization entrusted the state's Bureau of Statistics to carry out an independent survey of 80,000 citizens. The survey will examine satisfaction levels regarding the performance of cadres and the process of appointing cadres. The results of the social survey will influence future political appointments and promotions.[24] On August 20, 2008, all 12 districts in Guangzhou city carried out a survey whose results will impact the political life of local cadres. If the dissatisfaction rate reaches 50%, the cadre will be regarded as "disqualified."[25]

There are several limits to this evaluation. In Jiaojiang city, Zhejiang, the party organization stopped the evaluation practice in 1991 because the party secretary lost face when he received far fewer confidence votes than his colleagues. Nevertheless, it was forced to reintroduce the evaluation in 2003. In Zhejiang, the party secretary Zhang Dejiang did not endorse the idea of citizen evaluation and did not approve the proposal for the evaluation of all major leaders by citizens. Only deputy leaders of governmental departments were allowed to be evaluated by 21 leaders in 2002–2003.

Anticorruption Measures

The CCP has also been combating the real and potential corruption of absolute power in a one-party–dominated system through the introduction and development of intraparty democracy. There are several checks against any potential evil doer. The party discipline committee has more power than before; and the party secretary no longer controls the party discipline committee at his or her own level. The monitoring committee comprising permanent party representatives constitutes another important checking mechanism. The annual democratic evaluation meetings are also an important institutional safeguard against corruption; any party leader who does not gain above 70 percent of the evaluative votes will face internal party disciplinary warning and punishment, and officials who have gained a reputation for corrupt acts are now likely to lose their positions in the next internal party elections. There are signs these efforts are serious. In Chongqing in July 2008, 370,000 mobile phone users in one district received a message from the procuratorial organization offering a financial reward to anyone able to provide valuable information about official corruption. If the value of corruption was over 20 million yuan, the informant was promised a reward of half a million Chinese yuan.[26]

Limits to Intraparty Democracy

Serious reservations about the soundness of intraparty democracy are often raised, the most significant of which is the question of how a Leninist party can contribute to the democratization of itself. Obviously there are many limitations to intraparty democracy. Most new experiments have taken place at the township or county level.

The inherent limitations of intraparty democracy include continuing party domination, limited roles for active civil society, a failure to protect civic rights, and a lack of transparency and openness. An external mechanism to monitor party elections is absent. If internal democracy is not open to outside scrutiny, how can it push societal democracy or encourage pluralism and competition among parties? The problem is that the CCP still controls state power. Intraparty democracy is under the control of the party organization, in particular, the party's "four submissions" discipline.

Normally, state democracy precedes party democracy, with the assumption that it is only after a country consolidates state democracy that intraparty democracy becomes possible, when freedom and democratization in civil society encourage and allow ordinary party members to challenge party leaders. Given the lack of state democracy in China, many doubt that China can develop a meaningful party democracy. As Gang Lin points out, "in the absence of meaningful restraints on the Party's monopoly of power and the consequent blurring of lines between Party and state authority, China's institutional building is likely to be incomplete and fraught with theoretical inconsistency and strategic ambiguity."[27] It is commonly asked whether it is possible for China to achieve internal party democracy before it achieves state democratization, but this sequential thinking is mistaken. At the same time, it is also a mistake to say that there is no need for state democracy if the CCP has internal party democracy.

While I concur with many of the criticisms of intraparty democracy, I would like to stress that intraparty democracy is a much more important and significant institutional development than that of village or township elections. It is far from insignificant that 74 million party members, 0.056% of China's population, are now able to vote for their party representatives. If the proposal of intraparty democracy is to be thoroughly realized, the party itself would need to change into something new and the current nature of the CCP would be sacrificed. The party would become more powerful but also more legitimate. Even if a majority of Chinese people were still deprived of democratic processes, intraparty democracy would nevertheless constitute a big step. Intraparty democracy would improve the quality of one-party domination and prevent it from becoming an absolutely corrupt and tyrannical party.

Such a change might also lead to a fundamental change in the state-party relationship. If the party were democratized, the state would have been democratized as well, at least to a certain extent, because of the nature of the Chinese party state. Intraparty democracy would also pave the way for a rapid transformation to state democracy and strengthen reformers within the party. Beginning with intraparty democracy, one may look next for the democratization of the relationship between the party and the state. The CCP cannot afford to miss this historical opportunity, and western observers and China watchers need to be open to new possibilities for the future of the CCP.

Thinking the Unthinkable

It is a puzzling political phenomenon, which repeatedly surprises many commentators. After the events of 1989, it was predicted that the CCP would collapse in three years. When this did not happen, the prediction was revised to nine years, but this too proved to be wrong. The party not only survived but it also expanded its power by establishing party branches in newly established residential buildings[28] and privately owned factories.

The changes discussed above require a revisionist view of the party. To argue that the CCP is unchanged, monolithic, and utterly totalitarian is simply inaccurate. Without revision, the predictions of the demise of the CCP will fail again. Western liberals must therefore find the courage to see and adapt to the new Chinese reality. Western liberal presuppositions about the party prevent us from looking objectively at the Chinese path toward local democracy. The liberal political paradigm distracts us from paying sufficient attention to the mixed regime China has developed, and the focus on democratization strategies for civil society handicaps our inquiries into other paths toward democracy.

Not long ago, a special issue of the *Journal of Democracy* was devoted to the question of whether the CCP is able to renew itself or whether it is likely to suffer further decay.[29] He Qinglian argued that the CCP is morally and politically so corrupt and bankrupt that it cannot renew itself, let alone undertake the democratization of China.[30] Nevertheless, going beyond a simple dichotomy between renewal and decay, one needs to ask deeper questions, think the unthinkable, and view the party with a fresh eye.

Although the party is still Leninist in the sense that "Leninist organizational principles prohibit the formation of competing organizations that could challenge the CCP, and the Party enforces this prohibition strictly,"[31] the Leninist framework is inappropriate to apprehend fully the significant developments at the local level and is unable to explain the complex reality of party politics in China.

The conventional view in the West is that the presence of the party constitutes an obstacle to Chinese democracy, and that the CCP is expected to collapse as did its counterpart in the Soviet Union. In reality, however, the ideology of communism is gone, and the party ideology has been "secularized" from a principle-oriented party to a utilitarian party. The CCP is flexible enough to make substantial changes for its survival. Indeed, the membership of the party is changing in favor of the rich, the unchallenged domination of the party has been weakened, and the party has gradually learned to share power with elected village committees and representative assemblies, while increasingly adopting elections as an institutionalized measure to reinforce its legitimacy.

Of course we must ask whether the "nomenklatura" appointment system[32] has really changed at the local level. The answer is a qualified yes. Now, the local party organization appoints cadres outside the party, open nomination and elections play some role in appointing local cadres, and the local party, in particular, village party secretaries, have to share power with elected village chiefs. In these ways, the power of the party's organization has been slightly reduced and restricted, the sources of local power are being redefined, and elections and deliberation are increasingly becoming a new source of authority and legitimacy.

The CCP has undergone a transition from an overwhelmingly peasant-based party to one that attempts to represent all sectors of society, from opposition to private ownership to the support for privatization and the capitalist line. The CCP has recruited entrepreneurs and the new rich. The CCP has also transformed itself from a revolutionary party to a conservative ruling party, as was proposed in 1991 by Tai zi dang.[33] The move toward a conservative ruling party has followed the following steps: to abandon the communist goals and to adopt new nationalist and patriotic goals; to restore the traditional Chinese culture in order to discipline the masses and to unite all the Chinese people; to give up radicalism and political romanticism and to emphasize gradualism and realism.

In urban cities, local parties at the level of residential committee sometimes function like charity organizations; the local party boss develops a charity plan and persuades local business people to help the poor. During traditional Chinese festival periods, the poorest people may receive up to 2,000 yuan. Urban residential communities also provide welfare services by registering the jobless and the poor and helping them find jobs.

The idea that the party is a rational actor helps us to understand its choice of seeking to foster intraparty democracy under certain circumstances. In the long term, if these developments continue, the party's principles will be redefined and its nature changed, so that these elements will eventually open a path that may lead to a quiet and peaceful change in the Chinese authoritarian system.

CREATING A CHINESE MODEL OF DEMOCRATIZATION?

China's path toward democracy must be unique in human history not only because of the size of China's population and its long history of civilization, but also because of the Chinese experience of economic reform. China has experienced more than 30 years of economic reforms and has developed its own pattern and model. Due to the success of these economic reforms, the Chinese are becoming more confident in creating their own model, and they do not want to simply copy models such as the Kuomintang in Taiwan, the People's Action Party in Singapore, and the Liberal Democratic Party in Japan.

Will the CCP adopt a multiparty system? This seems to be a misleading and unproductive question in the current situation; instead it is better for us to understand fully the historical and conceptual restrictions on the development of a multiparty system in China. Such a review is enlightening. In the later Qing Dynasty, there was strong opposition to the formation of the party because, according to Confucian ethics, the western style of party was regarded as a group of people who pursue private interests (Pengdang 朋党). Gradually, the notion of party was accepted and China witnessed a variety of political parties. Despite the existence of plural parties, one party tended to regard itself as the only legitimate one and did not respect other parties. In the end, the CCP monopolized all powers and controlled states, society, and the army. Despite the separation discourse, since the 1990s, the CCP now firmly holds to the unity discourse, that all key political organizations should be unified under the party's leadership. Clearly, all these historical events demonstrate continuation of the Chinese tradition of so-called Great Unity. The centralization of power through one party has been regarded as an effective way to maintain national unity. The holistic concept of party as a whole was entrenched in the Chinese mindset and political institutions. This is a significant historical constraint on the development of a multiparty system in China.

Another constraint on the development of a multiparty system in China is cognitive. It is extremely difficult for the Chinese to break free of the holistic tradition, endorsing an individualistic concept of the party. In the history of well-developed democracies, different parties represent the different interests of social classes, which constitute a basis for a multiparty system. Today the CCP claims to represent the whole of society.

Given the above cognitive and historical conditions, one might think a realistic and productive question about the Chinese form of a multiparty system might be whether the current one party plus multiparty cooperation system[34] will develop into a functional equivalent of a multiparty system. In the system of one-party domination and multiparty cooperation, the CCP shares its power with other democratic parties in a limited way. Political consultation with democratic parties is made before making a decision, democratic parties are informed before announcing major decisions, the support from democratic parties is garnered after announcing major decisions, and some deputy posts are allocated to democratic party leaders. In this way the CCP is the head of a coalition including other parties.

China is developing a mixed regime in which different ingredients, such as the traditional Mandarin rule, one-party domination, the form of a people's party, functional factions representing different interest groups, and democratic elections and monitoring, are combined. The idea of a mixed regime provides a better framework for exploring new developments and examining the potential of intraparty democracy.[35] By thoroughly mixing these ingredients, China is in the process of creating its own model of political rule and democratization in the 21st century.

CHAPTER 6

Political Parties and Democracy in India

M. V. Rajeev Gowda and Eswaran Sridharan

INTRODUCTION

As the 21st century unfolds, political parties continue to play a key role in the Indian political system, and Indian democracy is very much alive. Competitive elections, a free media, and a vibrant civil society are all integral parts of the Indian political landscape. Although India's democracy can still be improved on many fronts, the results so far are impressive. Just over 60 years ago, when India obtained independence from British rule in 1947, conditions were not particularly favorable to the emergence and sustenance of democracy. The country itself had just been united—through the merger of British India with numerous kingdoms—and divided—with two regions in the east and the west becoming the Muslim majority state of Pakistan. More than half the population lived in abject poverty, illiteracy was rampant, and discrimination and distrust on the basis of caste and religion were widespread.[1]

Nonetheless, the new nation's Constituent Assembly—essentially a broad-based group of elites—established a secular, federal, democratic framework. It proceeded to endow all adults with fundamental rights and the vote. It established a bicameral national parliament and sometimes bicameral state legislatures, with power over budgets granted to the directly elected houses. In the 1990s, the 73rd and 74th amendments to the Indian constitution took democratic empowerment to the grass roots by establishing a third tier of elected local governments in both villages and cities (termed the Panchayati Raj institutions) and by devolving funds for development directly to them. Today Indians regard democracy as integral to their way of life.

The democratic experiment succeeded, in no small measure, due to the active participation of political parties and their embrace of democratic procedures. India's first prime minister, Jawaharlal Nehru, led the way by establishing democratic norms in the ruling Indian National Congress (hereafter, the Congress) and the larger polity. In spite of having an overwhelming majority in parliament, he ensured that opposition parties' views were heard and respected. India's political parties also have a strong tradition of leading open, public protests, continuing with practices established during the independence struggle; such protests sometimes lead to policy changes. Democracy has flourished in India except for a brief period between 1975–1977 when Prime Minister Indira Gandhi invoked the Emergency provision of the constitution, suspendig fundamental rights, and arresting leaders of opposition parties.[2] But Indira Gandhi did hold elections in 1977 and thereupon, when voters rejected her Congress party, the transfer of power to the victorious opposition alliance was smooth. Throughout India, political parties have learned to abide by the principles of democracy, although recent developments raise cause for concern about the quality of that democracy. But India has also developed strong, independent institutions such as the Election Commission of India (EC) that work to ensure that elections are free and fair.

This chapter will analyze the current relationship between political parties and democracy in India. It will address one central question: How do India's political parties currently facilitate or impede the work of democratic politics?[3] This chapter is structured as follows: First, we consider what political science theory has to say about political parties and how they enable the consolidation of democracy in multiethnic societies. Second, we turn to the details of the Indian political landscape, providing an overview of the diversity of political parties in India and their electoral performance. Third, we discuss the emergence of coalition politics as a standard feature of current Indian politics. Fourth, we examine a curious empirical feature of Indian politics—a persistent "anti-incumbency" effect at the level of individual candidates and constituencies. Fifth, we examine emerging patterns in how Indian political parties organize and run themselves. Sixth, we examine how other institutions, both official (the judiciary and the Election Commission) and nonofficial (the media and civil society), constrain political parties while enhancing democratic functioning. Seventh, we consider the relationship between political parties and Indian democracy against the backdrop of the theories presented in the first section. We conclude with a reflection on key issues and challenges that arise from our survey of political parties and democracy in India.

PARTIES AND THE CONSOLIDATION OF DEMOCRACY: WHAT EXISTING THEORY SAYS

This section discusses the political science literature relating political parties and the party system to the project of democratic consolidation in emerging, multiethnic democracies, summarizing the relevant comments of nine scholars (or teams of scholars).

We begin with Philippe Schmitter who argues that "in the effort to consolidate new or recent democracies . . . parties remain dominant in structuring the electoral process, governing and perhaps even in the 'symbolic integration' of citizens into the democratic process"[4] even though political parties are only one of three generic types of intermediaries between the citizen and the state: parties, interest groups, and social movements.[5]

The role of parties in the consolidation of new democracies is also stressed by Thomas Carothers.[6] He points out that efficacious democratic parties do not necessarily emerge out of repeated elections unless there are other factors present, such as mobilized mass publics, civic organizations, funds, and access to state resources.

What is important, argue Larry Diamond, Juan Linz, and Seymour Martin Lipset, is "not merely the number of parties but also their overall institutional strength, as indicated by Samuel Huntington's criteria of coherence, complexity, autonomy and adaptability."[7] They argue that consolidation of democracy depends on at least one party developing these characteristics and give the example of India's Congress party.

Political parties and citizens can be linked in four ways—participatory, responsive, clientelistic, and coercive—argues Kay Lawson, of which only the first two types of linkage are conducive to the capacity of parties to promote and consolidate democracy.[8]

On the crucial issue of ethnic pluralism and democracy, Larry Diamond and Marc Plattner argue that democratic consolidation requires that political parties find ways to reconcile the two (and related to this, minority rights and representation).[9] Ethnic conflict can be politically managed in ways that consolidate democracy. Arend Lijphart's consociational formula for managing ethnic differences consists of interelite agreements on power-sharing arrangements, of which the principal features are: grand-coalitional governments encompassing all ethnic groups; federalism in cases of ethnic groups having distinct territories and proportionality in the distribution of cabinet portfolios and public resources; minority veto powers; and internal autonomy for ethnic groups.[10] Donald Horowitz emphasizes the importance of well-designed federalism because it can have any or all of five functions to reduce ethnic conflict: it "disperses conflict," "generate(s) intra-ethnic conflict," creates "incentives and opportunities for inter-ethnic cooperation," "encourage(s) alignments on non-ethnic interests," and "reduces material disparities among ethnic groups."[11] In general his solution would be to design institutions, most particularly electoral systems, so as to reward moderate behavior. For example, systems in which politicians "cannot be elected on the basis of the votes of their group alone" or "systems that require candidates to achieve a regional distribution of votes, in addition to a national plurality, may foster conciliatory behaviour if territory is a proxy for ethnicity because groups are regionally concentrated."[12]

Aggregative parties have helped to consolidate democracy, as Benjamin Reilly has documented, showing how since the late 1990s majoritarian electoral systems have been engineered in Asia to produce less fragmented party systems, which have helped stabilize democracy.[13]

In an innovative conceptualization, Juan Linz, Alfred Stepan, and Yogendra Yadav conceive of India not as a nation-state or a multinational state but as a "state-nation"; in other words, a nation that is forged by state institutions and policies that respect and protect multiple and complementary identities and that is not limited to ethnolinguistic federalism.[14] They focus on how such policies engender identification with the state by all groups in the nation. It is related to power sharing in that it does not privilege any one identity. Linz, Stepan, and Yadav's focus, however, is not on parties and the party system.

Although all of the above approaches offer useful insights, we believe that in multiethnic developing countries (especially with distinct ethnic regions), the types of parties and ideologies, and type of party system, that are able to consolidate themselves have a major bearing on the stability and quality of democracy, by virtue of the inclusive character of politics or the lack thereof. Parties have to be seen, as many of these scholars have noted, in combination with other critical variables such as federalism, the electoral system, and the idea of the nation embodied in the constitutional framework, crucial to Schmitter's "symbolic integration." We return to this discussion later. We will also later assess the quality of India's democracy using the eight criteria to measure the quality of a democracy established by Larry Diamond and Leonard Morlino.[15] These criteria are: freedom, participation, competition, horizontal accountability, rule of law, equality, vertical accountability, and responsiveness.

THE PERFORMANCE OF POLITICAL PARTIES

We now turn to a brief historical overview of the electoral performance of the main players in the Indian political landscape (see Table 6.1).[16] Historically, the Congress has dominated the party landscape, building on its legacy as the all-encompassing movement that led India's struggle for independence from the British. After independence in 1947, the Congress won seven of the first eight general elections

Table 6.1 Performance of Major Political Parties in Elections, 1952–2009

	1952	1957	1962	1967	1971	1977	1980	1984	1989	1991	1996	1998	1999	2004	2009
Total seats	489	494	494	520	518	542	529	542	529	521	543	543	543	543	543
Indian National Congress (INC), (INCI) in 1980	364 (479) 74.4% 45.0%	371 (490) 75% 47.8%	361 (488) 73.0% 44.7%	283 (516) 54.4% 40.8%	352 (441) 68.0% 43.7%	154 (492) 28.4% 34.5%	353 (492) 66.7% 42.7%	415 (517) 76.6% 48.1%	197 (510) 37.2% 39.5%	232 (492) 45.0% 36.5%	140 (529) 25.8% 28.8%	141 (474) 26.0% 25.9%	114 (453) 21.0% 28.3%	145 (414) 26.7% 26.4%	206 (440) 37.9% 28.6%
Bharatiya Janata Party (BJP), (BLD) in 1977, (BJS) till 1971	3 (94) 0.6% 3.1%	4 (130) 0.8% 5.9%	14 (196) 2.8% 6.4%	35 (251) 6.7% 9.4%	22 (160) 4.2% 7.4%	295 (405) 54.4% 41.3%	—	2 (229) 4.0% 7.4%	86 (226) 16.5% 11.5%	120 (468) 23.0% 20.1%	161 (471) 29.6% 20.3%	179 (384) 33.0% 25.5%	182 (339) 34.0% 23.8%	138 (364) 25.4% 22.2%	116 (433) 21.4% 18.8%
Janata Dal (United) (JDU) in 1999, (JD) 1989–98, (SWA) till 1971	—	—	18 (173) 3.6% 7.9%	44 (178) 8.5% 8.7%	8 (56) 1.5% 3.1%	—	—	—	142 (243) 27.0% 17.7%	59 (307) 11.3% 11.8%	46 (196) 8.5% 8.1%	6 (190) 1.1% 3.2%	21 (60) 3.8% 3.1%	8 (33) 1.5% 1.9%	20 (55) 3.7% 1.5%
Communist Party of India (CPI)	16 (49) 3.3% 3.3%	27 (110) 5.5% 8.9%	29 (137) 5.9% 9.9%	23 (106) 4.4% 5.0%	23 (87) 4.4% 4.7%	7 (91) 1.3% 2.8%	11 (48) 1.8% 2.6%	6 (66) 1.1% 2.7%	12 (50) 2.3% 2.6%	14 (42) 2.7% 2.5%	12 (43) 2.2% 2.0%	9 (58) 1.6% 1.8%	4 (54) 0.7% 1.5%	9 (33) 1.6% 1.3%	4 (56) 0.7% 1.4%
Communist Party of India Marxist (CPM)	—	—	—	19 (62) 3.7% 4.4%	25 (85) 4.8% 5.1%	22 (53) 4.1% 4.3%	36 (63) 7.0% 6.1%	22 (64) 4.1% 5.7%	33 (64) 6.2% 6.5%	35 (60) 6.7% 6.2%	32 (75) 6.0% 6.1%	32 (71) 5.9% 5.2%	33 (72) 6.1% 5.4%	43 (69) 7.9% 5.7%	16 (82) 2.9% 5.3%
Lok Dal (LKD), (JPS) in 1980, (INCO) till 1977	—	—	—	—	16 (238) 3.1% 10.4%	3 (19) 0.6% 1.7%	41 (294) 7.7% 9.4%	3 (174) 0.6% 5.6%	0 (117) — 0.2%	0 (78) — 0.1%	—	—	—	—	—

(Continued)

Table 6.4 Performance of Major Political Parties in Elections, 1952–2009 (Continued)

	1952	1957	1962	1967	1971	1977	1980	1984	1989	1991	1996	1998	1999	2004	2009
Samajwadi Party (SP) in 1991, (JP) till 1989	—	—	—	—	—	—	31 (432) 5.9% 19.0%	10 (219) 1.8% 6.7%	0 (156) — 1.0%	5 (345) 1.0% 3.4%	17 (111) 3.1% 3.3%	20 (164) 3.7% 5.0%	26 (151) 4.8% 3.8%	36 (237) 6.6% 4.3%	23 (193) 4.2% 3.4%
Bahujan Samaj Party (BSP)	—	—	—	—	—	—	—	—	1.0%	—	11 (117) 2.0% 3.6%	5 (249) 0.9% 4.7%	14 (225) 2.6% 4.2%	19 (435) 3.5% 5.3%	21 (500) 3.9% 6.2%
Praja Socialist Party (PSP), (KMPP) in 1952	9 (145) 1.8% 5.8%	19 (189) 3.8% 10.4%	12 (168) 2.4% 6.8%	13 (109) 2.5% 3.1%	2 (63) 0.4% 1.0%	—	—	—	—	—	—	—	—	—	—
Samyukta Socialist Party (SSP), (SOC) till 1962	12 (254) 2.5% 10.6%	—	6 (107) 1.2% 2.7%	23 (122) 4.4% 4.9%	3 (93) 0.6% 2.4%	—	—	—	—	—	—	—	—	—	—
Others	47 9.6% 16.5%	31 6.3% 7.6%	34 6.9% 10.5%	45 8.6% 10.0%	53 10.2% 13.8%	52 9.6% 9.9%	3 9.1% 8.5%	79 14.6% 10.0%	44 8.9% 12.2%	55 11.0% 12.1%	115 21.2% 21.5%	141 26.0% 26.3%	143 26.3% 27.1%	140 25.8% 28.6%	128 23.6% 29.6%
Independents (IND)	38 7.6% 15.9%	42 8.5% 19.4%	20 4.0% 11.1%	35 6.7% 13.7%	14 2.7% 8.4%	9 1.7% 5.5%	9 1.7% 6.4%	5 0.9% 8.1%	12 2.26% 5.2%	1 0.2% 3.9%	9 1.7% 6.3%	6 1.1% 2.4%	6 1.1% 2.8%	5 0.9% 4.3%	9 1.7% 5.2%

Notes: Elections were not held in 13 constituencies: 12 in Assam and 1 in Meghalaya. Elections were not held in Jammu or Kashmir (6 seats), or Punjab (13 seats); 3 countermanded seats results excluded. Figures in parentheses are seats contested; first percentage is seat share, and second percentage is vote share. The number of seats contested is omitted for Others and Independents. BLD, Bharatiya Lok Dal; BJS, Bharatiya Jan Sangh; SWA, Swatantra Party; INCU, Indian National Congress (Urs); JPS, Janata Party Secular; INCO, Indian National Congress (Organised); JP, Janata Party; KMPP, Kisan Mazdoor Praja Party; SOC, Socialist Party; SJP, Samajwadi Janata Party.

Sources: Election Commission of India, *Statistical Report on General Elections*, 1 (Ver. I)—National and State Abstracts, for 1996, 1998, 1999, and 2004 and the Web site: www.eci.nic.in

from 1952 to 1984, except 1977, and it has governed India for 50 of 62 years. It had an unbroken domination for the first 30 years of free India and won pluralities of the vote of 40% and above against a fragmented and regionalized opposition. Even since 1989, it has remained the single largest party by vote share, although not seats, in each of the seven elections from 1989 to 2009. The Congress is a secular party that believes in a linguistically and culturally diverse notion of Indian nationhood and remains broadly acceptable to all segments of the population.

There are four other major categories of parties (although these groups of parties do not necessarily constitute a coalition). We classify them as: (1) Hindu nationalist parties (the Bharatiya Janata Party [BJP], and the Shiv Sena), (2) the communist parties, also termed the Left Front (including the Communist Party of India Marxist [CPI(M)] and the Communist Party of India [CPI], and the various CPI [Marxist-Leninist] splinters), (3) the agrarian/lower-caste populist parties (the Janata Party, the Janata Dal and its offshoots like the Samajwadi Party, Rashtriya Janata Dal, Rashtriya Lok Dal, Biju Janata Dal, Janata Dal [Secular], Janata Dal [United]), and (4) ethnoregional or ethnic parties based on particular regional linguistic groups or lower-caste blocs or tribes (in the northeastern states, in particular). Examples of such ethnoregional parties are the Dravida Munnetra Kazhagam (DMK) and the All India Anna Dravida Munnetra Kazhagam (AIADMK) of Tamil Nadu, the Shiromani Akali Dal of the Sikhs in Punjab, the National Conference and People's Democratic Party of Jammu and Kashmir, Asom Gana Parishad (AGP) of Assam, Telugu Desam Party (TDP) of Andhra Pradesh, the tribal Jharkhand Mukti Morcha of Jharkhand, and various small ethnic parties of the northeastern rim states, and the Scheduled Caste–based Bahujan Samaj Party (BSP).

In some states, there are regional parties that have been founded by influential leaders. The Nationalist Congress Party of Maharashtra and the Trinamool Congress of Bengal are examples. Most of these, and a large number of even smaller parties, are single-state parties and are officially termed regional parties. In the last general election (2009), there were 7 national parties, 39 state parties, recognized by the Election Commission and over a hundred minor parties. Rather than demonstrating political fragmentation alone, these large numbers reflect the underlying diversity of India and the political mobilization of groups that were hitherto not politically empowered (Table 6.1).

Since 1989, the pattern of Congress majorities based on vote pluralities has broken down. The Congress plurality fell from 39.6% in 1989 to as low as 26%, (in 1998) and this low share did not enable it to obtain a majority of seats. This decline was due to parts of the Congress base going over to regional, agrarian-populist, lower caste–based parties that reaped the benefits of identity politics and popular mobilization from below. The three electoral megatrends since 1989 are: (1) the decline of the Congress vote share from 40% to 29% in 2009, bottoming at 26% in 1998, although still winning a plurality of votes but not seats; (2) the rise of the BJP from 11% in 1989 to a high of 25% in 1998, and still 19% in 2009; (3) the rise of mostly single-state–based regional parties such that the combined vote shares of the Congress and the BJP were less than 50% in 1996, 1999, 2004 and 2009, and barely 51% in 1998. With the communist parties' vote share stagnant at under 8% and the decline of the agrarian populist Janata Dal, the bulk of the non-Congress, non-BJP vote now goes to ethnic or regional parties organized on the basis of regional, linguistic identities, or lower-caste coalitions. The rise of regional parties is even more pronounced in state assembly elections. Both the BJP and the Congress rule only a minority of states, even as part of coalition governments.

In terms of seats, both the Congress and the BJP have fallen well short of 206 seats (which the Congress obtained in 2009) in every election since 1996, although 272 seats are required to form a majority government. Indeed, both major parties obtained under 150 seats each in 2004. Thus coalition and minority governments have been the order of the day since 1989. In 1996, the single largest party in the ruling coalition had only 59 seats. All coalitions have been large, multiparty minority coalitions, often grouped together after the election and dependent on external support (although for the BJP-led National Democratic Alliance, the principal external supporter was a preelectoral coalition partner, the TDP).

Judging by vote and seat share, it is evident that the number of viable political parties is increasing. One measure that enables us to summarize this analytically is the Laakso-Taagepera index (N) of the number of effective parties. For Indian elections, the values of N by votes/seats were 4.80/4.35, 5.10/3.70, 7.11/5.83, 6.91/5.28, 6.74/5.87, 7.60/6.50 and 7.98/5.01 in 1989, 1991, 1996, 1998, 1999, 2004 and 2009, respectively. In contrast, in the eight general elections between 1952 and 1984 the effective number of parties by seats exceeded three only once (3.16 in 1967) and the effective number of parties by votes exceeded five only once (5.19 in 1967).[17] Thus, over time, India has clearly emerged as a multiparty democracy.

What are the underlying drivers behind these electoral megatrends and the emergence of multiparty coalitions? The social cleavage theory postulates that the party system will reflect the principal cleavages in society, as for example, between capital and labor in ethnoculturally homogeneous industrialized societies, with parties positioned on a left-right spectrum. In the Indian context, this theory would predict that political parties would emerge to capitalize on several politically salient cleavages, for example, caste or ethnicity, religion, language, and region (such parties are said to be indulging in "identity politics"). Yogendra Yadav argues that the rise of identity-based parties represents the political empowerment of historically marginalized groups and reflects favorably on the vibrancy of political entrepreneurship.[18]

On the other hand, the political-systemic theory, particularly the electoral rules theory, postulates that the electoral system's rules will be reflected in the number, relative weight, and ideological positioning of political parties,[19] creating varying disproportionalities between votes and seats, and hence, incentives for the coalescing or splitting of political forces.

A leading electoral-rules theory, Duverger's law, would predict that the single-member constituency, first-past-the-post electoral system will result in a two-party outcome, at least at the constituency level. In a first-past-the-post system, small parties would have an incentive to merge into larger formations to aggregate votes to obtain the winning plurality or alternatively to form preelectoral coalitions for the same purpose.

From 1967 onward, a consolidation of the non-Congress opposition took place, state by state, in tandem with such consolidation in state assembly elections. This bipolar consolidation was the key feature and driving force of the fragmentation of the national party system.[20] But this bipolar consolidation has been one of multiple bipolarities (e.g., Congress-BJP, Congress-Left, Congress-Regional Party, in different states), thereby contributing to fragmentation at the national level. Duvergerian dynamics were the drivers of these multiple bipolarities.[21]

In India's federal polity, states are typically linguistic and cultural entities, and parties that reflect such social cleavages flourish therein. Duvergerian dynamics can lead to bipolar systems at the state level due to the consolidation of the state-level opposition to the principal party at the state level, whether it is a national or regional party. This leads to a multiparty system nationally because the state-level two-party systems do not consist of the same two parties.[22] Indeed, they can consist of a variety of parties, some national, some purely state level. Further, because the division of powers between the center and states makes it sufficiently attractive to come to power at the state level alone, this too drives the bipolarization of state-level party systems.[23] The playing out of the Duvergerian dynamic has resulted in the consolidation of regional/linguistic or caste/ethnic identity-based parties in a large number of states. However, political fragmentation has not led to significant instability because of the Indian political system's ability to include these diverse parties in power-sharing arrangements.

For explanations emphasizing the division of powers between levels of government—national, state, and local—the argument goes as follows.[24] Other things being equal, the greater the political and economic powers of state governments in federal systems over decisions that most affect the lives of citizens, the greater a political prize the capture of power at the state level represents. Hence, the greater the incentive there is for political entrepreneurs to form state-level political parties and for voters to vote for such parties. Conversely, the more centralized the powers over decisions that most affect citizens are, the more incentive there is for political entrepreneurs to coordinate to form nationwide political parties and for voters to vote for such parties and to ignore state-level parties. Hence, a more multiparty system can be expected under the former circumstances and a less multiparty system can be expected under the latter circumstances. It is the former situation that prevails in India. Regional parties have also benefited from the fact that the national parties have developed highly centralized "high command" decision-making cultures that are renowned for their opacity. In contrast, it is easier in regional parties for local level leaders to access their party leaders and to influence their decision making. The emergence of a multiparty system with several regional parties is a development that makes Indian democracy more competitive and participatory and allows a large number of smaller interests and identities to find representation in the power structure.

COALITION POLITICS

Coalition governments have become an abiding feature of Indian politics over the past few decades. Following an outline of the evolution of coalitions, we will analyze what this means for the party-democracy relationship. The evolution of coalitions in India can be summarized as follows.[25] The first phase of broad-front anti-Congress in the 1960s and 1970s was characterized by intrastate coalitions. The component parties of these coalitions (e.g., the Jana Sangh, Bharatiya Kranti Dal/Bharatiya Lok Dal, Socialists, Swatantra, Congress) had their state units, strongholds, and interests and the coalitions had no programmatic glue.[26]

The second phase, again of broad-front anti-Congress, was that of the Janata Party. In the aftermath of the Emergency, the Janata Party platform unified ideologically disparate non-Congress parties in intrastate and interstate coalitions to ensure one-on-one contests aggregating votes at the constituency level. This reflected the imperative of aggregation to defeat the Congress and did not pay attention to the ideological differences between the parties that merged to form the Janata Party.

The National Front coalition, 1989–1990, was led by the Janata Dal and included four regional parties. It was supported from the outside by the BJP and the Left Front and was a new departure in three senses. First, learning from the Janata experience, it did not try to unify very different parties but put together a coalition of distinct parties based on a common manifesto. Second, it brought in the explicitly regional parties like the DMK, TDP, and AGP, and the left parties, unlike coalition experiments of the late 1960s and into the 1970s. Third, it also marked the beginning of interstate alliances of parties that were territorially compatible (i.e., where parties did not compete on each other's turf).

In 1996, a nine-party United Front (UF) minority coalition government was formed, led by Prime Minister Deve Gowda. Crucial outside support was provided by the Congress and most left parties. The UF was a territorial coalition but had ideological coherence in terms of secularism, as its component parties and outside supporters were ideologically opposed to the Hindu nationalist BJP. The Congress withdrew support in April 1997, forcing a change of prime minister, and then again withdrew support in November 1997, precipitating early elections in February 1998.

In March 1998, a 11-party BJP-led minority coalition government, based on a coalition consisting of 13 preelectoral (including three independents) and 1 postelectoral members of the government, and 10 postelectoral supporters and 3 preelectoral allies who opted out of the government, assumed power for a year.

In October 1999, the 12-party BJP-led National Democratic Alliance (NDA) won a decisive victory and formed a minority coalition along with postelectoral allies, despite some NDA constituents opting to support from the outside.

In May 2004, the nine-party Congress-led United Progressive Alliance (UPA) formed a minority coalition government with the external support of the four left parties and two others, plus external support of two preelectoral allies who opted to stay out.

In May 2009, the UPA won again and formed a minority coalition government with five allies and external support from 14 smaller parties (of which five were pre-electoral allies who opted to be external supporters) and three independent MPs.

All non-single-party majority governments in India have been minority governments, either single-party minority governments or minority coalition governments, dependent on external support. All the coalitions since 1996 have been interstate territorial coalitions. The clear emphasis of coalitions since the 1990s has been on territorial compatibility at the expense of ideological compatibility, particularly in the BJP-led coalitions of 1998 and 1999. The important point to note in this history of coalitions is that, with the exception of the Left Front (which is limited to three states), coalitions have been driven by the imperative to aggregate votes to win and not by ideological or programmatic cleavages, except for differences between the Congress/Left and the BJP on secularism.[27] Coalitions have reduced the sharpness of ideological differences as parties make compromises to win elections and form governments. Indeed, parties have, over time, learned "coalition dharma," or the norms and practices that enable diverse parties with disparate ideologies to function as a cohesive government, which has enabled a greater variety of regional, ethnic, and ideological interests to gain a share of power, thus broad-basing democracy, but at the same time making governance more complex and incoherent.

Coalition politics has also rewarded and ensured a share in power for smaller parties, and hence, access to power for the social groups that form the basis of many parties in a regionalized and ethnicized party system. Because they play a key role in the formation and survival of coalitions, small parties have been able to extract important ministerial positions for their members or increased federal allocation of resources to their states. Thus coalition politics has further consolidated the "ethnification" of parties and the party system. It has, by extension, also reinforced the clientelistic relationship between such parties and voters in which parties channel patronage toward their (increasingly) ethnically defined social bases in what has been called India's "patronage democracy."[28]

RESPONSIVENESS, PARTY COMPETITION, AND
ANTI-INCUMBENCY EFFECTS

Unlike in the United States and many other nations, where incumbents have an advantage in reelection, candidates for both parliament and state assembly elections in India face an incumbency disadvantage.[29] This is particularly the case since 1991, after the end of the long period of Congress hegemony at the national level. Table 6.2 shows a retention rate (of seats by incumbents in elections in the 1989–2004 period) of roughly 40% in elections to the Lok Sabha (lower house of parliament directly elected by plurality rule). Tables 6.3 and 6.4 show a retention rate (re-elected as a proportion of renominated MPs) of about two-thirds for the BJP and about nearly half for the Congress respectively over 1991–2009. However, this anti-incumbency effect at the constituency level does not translate automatically to an incumbency disadvantage for ruling parties at the national level. There is no clear pattern in this regard, although turnover in office has been more frequent since 1989. There is also no clear pattern regarding the disadvantage of incumbent candidates belonging to the ruling party in a particular election compared to incumbents belonging to opposition parties; both face an incumbency disadvantage. Why is this the case and how is it related to patterns of political party competition and responsiveness to the electorate? And, in turn, what does this mean for the relationship between parties and democracy?

The literature suggests that incumbency disadvantage is due to the inability of incumbents to deliver public goods and services in a manner that satisfies voters. Arvind Virmani links anti-incumbency to the lack of good governance since a minimal competence in governance is necessary to ensure effective provision of public goods and services on a widespread scale.[30] He observes that India has witnessed a gradual deterioration in the "quality and effectiveness of government

Table 6.2 Pattern of Seat Retention: Lok Sabha Elections, 1991–2004

Year of elections	Seats retained by same parties	Seats won by different parties
2004	247	296
1999	282	261
1998	267	276
1996	266	277
1991	302	241

Note: 2009 is not included because it is not comparable to earlier years because the delimitation (redistricting) of constituencies changed the boundaries significantly.

Source: Sanjay Kumar, "Increasing Fluidity in Electoral Contests: Is This Mere Anti-Incumbency?," in Indian Democracy Meanings and Practices, ed. Rajendra Vora and Suhas Palshikar (New Delhi: Sage Publications India Pvt. Ltd., 2004), 368–371.

institutions." The implication is that India's political leadership has lacked the executive capabilities required to ensure effective service delivery, and thus parties pay a heavy price at election time.

Keefer and Khemani link anti-incumbency to the pattern of party competition and to the credibility of the promises made by political parties. They argue that if "political competitors cannot make credible promises to the electorate, then elections can serve only the purpose of removing from power an incumbent who has performed poorly. Elections do not offer an opportunity to choose between alternative policy platforms offered by different parties."[31] They argue that promises to deliver public goods and services are not credible because of the lack of a history of actual delivery of such goods and services (except in exceptional states like Kerala where one of the competing forces, the Left Democratic Front, led by the Communist Party, has successfully mobilized and governed on this plank). They also fault social

Table 6.3 Performance of Bharatiya Janata Party's Incumbents: Lok Sabha Elections, 1991–2009

Year of elections	Sitting MPs	Renominated	Reelected	Incumbent won (%)	Other MPs of party in the present house	Turnover of MPs for the party (%)
2009	138	48	32	67	84	42
2004	182	147	74	50	64	46
1999	182	159	105	66	77	42
1998	161	144	100	69	82	45
1996	121	86	58	67	103	63

Source: Same as Table 6.2.

Note: MPs, members of parliament. In 2009, we look at the number of individual MPs reelected or not, and not constituencies because the latter changed due to delimitation (redistricting).

Table 6.4 Performance of Congress Incumbents: Lok Sabha Elections, 1991–2009

Year of elections	Sitting MPs	Renominated	Reelected	Incumbent won (%)	Other MPs of party in the present house	Turnover of MPs for the party (%)
2009	145	109	60	55	146	71
2004	113	69	30	43	115	79
1999	141	103	40	39	73	65
1998	140	101	52	51	89	63
1996	244	157	66	42	74	53

Source: Same as Table 6.2.
Note: MPs, members of parliament. In 2009, we look at the number of individual MPs reelected or not, and not constituencies because the latter changed due to delimitation (redistricting).

fragmentation on ethnic (primarily caste) lines and the poor quality of information available to voters, particularly in rural areas, for the lack of credibility of political parties' assurances of better governance.[32]

Although the evidence suggests that public goods and basic social services do matter to voters, political parties in office are geared instead to delivering "club goods" to their respective, often ethnic or ethnoterritorial, support bases.[33] This is partly a consequence of social fragmentation and political party formation on ethnic lines and the ensuing multiparty competition at the state level.

Thus, politicians are credible when they promise to provide club or private goods to their "client" groups with whom they have repeated interaction, whether these are ethnicity based or interest based. This leads to clientelistic relationships between parties/politicians on the one hand and grassroots members and voters on the other. It also is the root of incumbency disadvantage in that a large number of voters feel dissatisfied at the end of each term in office since this clientelistic pattern of private goods to particularistic interests leads to a low level of public goods provision overall. However, despite clientelism, parties do represent societal interests, whether ethnic or economic, and are successful in representing such interests in the national- and state-level power structures and extracting tangible allocative and policy benefits for them. Despite clientelist distortions, this still means that parties carry out their interest aggregation and representation functions in a way that connects them to citizens.

ORGANIZING AND SUSTAINING PARTIES

India's political parties have evolved less on ideological lines and more as amorphous collections of political activists, coming together for the sake of winning elections and often rallying around an ethnic or identity-based agenda. The key exceptions would be the cadre-based parties of the left and, to a lesser extent, the BJP. Cadre-based parties have various wings—from student wings to farmer wings to trade unions—through which ideologically committed activists enter, participate, gain recognition, and rise through the ranks. Other political parties have such wings too, but their internal organizations are not usually disciplined enough nor do they provide clear paths to political growth for ambitious activists. In almost all parties, internal elections are stage managed by the leadership, often with "consensus" candidates chosen without contest, to the extent that such elections are held at all.

The imperative of securing electoral victory has led parties to launch a wide search for candidates, using "winability" as the key criterion. Winability is measured by the resources the candidate has to spend on elections, whether he hails from a numerically powerful caste, or has a track record of success in other fields or as a politician, or is some sort of celebrity. Locally powerful politicians, and even criminals, have emerged as candidates based on this criterion. Reflecting the decline of ideology in Indian politics, defectors also routinely find openings in other parties if they are regarded as having winability.

The activists who hover around potential candidates are typically motivated by the desire to obtain power, prestige, and influence, either directly for themselves or indirectly, through the election of their leader. A leader's worth is measured by his ability to be a patron, to bend bureaucracy to his will, and to obtain lucrative contracts or other income for his followers.

The mandatory introduction of Panchayati Raj—the third or local tier of government—since 1993, has been a boon to political parties organizationally. Now, in every village, there are at least some people interested in winning local office. To enhance their own support, such local activists gravitate to one party or another. Thus the systemic change ushered in by decentralization has had the side effect of allowing parties to develop a support base at the grass roots without significant efforts at mobilization.

Over time a large number of Indian political parties are becoming dynastic—that is, led and controlled by a family. There is an inexorable logic to this, starting with the rapid rise in the cost of elections. Established political leaders have an advantage in terms of fund raising, often through illegitimate methods. Among them, those leaders who are seen as potential chief ministers or prime ministers attract political funding from entities that want to use the political system for economic gains. These leaders tend to centralize control within their parties and allow party organizations to weaken in order to prevent the emergence of challengers. They also look within their own families for trusted individuals to manage their funds. Dynastic succession is also spurred by the fact that a well-known leader has a brand appeal and a political network that can be built upon by the successor.

Dynastic domination has resulted in the decline of internal democracy in political parties. Therein is the paradox: the same political parties that so crucially contribute to the success of India's democracy are internally undemocratic and have few options for discussion and dissent. Leaders who disagree with the family that runs the party typically have exit, not voice, as their only option. The dynasty maintains its domination by encouraging competing factions at lower levels of the party who then come to the "high command" to resolve disputes, thus enhancing the latter's power and control. However, given the large scale of India's political parties, even a high command-driven party presents substantial opportunities for political maneuvers and bargaining among factions, thus providing some semblance of internal democracy.

INSTITUTIONS THAT AFFECT PARTIES
AND ENHANCE DEMOCRACY

Despite the difficulties India has faced, it has maintained an evolving multiparty system, free elections, and the peaceful transition of power, and has curbed corruption significantly as well. Credit for these accomplishments must go to institutions other than the parties.

An independent judiciary adjudicating cases of electoral fraud has helped provide a check on electoral malpractices, but the most significant institution for ensuring free and fair elections has been the Election Commission. This constitutionally independent authority has substantial powers during elections that it has exercised neutrally and aggressively over the past two decades. However, some aspects of the EC's activities have been counterproductive, basically because aspects of the underlying law it has enforced are flawed. The EC has strictly tried to enforce ceilings on election expenditures by candidates and parties. Because these expenditure limits are too low when compared to what it would cost to communicate a political agenda to an electorate, candidates resort to underground expenditures in cash and kind to influence voters. An even more basic flaw is that parties are, in effect, outside the election expenditure ceiling, rendering it farcical.

The vibrant Indian media also provides substantial coverage of politics and mediates crucially between the electorate and its representatives in matters of public importance. Generally the Indian media have been independent and performed a watchdog role—this applies both to respected broadsheets and muckraking tabloids. There are also numerous print publications and television channels with ideological or party affiliations. In any case, political parties and their activities, in and out of office, are under the media's scanner, and this provides a check against excesses or flagrant corruption.

However, as in the case of the EC, the role of the media in enhancing Indian democracy is not always positive. Television is regarded as having spurred the rise of Hindu nationalism following the screening of a mythological serial that had huge audiences around the country.[34] The vernacular media are regarded as having spurred the occurrence and escalated the virulence of communal riots. Other media activities are questionable but do produce positive results. In recent times, sections of the media have indulged in "sting" operations, clandestinely capturing politicians' misdeeds on hidden cameras. The president of the BJP was forced to resign in 2001 after he was captured on hidden camera accepting bribes from reporters posing as representatives of a fictitious company. The strong investigative component of the media and its ability to broadcast its embarrassing findings has ensured that politicians are wary of entrapments and that corruption is a significant enough issue to warrant resignations and the premature termination of a political career.

India's vibrant and diverse civil society also plays an active role in checking the power of political parties and in enhancing democracy. For example, a civil society group called the Association for Democratic Reforms (ADR) decided to confront the increase in the number of criminals participating in the electoral process, often as candidates of mainstream parties. ADR filed a "public interest litigation" petition in the Supreme Court of India arguing that citizens had a right to know the credentials of their candidates. The Supreme Court, in 2002, ruled in ADR's favor, and thereafter, Parliament passed a law that made it mandatory for candidates to reveal their education, assets and liabilities, and their criminal record, if any.[35] The EC now publishes this information online and highlights are published by the media, thus increasing voters' awareness about candidates. More recently, civil society activists have gotten the Central Information Commissioner to rule that the financial accounts of political parties must be made public.[36] Overall, civil society, in conjunction with other institutions, has had a positive impact on India's democracy and enhanced its self-correcting properties.[37]

THEORY IN CONTEXT: POLITICAL PARTIES AND THE CONSOLIDATION OF INDIAN DEMOCRACY

A number of factors affect the consolidation of democracy in multiethnic developing countries. These include the types of parties and ideologies, and type of party system, and whether these are inclusive in character. Other critical variables include federalism, the electoral system, and the idea of the nation embodied in the constitutional framework. This section examines the Indian case using the theoretical frameworks enunciated at the beginning of the chapter. We also assess the impact of political parties on the quality of India's democracy as measured against the eight criteria of Diamond and Morlino (listed earlier).

India's population has a multiethnic composition (defined broadly to include religious and linguistic divisions), with distinct ethnic concentrations in different regions. India thus potentially faces the danger of structural ethnopolitical majorities emerging and creating exclusionary political outcomes that would be counter to national integration and political stability. This could happen if religious, linguistic, and other ethnic divisions were to coincide wholly or largely with political or party identification, thus leading to clear ethnopolitical fault lines, and if political elites of the leading ethnic party follow an exclusivist strategy or have an exclusivist idea of the nation.

The single-member district, simple plurality (SMSP) system used in India can also lead to exclusionary outcomes. Once ethnic identities harden, the SMSP system offers only weak mechanisms for accommodation and stable coalition building. It is vulnerable to political mobilization strategies that deliberately seek to divide people on "ethnic" lines, along with their inevitable ideological package of political mythologies and mythologized histories. The SMSP system is particularly hard on minorities that are not geographically concentrated enough to be politically decisive at either the state or constituency level. This is indeed the case for Muslims in India who constitute 13% of the nation's population but are a majority in only a minuscule number of seats. On the other hand, the SMSP system can also work against exclusion, because it requires political parties to aggregate the pluralities necessary for winning seats. This leads to bargaining and compromise among groups. The crucial determinants seem to be whether political and ethnic identities are consolidated along the same lines as ethnic cleavages, and whether the vision and strategies of political elites are exclusionary along ethnic lines.

In terms of political participation, India has had a large number of political parties that contest competitive elections at the national and state levels. India also has a large number of social movements, which may or may not be linked to parties, whose fortunes ebb and flow. But India does not have a large number of formally organized interest groups such as trade unions, farmers' unions, and business associations. In line with Schmitter and Carothers' observations, it is political parties that have been the key contributors to democratic consolidation in India.

Historically, India's political parties have played a major role in both the symbolic (as per Schmitter) and actual integration of citizens into the democratic process. Indeed, because they have overwhelmingly respected and nurtured democratic norms, both in elections and in governance, they have helped establish the broad, inclusive, participative

Indian state. India's political parties have helped, in Linz, Stepan, and Yadav's terms, to build India as a "state-nation." A state-nation is one created by state institutions and policies that respect and protect multiple and complementary identities, beyond just ethnolinguistic federalism.[38] Indian political parties have, in the main, ensured power sharing that does not privilege any one identity, thus helping diverse groups in the nation to identify and believe in a democratic India.

In congruence with Diamond, Linz, and Lipset, and with Lijphart, we see that the Congress was a leading contributor to India's democratic consolidation because during the decades that it was dominant, it nurtured a power-sharing political system. In doing so, it was carrying forward the umbrella character that it had developed during the freedom struggle. The Congress's electoral dominance ensured that politically salient cleavages did not translate into ethnic party formation during the first two decades after independence. The Congress-dominated Constituent Assembly (1946–1950) institutionalized cultural autonomy for all religious groups, granting a de facto minority veto on issues vital to minority rights and autonomy. Specific Congress policies and practices of a semi-consociational nature include linguistic federalism, educational autonomy, and separate personal laws for religious minorities; roughly proportional accommodation of linguistic and religious groups in cabinets; and reservations for Scheduled Castes and Scheduled Tribes. In fact, Lijphart argued that India's democracy consolidated itself, despite the absence of the usual preconditions, precisely because it was consociational.[39]

Atul Kohli supports Lijphart's power-sharing explanation for India's democratic success stating, "moderate accommodation of group demands, especially demands based on ethnicity, and some decentralization of power strengthens a democracy."[40] Rudolph and Rudolph also argue that Indian politics is persistently centrist because of, among other factors, the marginality of class politics, the fragmentation of the confessional majority, cultural diversity and social pluralism, and the single-member plurality system.[41]

In terms of Lawson's classification of political parties, the major Indian political parties have essentially been clientelistic in their relationship with voters.[42] However, we argue that, given the high turnover of parties in power, especially since 1989, the growth of literacy, education, the middle classes, and media exposure, particularly the spread of television and investigative journalism, parties are under increasing pressure to evolve from clientelistic relations to increased responsiveness in their relationship with voters.

Kanchan Chandra argues that the Indian political economy is conducive to the ethnification of parties, but that this enhances the stability of democracy. She argues that India is a "patronage democracy," defined as one in which most modern sector jobs and services are in the public sector and public officials have discretion in the allocation of public jobs and services. "An ethnic party is likely to succeed in a patronage democracy when it provides elites from across the 'subdivisions' included in its target ethnic categories with greater opportunities for ascent within its party organization than the competition, and when voters from its target ethnic categories are numerous enough to take the party to a winning or influential position."[43] We can see that this incentivizes political mobilization, including party formation, on a caste basis for numerically large caste clusters at the state level or for regional-linguistic groups in India.

Over the past two decades, political mobilization in India has indeed revolved around "identity." Given the explicit repudiation of identity-based divisions in the Indian Constitution, this development raises questions about whether we are witnessing the rise of essentially anti-system parties. Giovanni Sartori coined the term "anti-system" to refer initially to communist parties that take part in the electoral process with the avowed aim of coming to power and then moving from democracy to communist rule. In the Indian context, along with the communists, we could argue that religiomajoritarian parties are fundamentally anti-system, because their ideologies are contrary to the secular, nonethnic basis of the Indian state. The BJP, for example, would prefer to mold India into a "Hindu Rashtra," where the Hindu religion would dominate, to the disadvantage of various religious minorities. The BSP aggressively promoted lower-caste political consolidation that targeted upper-caste Hindus, who it characterized as historical oppressors. The Shiv Sena has changed its choice of enemy—from South Indians in Mumbai, to Muslims, and, seemingly now, to North Indians in Mumbai— each time aiming to consolidate the native Marathi speakers against a perceived adversary. These divisive political agendas are contrary to the inclusive essence of Indian democracy.

However, the exigencies of forming political coalitions have ensured that particularly divisive, anti-system ideological agendas have been removed from governance agendas. The BJP, when it led the NDA coalition, was forced by secular partners to drop contentious issues that were regarded as anti-minority (e.g., building a temple for Rama at the site of the demolished Babri Masjid, shelving Article 370 that gives special status to the Muslim-majority state of Jammu and Kashmir, and proposing a uniform civil code taking away minorities' rights to govern themselves according to their own religious traditions). Similarly, the BSP, in its quest to come to power, has toned down its anti–upper-caste rhetoric and is now making successful efforts to create broad, multicaste coalitions—its alliance with a section of upper-caste Brahmins has helped it secure a simple majority in the state legislature of Uttar Pradesh, India's largest state. The mainstream communist parties too seem to have been tamed by the system and have long sought to work toward their policy goals within the constitutional framework. But a small number of extremist, radical communist factions (often termed Naxalites) typically choose to bypass the electoral process and instead run their own parallel administrations in certain pockets using tactics such as armed insurrection.

The question arises as to whether regional/linguistic chauvinist parties and caste-based reservationist parties articulating lower-caste interests can be described as anti-system since linguistic states are part of the constitutional design and most such parties are not secessionist. Further quotas in public sector employment and in education have been enshrined in the Constitution for SCs (Scheduled Castes or ex-untouchables) and STs (Scheduled Tribes or aboriginals), and from 1990, for "Other Backward Classes" defined mainly on the basis of caste. Perhaps one can describe such parties as anti-system only if they articulate an ideology of permanent hatred of any other group, a criterion that could describe the early BSP at the height of its anti–upper caste rhetoric, or the 1950s and 1960s DMK at the height of the anti-Brahmin movement.

How have such anti-system parties, variously defined, fared in terms of seats and votes, in the past and the present, in Indian politics? If one looks at vote shares in 2009, the explicitly anti-Muslim Hindu nationalist parties, BJP and Shiv Sena received 21% of the vote between them, and the two communist parties 7%. Thus, nearly 30% of the votes went to parties of the right and left extremes, whose core beliefs and preferences, despite formally adhering to the Constitution, deviate sharply from liberal-democratic norms and can be considered anti-system. This is a very significant fraction of the vote and has come down from an even higher one-third in 2004.

In India, the present party system at the state level, for both state assembly and parliamentary elections is essentially bipolar if not bipartisan (that is, either two coalitions led by a leading party, or one party versus a coalition, or a two-party rivalry). Therefore, a party has to be one of two leading parties in a state to be able to win most of the seats in the state. We thus need to look at the number of states in which an anti-system party is one of the two leading parties, and then the share of such states in Lok Sabha seats, to get an idea of the share of seats that could be won by anti-system parties.

In 2009, the centrist Congress party was one of the two leading parties in 31 (out of 35) states and Union (federal) territories, totaling 63% of the Lok Sabha seats.[44] The BJP was one of two leading parties in 16 states and Union territories totaling 31% of Lok Sabha seats and the CPI(M) one of the two leading parties in three states with 12% of Lok Sabha seats (these are not the same states in which the BJP is one of the two leading parties). Theoretically, if electoral swings went their way, anti-system parties could win the majority of seats in states whose representatives would total 58% of the Lok Sabha, although they would not form a coalition for ideological reasons. This amounts to a significant potential presence of anti-system parties in parliament and in ruling coalitions as partners or supporters, and thus is a matter of concern into the future.

We now assess the impact of political parties on the quality of India's democracy as measured against the eight criteria of Diamond and Morlino (listed earlier).[45] India's political parties have enjoyed fairly complete freedom to engage in political activities. The political environment has also been unfettered, with free and fair elections and a vigorous, independent media. Political parties have sometimes misused their freedom by constraining the freedom of citizens. This has happened when parties call for *bandhs*—shutting down all economic activity as a mark of protest—which are enforced by the threat of violence against anyone who violates the shut down.

In terms of participation, political parties across the spectrum have seen increased involvement of socially and educationally backward classes, in effect, backward castes, or lower castes that are above the Scheduled Castes in the traditional social hierarchy. This has been partly owing to the nature of elections to the third tier of government. At this level, reservations (quotas) have been created for women, minorities, and backward castes, in addition to the Scheduled Castes and Tribes. These reservations have ensured that parties now have activists and representatives from across the social spectrum at the grass roots.

In terms of competition, we have seen that anti-incumbency effects ensure that there is vibrant competition between parties at the constituency level. At the state level, multiple bipolarities have typically emerged, with strong competition between the opposing fronts (including in West Bengal, although the communist parties have won the state continuously since 1977). On the national stage, the vibrancy of competition can be seen in the decline of the Congress and the inability of the two largest national parties to win a majority of parliament seats between them.

Horizontal accountability is essentially about the ability of various democratic institutions to check and balance one another. Within parliament and state legislatures, opposition parties have a voice that the party in government cannot ignore; this acts as a check on ruling parties. In terms of the branches of government, over time, the influence of the executive (and by extension, the ruling party) over other branches has declined. The judiciary is independent and constitutional bodies such as the EC demonstrably constrain the electoral excesses of political parties.

On equality, the influence of the poor and rural, Scheduled Castes and Scheduled Tribes, and minorities and women has increased due to greater opportunities for electoral participation and these groups' greater importance to smaller parties. The rise of an implicitly anti-Muslim party like the BJP and of upper-caste backlash to the assertiveness of lower castes, on the other hand, has threatened not only the equality formally enjoyed by minorities, Scheduled Castes, and Scheduled Tribes, but often even the rule of law in states where such parties or movements are dominant. An example is the state of Gujarat, where perpetrators of large-scale violence against Muslims in 2002 have gone unpunished.

In terms of the rule of law, it has both been strengthened by greater party competition, voter participation, and the strengthening of some institutions, as well as weakened, for example, by attempts of lower-caste parties to use state power to further their social bases' interests in a manner that damages norms and institutions (such as in Bihar and Uttar Pradesh). The fact that parties continue to field candidates with criminal records is another feature contributing to the decline of the rule of law, although the law does prohibit candidates who have been sentenced to jail terms of over two years from participating in elections. Another aspect of party politics that has diminished the rule of law is the raising of electoral funds illegitimately. In a larger sense, such practices have led to the decay of democratic institutions, ensnared even the common citizen in the web of corruption, and resulted in a decline in the overall quality of governance.

The fact that political parties and individual candidates are often rejected at reelection time suggests significant vertical accountability in the system. However, it could also be an indicator of these parties' ineffectiveness on the criterion of responsiveness. Parties may only be selectively responsive to some sections of voters, partly as a result of their ethnification. This does not enhance the quality of democracy overall.

CONCLUSIONS

What do the features and recent trends outlined in this chapter imply for the relationship between political parties and democracy? On the whole, we can say that political parties have contributed to greater political participation and have strengthened democratic processes, including free and fair elections, aided by the judiciary, the EC, and a vibrant media and civil society organizations. Elections have become notably freer and fairer, and politicians and parties are not able to rig elections, even locally, as happened in some instances in earlier decades.

Are democratic norms getting gradually eroded and diluted due to the huge weight of anti-system parties, for example, the passive acceptance by the public of violence and hatred propagated against religious minorities, or the systematic use of violence by communist cadres in their strongholds? Or does it mean the opposite, that is, the taming of extreme parties by the "system" and their drift toward the political center so as to become acceptable coalition partners before elections and in formation of national and state governments in an era when pre-electoral and government coalitions are necessary for electoral victory and political power? The available trends are mixed and can be read both ways. It is too early to say whether anti-system ideologies will gain mainstream acceptance and if they do so whether this is certain to weaken democratic norms. It should be noted that even religiomajoritarian and communist parties accept democratic verdicts, operate within the law most of the time and in most places, and exit office at the national or state level when voted out.

A key weakness in the relationship between parties and democracy in India is the lack of internal democracy. Nowadays most parties observe some perfunctory rituals of internal democracy for the sake of formality, as certain practices are mandated by the EC of India for maintaining a party's official recognition, but true internal democracy cannot be said to exist and all parties are essentially top-down in their functioning. This is a great weakness because internal democracy, in Lawson's terms, enhances both participation and responsiveness, and thus strengthens democracy overall.[46]

Does the observed incumbency disadvantage mean that democracy is being strengthened? We can relate the observable anti-incumbency effects to the relationship between political parties and democracy by observing that party-voter relations remain clientelistic rather than participatory or responsive, to use Lawson's framework. The probable remedy for this is some combination of decentralization of provision of public services and internal democracy within parties. That would ensure participation and responsiveness and thereby counter the capture of goods and services by particularistic interests. This will help move the party-voter relationship from the present clientelism to responsiveness and, eventually, participation.

However, we can also argue that anti-incumbency effects actually enhance the competitiveness of Indian democracy. Fundamentally, competitive elections require that competing candidates (and their backers) believe that they have a reasonable chance of winning elections. Given the constituency-level anti-incumbency effects observed in India, we argue that this emboldens challengers to contest, thus ensuring competitive elections.[47] All in all, the evolution of the party-voter relationship and the larger impact of political parties on democracy is, in our judgment, moving in the direction of greater consolidation and improvement in the quality of democracy, particularly over the past two decades which have been dominated by minority and coalition governments.

CHAPTER 7

Fledgling Two-Party Democracy in Japan: No Strong Partisans and a Fragmented State Bureaucracy

Takashi Inoguchi

INTRODUCTION

The central question addressed in this chapter is: How do the parties of Japan facilitate or impede the work of democratic politics? This question is interesting in the case of Japan for three reasons: (1) Japan is the first non-western democracy of long duration, so the question naturally arises as to whether and how on the whole party politics might facilitate or impede democratic politics,[1] (2) Japan's party politics is that of one-party dominance,[2] so the question naturally arises as to whether one-party dominant party politics might facilitate or impede democratic politics, and (3) Japan's party politics is based on the pivotal weight of central bureaucracy that carries out both its prelegislative task and its executive task.[3] By prelegislative work I mean that the central bureaucracy monitors and identifies where legislation is necessary, desirable and feasible and drafts bills for the elected cabinet before that body, headed by the prime minister, and decides which bills to present to the National Diet; the question naturally arises as to whether this type of party politics might facilitate or impede democratic politics.

To answer these and other related questions, it is necessary to take a quick glance at the historical and institutional dimensions of Japanese political development since its early modern period onward (i.e., 1603–1867) as well as its prewar modern development (i.e., 1868–1945).[4] Thus I give a brief historical account of political development in the early modern and modern periods before focusing on the contemporary period of 1945–2010. Then I try to answer the questions on the basis of historical accounts, as summarized in Table 7.1.

EARLY MODERN PERIOD, 1603–1867: PAX TOKUGAWANA

It may be surprising to some that I begin by saying that the late 16th century should be considered as the time when Japanese democratic politics began, especially since the end of the 16th century was a period in which the Hobbesian postulation, war of all against all, was a reality. However, out of this warring period rose an ambitious unifier, Oda Nobunaga, who defeated most other feudal warlords, crushed merchant city republics, massacred armed Buddhist monks, thus monopolizing the weapons of violence for himself alone, and made excellent use of western technology and knowledge, thus facilitating commerce both internal and external. Nobunaga was assassinated midway to a final unification.[5] His successor Tokugawa Ieyasu completed national unification by 1603 with an important early modern feature kept largely intact. That is, Ieyasu and his Tokugawa family reigned supreme over matters of defense, diplomacy, and external commerce while allowing 300 odd domains to keep autonomy as long as they kept peace in their respective domains and did not challenge the Tokugawa hegemony.[6] Herein lies the quasi-democratic momentum hidden beneath domain autonomy during the early modern period.[7]

In the period of transition from the warring to early modern periods, governing elites were fairly frequently relocated from one domain to another, reflecting the geopolitical calculi of victorious power coalitions,

---

Table 7.1 Political Parties and Democracy: A Chronological Relationship

Early Modern Period 1603–1867: Pax Tokugawana
- Bureaucratic authoritarianism developed in 300 feudal domains
- Democratic potentials fostered for better governance

Modern Period 1868–1945: Parliamentary Monarchy with Bureaucratic Authoritarianism
- 1868–1874 Rebellions suppressed
- 1875–1890 Political parties as opposition
- 1890–1910 Parliamentary politics as means of maintaining control
- 1910–1925 Emergence of two-party system
- 1925–1941 From expanded suffrage to a stronger left to military rule and war

Contemporary Period 1945–2008: Parliamentary Democracy with Fragmented Bureaucracy
- 1945–1952 Military occupation with Japanese bureaucratic authoritarianism
- 1952–1985 One and a half party democracy
- 1985–2008 Fledgling two-party system without partisans

especially the Tokugawa hegemonic family coalition. The Tokugawa transferred their enemies to locations far from Edo (later Tokyo), its capital, while it assembled its friends located at key pivotal places that led to Edo and to Kyoto where the emperor resided. What this means at the grassroots level is that peasants stayed in the same domain but governing elites in each domain, numbering from a few hundred to a couple of thousand (i.e., 2% to 5% of the population), relocated. Given the increasing administrative, fiscal, and penal tasks they had to shoulder as governing elites, who were drawn only from the warrior classes, they came to rely heavily and steadily on local elites in the domain, that is, on the governing networks of rich merchants and rich peasants.[8] Therefore, they had to be attentive to people's grievances and manifest a sense of justice to a certain extent.

This early modern period of 1603 to 1867 was a period of relative peace, except for two Tokugawa military interventions, one against Christian dissidents in the mid-16th century, the other against the anti-Tokugawa rebellion of the Choshu domain in the mid-19th century.

MODERN PERIOD 1868–1945: PARLIAMENTARY MONARCHY WITH BUREAUCRATIC AUTHORITARIANISM

The Tokugawa system collapsed in 1867 due to the onslaught of anti-foreign forces aroused by the opening of ports and the country in 1853 and 1858. Once the anti-Tokugawa forces took power in 1868, a parliamentary monarchy was designed and established. The emperor was instructed to declare that he was in charge, that domains were to be abolished and replaced by 69 prefectures by 1872 (latter modified to 46 by 1889) with governors appointed by Tokyo, and that he would listen to the voice of the people.[10]

To prepare a national parliament, local parliaments were set up first, and popular elections took place in the 1880s. Local assemblymen consisted of unemployed former warriors and disgruntled rich landlords and peasants who shouldered most of the tax burdens.[11] Together these groups formed the first political parties, mostly in opposition to the government.

The modernizing Meiji government shifted its emphasis from the emperor's personal direct rule to that of bureaucratic rule. They found the enormity of government tasks beyond the emperor's capacity and looked at the popularly elected parliament with deep suspicion as to its probable loyalty and competence. They therefore invented the idea of a meritocratically recruited central bureaucracy.[12] The pool of bureaucratic talents was to be developed in seven imperial universities, and an imperial service examination would determine who would be assigned which posts, on the basis of merit.

Each bureaucratic agency was made semisovereign as far as its own jurisdiction was concerned.[13] However, the meritocratic system of recruitment could not be established immediately, with the result that in the beginning the existing spoils system prevailed: Friends were chosen for key posts, by and large from the literate and disciplined warrior class, and each cabinet leader chose persons from his own domain. Hence the army was dominated by men from the Choshu domain (the leader of the anti-Tokugawa forces), the navy from the Satsuma domain (the coleader of the anti-Tokugawa forces), the police from the Higo and Aizu-wakamatsu domains, and the accounting office from the Hizen domain. In this way the geographically decentralized feature of the Tokugawa system was transferred into the functionally decentralized Meiji system.

Power was also decentralized. The idea of the emperor's personal direct rule permeated the Imperial Constitution, but at the same time he was expected to aggregate a wide range of views and actions and to carry out his rule with the assistance of many subjects including the Council of Senior Statesmen, the Privy Council, the prime minister, the army, the navy, cabinet ministers representing bureaucratic agencies, and so forth. Furthermore, every subject was to be considered equal under the emperor. Theoretically, every cabinet minister was almost on par with the prime minister, and, since consensus was one of the preconditions of any cabinet decision, one dissenting opinion from any member could topple the cabinet and force the prime minister to announce the resignation of the entire cabinet.[14]

The budding quasi-democratic feature of the Tokugawa system, which had given domains autonomy and led the governing elites to coopt rich merchants and landlords into their governing networks and to foster domain identity by carrying out projects of school construction, flood prevention, and irrigation, now set the stage for the Meiji modernizing government reforms, including democratization. The Imperial decree of 1868 made it clear that the government must listen to the people and make its decisions only after collective discussion. Accordingly, prefectural assemblies were established by elections in the 1880s and political participation at the local level was realized.

The Imperial Diet House of Representatives elections took place in 1890 with electors who paid taxes above a certain level. Only the very rich were electors and the entire electorate was only a small percentage of the entire adult male population. That percentage increased steadily as industrialization made progress, and by 1925 the law to accord universal suffrage was legislated whereby the entire male adult population, amounting to 12.4 million, became electors.[15] The House of Peers consisted of those appointed by government. In 1946, when the first House of Representatives elections took place under the occupation of the Allied Powers, the entire adult female population was accorded the right to participate in elections.

During this period (1868–1945), the place and role of political parties in the Japanese political system grew. Political parties came to the fore in the 1880s, after the antigovernment dissidents and rebels were suppressed in the mid-1870s and the government introduced local assemblies in each prefecture. Politically disgruntled, those rallying around political parties were by definition in the opposition. But during the 1880s and through the 1890s, the government was more or less barricaded against the parties in the Imperial Diet, ruling instead via executive institutions such as the bureaucratic agencies, the army, the navy, the Privy Council, the police, and so forth. Only slowly did the government come to terms with the political parties, moving from a long period of authoritarian intimidation to more utilitarian means of control, offering parliamentary party leaders government positions or favoring pork barrel legislation, as policies developed during the 1900s and 1910s.[16]

In the 1920s and 1930s, a two-party system emerged, with power alternating between two major parties, the Seiyu Party and the Minsei Party, each representing a mix of traditional and reformist strands of Japanese political persuasion.[17] Reflecting on the rise of industry and leftist forces amid the Great Depression, the Social Mass Party, the first social democratic party representing interests of workers and farmers, won 47 seats in the 1930 House of Representatives election.[18] Extreme right-wing forces pushed their assertion aggressively in response to this leftist thrust into national political scenes in the form of a military coup d'état in 1930. Amid long economic depressions came the Japanese occupation of the three northeastern provinces of the Republic of China and establishment in 1931 of a puppet state called the Manchukuo, which was carried out by an army lieutenant and his comrades. Political parties were steadily rallying around two policies: boosting the economy by government spending and following a hawkish foreign policy vis-à-vis China and gradually the United States as well. The latter policy led to the Second Japan-China War of 1937–1945 and the Pacific War of 1941–1945. During the war the parties abandoned their own identities, joining what was called the Council to Assist the Emperor to Carry Out the Great Task. Thus at the height of the success of party politics and the solid advance of the center-left party, parties actively participated in their own demise.[19]

CONTEMPORARY PERIOD 1945–2008: PARLIAMENTARY DEMOCRACY WITH FRAGMENTED BUREAUCRACY

Modern Japanese politics were entirely transformed during the period of military rule of the Allied Powers in 1945–1952. Defeat in war and U.S. military rule had an enormous impact on Japanese politics.[20] First, the realm and role of political parties was enhanced by a wide range of reforms. The political purge of war-tainted elements meant the disappearance of the Japanese military, the authoritarian security police, the aristocratic system assisting the emperor, and pro-war politicians, bureaucrats, opinion leaders, and business leaders. The constitutional provision of extensive freedoms allowed political parties to become a strong element to sustain further democratization under military rule.

The 1925 provision of universal male suffrage coincided with the legislation of the Internal Security Act, whereby expressions and conduct considered improper were regulated by the government. In 1946 the new constitution adopted a thoroughly progressive liberal view of freedom of expression, including the formation of political parties. Thus the first House of Representatives elected in 1946 saw the mushrooming of political parties and an enormous number of candidates competing. Reform also meant the disappearance of the emperor worship system and the introduction of a liberal form of education, which contributed immensely to socializing citizens to participate in politics. Now the citizens, not the state, became primordial in politics.

Other wide-ranging reforms were carried out in such areas as land reform (all tenants were transformed into land-owning farmers), union reform (freedom of unions in business firms), tax privileges to owners of small shops and factories, and gender equality whereby females were made legally equal to males in all respects.[21] Political participation increased, education levels rose, and the working female population grew. Not all reform measures were fully implemented deeply at the grassroots level, but there as well political parties played a key role, embodying the idea of popular sovereignty, the key notion of democratic politics.

1952–1985: One and One Half Party Politics

Mushrooming political parties formed, split, and formed again over the next 10 years, eventually creating what is often called the one and a half party system.[22] Long-suppressed parties like the Japanese Communist Party and other leftist parties competed to take power in the early postdefeat years, when it could be said that the conservatives were on the defensive while the progressives were on the offensive. Many politicians tainted by war collaboration were removed from the political arena, and those who had been jailed or placed in home custody before 1945 were now treated as heroes.

However, as the East-West confrontation grew intense in the late 1940s, it permeated domestic politics as well, with significant effects. Mergers by parties on the left and the right accelerated as both sides sought victory. The United States took the side of the conservatives after progressives manifested their dismay with the East-West confrontation, with the peace treaty finally concluded with allied powers minus the

Soviet Union, and with the Japan-United States security treaty, which allowed U.S. forces to stay on in Japan even after independence, now planned for 1952. Economic recovery and high growth enabled the conservatives to gain self-confidence, especially land-owning farmers, shop and factory owners, and fast growing numbers of office and factory workers who leaned steadily to the side of the conservatives. The net result of these and other social forces was the one and a half party system. The center-right Liberal Democratic Party (LDP) was established in 1955 in response to the merger of the right-wing and left-wing socialist parties earlier in 1955, and this set the basic pattern of Japanese modern party politics. The LDP occupied slightly more than 50% of the seats in the House of Representatives, whereas the Japan Socialist Party and the Japan Communist Party occupied about 30% combined. The rest of the seats were occupied by minor parties and by those who had not been able to become party-designated candidates but won election anyway—many of the latter candidates joined the LDP after victory. Thus instead of a more familiar two-party politics, Japan created the one and half party politics system, with the LDP continuously in power from 1955 until 1993.

This period was one of state-led industrialization,[23] during which Japan experienced high developmental momentum with vibrant demographic growth. The business community wanted business-friendly legislation and the central bureaucracy wanted to carry out those tasks that would facilitate developmental momentum to bear fruit as planners and monitors of recovery and growth. This situation meant that parliamentary politics where political parties are key actors of legislation tended to play a secondary role to bureaucratic politics.[24] Since the majority party held a comfortable lead in both houses, the central bureaucracy developed the habit of simply briefing the governing party outside the National Diet when there were key issues that required legislative action.[25] Parliamentary committees, where representatives of both governing and opposition parties deliberated together, did not have a high priority.

Furthermore, the length of parliamentary sessions was (and still is) relatively short, about half a year, a factor that has two major implications.[26] First, within parliament the government is easily made subject to the intimidation of opposition parties, which can prolong discussions in committee and plenary sessions and disable the governmental legislative schedule. For the government to get legislation passed quickly and well, it had either to accommodate opposition preferences by modifying legislative draft bills—a sign of democratic governance—or simply use its majority to evade full debate in the Diet—a sign of willingness to bypass democratic politics.

Toward the end of the period of one and a half party system, its malaise was clearly manifested at times, most importantly in serious scandals that brought an end, at least temporarily, to one-party dominance in 1993 (Table 7.2).

The scandals coincided with the time period when money flooded the Japanese economy in a most rampant fashion, 1985–1991. The Plaza Agreement of the Group of Seven of 1985 played a role by showing how the high economic growth rates for these years were achieved. A series of scandals was revealed, leading to the activation of civil society and nongovernmental organizations on a scale unprecedented since 1955. One of the movements, led by Morihiro Hosokawa, former governor of Kumamoto Prefecture and a distant relative to the Imperial family, seized the moment and defeated the LDP in many districts. Hosokawa's winning coalition was formed with sizable defectors from the LDP. As prime minister, Hosokawa's key reformist legislation was about elections and political parties.[27] The huge amount of money needed to carry out campaigns is now made available by the central government, via the Ministry of Internal Affairs and Communication, with the amount depending on the number of party members registered at the end of each year. At the same time, the regulations have been tightened. The number of campaign posters put out in districts is strictly limited, as are the length of television campaign speeches and the wages paid to campaign helpers. Legislators are now strictly regulated when giving or receiving money from anywhere. Pork barrel politics—the explicit linkage of legislative action and electoral support, such as when legislators bring central government projects to districts in return for electoral support—has become far less common if only because of the expectation of strict punishment if caught. In Osaka, for example, a legislator known to give a gift to a district supporter at a funeral was punished. Most fundamentally, transparency is required,

Table 7.2 General Election of 1993 by Political Party

Political party	Number of seats	
Liberal Democratic Party	223	Lost power
Japan Socialist Party	70	Coalition government
Renaissance Party	55	formed with leaders
Komei Party	51	from Japan New Party
New Japan Party	35	and New Harbinger
Democratic Socialist Party	15	Party
New Harbinger Party	13	
Social Democratic Alliance	4	
Independents	30	
Japan Communist Party	15	Stayed out
Total	511	

as is strict and full accounting for all money that comes from any-where, including that from the central government for party use.

In addition, the electoral system was transformed from what is called the medium-sized district system to the combination of what is called the small-sized district system and the proportional representation sys-tem for the House of Representatives. The medium-sized district elects two to five persons with one vote for each elector. In the past the govern-ing LDP had more than one candidate in the same district and their com-petition tended to encourage pork barreling, strengthen clientelistic networks, and reduce the programmatic components of party competi-tion. The small-sized district system is the system of choosing a legislator with one nontransferable vote for one person, as in the Anglo-American system. The party candidate is now chosen by the party headquarters, more specifically its secretary general.

The party manifesto is now drafted more carefully in preparation for the annual conference in January and it is treated seriously. The postal privatization issue in 2005 was a case in point.[28] Prime Minister Junichiro Koizumi tabled its bill to the National Diet. There a sizable number of governing party member legislators defected in voting in the House of Councillors. Koizumi said that if legislators were not happy with postal privatization, he would have to ascertain citizen con-fidence in the prime minister. He dissolved the House of Representa-tives immediately and then, referring to the LDP's party manifesto promulgated earlier in the year, removed all the legislators from the LDP and fielded new party-backed candidates to compete with defec-tors. The result was a resounding victory for Koizumi in the 2005 gen-eral election. It is important to note that in order to mitigate the possible and probable underrepresentation of minor parties that occurs under the Anglo-American system, the Japanese reformist legislation juxtaposed the Anglo-American system and the continental European system by setting up the proportional representation system both nationwide and in the regions. It is no less important to note that those defeated in the Anglo-American system have been enabled to capture a seat in the proportional representation system in the regions, via *hirei fukkatsu* (resuscitation by the proportional representation scheme). Thus, even if a candidate is defeated in one Tokyo district, the same candidate can be elected in the Tokyo bloc proportional representation scheme in the Tokyo regional bloc, as long as the candidate is listed high in the LDP party list. How many are elected depends entirely on the number of votes the LDP has garnered in the Tokyo regional bloc and on the ranking of the candidate in the LDP party list.

The Hosokawa- and Hata-led reformist administrations collapsed perhaps prematurely in spring 1994. Internal feuds, policy incompe-tence, and political naiveté manifested in reformist conduct inside and outside the National Diet led to the slow comeback of the LDP in the general election of 1994. Although the LDP was the largest, if not majority, party in the House of Representatives 1994 election, the reformed electoral system, especially the mixed system of using both the Anglo-American system and the continental European system plus the *hirei fukkatsu* seems to have contributed to the relative continuity and stability of parliamentary representation by political parties and, hence, the revival of the LDP in a short period of time after its initial demise as the governing party. Just as the economic boom period from 1985 to 1994 coincided with the declining popularity of the LDP and the increasing popularity of the rest, so too the period of economic recession, 1994–2006, coincided with the slow comeback of the popularity of the LDP. (However, see Epilogue.)

Table 7.3 summarizes how political parties and democracy have been linked over time.

A TWO-PARTY SYSTEM WITH NO PARTISANS: THE PERSONALIZATION OF PARTY POLITICS UNDER GLOBALIZATION (1994–PRESENT)

Today the debate continues as to whether Japan has become a two-party system.[29] What is clear, however, is the importance of two major changes, regardless of the number of parties: the personalization of party politics and the impact of globalization.

Table 7.3 Political Parties and Democracy in Japan: Key Features of the Links Between Them Over Time

Early Modern Period 1603–1867
1. Tokugawa fledgling democracy: bureaucratic authoritarianism with democratic potentials, 1603–1867

Modern Period 1868–1945
2. Meiji modernizing democracy: political parties grew from antigovernment social movements, 1868–1890
3. Taisho democracy: political parties as parliamentary opposition by definition, 1890–1914
4. Former Showa democracy: political parties accelerated democratization, 1914–1931
5. Death of democracy: political parties destroyed democracy, 1931–1945

Contemporary Period 1945–2008
6. Occupation democracy: political parties as critical vehicle of democratization, 1945–1952
7. Later Showa democracy: political parties as positive links to sectors (business and bureaucratic) in state-led developmentalism, 1952–1985
8. Heisei democracy: political parties as positive links to citizens under globalization 1985–2008

Globalization is a force that is steadily causing the disintegration of the forces in the national community and the reintegration of its fractured subunits, again in two directions, upward and downward. The driving force is technological progress: those units or subunits with technological prowess move upward; those without move downward and tend to be marginalized. Party politics is not immune from the tide of globalization.[30] Two major social forces have undermined the sociological bases of the key supporters of both governing and opposition parties. In its earliest days the sociological bases of the LDP were land-owning farmers and shop and factory owners. They were undermined by forces of state-led industrialization, making it impossible for them to compete. Many were absorbed by the factories and offices that helped Japan produce and sell manufactured goods to the rest of the world.

Under these circumstances, the LDP shifted its support bases from rural to urban centers where a large number of what was called the new middle mass resided and worked.[31] Their income level soared; their class consciousness was that of a middle class without class-related contents; their cherished norms and values were now optimistic conservatism, risk aversion, and high investment in educating children, all based on growing income level, nuclear family, life-long employment, and a stable government.

The Socialist Party, on the other hand, shifted its support base from union members to nonunion members, as the number of the former drastically decreased. Although their cherished norms and values now also reflected the mindset of what was called the new middle mass, they placed greater stress on such issues as job retention, anti-tax hike, and pro-alliance policies that ruled out war participation. Such shifts on both sides of the spectrum were further accelerated by the relentless permeation of globalizing forces. Local chapters of many parties ceased to function as key vehicles of electoral mobilization, whether based on a business council, neighborhood community, or union. A growing number of the population have became part-time workers, now approximately 30% of the entire working population. Such workers tend to be indifferent to political participation in normal times, yet volatile in extending their support once their attention is gained.

A steadily increasing elderly population ranging from 65 to 95 years old now forms about 20% of the total electorate. They actively participate in politics and volunteer work and know how to voice their grievances collectively. They focus on social policy, pension, medical and other insurances, welfare facilities, and tax reduction privileges.

Given the possibility voters have of identifying, however sporadically, with one or another of these groups, it is now much more difficult for political parties to gain electoral support on the basis of local chapters or sectoral supporters lists. Chanting the names of the candidates and political parties from the campaigning wagon in electoral districts has ceased to function as electoral mobilization.[32] Something much more personal, capable of attracting positive sympathetic responses, has become necessary. Voters are affiliated with many organizations and associations with thin and widespread identity and are preoccupied with mundane and not so mundane issues, so political issues only sporadically come to the fore of their attention. To strike a chord the candidate needs a meticulously well-calculated set of manners, expressions, and actions, orchestrated around a single thematic focus, transforming his audience into virtual participants.[33] One can see an increasing array of political leaders who successfully give politics personalized dimensions, bringing solace, however artificial, to citizens caught up in mercilessly globalizing daily routines that fill them with uncertainties and apprehensions, such as Taksin Sinawatra and Junichiro Koizumi, in ways similar to those used by others on the world stage.[34] As ideological and policy differences between the parties grow less pronounced, the party whose leaders are most capable of personalizing politics is likely to be the most successful.

The driving force of this personalization of politics is globalization and the ways in which it permeates the national political system. Jean-Marie Guéhenno argues that globalization is a key factor that is putting an end to democracy, which has in the past been organized within each national political unit. Capital now moves abroad, seeking its location based on lower taxes, comparative advantages, and other considerations.[35] What was once the tightly organically linked national economy has been disintegrating steadily and some of the subunits have been reintegrating themselves with other subunits abroad. Perhaps things have not gone as far as Guéhenno argues, but it is quite clear that the relative weight of domestic politics has gone down significantly. Regional and global political actors are ever more influential, and in these circumstances national political parties cannot avoid their own relative decline.

To answer the question of whether personalized party politics facilitate or impede democratic politics one needs to consider the social group-political party relationship as perhaps now more important than the citizen-leader relationship. Both voters and candidates are far more atomized and fragmented during the phase of relentless globalization than during the previous phase of political development under state-led industrialization.[36] What unites electorates, if only temporarily, is the strong appeal of a rather simplified yet seductive message assuaging their key concerns. Choosing a leader is like forming an ad hoc coalition of the temporarily willing, each with a single issue and mood. Insofar as choosing a leader is based on free and democratic election, one can argue that party politics facilitates democratic politics. However, populist party politics, that is, political appeals that rely on a single leader's appeal, whether that appeal is based on message, mood, or rhetoric, rather than on a hard working party organization, a party manifesto, or the pursuit of political careers within the party, may impede democratic politics.[37]

Given how strongly the forces of globalization have impacted the weight and nature of Japanese parties today, have they simply become mirror images of each other? Table 7.4 suggests that there may be a strong tendency in that direction but that important differences do remain in the nature of their internal organization. Nonetheless, overall, as the parties decline in weight, the pattern of gradual convergence is undeniable.

CONCLUSIONS

Thus far I have focused on political parties and democracy in Japan. To conclude I will briefly consider how these two institutions fit in a broader framework, that of the state and citizens or civil society. The features of the Japanese modern state and its relationship with civil society are quite distinct. They include the following:

1. The state contains what may be called the state-servicing class called warriors during the early modern period and bureaucrats in the modern period since the mid-19th century. They continue to be the key actors in Japanese politics.

2. Civil society in Japan has always been relatively weak vis-à-vis the bureaucracy. Indeed in the past there were only two categories of political actors: governmental institutions and nongovernmental individuals.

3. Political parties first emerged in the mid-19th century from civil society as agencies of opposition to the bureaucratically led government in parliamentary bodies, local and national.

4. The state organized civil society as if the latter were a set of appendices of each bureaucratic agency during much of the 20th century.

5. Over the years the slow but steady democratization of the government has given the parties ever more significant roles, especially since 1945.

6. The tide of globalization has loosened the grip of power of the state and its agencies servicing social groups over nongovernmental organizations, including the parties. The latter have grown stronger in tandem with democratization and globalization.

The strong state tradition vis-à-vis citizens may have retarded the full-fledged development of political parties in Japan. However, it prepared a solid basis of democratic development for later days by producing effective state-servicing bureaucrats and institutions (civil servants), by ensuring a high literacy rate throughout the population, and by

Table 7.4 Comparing the Two Major Parties: The LDP and DPJ Today

	Liberal Democratic Party	Democratic Party of Japan
Membership	• Open. • 1.2 million.	• Open. • A few hundred thousand.
Internal organization	• Loose. • Clientalist-oriented factions losing weight since reform.	• Loose. • Strong groups originating from their previous party membership (formally, Socialist, Liberal, New Progressive, New Japan, Democratic Socialist parties).
Candidate recruitment	• Public announcement and recruitment with interviewing. • Those with backgrounds of political family. • Those with backgrounds of local politicians and secretaries to legislators of both houses abound. • Those with backgrounds of local public sector and self-employed business leaders abound.	• Public announcement and recruitment with interviewing. • Those with backgrounds of bureaucrats, lawyers, NGO leaders, and journalists. • Those with backgrounds as local politicians and secretaries to legislators of both houses abound.
Openness of the nomination process	• Party endorsed candidate nomination carried out by secretary general with concurrence of president on the basis of draft list made up by electoral strategy headquarters chairman in Tokyo. • Local chapters used to take the lead in nomination process before reform.	• Party endorsed candidate nomination carried out by president with concurrence of a few key factional leaders. • Local initiatives strong especially where there is no DPJ seat.
Program in terms of who writes it	• Party manifesto announced in party annual convention drafted by manifesto drafting committee on the basis of key policy lines articulated by president.	• Party manifesto announced in party annual convention drafted by manifesto drafting committee on the basis of key policy lines articulated by president.

	• Party militants do take parts in its formation, but their credibility and strength are measured in daily party committee meetings on each specific policy; party discipline strengthened in parliamentary voting after reform; defiance meaning marginalization and at times loss of party membership.	• Party militants do take parts in its formation, but their credibility and strength measured in party committee meetings.
Electoral strategy	• Campaigning allowed only during the two-week period after official announcement; campaigning allowed only with those forms and frameworks stipulated in the Public Election Law and in the Political Money Law. • Besides the formal campaigning period, semicampaigning takes place in districts focusing on speeches, discussions, participation in funerals, marriage ceremonies, school events and community events, focusing on weekend.	• Campaigning allowed only during the two-week period after official announcement; campaigning allowed only with those forms and frameworks stipulated in the Public Election Law and in the Political Money Law. • Besides the formal campaigning period, semicampaigning takes place in districts focusing on speeches, discussions, participation in funerals, marriage ceremonies, school events and community events, focusing on weekends.
Votes won in local, regional, and national	• Votes won evenly in local, regional, and national elections; votes lost at times of major scandals and great economic upheavals; votes won when charismatic leaders lead the country.	• Votes won when LDP loses credibility whether it is attributable to scandals, dissonant policy thrusts, or lack of leadership.

providing the checks-and-balance nature of central bureaucracy at the highest level. Within this state-and-society framework, political parties were able to grow and facilitate the growth of democracy. This growth took place in stages. During the 1870s and 1880s antigovernment social forces moved from violent rebellions to nonviolent opposition in parliament; in the 1890s and 1900s antigovernment political parties pressed the government in the direction of normal parliamentary politics by alternating their power positions by elections; in the 1910s and 1920s two-party politics began to be practiced normally until cut short by military takeover and a 15-year period (1931–1945) when party growth was arrested; in the 1940s and 1950s the purge of pro-war actors and institutions and the democratic institutional reforms insisted upon by the occupying powers after military defeat facilitated the rapid growth of the party system; in the 1960s, 1970s, and 1980s the evolving one and a half party system created a stable and mature democratic party system, albeit increasingly flawed by corruption. The subsequent reforms were accompanied by increasing globalization, and both strongly influenced the development of present day party politics, leading to the final stage in which the party system appears to be evolving into a system of parties without partisans, as voters are more inclined to respond to personalistic seduction of leaders rather than the programmatic appeals of party manifestos, the organization, or the arguments of the candidates.

The links between political parties and democracy have been positive and strong in Japan for the past century and a half. Yet the weakening of the centripetal force of the Japanese state and nationally integrated economic structure has contributed to dilution of the importance of political party organization in politics. Revitalizing the role of political parties in democratic development seems to depend on how well the parties themselves can enhance their appeal and utility to somewhat fragmented and atomized citizens without evoking excessive partisan emotions and spirits.

EPILOGUE

On August 30, 2009, a general election took place. A massive number of voters turned to the major opposition party, the Democratic Party of Japan (DPJ), replacing the LDP, which had been in power since 1955 with the one-year exception of 1993–1994. The former won 208 seats of the total 480 seats in the House of Representatives, whereas the latter won merely 118 seats. The DPJ got the largest share of seats in the House of Representatives for any party since the first election took place in 1889.

What factors contributed to this? Much still remains to be analyzed, yet the following factors are widely accepted. First, the LDP's three latest prime ministers, Shinzo Abe, Yasuo Fukuda, and Taro Aso, evaded facing the judgment of popular votes successively for the period between 2006 and 2009. People witnessed the quasi-illegitimate continuation of power. Second, the global financial crisis that erupted in September 2008 hit the Japanese economy hard. Unemployment soared to the unprecedented level of 6 percent and income levels went down tangibly. Third, astronomically accumulated government deficits forced the government to cut the budget on social and economic policy, with the effects of sharply raising popular antipathy to the government. Fourth, the deepening tide of globalization eroded the unity and solidarity of social and institutionalized groups, including the once entrenched governing party (the LDP) so that electors were not collectively anchored but rather left in isolation from one another. Last, but not least, the United States's continuing quest for primacy, despite the economic recession and antiterrorist wars in Afghanistan, Iraq, and other places, and the rise of other nations including China have raised anxiety about Japan's reduced standing in the world, especially since none of the past three prime ministers has been seen as making deft judgments or exercising decisive leadership.

The major lessons are first that democracy matters and makes a difference and second that electors in the globalizing world tend to make big swings especially when the electoral system is based on the Anglo-American scheme of choosing only one person in each district.

CHAPTER 8

The Politics of Ethnicity: Authoritarianism, Development, and Social Change in Malaysia

Edmund Terence Gomez

INTRODUCTION

The results of the general elections, held on March 8, 2008, suggested unprecedented and imminent change in Malaysia's political system, in particular the beginning of the end of an authoritarian form of governance. In contrast to other industrialized countries in East and Southeast Asia, such as South Korea, Taiwan, Thailand, the Philippines, and Indonesia, that had begun to democratize from the mid-1980s, Malaysia had not been subject to political liberalization of a similar nature in spite of the rise of the *reformasi* (reformation) movement in 1998. A large segment of the Malaysian electorate, particularly the urban middle class, had then been in the forefront for social change, but this movement was eventually stifled through highly authoritarian, even oppressive measures.[1] A decade later, the results of the 2008 general election suggested that the electorate had, through the ballot box, once again voiced a desire for political reforms involving an open, accountable, and nonracialized form of governance.

The results of this general election also drew attention to transitions in a society undergoing economic progress, indicating the need for political parties long in power to review their pattern of organization and mobilization. These socioeconomic transitions were also a consequence of key government policies, such as affirmative action, as well as those introduced during the 1980s to rapidly industrialize Malaysia and promote the rise of domestic capitalists.

This chapter first provides a brief history of Malaysia's political system and the main political parties. This overview further offers insights into the structure of the state and the mechanisms that have been adopted to limit the space for growth of a democratic state and a democratic party system.

I turn next to an appraisal of the role of Malaysia's parties in developing or hindering democracy by studying electoral trends since 1990. Next I draw attention to the outcomes of major economic policies on society and how these influenced the democratization of the state and the party system. The chapter ends with an evaluation of the results of the epochal 2008 general election, arguing that the results portend political reforms that may lead to the emergence of a stronger and more democratic party system in Malaysia.

POLITICAL SYSTEM AND PARTIES: A BRIEF HISTORY

Malaysia, formerly known as Malaya, is a constitutional monarchy with a system of federalism divided between a central government and 13 state governments,[2] although the distribution of power overwhelmingly favors the federal government. The country's bicameral parliament consists of a Dewan Negara (Senate) comprising 70 senators and a Dewan Rakyat (House of Representatives) of 222 parliamentarians. The election of members to the Dewan Rakyat, from territorially delimited constituencies through the single-member plurality system, is required to be held by universal adult franchise at intervals no longer than five years from the date on which parliament was first convened.

The government is formed by that party or coalition of parties whose individual members are able to command a majority in the Dewan Rakyat. The prime minister is by tradition the leader of the party or coalition of parties that secures the most seats in parliament. Since the prime minister is to be selected from among the elected members of the legislature, this weakens the system of checks and balances envisaged in the constitution since the executive branch is hardly accountable to parliament. The prime minister is traditionally also the president of the United Malays' National Organization (UMNO), the leading party in the ruling coalition, the Barisan Nasional (National Front), which comprises about a dozen, mostly ethnically based parties. The Barisan Nasional and its predecessor, the tripartite Alliance coalition—UMNO's partners then were the Malaysian Chinese Association (MCA) and the Malaysian Indian Congress (MIC)—have consistently maintained control over the government since general elections were first held in 1955.

The character and constitution of Malaysian political parties are deeply influenced by the multiethnic feature of its population. Of Malaysia's almost 27.7 million people in 2008, Bumiputeras[3] accounted for 65%, while the Chinese constituted about 26% and the Indians 8%; the remaining 1% is made up of other minor ethnic groups.[4] One outcome of the multiethnic constitution of Malaysian society has been the creation of political parties that are primarily ethnically based, although the governing Barisan Nasional is a multiracial, multiparty coalition. UMNO has, however, remained the hegemonic party in the Barisan Nasional (and the Alliance). The ethnic factor similarly shapes opposition politics. When the multiracial Pakatan Rakyat (People's Alliance) coalition was created in 2008, its principal members included the predominantly Chinese-based Democratic Action Party (DAP), the Malay-based Parti Islam SeMalaysia (Malaysian Islamic Party [PAS]), and the ostensibly multiethnic but Malay-dominant Keadilan Rakyat Malaysia (Malaysian Justice Party).

The third arm of the government, the judiciary, is constitutionally vested with the power to ensure an adequate division of powers, to sustain a system of checks and balances, and to ensure that the political liberties and rights of members of society are protected. The Constitution also tries to ensure the independence of the judiciary by securing the tenure and remuneration of its members. Although all senior judicial appointments are made by the king (who exercises no discretion in judicial matters), such appointments are made based on the recommendation and advice of the cabinet. The king is similarly vested with the authority to remove a judge from office.[5]

Ruling Coalition: From Alliance to Barisan Nasional (1955–1973)

Malaysia's ethnic pluralism was a consequence of British colonialism that commenced in 1786. In pursuit of their economic interests in the peninsula dominated by peasant-based Malays, the British encouraged the mass migration of Chinese and Indians to provide labor for their fledgling tin and rubber industries. By the mid-1930s, the population ratio of non-Malays to the indigenous community was almost even, while the Chinese had developed an economic presence, involved as they were primarily in small-scale trade and middleman business ventures, although their business interests were not as extensive as those of the British. Some Chinese had, however, emerged as rubber barons and prominent tin miners.[6]

In the aftermath of World War II, when the British returned to reclaim control over Malaya following the surrender of the Japanese, they proposed a unitary Malayan Union scheme that involved placing under one government all the nine Malay states and the Straits Settlements of Penang and Malacca. Singapore, the other remaining Straits Settlement, was to be left out of the Union. The Malays vehemently opposed the idea of the Union, renouncing it as a British ploy to abolish the Malay sultanate. The Malays also objected to the Union's intention to provide citizenship with equal political rights to all Malayans, irrespective of race, as long as they professed loyalty to and regarded Malaya as their home.[7]

In May 1946, an assortment of Malay clubs, associations, and political organizations merged to form UMNO to oppose the Malayan Union. Spearheaded by Malay aristocrats, UMNO managed to marshal widespread opposition to the Union.[8] UMNO's key role in preventing the implementation of the Malayan Union made the party the leading political force in Malaya, particularly in rural areas. Even presently, in the late 2000s, despite a membership totaling more than 2 million, making the mass-based UMNO the largest local political party, its bastion of support still remains rural Malays.

Although the British had collaborated with the predominantly Chinese-based Malayan Communist Party (MCP) during the world war (the party had gained a reputation among Malayans for its role in opposing the Japanese during that time), they were fearful of the growing impact of the party and the influence of other left-leaning organizations on the Chinese. As tension mounted between the British and the MCP and as a state of emergency was declared over the entire country in 1948, the British need for an alternative Chinese party that was conservative yet pliant to British interests had become imperative. To initiate the formation of such an alternative Chinese party, the British turned to leading Chinese businessmen who, like them, would have vast interests in the economy to protect after independence was gained. When the MCA was established in February 1949, the main, if covert, preoccupation of its leadership, which comprised some of the wealthiest Chinese businessmen and professionals in the country, was to ensure the protection of their economic interests through some form of political involvement.[9] In view of the bourgeois nature of the MCA leadership and the subservient role it has always played to UMNO, the party has had great difficulty mobilizing and sustaining the support of working-class and middle-class Chinese.

The MIC was led by left-leaning, middle-class, noncommunal members when it was established in August 1946. When it became apparent that multiracial parties received little electoral support, in 1954 the MIC became the third partner in the Alliance, a coalition that UMNO and the MCA had formed on an ad hoc basis two years earlier to contest municipal-level elections. The MIC's entry into the Alliance was precipitated by fears over its political survival, since the party represented a small fraction of a community that was well dispersed in the electorate.[10]

When the Alliance was officially formed in 1954, it was because of the colonial government's condition that independence would only be granted to a multiethnic leadership. The Alliance was also aware of the appeal of a multiracial coalition of parties to the electorate. There were other important reasons for forming the Alliance. UMNO was continually bedeviled by financial problems as the party's mainly rural, peasant membership could not provide it with sufficient funds to allow it to participate effectively in electoral contests. UMNO would come to rely heavily on cash-rich MCA to fund the Alliance. At the same time, the MCA needed UMNO to win seats as the Malays were heavily overrepresented in the electorate. During the federal election in 1955, for example, only 11% of the 1.28 million voters were non-Malays, while only 2 of the 52 parliamentary seats were non-Malay majority seats. Yet, a third of the Alliance's candidates were non-Malays, 15 from the MCA and 2 from the MIC.[11] The Alliance took control of government when independence was granted in 1957.

Since the Alliance members were ethnically based, their aims and objectives were devoid of a strong ideological orientation. Brown referred to these parties as having "ethnic ideologies."[12] Given the bourgeois nature of these parties' leaders, the use of such an ethnic ideology served to camouflage class dominance and helped them present themselves as racial patrons, even though such an ideology has seldom been of much significant material value to the working classes of these communities.[13] By the late 1960s, with the declining popularity of the Alliance and increasing factionalism in all three component parties, newly established opposition parties began to make inroads into the coalition's electoral base. In the 1969 general election, the Alliance's control over government was severely threatened when it obtained the support of only half the Malay population and a third of the non-Malay vote. Although it was the MCA that sustained the heaviest defeat, UMNO's support had so declined that the Alliance managed to secure a mere 48.5% of the popular vote. The Alliance retained control of the federal government only because of the communally divided nature of the opposition, the rural bias of the heavily gerrymandered electoral system, and the inability of the opposition in peninsular Malaysia to forge meaningful links with possible allies in Sabah and Sarawak, despite the prevailing discontent in those states. Nevertheless, the states of Penang and Kelantan fell to the opposition, while the Alliance barely secured majorities in the Selangor, Terengganu, and Perak legislatures.

Since the Alliance had retained control of the federal government with a severely diminished majority, communal tensions ran high as the election results were perceived by some quarters in UMNO as a reflection of the diminution of the party's and, hence, Malays' hegemony. These tensions heightened following "victory" processions held by opposition parties and UMNO in Kuala Lumpur. Inflamed racial sentiments eventually triggered the race riots of May 13, 1969, which spread quickly from Kuala Lumpur to other major towns. The riots led to the proclamation of a state of emergency on May 15. Parliament was suspended and power was vested in a National Operations Council (NOC), swiftly established by the government to restore order. Led by Deputy Prime Minister and UMNO Deputy President Abdul Razak Hussein, the NOC comprised mainly Malay senior bureaucrats and Alliance leaders.

UMNO's narrow retention of power precipitated a struggle between the party's young Turks and its conservative factions, which led to the resignation in 1971 of the long-standing prime minister and UMNO president Tunku Abdul Rahman. His successor, Razak, embarked on a round of discussions with all major political parties to regroup the Alliance into an enlarged coalition, the Barisan Nasional, which was registered as a party in June 1974, just two months before a general election was called.[14] Apart from the DAP, most opposition parties, including the main Malay opposition party PAS, the Gerakan Rakyat Malaysia (Gerakan or People's Movement Party), and the People's Progressive Party (PPP), were coopted into the Barisan Nasional. Their leaders were convinced by Razak's argument that warring political parties needed to stop "politicking," transcend their ideological differences, and come together to forge a nation that had been torn asunder by racial strife. UMNO's system of consociationalism, provided through the Barisan Nasional, meant, however, that the huge Chinese support enjoyed by the Gerakan and the PPP had eroded the MCA's influence in government.[15] Meanwhile, the incorporation of PAS, which was very influential on the east coast of the peninsula, enhanced Malay electoral support. UMNO's refusal to allow PAS to increase the number of seats it contested in the subsequent general election of 1974 further strengthened UMNO's hegemony in the coalition. PAS returned to the opposition in 1977.

The Barisan Nasional's objectives are broad, ranging from fostering and maintaining a united Malaysian nation to striving for a fair and just society. The coalition's conception of democracy in the Malaysian political system is not compatible with western models of liberal democracy. Malaysian prime ministers, particularly Mahathir Mohamad, who held this office from 1981 until 2003, have often publicly derided the procedural messiness and sluggishness of western democratic institutions, claiming that a working majority in parliament (by this he meant a more than two-thirds majority) was needed to ensure effective governance, political stability, and sustained economic development. For Mahathir, Malaysia's political system was based on a different kind of democracy, an "Asian" form of democracy, a notion also subscribed to by Lee Kuan Yew and Suharto, former leaders of Singapore and Indonesia, respectively.

The notion of cultural difference was used to justify this "Asian" form of democracy and has served as a convenient, even logical, explanation for the need to maintain authoritarian rule. Asian democracy ostensibly helps maintain ethnic harmony and political stability, both crucial for drawing foreign investments required to expedite industrial development. Mahathir would claim that historically, Malaysian—and, in particular, Malay—social and political structures have been authoritarian, hierarchical, and highly stratified. Malay political norms include loyalty to the ruler over and above individual freedom and rights, and the community tends to avoid adversarial relations and favor order over conflict. Such arguments have been used to justify extensive limitations on civil liberties, such as freedom of the press, assembly, and expression.

During Mahathir's long rule, considerable transformations had also occurred involving the autonomy of government institutions. The monarchy, judiciary, and parliament were reputed to have lost the capacity to check the executive, while the bureaucracy, military, and police had become extremely subservient to the office of the prime minister where enormous power had become concentrated. The capacity of the prime minister to undermine democratic norms by circumventing constitutional constraints on the office of the executive has emerged as one key feature of Malaysia's political system.

Under the Barisan Nasional, more pronounced Malay-based policies have been formulated. This was seen in the importance of the term *Bumiputeraism*, reflected specifically in the New Economic Policy (NEP), which was primarily devoted to the creation of a Bumiputera capitalist class through positive discrimination. The other goal of the NEP, to be implemented over 20 years from 1970, was to eradicate poverty irrespective of race.

In Sarawak, the leading Barisan Nasional component party is the Parti Pesaka Bumiputera Bersatu (United Bumiputera Party [PBB]), led by its long-standing president Abdul Taib Mahmud, the state's chief minister. Taib has progressively become a dominant force in Sarawak and maintains close ties with senior UMNO leaders. Other Barisan Nasional members in this state include Chinese-based Sarawak United People's Party (SUPP) and the Sarawak National Party (SNAP), which claims to represent the ethnic Iban community. SUPP is the state's first legal party, formed in 1959 and open to all ethnic communities but led predominantly by the Chinese; its original membership, however, included Malays, Ibans, and Dayaks.[16] Another component member is the Parti Bangsa Dayak Sarawak (or Sarawak Dayak People's Party [PBDS]), a breakaway from SNAP. None of these parties has any influence outside Sarawak.

In Sabah, the Chinese-based parties include the Sabah Progressive Party (SAPP) and Liberal Democratic Party (LDP), while the ethnic Kadazan-based parties include the Parti Bersatu Sabah (United Sabah Party [PBS]), Parti Bersatu Rakyat Sabah (United Sabah People's Party [PBRS]), and the Parti Demokratik Sabah (Sabah Democratic Party

[PDS]). While UMNO has no presence in Sarawak, it emerged as a major political force in Sabah in 1994 when it secured control of the government following defections from the opposition to the Barisan Nasional.

The Opposition

The DAP is an offshoot of the People's Action Party (PAP), the ruling party in Singapore. After Singapore left the federation, the Malaysian branch of the PAP adopted the name Democratic Action Party in March 1966. The DAP's identity as a "Chinese" party is due to the common perception that it raises primarily Chinese-based issues, although it has, since its inception, espoused a commitment "to the ideal of a free, democratic and socialist Malaysia, based on the principles of racial equality, and social and economic justice, and founded on the institution of parliamentary democracy."[17] Despite this espousal of economic justice, the DAP has failed to deliver viable or well-received economic policy alternatives. The party has consistently couched its ideals in its commitment toward creating a "Malaysian Malaysia," entailing the denunciation of the supremacy of one particular race in favor of the creation of a transethnic national identity. The DAP places great emphasis on the need for greater democratization, arguing that this would constitute the primary means for establishing unity among the various ethnic communities. The party has also argued that concentration of power has contributed to significant inequities in the distribution of wealth.

PAS, a breakaway UMNO faction, was formed in 1951 and is the main opposition party with the capacity to undermine the Barisan Nasional's influence among rural Malays.[18] PAS was originally led by leaders of the left-leaning Malay Nationalist Party (MNP) and comprised primarily rural teachers. Its objective at the outset was to secure mass rural-based Malay support through the propagation of a Malay nationalist agenda.[19] In 1982, following a radical change of leadership, PAS began adopting a predominantly Islamic posture.

Currently, PAS's key leaders are *ulama* (religious teachers), and its area of influence is limited primarily to the Malay heartland states of Kelantan, Terengganu, and (rural) Kedah. PAS first secured a majority in the Kelantan state legislature in the 1959 general election and governed the state until 1978. PAS also clinched power in Terengganu in 1959, but had to relinquish control of this state government in 1961 following defections from the party to UMNO. During the 1990 general election, PAS swept back to power in Kelantan with the aid of the then newly established Malay party Parti Semangat '46 (Spirit of '46 Party) led by Tengku Razaleigh Hamzah, a prince from Kelantan.[20] Razaleigh, a long-standing UMNO vice president (and treasurer), had formed

Semangat in 1988 after being forced out of the ruling party by then president Mahathir, following a bitter and divisive leadership contest in 1987.[21] PAS's electoral performance in Terengganu in 1990 also improved appreciably following its collaboration with Semangat.[22]

Among opposition parties, PAS has the most strongly defined objective. As a party motivated by Islam, PAS is principally devoted to the formation of an Islamic state in Malaysia. Accordingly, it espouses policies and ideas that are rooted in Islam. Adopting this preponderant Islamic posture, PAS has been offering Malaysians, Muslim Bumiputeras in particular, a vision of a society reformed through legislative changes based on religious tenets. The establishment of an Islamic state, according to the party, will bring about spiritual regeneration and lead to the development of a more just, democratic, moral, principled, and socially conscious society, devoid of repressive legislation and unhealthy economic activities such as gambling. For PAS, its ideas and motivations stem from Islam, as the party perceives it. Democratic ideals, the party believes, are acceptable only within a secular context because they would automatically feature in an Islamic theocratic state, since this system is inherently just. Yet, it has been observed that PAS will, in all likelihood, reject the concepts of majority rule and individual choice because the former can permit the implementation of morally wrong tenets while the latter embodies the assumption that individuals are all-knowing.[23] Most urban-based Malaysians, including many Muslims, find PAS's policies, particularly its social policies, profoundly rigid and inflexible. For example, in view of PAS's strict interpretation of Islam, the party has denounced as evil not just the numerous forms of western culture adopted by Malaysians, such as music, dance, and fashion, but has also seen fit to ban in Kelantan any performance of the *joget*, a traditional Malay dance. Nevertheless, PAS has been able to muster the support of rural Malays through active propagation of its conviction that religion and politics are inseparable in Islam and that religion should be thought of as a worldview, a value system, a code of ethics, even as an ideology. The reason for PAS's strong influence is partly due to the respect commanded by its leaders' rigorous Islamic training, many of whom are graduates of the esteemed Al-Azhar University in Cairo.

In the Malay heartland, particularly in Kelantan and Terengganu, PAS has consistently enjoyed staunch support, estimated at 35% to 40% of the electorate.[24] By working with Semangat, and later Keadilan, PAS was able to mobilize sufficient support to secure control of the Kelantan state legislature in 1990 and retain control of it in all general elections since then. In 1999, PAS, in coalition with other opposition parties, secured control of the Terengganu state government before losing power in the subsequent general election in 2004. In the 2008 general election, for the first time in its history, PAS helped form the government in the states of Perak, Selangor, Penang, and Kedah, with the DAP and Keadilan.

Keadilan, led by Anwar Ibrahim, has its roots in a power struggle in UMNO, which erupted following a currency crisis in 1997. This currency crisis evolved into an economic crisis the following year, which eventually led to a major political upheaval known as the *reformasi* in September 1998. This upheaval arose out of the controversial dismissal of Anwar as deputy to Mahathir, then the prime minister. Anwar was also removed from his post as deputy president of UMNO. Anwar was subsequently arrested and charged with sexual impropriety and corruption, allegations that were leveled at him, many believe, solely to remove him from public office.

The primary concern of the *reformasi* was to transform the way authority was exercised, that is, to check Mahathir's domination of the state. The resistance drew attention to a prevailing feature of the Malaysian state that had become quite manifest with the ouster of Anwar—unaccountable abuse of power to protect vested political and economic interests. These post-1998 developments led to public discourses on the nature of democracy and form of economic development that had been accompanied by rampant corruption and nepotism. But while a similar *reformasi* in neighboring Indonesia had managed to remove the long-standing authoritarian President Suharto from power, this movement in Malaysia failed to overthrow Mahathir.[25] The *reformasi* did, however, manage to become a major site of resistance to Mahathir and his form of governance, badly tarnishing his reputation. The *reformasi* initially involved random mass street demonstrations, but these protests were soon institutionalized with the formation of a multiparty opposition coalition, the Barisan Alternatif (Alternative Front). This coalition comprised the leading opposition parties, that is the then newly formed Parti Keadilan Nasional (National Justice Party), led by Anwar's wife, Wan Azizah Wan Ismail, PAS, and the DAP. Another member of this coalition was the Parti Rakyat Malaysia (Malaysian People's Party [PRM]),[26] which eventually merged with Keadilan when its present name Parti Keadilan Rakyat was adopted.

Keadilan's capacity to draw support is attributable to the more inclusive form of politics it has propagated. Among those who have stood behind this party and the coalition it leads (first the Barisan Alternatif and subsequently the Pakatan Rakyat) were people from groups that had hitherto felt marginalized, including the young and women, as well as the Malay rural electorate and the new middle class, which was increasingly frustrated with wealth concentration and cronyism in government. Keadilan members include a faction from UMNO, mainly Anwar's supporters who had been consigned to the margin after his fallout with Mahathir. Members of this UMNO faction were upset that Anwar's departure had hindered their hopes of developing their own economic interests, a factor that contributed to their move to the opposition. However, although UMNO was deeply divided following Anwar's ouster, there was no mass exodus from the party to Keadilan. UMNO members were well aware that other ousted party leaders who had formed opposition parties had not fared well. Some of them, including the very influential former finance minister Razaleigh, had spent an unfruitful time, nearly a decade, in the opposition, in alliance with PAS, only to return to UMNO in 1996.

The political liberalization and reforms that the rise of the opposition coalition portended did not, however, materialize when the Barisan Alternatif failed to make an impact in the 1999 general election. The opposition did not even manage to deny the Barisan Nasional its customary two-thirds majority in parliament. One major reason for the dismal performance of the opposition was the structure of the electoral system, an issue to which we now turn.

ELECTORAL SYSTEM, ELECTIONS, AND CAMPAIGNS

In Malaysia, two kinds of elections are held on a regular basis: the parliamentary and state elections. Municipal elections were conducted regularly until 1964 when it became apparent to the ruling Alliance that it was in danger of registering embarrassingly high losses in most urban areas. Federal and state elections are conducted through the first-past-the-post system in single member territorial constituencies. The costs incurred for conducting an election are borne by the government, although individual candidates or parties are responsible for funding their own campaigns. Voting is not compulsory, but the principle of universal suffrage applies to all Malaysians above the age of 21.

This single member system of election for a seat in the Dewan Rakyat and the state assemblies has been in use since the first federal election in 1955. Since then, elections have been conducted without fail as constitutionally required, and the electoral participation of citizens has consistently been high. Elections are competitive as a number of parties compete in the electoral process and the outcome of an election can result in a change of government. Since it is possible for the Barisan Nasional to be voted out of office, and this has transpired on a few occasions during state-level elections, this has legitimized the coalition leaders' claim over their right to rule.

The conduct of campaigns tends, however, to favor heavily the Barisan Nasional, undermining government claims that elections are fair. The major factors at play during a campaign that help Barisan Nasional retain control of government have been commonly termed the 3Ms—money, media, and machinery. This has involved complaints during electoral campaigns about the ruling coalition's excessive use of funds, abuse of its control of the country's leading newspapers, television, and radio networks, and misuse of the government machinery.[27]

In the case of the media, legislation to control the press has been effective in curbing dissent and criticism of the Barisan Nasional's performance in government. The government's direct control over the electronic media—TV1, TV2, Bernama, the national news agency, and the radio networks—has also been flagrantly abused by the Barisan Nasional to cast the opposition in an unfavorable light. Barisan Nasional component parties have direct and indirect control over the private media—the television and radio networks and the major Malay, Chinese, Tamil, and English newspapers. UMNO, for example, has a majority stake in Utusan Melayu, which publishes the influential Malay newspaper *Utusan Malaysia*. UMNO has indirect control of TV3 and The New Straits Times Press, which publishes major English and Malay newspapers—*The New Straits Times* and *Berita Harian*, respectively. The MCA has a controlling interest in Star Publications, which publishes the popular English tabloid *The Star*, while *The Sun*, another English tabloid, is controlled by a businessman with strong ties to UMNO. Most Tamil newspapers are controlled by leaders of the MIC, while the leading Chinese newspapers, including the *Nanyang Siang Pau* and *The China Press*, are controlled by businesses sympathetic to the MCA and the Barisan Nasional. The *Shin Chew Jit Poh*, the country's best-selling Chinese newspaper, is controlled by a Sarawak-based tycoon who is also a Barisan Nasional senator.[28]

The mainstream press has remained under such tight control that the tradition of investigative reporting is very weak, particularly if it affects the interests of the ruling elite, while reports on political news are generally very cautious, unless they apply to the opposition. Opposition parties persistently complain that given the ownership patterns of the mainstream media they are unable to get their manifestos publicized during election campaigns; and, on those occasions when the press does publish articles on them, their statements are either taken out of context or falsified. Major newspapers are used to carry full page advertisements, usually in color, on the Barisan Nasional's manifestos and accomplishments, and the views of government leaders are given wide coverage.[29]

The Barisan Nasional abuses the government machinery in several ways. Since the timing for the dissolution of parliament is the sole prerogative of the prime minister, provided that the general election is called for within the five-year period, the Barisan Nasional is given an undue advantage. The Election Commission decides the length of the campaign period, and ensuring that this time period is kept very short—normally just over a week—justified on the grounds of maintaining ethnic harmony, has proven of greater benefit to the Barisan Nasional. Since the banning of open rallies following the 1969 general election, campaigns have been restricted to those held indoors. Yet Barisan Nasional leaders give overt campaign speeches at huge rallies while ostensibly making an official address at government-organized functions or when opening public projects. Through their control of the federal and state governments, Barisan Nasional leaders often promise to provide funds for development projects, which are reinforced through public aid during electorate campaigns.

Compared to the opposition parties, the Barisan Nasional's campaign machinery, especially that of UMNO, is efficiently run during elections. The efficacy of the Barisan Nasional's machinery is, however, attributable to its easy access to funds. Since public rallies are banned, door-to-door canvassing, which is labor intensive, is the most common form of campaigning. Most Barisan Nasional campaign workers are remunerated, while the opposition relies heavily on unpaid voluntary help. In spite of the legal requirement to disclose how funds are spent during campaigns, allegations abound that the money spent usually far exceeds the permitted amount.[30]

The electorate in parliamentary constituencies is disproportionately smaller in rural, predominantly Bumiputera, areas compared to Chinese-majority, urban constituencies. For example, although the Malays accounted for just 55.2% of the total electorate in 1990, such a division of the electoral boundaries, which amounts to almost one rural vote for every two urban votes, favors the Barisan Nasional, especially UMNO. This pattern of creation of electoral boundaries is seen as a key factor for the Barisan Nasional's consistent victories in federal-level elections.[31] In the 1960s, Bumiputera-majority constituencies constituted 57% of the total number of parliamentary seats; by the early 1980s, this figure had risen to 65%. The overrepresentation of Sabahan and Sawarakian Bumiputeras has helped enhance Bumiputera dominance in parliament. In 2008, for instance, although only 15% of the population resided in Sabah and Sarawak, the 57 constituencies in these two states constituted 26% of the seats in parliament; more importantly, Bumiputeras in the Borneo states, particularly Sarawak, tend to support the Barisan Nasional. This means that any party in the peninsula that can command the support of most Bumiputeras would be able to control the federal government, and if it cooperated with Bumiputera parties of some influence in Sabah and Sarawak, it would also be able to command a comfortable majority in parliament. UMNO has a strong base in Sabah in Muslim Bumiputera-majority constituencies, while its relationship with PBB, Sarawak's long-standing ruling party, is particularly strong. This situation also means that even if the opposition manages to garner strong electoral support in terms of the total number of votes cast, the number of seats it secures in parliament may not necessarily be very large.

In spite of allegations of extensive gerrymandering and abuse of money, media, and machinery during the campaign period, the actual conduct of elections on polling day has been subject to fewer criticisms. However, the most common allegation made during elections is that funds are used to buy votes, causing the expenditures during campaigns to far exceed the stipulated maximum of 50,000 ringgit for a parliamentary constituency and 30,000 ringgit for a state seat. Although such allegations usually come from the opposition, the Barisan Nasional has on occasion lodged similar complaints against the opposition.

The Barisan Nasional has consistently argued that the need to ensure communal coexistence and sustain rapid economic development justifies such inequities and irregularities in the electoral system. To resolve inequities between communities, the government's main proposition has been to introduce policies within the economy that positively discriminate in favor of the Bumiputeras. Police who target Bumiputeras in need of help have, however, been abused in order to serve the vested interests of UMNO members or the well connected, a further reason for the need for serious restrictions protecting civil liberties.[32] However, such targeting through affirmative action has contributed to serious intra-Bumiputera and intraclass divides, leading to the rise of new wealth and income inequalities. The emergence of new intra-Bumiputera inequalities has had major economic and political significance.

AUTHORITARIANISM, ETHNICITY, AND DEVELOPMENT

Although Barisan Nasional has not denied that it has adopted authoritarian measures in the running of government, it has also maintained that such restrictions are necessary until parity in equity ownership among all ethnic communities is achieved. Redistributive policies, based as they are on ethnic identity, have aided UMNO's capacity to mobilize Bumiputera support and consolidate its position in the Barisan Nasional. For this reason, even though a multiparty system prevails in Malaysia, and the Barisan Nasional comprises about a dozen parties, the political system is dominated by UMNO.[33] Two major features of the political system are the scale and scope of authoritarianism and of Malay hegemony through UMNO.

The enfeeblement of civic culture and the gradual heightening of authoritarianism commenced notably with the banning of local elections in the early 1960s. When state and federal elections results also began to swing in favor of the opposition in the late 1960s, the rules were changed, primarily through amendments to the constitution. It was, for example, prohibited, even in parliament, to question "ethnically sensitive" issues, which included any reference to Malay special rights, non-Malay citizenship, the status of the national language, Islam, and the constitutional provisions pertaining to the sultans. Meanwhile, recognizing the ethnically divided nature of the electorate, an enlarged

Barisan Nasional coalition was formed, ostensibly to share power, although as Mauzy has noted, it was in effect "accommodation on essentially Malay terms."[34] UMNO openly asserts that it can rule alone, but prefers to "share" power in the interests of national unity. Malay hegemony has been justified on the grounds that UMNO represents the interests of the largest ethnic community.[35] And government leaders regularly argue that Barisan Nasional's consociationalism has enabled them to manage and resolve race-related problems.

This suggests that a distinction should be made between cooption and power sharing within the Barisan Nasional.[36] Although Malaysian prime ministers have stressed that power sharing prevails within the ruling coalition (Mahathir, for instance, had said that, "[p]ower sharing in Barisan Nasional means giving our power to the minority groups so they can have a meaningful part to play in all our deliberations and decisions"[37]), this is not entirely true. UMNO coopts major parties into the Barisan Nasional to project a multiracial image, as this has been found to be an effective means of perpetuating its power.

This system of consociationalism diminishes open debate, while the Barisan Nasional component parties seldom speak out in favor of the groups they represent, particularly if this would entail taking UMNO to task over government policies. And in spite of the representation of numerous Barisan Nasional parties in parliament, legislators do not play a meaningful role in drawing up new legislation. This function is left almost entirely to the bureaucracy, dominated by the UMNO-led executive. In view of strict party discipline, Barisan Nasional parliamentarians usually endorse new legislation and policies, customarily with minimal or no protests.

Under UMNO hegemony, policies such as affirmative action were implemented, presumably to equitably redistribute wealth among ethnic communities.[38] Although implementation of affirmative action has appreciably improved the economic position of the Bumiputeras, the policy should also have moved toward rendering inoperative the racist or ethnicized ingredient with respect to allocation of resources for two reasons. Affirmative action has proven to be an indispensable avenue through which UMNO has managed to secure Malay support. Second, UMNO members have exploited resource allocation through affirmative action to develop and consolidate their position in the party and continue to argue for the need for affirmative action-like policies on the grounds that economic differences still exist between communities, in spite of the emergence of an influential Malay middle class.[39]

Since political participation is permitted, which has enabled the emergence of new opposition parties, most studies characterize the Malaysian state as semiauthoritarian,[40] semidemocratic,[41] or quasi-democratic.[42] These qualified terms on the state of authoritarianism in Malaysia suggest that some democratic forms still prevail, but, as noted above, most are simply the minimal conditions necessary for the practice of democracy. Further, as Crouch points out, even the minimal democratic procedures that exist are permitted only if the power of the ruling elite is not undermined and they have been "quickly modified or abolished when elite interests were threatened."[43] This has been true both in the case of amendments to UMNO's constitution and the federal constitution as well as other legislation.

In 1987, for example, when Mahathir's legitimacy to rule was seriously undermined after he narrowly secured the UMNO presidency through questionable means following a factional struggle, government leaders dismissed genuine grievances against key policies by opposition parties and nongovernmental organizations as mere communal agitation. Mahathir employed this argument to justify authoritarian measures to help him stay in power. Using the draconian Internal Security Act (ISA), which allows for indefinite detention without trial, 119 Malaysians were detained in late 1987, most of them accused of having incited racial tension.[44] Subsequently, the already docile press was further intimidated, with the suspension of the publishing licenses of several leading English and Chinese newspapers. When the judiciary posed a threat to the UMNO elite, the lord president and two Supreme Court judges were removed from office under unprecedented and suspicious circumstances.[45] Later, the power vested in the executive arm of the government was increased through constitutional amendments, which further circumscribed the powers of the judiciary and the monarchy.[46] The result of these actions was severe, and the independence of the judiciary has been so fundamentally compromised that it has led to growing skepticism about the capacity of the judicial system to administer justice.

New Middle Class, But Limited Democratization

Modernization theorists argue that developing countries need an authoritarian political system where power is concentrated to ensure rapid economic growth and the creation of conditions that help promote the consolidation of democracy.[47] This strong state would face little resistance from social groups within society and in the political arena, such as trade unions, opposition parties, and NGOs, allowing the government to implement economic policies that would facilitate rapid development. Economic progress would contribute to the rise of a new, economically independent middle class whose tolerance for autocratic rule would diminish. This new middle class, now highly educated, well informed, and self-sufficient economically, would eventually develop a worldview that would compel them to act as the vanguard to dismantle the strong state.

To a certain extent, we can see this process at work in Malaysia. As the class structure between Bumiputeras and non-Bumiputeras was bridged, greater intraethnic Malay problems have emerged. This has been manifested in the continuous splits within UMNO, which have twice led to the formation of new opposition parties in the 1990s by breakaway factions. These splits had a distinct class dimension and could have been expected to bring about greater democratization, as the Bumipiteras who are achieving middle-class status now have more in common with middle-class non-Bumipiteras, creating a serious threat to Malay hegemony. This, however, has not worked out as expected. UMNO's hegemony over the state facilitated the concentration of political and economic power at the top of the party hierarchy, and this contributed to increased friction among leading politicians over access to lucrative state rents. As the ties between capital and politics grew, the rent-seeking activities of politicians led to conflicts within the business class, predominantly among a breed of new well-connected Bumiputera capitalists who had emerged through extensive state patronage. Such rivalries have transpired despite the admission by government leaders that although Bumiputera capitalists have been created through state policies and patronage, genuine and competent indigenous entrepreneurs have failed to emerge in satisfactory numbers.[48] Without much transparency, the abuse of power for vested interests continues to prevail even though the rapidly burgeoning middle class is increasingly concerned over such issues.

In spite of the rapidly changing socioeconomic conditions, such as the growth of a multiethnic middle class, the resentments of less-favored business interests, and growing cultural and lifestyle disparities among Bumiputeras, as well as growing tensions between the authoritarian state and civil society, more democratic measures and institutions have not been introduced. Why has this been the case in Malaysia?

Academics such as Samuel Huntington have ascribed this lack of democratization in Asia, in spite of the emergence of a middle class, to the "cultural factor." In his opinion, while Protestantism (in the European tradition) allowed for compromise and equality, thus making it conducive to democratic transformation, Islam and Confucianism (in the Eastern tradition) were more hierarchical in character, therefore providing obstacles to change.[49] Another culture-based argument posited that "whereas the experience of liberal capitalism helped to nurture an entrepreneurial middle class grounded in a culture of competitive individualism in West Europe, in East Asia the experience of static economic paternalism has produced a middle class grounded in a culture of dependence; these cultural traits in turn produce a middle class constantly anxious about instability and insecurity."[50]

The most routinely offered explanation for the persistence of authoritarian rule is the ethnic factor: the still limited cooperation among middle-class Malaysians, due to the still relatively undiminished ethnic polarization, has inhibited political mobilization. Another argument is that the bulk of the middle class in Malaysia is depoliticized and materialist and therefore hardly reformist.[51]

Analysts who dismissed cultural-based arguments used to analyze the Malaysian political system proffered the contention that given the inability of the opposition to combine forces in a meaningful way, if change leading to greater democratization was to come about, it depended primarily on machinations within UMNO, arising from the deeply divided nature of the party and growing unrest with Mahathir hegemony and his long rule.[52] Democracy was possible only if UMNO became more open and internally democratic, thus forcing the government to be more responsive and accountable.

Another key reason why democratization has not been achieved is because the government has been able to provide for commendable economic growth and has had relative success in eradicating poverty, raising real incomes, and reducing wealth disparities among ethnic communities. This factor had helped to shore up the regime and even legitimize authoritarian rule until the onset of the economic crisis in 1997. However, growing intra-Malay economic disparities appear to have contributed most to emerging calls for political reforms. One major consequence of the government's development agenda, involving also the implementation of affirmative action, was the rise of a middle class that included an independent, dynamic, mainly professional Malay community. This new Malay middle class was reputedly a disgruntled community because they could not break into the elite cohort that was capturing most state rents,[53] created to attain Mahathir's goal of promoting the rise of Malay-owned capital. This Malay middle class eventually became the primary supporters of Keadilan, after it was formed in the late 1990s.

Despite affirmative action, which aspired to eradicate poverty by 1990, when Mahathir retired from public office in 2003, the persistence of this problem remained a serious issue among rural Malays who had long provided staunch support to UMNO. By the mid-1990s, these Malaysians, situated in the Malay heartland of Kelantan, Terengganu, Kedah, Perlis, Pahang, and northern Perak, had begun to question why affirmative action had not helped them. These Malays increasingly saw UMNO not as their "protector"[54] but as having offered nothing more than a series of broken promises. They viewed the government's focus on heavy industries, privatization, and the promotion of big business as policies contributing little to alleviate the plight of the poor, especially those still involved in agriculture, fishing, and cottage industries.

Rural Bumiputeras were also growing anxious over the influence of western-style modernism on the Malaysian, especially Muslim, society. By the mid-1990s, rapid urbanization and modernization led to new social problems, including a rise in divorce rates among Malays, *bohsia* (promiscuous behavior), and *lepak* (loitering in malls), primarily by Malay youths, escalating gangsterism among poor ethnic Indians who had migrated to urban shanty areas, and a burgeoning drug problem among youths, including the abuse of the drug Ecstasy, by young ethnic Chinese. These factors contributed to growing support for the Islamic party PAS, from the early 1990s, as the party offered Islam as the answer to the social malaise enveloping the country.[55] By the late 1990s, feelings of marginality and exclusion were being expressed more by Malays than by non-Bumiputeras, an indication of the emergence of new intraethnic class divisions as a consequence of policies implemented to promote rapid industrialization.

Within the corporate sector, as a result of the rapid rise of a number of big businesses—the supposed new "captains of industry"—where much wealth was concentrated, allegations of unbridled corruption in politics and business were hurled at Mahathir. Following the 1997 currency crisis, when a number of these large enterprises nurtured by the government required state support to fend off bankruptcy, further allegations of favoritism, nepotism, and abuse of power by UMNO arose. By the time Mahathir announced in late 2002 his desire to step down as prime minister the following year, he was ready to acknowledge that his attempts to develop new privately owned Malay conglomerates had failed.[56] There was evidence to support Mahathir's admission that his efforts to promote Malay capital and effectively privatize and industrialize Malaysia were unsuccessful. In 2000, of the top 10 firms quoted on the Malaysian stock exchange, the government had majority ownership of seven.[57] The remaining three firms were Chinese owned.[58] None of these top 10 companies was owned by Malays. No company in the top 10 was involved in the industrial sector, indicating that the government had failed to develop large enterprises with an active participation in manufacturing. Among the top 20 firms, only two were involved in manufacturing: the once-privatized but subsequently renationalized Proton, manufacturer of the Malaysian car, and foreign-owned Rothmans, producer of cigarettes.[59]

Other evidence to substantiate Mahathir's argument that the enterprises his government had scrupulously nurtured were not sustainable was the impact of the 1997 currency crisis on these firms. Among the companies that were reportedly "bailed out" was Renong, a firm controlled by Halim Saad and reputed to represent the rise of Malay capital. Halim's companies had been privy to a number of lucrative privatized projects, including the multibillion ringgit North-South Highway. The loss- and debt-ridden Malaysian Airlines (MAS), the nation's privatized airline, had to be renationalized to rescue it from imminent bankruptcy. MAS was then controlled by the well-connected Tajuddin Ramli who also owned the privatized mobile phone operator Celcom, which was taken over by government-controlled and publicly listed Telekom. The government's acquisition of debt-ridden businesses owned by Mirzan Mahathir, Mahathir's eldest son, was mired in much controversy. Mahathir's deputy, Anwar, had objected to Mirzan's bailout, an issue that reputedly contributed to the split between the two leaders.

On November 1, 2003, Mahathir retired from public office, handing the premiership to his chosen successor, Abdullah Ahmad Badawi. During his more than two-decade−long tenure, the structure of the state had become so extremely personalized that the term Mahathir hegemony was liberally applied in most analyses of Malaysian politics.[60] Immediately after Abdullah took office, he astutely adopted a populist agenda, voicing his desire to liberalize the political system by devolving power. Abdullah had recognized that society was increasingly concerned about the authoritarian and unaccountable nature of the political system under a hegemonic UMNO, evident in particular during the 1999 general election. Abdullah also promised to rein in corruption, which had thrived because of Mahathir's form of selective patronage.

Other key pledges Abdullah made included eradicating poverty by promoting agriculture, a sector in which many rural Malays were involved. Unlike Mahathir who was deeply committed to the development of big business, Abdullah actively promoted small- and medium-scale enterprises (SMEs). Abdullah went so far as to suggest that his government would provide little support to big capitalists. While it appeared that Abdullah was distancing himself from the excesses of the Mahathir administration and some of the latter's controversial and unpopular developmental plans, the new prime minister had, historically, shown little support for his predecessor's entrepreneurial and industrial agenda. Prior to the first general election during Abdullah's tenure, in 2004, the themes of equitable economic development and good governance were publicized as his government's priorities, key issues that had preoccupied the minds of the middle-class and rural Malays, two groups that had supported Keadilan and PAS, respectively, in the previous election in 1999.

Abdullah was clearly aware of the call from society for a new type of politics and had responded accordingly. Abdullah's policy agenda helped the Barisan Nasional retrieve the electoral support it had been losing, although it was also clear that the electorate had expected him to deliver on his pledges. He would, however, fail to deliver on most of them, which would cost him and his party dearly in the next general election.

MALAYSIA IN TRANSITION?

The results of the election of March 8, 2008, were unprecedented for the Barisan Nasional, which registered considerable loss of support.

Although the coalition had secured 90% of the seats in parliament in 2004, its presence there was reduced to 63% in 2008. In the state-level election, for the first time in Malaysian history, the opposition secured control of five states. Apart from Kelantan, opposition parties, in coalition, formed the government in Penang, Selangor, Perak, and Kedah; the former three states being among the most highly developed in the peninsula.

In 2008, Barisan Nasional obtained only 51.2% of the popular vote, compared to 64.4% in 2004. UMNO's presence in parliament fell from 109 to a meager 79 seats, a shock for a party accustomed to regularly holding more than half these seats. UMNO's main Barisan Nasional partners, the MCA and MIC, fared worse. MCA won just 15 seats, a massive drop from 31, and MIC was down to 3 parliamentarians from its previous 9. Barisan Nasional had a majority in the Dewan Rakyat only because it won 55 of the 57 parliamentary seats in the east Malaysian states of Sabah and Sarawak. In the peninsula, Barisan Nasional obtained a mere 49.8% of the total votes cast, meaning that the opposition had more popular support in this part of the country.

Keadilan benefited most from Barisan Nasional's decline. Although Keadilan held only one parliamentary seat going into this election, it emerged unexpectedly victorious in 31 constituencies. PAS secured 23 seats, compared to its seven in 2004, while the DAP won 28 seats, 16 more than before. A review of electoral trends from 1990 will put in perspective the Barisan Nasional's shocking electoral loss.

Between 1990 and 1995, when the Barisan Nasional secured its best electoral victory with 65% of the popular vote, Malay support for it had already begun to fall (Table 8.1). This was in spite of the fact that the economy had grown phenomenally over that five-year period, a factor in the unprecedented non-Malay swing to the coalition in 1995 (Table 8.2). The Barisan Nasional continued to lose Malay support after the *reformasi*, but following Mahathir's departure, the coalition registered in 2004 increased support in all Malay-majority seats, only narrowly failing to regain control of Kelantan, and recouped non-Malay support it had lost in the previous election. In 2008, Barisan Nasional's support in most Malay-majority seats declined, while a large segment of non-Malays swung to the opposition.

The percentage point difference in times of electoral victory and loss in numerous Malay-majority areas has, however, consistently been below 10, suggesting swings in support between UMNO and PAS. The swings against UMNO were registered when it was perceived to have failed to deliver economically. The voting trend suggests other anomalies. Although Barisan Nasional lost Malay support in 2008, Terengganu state did not fall to the opposition as it had in 1999, although another state, Kedah, did for the first time in its history. The results

Table 8.1 Difference in Support for BN in Malay-Majority Parliamentary Constituencies, 1990–2008 (%)

State	1990	1995	Difference	1999	Difference	2004	Difference	2008	Difference
Kedah									
Baling	61.4	55.7	-5.7	48.0	-7.7	53.5	5.5	43.7	-9.8
Sik	59.4	53.6	-5.8	49.0	-4.6	50.5	1.5	49.3	-1.2
Jerlun	59.5	53.9	-5.6	49.0	-4.9	52.9	3.9	53.0	0.1
Padang Terap	58.4	54.4	-4.0	48.0	-6.4	53.9	5.9	49.4	-4.5
Pendang	52.9	51.0	-1.9	46.0	-5.0	49.9	3.9	46.0	-3.9
Yan	57.2	55.7	-1.5	50.0	-5.7				
Kubang Pasu	75.4	74.2	-1.2	65.0	-9.2	67.3	2.3	58.6	-8.7
Kuala Kedah	52.8	52.3	-0.5	49.0	-3.3	58.1	9.1	44.5	-13.6
Pokok Sena	53.8	54.0	0.2	46.0	-8.0	56.9	10.9	44.6	-12.3
Terengganu									
Kemaman	62.9	57.6	-5.3	48.0	-9.6	63.9	15.9	60.3	-3.6
Kuala Nerus	53.6	51.5	-2.1	40.0	-11.5	54.5	14.5	51.3	-3.2
Dungun	54.0	50.5	-3.5	39.0	-11.5	55.1	16.1	54.7	-0.4
Marang	48.2	47.6	-0.6	37.0	-10.6	50.1	13.1	47.9	-2.2
Hulu Terengganu	53.1	52.5	-0.6	43.0	-9.5	59.7	16.7	61.6	1.9
Setiu	55.7	55.5	-0.2	46.0	-9.5	58.5	12.5	57.9	-0.6
Besut	50.4	54.6	4.2	45.0	-9.6	59.7	14.7	61.0	1.3
Kuala Terengganu	45.3	53.5	8.2	35.0	-18.5	51.6	16.6	50.5	-1.1
Kelantan									
Tumpat	33.1	46.1	13.0	35.0	-11.1	48.3	13.3	42.7	-5.6
Pengkalan Chepa	26.1	29.6	3.5	25.0	-4.6	41.1	16.1	36.6	-4.5
Rantau Panjang	38.1	40.4	2.3	36.0	-4.4	48.8	12.8	43.4	-5.4
Bachok	32.8	42.0	9.2	38.0	-4.0	53.5	15.5	47.4	-6.1
Kuala Krai	30.8	42.5	11.7	43.0	0.5	53.4	10.4	44.1	-9.3
Kota Baru	29.3	41.6	12.3	38.0	-3.6	51.9	13.9	39.3	-12.6

Pasir Mas	33.9	44.3	10.4	39.0	−5.3	40.7	1.7	40.7	0.0
Tanah Merah	33.7	46.9	13.2	43.0	−3.9	54.3	11.3	47.6	−6.7
Pasir Puteh	35.0	44.1	9.1	40.0	−4.1	46.2	6.2	46.2	0.0
Machang	32.6	43.4	10.8	40.0	−3.4	50.2	10.2	48.2	−2.0
Peringat	35.3	50.5	15.2	43.0	−7.5	—		—	
Gua Musang	22.7	21.9	−0.8	56.0	34.1	66.1	10.1	59.3	−6.8
Jeli	—	51.1		49.0	−2.1	63.8	14.8	57.4	−6.4
Kubang Kerian	—	33.5		27.0	−6.5	42.4	15.4	37.8	−4.6

— indicates new seats created in the 1995 general election.

Table 8.2 Difference in Support for BN in Non-Malay Parliamentary Constituencies, 1990–2008 (%)

State	Percentage non-Malay electorate in 2008	1990	1995	Difference	1999	Difference	2004	Difference	2008	Difference
Penang										
Tanjong	95.2	29.1	40.7	11.6	45.0	4.3	44.8	-0.2	25.7	-19.1
Bukit Bendera	86.2	36.6	51.8	15.2	50.0	-1.8	61.7	11.7	32.6	-29.1
Bukit Mertajam	81.5	46.7	60.9	14.2	47.0	-13.9	40.2	-6.8	44.2	4.0
Jelutong	80.4	39.2	48.2	9.0	51.0	2.8	58.8	7.8	31.2	-27.6
Bagan	85.0	45.9	48.7	2.8	47.4	-1.3	45.7	-1.7	25.7	-20.0
Bayan Baru	59.6	46.6	54.5	7.9	58.0	3.5	73.6	15.6	37.5	-36.1
Nibong Tebal	56.4	50.7	59.4	8.7	46.6	-12.8	59.5	12.9	45.9	-13.6
Perak										
Ipoh Timur	91.2	40.6	49.4	8.8	52.0	2.6	39.8	-12.2	29.2	-10.6
Ipoh Barat	87.1	—	54.2		54.0	-0.2	49.3	-4.7	34.3	-15.0
Batu Gajah	89.9	37.1	50.5	13.4	47.0	-3.5	41.9	-5.1	27.7	-14.2
Kampar	74.5	48.1	65.6	17.5	59.7	-5.9	62.9	3.2	53.7	-9.2
Beruas	67.9	50.1	65.9	15.8	52.0	-13.9	58.4	6.4	46.9	-11.5
Gopeng	58.5	60.6	71.0	10.4	57.5	-13.5	65.8	8.3	42.9	-22.9
Lumut	53.2	50.9	77.9	27.0	50.7	-27.2	63.4	12.7	50.3	-13.1
Teluk Intan	63.84	51.5	65.5	14.0	54.0	-11.5	55.5	1.5	47.9	-7.6
Johor										
Bakri	56.2	52.5	60.5	8.0	68.0	7.5	74.1	6.1	49.1	-25.0
Kluang	63.7	52.4	70.6	18.2	71.0	0.4	69.8	-1.2	53.6	-16.2
Gelang Patah	66.6	—	72.1		74.0	1.9	81.5	7.5	57.6	-23.9
Segamat	59.4	51.7	68.4	16.7	62.0	-6.4	63.9	1.9	55.2	-8.7
Kuala Lumpur										
Kepong	96.5	29.2	44.2	15.0	47.2	3.0	47.9	0.7	24.8	-23.1
Seputeh	95.2	28.7	43.7	15.0	44.5	0.8	37.6	-6.9	18.5	-19.1

Cheras	90.9	40.0	33.5	−6.5	40.0	6.5	37.2	−2.8	21.8	−15.4
Bukit Bintang	87.0	20.8	41.5	20.7	48.0	6.5	48.0	0	31.9	−16.1
Segambut	64.9	—	65.9		60.0	−5.9	71.6	11.6	40.9	−30.7
Selangor										
Serdang	65.6	45.8	54.3	8.5	53.0	−1.3	59.8	6.8	35.8	−24.0
Klang	66.9	42.0	52.1	10.1	54.6	2.5	63.0	8.4	34.8	−28.2
PJ Selatan	63.2	—	61.3		54.0	−7.3	66.6	12.6	44.5	−22.1
Negeri Sembilan										
Rasah	73.6	51.4	58.1	6.7	51.0	−7.1	55.0	4.0	38.1	−16.9
Seremban	60.9	48.3	62.1	13.8	58.0	−4.1	64.3	6.3	46.8	−17.5
Telok Kemang	63.4	66.6	72.1	5.5	61.0	−11.1	72.7	11.7	46.2	−26.5
Malacca										
Kota Melaka	69.4	35.6	44.0	8.4	42.0	−2.0	50.2	8.2	41.4	−8.8
Pahang										
Bentong	59.4	65.7	73.6	7.9	65.0	−8.6	72.5	7.5	66.6	−5.9
Kedah										
Alor Setar	41.6	54.3	68.6	14.3	68.0	−0.6	67.2	−0.8	50.2	−17.0

— indicates new seats created in the 1995 general election.

suggest UMNO could well regain control of Malay heartland states in the next election if it addresses the economic needs of rural Malays.

There were similar inconsistencies in voting patterns in non-Malay majority seats. Although Barisan Nasional lost much support in two-thirds of these seats between 1995 and 1999, then opposition leader Lim Kit Siang of the DAP and prominent allies registered defeats. Even though the opposition retained its Chinese-stronghold seats in Kuala Lumpur, Barisan Nasional increased its support there. In 2004, Barisan Nasional secured greater support in 22 non-Malay majority constituencies, with a decline in only 10. However, DAP secured two more parliamentary seats and Lim was returned as opposition leader. In 2008, Barisan Nasional recorded a phenomenal double-digit percentage point drop in support in most non-Malay constituencies. There was a reason for these unusual electoral patterns in both non-Malay and Malay-majority constituencies.

The results of the epochal 1999 elections following the *reformasi* reflected an ambivalence among the electorate. Although the urban, particularly non-Malay, electorate supported the demands for political reform made by the *reformasi*, it was also uneasy over the awkward constitution of the opposition coalition. The major opposition parties had then coalesced to form Barisan Alternatif. Lim, who lost in his own constituency, would later admit his decision to take DAP into the Barisan Alternatif had been repudiated by the electorate. Barisan Alternatif subsequently fragmented when DAP left, citing irrevocable differences with PAS over the latter's insistence on propagating an Islamic state.

The subsequent 2004 electoral results reflected a number of pertinent issues. First, the results confirmed that Barisan Alternatif was not seen as a viable alternative to many Malaysians. Second, the results supported the argument that Mahathir's focus on heavy industries and corporate accumulation had steadily alienated rural Malays and contributed to PAS's growing influence in the Malay heartland. Third, they suggested that Barisan Nasional's phenomenal victory was due to problems within the opposition, specifically its inability to articulate a common stand to unify Malaysians. DAP's departure from Barisan Alternatif and PAS's Islamic state ideology had alienated non-Muslims and hindered Keadilan's capacity to secure victories in non-Malay majority constituencies. Prominent Keadilan leaders would later publicly acknowledge that it was PAS's brand of theocratic politics that had stymied Barisan Alternatif.

While PAS remained UMNO's primary opposition, electoral trends between 1990 and 2004 suggest that it was not the Islamic party's religious stance that posed a threat to Barisan Nasional. PAS has little national influence, with limited capacity to win seats outside the Malay heartland. After its victories in 1990 and 1999, PAS had become aware that it fared well only when it contested elections in a coalition.

Although PAS has a strong core base comprising about 40% of the Malay heartland electorate, it recognized the need to modify its discourse if it was not to be viewed merely as a party to support in protest of Barisan Nasional. PAS subsequently began emphasizing the need for a welfare state.

Among politicians, it was Anwar who best responded to transitions in society. His 2008 campaign had two key rallying points. He would institute a genuine form of multiethnic governance, without Malay hegemony, and his party would dispense with affirmative action along racial lines. Although affirmative action had reduced interethnic income and wealth disparities, Anwar was aware that its long-term implementation had dissatisfied many Malaysians. Poor Indians had manifested their anger over their continued marginalization in a mass demonstration, while the Chinese had been particularly critical of affirmative action after 1990 when the policy was sustained indefinitely, even though Barisan Nasional had promised in 1970 that it would practice positive discrimination for only the next 20 years. Rural Malays were upset that the policy had contributed to huge intraethnic income and wealth disparities.

In response to calls for a new type of politics, Abdullah had mounted an effective campaign in 2004, advocating an open and inclusive form of governance that would promote the well-being of all Malaysians. By 2008, however, UMNO had shown that it had little interest to change its brand of highly racialized politics. Although Abdullah had introduced economic policies in 2004 to advance the rural Malays, there was little evidence of adequate support for their cottage and agricultural industries. This was attributed to the bureaucracy's poor delivery mechanism, a problem significant enough to warrant discussion of institutional reforms required within the civil service. And corruption continued to fester, with Abdullah patently reluctant to act decisively against errant but influential politicians. Inevitably, the huge swing against the Barisan Nasional was seen as Malaysians stood cohesively in opposition to Abdullah for failing to deliver on his pledges.

CONCLUSIONS: NATIONAL IDENTITY, RACE, AND IMPENDING POLITICAL CHANGE

The unexpected rise of multiracial Keadilan in 2008 (it secured the most number of seats among opposition parties) suggests the need for all parties to seriously consider the concept of *Bangsa Malaysia*, a Malaysian nation that transcends ethnic identity. The concept of *Bangsa Malaysia* was conceived by Mahathir in 1990, probably as mere rhetoric, but it captured the imagination of Malaysians. National identity appears important, as a recent poll indicates, although experiences of exclusion, discrimination, and marginality shape how it is understood by Malaysians. In spite of their public endorsement of *Bangsa Malaysia*, past and present UMNO presidents have had to contend with repeated calls from within the party for *ketuanan Melayu* (Malay supremacy).

What further complicates the idea of a *Bangsa Malaysia* for UMNO is that it recognizes the serious need to redress its own policies that have exacerbated spatial imbalances, between highly developed urban areas and the underdeveloped Malay heartland. The factors contributing to such inequities in the Malay heartland include the people's weak asset base, low income and employment security, and the region's poor infrastructure as well as limited access to the national and global economy. Since politics in the Malay heartland has persistently been ethnically based and because the region remains one of Malaysia's poorest, it is likely that UMNO will continue to insist on a targeted form of affirmative action, rather than consider alternative policies for lessening inequality. It is plausible that UMNO believes that the propagation of race-based politics or policies to resolve these spatial and class cleavages remains the best strategy to mobilize rural Malay support and reinforce its legitimacy as a Malay-based party. Racializing Malay poverty would, moreover, allow influential UMNO members continued access to government concessions. This will only serve to foreclose other forms of political identification, such as *ketuanan rakyat* (people supremacy) that the opposition is trying to promote. But Barisan Nasional also has to contend with explicit calls for nonethnic and nonreligious-based politics from an increasingly vocal urban middle class. The non-Malay poor, notably the well-dispersed Indians, face the same problems that bedevil underprivileged rural Malays, while income and wealth inequalities in urban areas have evolved differently. All this suggests the need for universal-type policies rather than those that target specific communities.

Members of the Barisan Nasional−led national government and the state governments under the opposition are aware that how their form of governance unfolds is under scrutiny, and that the coalition that appears less racially oriented would probably secure ascendancy in the next election. Opposition parties have addressed this by creating Pakatan Rakyat, a tripartite coalition with all parties standing equal. But a crucial fact haunts Pakatan Rakyat. The DAP, which contested as a single party, performed extremely well in non-Malay majority constituencies, a result it had expected but not secured in 1999 when in the Barisan Alternatif. The DAP's participation in Pakatan Rakyat has yet to be endorsed by the electorate, and unless the coalition members transcend their ideological differences, they could well lose the electoral gains that have unexpectedly led them to power. The dual-type society that has now emerged in the peninsula, in multiracial urban areas and in the rural Malay heartland, though numerous class and other cleavages exist within both spatial areas, poses a complex challenge to Pakatan Rakyat, which has to navigate the difficult terrain of understanding cultural and national identity before articulating a discourse of politics and promulgating policies that all groups would welcome.

In spite of its poor showing, UMNO has shown no move toward reforming Barisan Nasional to allow its partners meaningful participation in policy planning and decision making. The MCA and MIC, realizing their growing irrelevance following their dismal electoral showing, have become overtly, and unconventionally, critical of government plans and of UMNO. There also appears to be little willingness on UMNO's part to accommodate the demands by Barisan Nasional component parties from Sabah for larger representation in the executive and for greater autonomy over royalties from its mineral resources, particularly oil and gas, which are desperately required to alleviate poverty in this state.

What is clear from the recent electoral trends is that Malaysian society has sent a clear message to all parties about its desire for greater democratization and for politicians to dispense with race-based politics. The electorate's younger cohort has been particularly vocal about a more participatory form of politics. These two points have been acknowledged by all non-Malay parties in the Barisan Nasional and the opposition. Although UMNO remains reluctant to change and PAS has been reticent about reviewing its Islamic state goal, and both these parties need to consider carefully their respective positions, as this would have a bearing on their capacity in order to retain the support of their coalition partners.

Government policies that bear centrally on nation building and equitable distribution of wealth also have to be reevaluated, as they have failed to promote social cohesion. The opposition, with its control of five state governments, now has an opportunity to provide alternative policies, although its capacity to conceive viable inclusive policies remains under question due to the ideological differences of the Pakatan Rakyat members.

Malaysian political history suggests the key factor that has contributed to racial tensions is the politics of ethnicity propagated by politicians. This history further suggests that democratic institutions can help promote ethnic harmony as well as curb forms of political mobilization that exclude communities, especially minorities, from mainstream society. A truly consociational system espouses moderation as well as accommodates difference and institutionalizes a government led by a coalition of parties representing different interest groups that promotes dialogue and encourages politicians to seek compromises that will eventually benefit all communities. Authoritarianism in multiethnic developing Malaysia is not necessary because of inherent inequalities in the economy. While economic inequities between ethnic groups can contribute to conflict, a government need not curb civil liberties until equality in wealth distribution is achieved. Indeed, doing so may serve as a justification to perpetuate an authoritarian and unaccountable form of governance.

CHAPTER 9

Political Parties and Democracy in South Korea

Hoon Jaung

INTRODUCTION

Throughout the spring and summer in 2008, tens of thousands of protesters filled the Seoul City Hall Square, once a shrine of democratic movement during the 1987 transition in Korea. Twenty-one years earlier, half a million protesters had packed the City Hall Square demanding free and fair elections, which eventually led to the end of the authoritarian regime in one of East Asia's economic miracle countries. This time around, protesters called for more accountability of the newly elected president, Lee Myung-Bak, on the issue of lifting the ban on imported beef from the United States, which had an allegedly high risk of BSE (bovine spongiform encephalopathy). Protesters were more diverse than those in 1987, comprising not just young activists but also housewives, office workers, and teenage students.

On the one hand, the mass protests in 2008 suggested the vibrant base of democracy, manifesting civic engagement and the participatory impulse of the public. On the other hand, they testified to the weaknesses of political parties, which are supposed to translate the public's demand to government and legitimize governmental decisions to the public. Not surprisingly, angry protesters did not allow National Assembly members of the Democratic Party, the main opposition party, to join the protests at Seoul Square by angry protesters.

The beef import protests raised several questions about the roles, structures, and limits of party politics and its place in South Korean democracy. To what extent have political parties enhanced their capacity to aggregate the public's demands over the past two decades? Does the electorate show sufficient trust in political parties as crucial mediating links between the government and the public? Do parties sustain proper roles in governmental policy-making process? Are parties cohesive enough to serve as reliable and stable institutions in terms of organizations and party programs?

By addressing questions like these, this chapter will explore both the strengths and weaknesses of political parties in South Korean democracy. More specifically, I will demonstrate that South Korean democracy has gradually moved away from majoritarian to consensual democracy with increasingly greater emphasis on representativeness than on governability. I examine how party politics contributes to South Korea's modification of majoritarian democracy with the evolving institutional and political infrastructure of political parties. I investigate such changes at three levels: the party in the electorate, the party as organization, and the party in government. By doing so, I will evaluate the roles and contributions of party politics on the South Korean road to a stable, consolidated democracy. After a brief summary of the early years of party development, the chapter will concentrate on the evolution of parties and democracy over the past two decades, from 1987 to 2008.

BETWEEN REPRESENTATIVENESS AND GOVERNABILITY: THE SOUTH KOREAN DEMOCRATIC EXPERIMENT

Just as politicians and the public pursue extremely different goals in democratic governance, so too there has been continuous scholarly debate to delimit crucial dimensions of democracy. Robert Dahl provided arguably the most seminal characterization of democratic regimes, focusing on the two pillars of inclusion and contestation.[1] Then, Arend Lijphart and others offered an influential analysis classifying 36 countries along the dimension between consensual and majoritarian democracy.[2] Whereas a consensual democracy emphasizes fair and proportionate representation, a majoritarian model leans toward providing governing effectiveness via institutional design.

Influential studies on the third wave of democracy have followed the lines of Dahl and Lijphart. For instance, Diamond posited representativeness and governability as the two conflicting goals of new democracies as well as established democracies.[3] Linz and Stepan postulated five arenas of consolidated democracy along the representativeness and governability spectrum in their sweeping discussion of democratic consolidation.[4] In this vein, this chapter will use representativeness and governability as the main criteria in evaluating the evolution of party politics and changing nature of South Korean democracy. Representativeness means the democratic responsiveness of representative institutions to civil demands. On this dimension, party politics is evaluated by how exactly social demands and conflicts are reflected in the party system. Governability involves stability and coherence for elected government through "sufficient concentration and autonomy of power to choose and implement policies."[5] On the governability dimension, party politics is assessed by the extent to which it provides stability and coherence necessary for managing government effectively. In general terms, it has been often observed that there is a tradeoff between governability and representativeness. The discussion of the South Korean case will reveal a new democracy's search for a fine-tuning between governability and representativeness.

When South Korea joined the third wave of democratization in 1987, there arose a strong expectation about the development of party politics and its contribution to democratic consolidation. For more than two decades of authoritarian rule (1963–1987), political parties suffered from diverse symptoms of underdevelopment. As the authoritarian regime took the form of personal rule rather than military-based or institution-based rule, political parties were largely feeble and ineffective in terms of social rooting, institutional stability, and policy-making capacity. The governing Democratic Republican Party, the longest surviving party in South Korean political history (1963–1980), was largely marginalized within the regime as the authoritarian regime was highly centralized around the personal leadership of Park Chung Hee (1963–1979) and Chun Doo Hwan (1980–1988), the protégé of Park. All that was expected from the DRP (and its successor Democratic Justice Party, 1980–1987) and opposition parties was to provide the facade of electoral legitimacy. As such, political parties had long suffered from incompetence, weak relevance, and lack of autonomy, which were crucial for vibrant party organizations.

The democratic transition in 1987 was largely expected to provide a watershed opportunity for party development as electoral democracy was fully recovered from its dark past. Yet, party development in democratic South Korea has been mixed. On the one hand, political parties expanded social rooting by means of addressing the regional cleavage and enhancing their relevance as the central organizer of electoral competition. On the other hand, as successor parties from the authoritarian era dominated the stage of party politics, some old symptoms persisted. Party leadership based on personal charisma obstructed institutionalization of party organizations, which led to the rise of a fluid party system. With the ups and downs of party leaders, political parties had to go through mergers, splits, and dissolutions from time to time. For instance, Kim Dae-Jung, the Nobel Peace Prize-winning democratization movement leader, has established and then dissolved political parties more than four times since 1987.

Despite the old problems, South Korean political parties have increased stability and consistency in terms of structuring electoral competition, providing electoral legitimacy and offering channels of political expression and aggregation. This process began when South Korea joined the third wave of democratization in 1987 and its institutional choices largely followed the majoritarian model of democracy with a strong emphasis on governing effectiveness over responsiveness of political institutions. The electoral system was basically designed to follow plurality rules in order to sustain governing efficiency while obstructing the proliferation of the number of parties. Presidential election was characterized by simple plurality without any further qualifications such as holding runoff elections. Most parliamentary members were to be elected by simple plurality rule in single-member districts, while a small portion of them would be elected by voting for party lists.[6] As a result, the effective number of parties was limited to about three in the transition election in 1988 and the following elections. Also, a unitary, not federal, system of government was sustained with a high degree of centralization between the central government and regional governments. The National Assembly was unicameral and the executive branch was given many institutional advantages over the legislative body.

Kim and Lijphart's study found that the South Korean democratic system was strongly tilted toward a majoritarian model after the democratic transition. Their analysis of the nation's eight dimensions of the majoritarian-consensual model revealed that South Korea was inclined to a strong majoritarian democracy. Only New Zealand and Britain showed a greater inclination toward majoritarian democracy than South Korea among 25 democracies over the period 1945–1996.[7]

There were two main reasons for the choice of a strong majoritarian model. First, a remarkable continuity from the authoritarian regime was responsible for this inclination. As South Korea moved along the path of compromised democratization, without a violent and outright toppling of the old authoritarian regime, there were significant continuities from the past.[8] Political institutions in authoritarian South Korea possessed several traits of the majoritarian model, although their functions were far short of what was required for democratic representation. The compromised democratization following authoritarian rule sustained a high concentration of power for the government by majoritarian institutions in democratic South Korea.

The other reason for the majoritarian inclination had to do with the relatively closed process of transition negotiations in 1987. While there were massive uprisings by protesters until June 1987, the actual transition negotiations thereafter were dominated by political elites from both the old regime and the democratization movement.[9] Labor leaders and most civic movement activists were largely excluded from the negotiation process. As the extant political elites dominated the transition negotiation, they were more interested in sustaining the pace of transition than in enhancing responsiveness of political institutions to various social forces.

However, the initial choice of a majoritarian model of democracy was soon confronted with mounting pressure for modifications, if not a shift to a more consensual model. As South Korean democracy has struggled toward a stable and consolidated democracy, demands for more responsiveness of political institutions have grown on several fronts. Most of all, a low level of inclusiveness frustrated various political minorities. As successors to the old regime and the democratization movement forces dominated political competition, with the help of majoritarian institutions, it has left various forces, most importantly labor, unrepresented in the party system. Those who participated in the transition negotiations established a cartel party system in which successor parties both to the old regime elites and to old opposition parties dominated the party system and did not permit newly emergent forces to join.[10] Obstructed by institutional barriers in the representative system, the labor movement could neither establish its own party nor receive representation in the party system until 2004. For instance, the Campaign Law, requiring each political party to sustain local chapters in more than one-third of all districts, put serious constraints on minor parties in terms of organizational and personnel resources.

In addition, both political reform activists and many experts called for movement toward consensual democracy, pointing out the problems with the initial choice. Citing the significant size of the nation and the not-so-simple structure of social cleavages, as well as the very low level of civic trust in representative institutions, they argued for enhancing the responsiveness of political institutions to various social forces and needs.[11]

ENHANCING REPRESENTATIVENESS IN THE PARTY SYSTEM: MODIFYING INITIAL CHOICES

Faced with mounting pressure to modify the majoritarian system, party politicians began to introduce changes to the initial institutional choices. Each new president introduced some "reforms" to political finance, party organizations, and electoral campaigning in the early phase of his tenure. Yet, such reforms were pursued in a gradual and piecemeal manner. A major breakthrough in political reforms came in 2002. The end of the presidential tenure of Kim Dae-Jung spelled the conclusion of the 1987 system, which was established by institutional choices during the 1987 democratic transition. As the democratization leaders, Kim Dae-Jung and Kim Young Sam, retired from politics, politicians had to search for new rules of the game among themselves. And these searches had to be done in the context of accommodating social demands to address the problems within the strong majoritarian system. As a result, there came a series of reforms in the field of political finances, party organizations, nomination processes, and election campaigns from 2002 to 2004,[12] with the purpose of enhancing the responsiveness of political institutions. The sections that follow examine three such democratizing reforms more closely: decentralizing the nomination process, modifying the mixed member electoral system, and easing entry barriers for minor parties.

Decentralizing the Nomination Process

The first reform effort was to decentralize the party nomination process in order to enhance the involvement of party members and supporters. Even after the democratic transition in 1987, South Korean parties sustained a highly centralized structure in most arenas of party organizations and functions. Following the tradition of personalized dominance and weak institutionalization,[13] party leaders continued to dominate candidate nomination, political finance, and the administration of party organizations. For instance, the process of presidential candidate nomination was not more than self-nomination by predominant party leaders like Kim Young Sam and Kim Dae-Jung, the leaders of the democratization movement. They particularly chose delegates who had no choice but to show support for party leaders at the nomination convention. Party leaders also dominated the process of parliamentary candidate nomination. As party leaders sustained enthusiastic support and loyalty from their regional home base, most candidates for parliamentary seats were highly dependent on regional party leaders. Since their endorsement virtually guaranteed electoral success in the regional home base, party leaders practically monopolized the nomination process no matter what rules the party had. In this sense, the party in the electorate did not represent a democratic linkage between party organizations and supporters. The linkage was seriously distorted by charismatic party leaders who relied on personal rule and subordination.

In early 2002, there came a sea change in the party nomination process. The change began within the governing New Millennium Democratic Party (NMDP), over which President Kim Dae-Jung had personally ruled since its establishment. In an effort to address voters' demands for party decentralization and to cope with the lack of a prominent successor to Kim Dae-Jung, the NMDP adopted the U.S.-type primary system to nominate its presidential candidate for the coming election in December 2002. The Grand National Party (GNP), the main opposition party, followed suit. The new primary system not only guaranteed participation of party members and nonmember supporters in the nomination process, but it also ensured fair representation by gender, age, and region in selecting delegates. Specifically, the nomination rule of NMDP allowed nonmember voters to elect half of the delegates (35,000), while party members elected 30% (21,000) of the delegates. The remaining 20% were selected by party elites like parliamentary members. Also the new rules attempted to enhance representativeness in delegate composition, requiring that female delegates should comprise at least 30% and delegates under 40 should make up at least 30% of the whole.[14]

The first provision of the new nominating rules specified retirement rules for party leaders. As the constitution allowed a single five-year term for president, Kim Dae-Jung could not seek reelection at the end of his tenure in February 2003.[15] Faced with the retirement of Kim Dae-Jung, the NMDP had to rejuvenate itself. The party chose to respond to social demands to open the nomination process rather than to stick to the old system. In this sense, potential successors to Kim Dae-Jung welcomed and cooperated closely with reform groups within the party.

Another source of change was a party reform coalition comprising political reform activists and party studies experts. U.S.-trained academics became as frustrated by the personalized predominance of party leaders as did the disgruntled voters. They provided ideational support for party reform efforts, sustaining close cooperation with reform activists such as People's Solidarity for Participatory Democracy (PSPD) and other NGOs. Together with supporters' desire to participate in party activities, the party reform coalition exerted pressure on parties to adopt U.S.-type primaries rather than the European-type member-centered nomination process.

The new nomination system was fairly successful in enhancing participation and responsiveness. Most of all, it drew a dramatic rise in participation for the nominating primaries. In a stark contrast to lukewarm commitment to parties in the past, about 1.8 million voters participated in NMDP's nomination process to select 35,000 delegates (nonmember delegates). Sixteen regional primaries of the NMDP attracted vigorous attention and participation across the nation throughout March–April 2002. Thus the nomination process shifted from an all but certain self-nomination of party leaders to open and passionate competition for supporters' choices among candidates.

The leading candidate in the NMDP primaries, Roh Moo Hyun, even saw the abrupt rise of a voluntary support organization for himself, NOSAMO,[16] and a grassroots movement to raise campaign money over the course of primaries. Given the long history of Korean parties as top-down mobilizing organizations, such voluntary movement was no less than a major breakthrough in party development. Eventually, Roh Moo Hyun won the general election in December, demonstrating the impact of party reform on electoral competitiveness.[17]

In addition, nomination reform helped parties to improve moderately, if not significantly, their ideological representation of supporters.

For instance, NMDP has improved its congruence with supporters on policy positions following the nomination reform in 2002.[18] The policy distance on the 10-point scale has slightly narrowed from 1.23 in 2000 to 1.15 in 2004 between NMDP supporters and NMDP parliamentary members. In contrast, the GNP did not narrow such a gap with its lukewarm reform in the nomination process.[19] The distance was rather enlarged from 1.11 in 2000 to 1.39 in 2004 between conservative voters and the MPs of GNP.[20]

Overall, however, decentralizing the party nomination process has achieved remarkable progress in terms of the "party in the electorate." In addition to the astonishing rise of participation by supporters in the nomination process, both the NMDP and the GNP improved the representativeness of party delegates by enhancing representation of female and young delegates to a remarkable extent. And the NMDP has moderately enhanced ideological representation of its supporters.

Modification of Mixed Member Electoral System

Another significant change involved a crucial modification of the electoral system. After reforms in party law, political finance law, and campaign law in 2004, South Korean political parties agreed to introduce a major modification in the electoral system. Since the 1987 transition, the electoral system had been a variant of the mixed electoral system, designed to produce a majoritarian outcome. The list tier and the nominal tier were linked, since share of the votes in the nominal tier determined the list seat allocation. And the allocation method gave a huge bonus to the largest party for the purpose of obtaining a majority.[21] For instance, the party that collected the most district seats was entitled to have the first half of the list seats, even if the party's share of district seats was less than half of the whole.

The change in 2004 was to adopt a more common form of mixed member electoral system. Like Japan, Mexico, Russia, and Thailand, the new South Korean election system now gave voters separate ballots for list and nominal tiers and seat allocation, and voting in the two tiers was no longer linked (Table 9.1).[22] By joining this global trend, both political elites and voters expected that the new electoral system would enhance the responsiveness of the party system. Specifically, the new mixed member electoral system (MMES) was expected to bring a more proportional translation of electorates' votes into parliamentary seats and thereby to provide a better chance for small parties to have fair representation.

Like other political reforms, the major driving force came from a coalition of NGO activists, academics, and political minorities such as labor. Along with this reform coalition, two unusual actors played key roles in bringing about the electoral reform. One was the Constitutional

Table 9.1 Classification of Mixed Member Electoral Systems

Seat linkage		Vote linkage	
No	Yes	No	Yes
Japan	Bolivia	Argentina	Hungary
Lithuania	Germany	Georgia	Italy
Macedonia	New Zealand	Thailand	
Mexico	Venezuela	Ukraine	
Russian Federation			

Source: Matthew Shugart and Martin Wattenberg, Mixed Member Electoral Systems: The Best of Both Worlds? (Oxford: Oxford University Press, 2002), 15.

Court, which triggered the electoral reform debate by a significant decision in 2001. When the Democratic Labor Party and electoral reform activists filed a case on the constitutionality of the old electoral system, the Constitutional Court found the old electoral system to be partially unconstitutional.[23] The ruling stated that it was unconstitutional to distribute list seats based on district voting without separate ballots for party list.[24] It also ruled that it was improper for a voter not to have separate ballots for list and district voting, given the possibility of split preference of voters for list and nominal tiers.

The Constitutional Court ruling in 2001 did not bring about immediate change in the electoral system due to the politics of delay by parliamentary members who did not welcome an abrupt change of electoral system for fear of unpredictability. It was the speaker of the National Assembly, Park Kwan Yong, who provided issue entrepreneurship for electoral reform. As the official Political Reform Committee in the National Assembly stalled due to partisan conflict, he organized a special Commission for Political Reform in late 2003. Since this commission was composed of academics, political reform activists, and journalists, it could offer recommendations to the National Assembly not plagued by partisanship and political calculation. Given mounting pressure from voters, the National Assembly passed the new Election Law, Party Law, and Political Finance Law following the recommendations in March 2004, just one month before the 2004 parliamentary election.

The new electoral system represented not a drastic break with the past but a significant modification of the electoral system. Now voters were given two separate ballots for list tier and nominal tier (with single member district voting for the latter). List seat allocation was to be based on each party's share of list voting. Second, the number of list seats was moderately increased from 46 to 56.[25] As a result, the share of list seats was slightly enhanced from 16.8% to 18.7%. Third, the threshold for list seat allocation was reduced from 5% to 3% of the votes (Table 9.2).

Table 9.2 The Mixed Member Electoral System in South Korea, Japan, and Taiwan

	District seats	District system	List seats	Total seats
South Korea (before 2004)	227	Plurality	46	273
South Korea (after 2004)	243	Plurality	56	299
Japan (1994)	300	Plurality	180	480
Taiwan (2005)	73	Plurality	34	113[1]

[1] Includes six additional seats reserved for aboriginal minorities.
Source: Benjamin Reilly, "Electoral Systems and Party System in East Asia," *Journal of East Asian Studies* 7 (2007): 194.

The first major goal of the new electoral system was to enhance the proportionality of the representative institutions by increasing the congruence of the voters' choice and their representation at the party system. Every electoral system strikes its own balance between governing efficiency (plurality) and representativeness (PR). While the former emphasizes efficiency by constraining the number of parties, the latter favors proportionate representation rather than efficiency. However, the proportionality of the party system has not improved dramatically after the electoral reform in 2004. While the proportionality index has hovered between 85 and 90 since the democratic transition,[26] it has remained at a similar level after the 2004 reform. The index figure was 87.9 in 2004 and 85 in 2008 (Table 9.3).

The second goal of the new MMES was to provide a better chance for political minorities, such as labor, to have representation in the party system. Given the substantive size of organized and unorganized workers,[27] the nonexistence of a labor party meant that a significant social force did not have political representation in the party system.

Table 9.3 The Proportionality Index of South Korean Election and Party System

1973	72.1
1978	69.3
1981	78.2
1985	81.7
1988	88.0
1992	85.5
1996	90.1
2000	90.2
Average between 1988 and 2000	88.5
2004	87.9
2008	85.0

Source: Hoon Jaung, "Honhaphyung Seongeojedoeui Jongchijok Hyokwa" ["Effects of the New Mixed Electoral System"], *Korean Political Science Review* 40 (2006): 191–213 (in Korean).

The new system attempted to facilitate minorities' representation by two main changes. On the one hand, since each voter has two separate ballots for list and district voting, minority parties like the Democratic Labor Party were expected to perform better than before. Specifically, it has been widely reported that voters are likely to support established big parties rather than minor parties for the sake of effectiveness in the plurality system.[28] When voters have two different ballots, support for minor parties is expected to increase through split-ticket voting.[29] For instance, while the Democratic Labor Party collected only 3.9% of the vote in the presidential election, the plurality election garnered 11.8% of the list vote in the 2002 local elections.[30]

In fact, the new MMES brought about a remarkable rise of the Democratic Labor Party in the 2004 parliamentary election. For the first time in democratic history, the Democratic Labor Party obtained representation in the National Assembly, as 10 of its candidates were elected. Whereas only two candidates won in district elections, eight candidates were elected through party lists. In a stark contrast to its unimpressive performances in district voting, the Democratic Labor Party obtained 13% of the vote in list voting. The phenomenal rise of the Democratic Labor Party was clearly linked to growing split-ticket voting among voters. One postelection survey revealed that 20% of the whole electorate split their ballots between district and party-list voting. In particular, 40% of these split voters supported the Democratic Labor Party in list voting while supporting candidates either of the GNP or of Uri Party, the two main parties, in district voting.[31]

The presence of 10 Democratic Labor Party members in the National Assembly signaled a notable change going beyond the entrance of a small party. Given its strong party discipline, the Democratic Labor Party played a pivotal role between the conservative GNP and the liberal Uri Party as neither of them controlled a majority of the 17th National Assembly (2004–2008).[32] Progressive legislation often depended on the Democratic Labor Party's 10 votes for passage. The party succeeded, with the help of the Uri Party, in passing the Citizen Recall Act and Taxation on Global Hedge Fund Act in 2006, two bills that had been on its agenda for a long time. The party system has improved its ideological representativeness to a remarkable extent with the rise of the Democratic Labor Party.

Easing Entry Barriers for Minor Parties

Whereas the extant political institutions discouraged the proliferation of political parties to sustain governing efficiency, the new system eased to a considerable extent the entry barrier for minor parties for the sake of representativeness of party system. First, as noted, the new electoral system lowered the electoral threshold for list seat allocation from 5% to 3% of the vote. As discussed above, the Democratic Labor Party has broken the mold due to the new MMES. Another small party beneficiary of the new electoral law was the Pro-Park Coalition, a splinter party from the GNP,[33] which obtained 13% of votes in the list tier, enabling it to get eight seats from the list tier. The Party for Advanced Korea (PAK), a newly emergent small party, collected two list seats with its 3.8% of the vote, whereas under the old system, it would not have had a single list seat (Table 9.4).

A new Political Party Law also contributed to easing the entry barrier for minor parties. Hitherto the Political Party Law had maintained detailed regulations with regard to party organizations, party finances, and policy activities. The 2004 reform did not dramatically diminish overall regulatory scope but lowered the organizational requirements for political parties. Initially, the main goal of such change was to reduce demand for political finance by downsizing party organizations. Changes in organizational requirements included: (1) prohibiting any party organization from establishing district offices, (2) reducing the minimum organizational requirement for parties from 26 district offices to 5 regional offices, and (3) limiting the number of paid staff members for national headquarter offices up to 100 and for regional offices up to 5. Downsizing all party organizations helped minor parties compete against established parties, as fewer financial and human resources were now required.

Another boost to minor party participation came from changes introduced by the Campaign Activity Law in 2004, which encouraged less capital-intensive campaigning methods. Specifically, the new Campaign Activity Law prohibited outdoor mass rallies upon which political parties used to spend huge amounts of money, mobilizing supporters by gifts and free transportation. Now the Campaign Activity Law provided financial and technical assistance for candidates to focus on Web-based campaigning and to have televised debates. Like the new Party Law, such changes were initially designed for other purposes, such as to restrain lavish campaign spending among political parties. Yet it also helped minor parties with low treasuries compete more effectively.

In sum, the 2002–2004 political reforms enhanced the representativeness of political parties in various ways. At the "party in the electorate" level, reforms secured active participation among supporters in

Table 9.4 Minor Parties in the 2008 Election

	Share of list voting (%)	Number of list seats	Number of district seats	Total number of seats
Pro-Park coalition	13	8	6	14
Labor Party	5.6	3	2	5
Party for Advanced Korea	3.8	2	1	3

Source: Data drawn from National Election Commission Database.

the party nomination process. At the level of "party as organization," a fairer representation was achieved with regard to delegate composition in the nomination process. And at the "party in government" level, the new electoral system provided enhanced representativeness by allowing minor parties to be present in the National Assembly.

SUSTAINING GOVERNABILITY IN A DEMOCRATIZING PARTY SYSTEM

As there is often a tradeoff between representativeness and governability, a critical concern for both political elites and the voters has been how and to what extent reforms for enhanced representativeness would affect governability. In fact, political reforms in South Korea have not seriously jeopardized governing efficiency while constraining proliferation and fractionalization in the party system. However, some changes in intraparty politics have led to new problems in the party-government nexus. Here we examine two concerns: (1) the number of parties and the problem of divided government and (2) the relationship between parties and government.

The Number of Parties and Divided Government

The first dimension of governability has to do with the effective number of parties. Conventional scholarly wisdom has it that the greater the number of parties, the less the governing efficiency of the political system.[34] Majoritarian political systems across the globe discourage proliferation of political parties by various institutional means to sustain governing efficiency.[35] Thus when South Korea modified the electoral system to enhance representativeness, its impact on the number of parties was one of great concern from a practical as well as academic perspective.

In fact, the new MMES has not increased the number of parties dramatically nor hampered governability to a great extent. As Table 9.5 shows, the number of effective parties was around three before the 2004 electoral reform.[36] This figure did not change remarkably after the electoral reform, as the effective number of parties was 2.0 in 2004 and 2.98 in the 2008 parliamentary elections.

Since the electoral reform has not led to a remarkable rise in the number of parties, governing efficiency was largely preserved under the MMES. Yet, if we view the South Korean case from a comparative perspective, the prospect for governing efficiency is neither disastrous nor promising. On the one hand, comparative studies of presidential systems have found that most stable presidential democracies tend to have a two-party system. For instance, the average effective number of parties was 1.9 in the United States, 2.1 in Colombia, and 2.2 in Costa

Table 9.5 Party Systems in South Korea and Presidential Democracies

Country	Elections	Mean number of effective parties	Mean share of legislative seats of president's party (%)
United States	1968–1986	1.90	45.8
Colombia	1974–1986	2.09	52.2
Costa Rica	1974–1986	2.45	50.9
South Korea	1988–2000	2.97	46.2
South Korea	2004–2008	2.49	53.5
		(2.0 in 2004)	
		(2.98 in 2008)	

Sources: Scott Mainwaring, "Presidentialism, Multipartism, and Democracy: The Difficult Combination," *Comparative Political Studies* 26 (1993): 213; and Korean National Election Commission, Election Data.

Rica over the 1960s to 1980s.[37] On the other hand, several frail presidential systems in Latin America have multiparty systems. Due to various reasons such as list voting, complex social cleavages, and strong regionalism, Brazil, Peru, and Chile have sustained multiparty systems since the democratic transitions of the 1980s and 1990s.[38] The proliferation of political parties meant that legislative support for presidents often fell far short of a majority in parliament. As a result, presidents had to face serious constraints from divided government. However, in South Korea the number of parties is not so great as to prevent a stable presidential system.

In presidential systems, the number of parties should be viewed along with the presidential party's share of seats in the legislative branch. If a president has majority support in the legislature, governing efficiency would be high even in pluralistic party systems with more than two parties. As can be seen in Table 9.5, the presidential party's share of legislative seats is above or around 50% in stable presidential democracies. The figure is slightly under 50% in the United States (45.8%) and it is above 50% in Colombia and Costa Rica.

South Korea shows a very interesting pattern before and after the electoral reform. While the number of parties has not changed remarkably, the share of seats of the president's party has increased moderately following the electoral reform in 2004. Until 2004, the president's party's share of seats has averaged around 45% to 48% while the president's party has never obtained a majority of legislative seats by itself.[39] In other words, South Korean presidents have invariably suffered from a divided government as they confronted a National Assembly controlled by opposition parties. Whereas U.S. scholars have presented conflicting views about the governing efficiency of divided government in the United States,[40] divided government in South Korea has undermined governing efficiency on various fronts. Given strong party discipline, South Korean presidents have found it difficult to pass their policy agenda against an opposition controlled National Assembly. Crucial nominations such as those for the chief justice or prime minister were often obstructed or delayed protractedly by opposition parties. Although ideological positions among political parties have not been great, strong party discipline so dominated party politics that legislative roll-call votes were largely party line voting, with very rare exceptions. That is, there was very little opportunity for presidents to pursue the so-called politics of persuasion to draw support from opposition parties. Given such difference in the usefulness of the politics of persuasion, governing efficiency has been much greater under a unified government.

In contrast, since the 2004 reforms, the president's party has often obtained legislative majorities, abetted by the new or stronger minority parties facilitated by the allocation of list seats. In 2004, President's Roh Moo Hyun's Uri Party collected 152 of 273 seats (56%). President Lee Myung-Bak's GNP obtained 153 of 299 seats (51%) in 2008.[41] Thus when minor parties gained representation in the National Assembly through the list-tier system, support for the president's party slightly increased rather than diminished. In this sense, voters seemed not to want to undermine governing efficiency while enhancing representativeness of the party system through MMES. They seemed to favor instead a balance between governability and representativeness, while not leaning strongly toward either of the two alternative models.

The Relationship between Parties and Government

Given the rareness now of divided government and the constrained number of parties, governing efficiency has not been seriously undermined at the party system level since the 2004 reform. However, when we look at the party-government relationship, we do see some undermining of governing efficiency. The problem stems from the changing relationship between the president and the governing party. In the past, the tradition of "imperial leadership" helped a president sustain his control over the presidential party. This has changed with the political reforms taking place over the 2002 to 2004 period. Party leadership is no longer the same, and the president can no longer maintain imperial domination over the governing party.

The decline of the imperial party leader resulted from the interplay of reforms in party nomination, political finance, and party organizations. The first wave of change has to do with the decentralization of the nomination process, meaning that party leaders could no longer personally control the choice of legislative candidates. Party members, supporters, and general voters became involved in selecting legislative candidates. As a result, party leaders have lost crucial leverage over their party's MPs. Given the lack of an alternative base, such as strong ideological solidarity, this has led to the weakening of internal cohesion more than ever before.

The second reason for the decline of imperial party leadership came from political finance reform. The new Political Finance Law has diminished party leaders' conventional leverage over legislative members by prohibiting corporate political contributions altogether. Initially, this prohibition was designed to constrain the skyrocketing of political finances, as corporate contributions constituted by far the greatest share of rapidly growing political money. To restrain this growing trend and to provide a level ground for all political parties, the new Political Finance Law prohibited not just big conglomerates but also all types of organizations like labor unions from making any type of political contribution.[42] Of course it can be argued that such a provision represented a significant breach of freedom of expression if we assume a political donation is a way of expressing one's political inclination. Yet, both corporate and social organizations accepted, indeed often welcomed, such a prohibition. As corporate leaders sometimes went to jail for violating unreasonably low contribution limits several times in the past,[43] they were more than willing now to accept this limitation on their freedom of expression.

The disappearance of huge illegal funds from the corporate sector led to the end of imperial party leadership. Along with domination over candidate nomination, distributing political finance was a major channel for party leaders to sustain a patron-client relationship with parliamentary members within parties. However, the passing of corporate money brought about decentralization in the flow of political money. Parliamentary members have become more reliant on their own support organizations rather than on illegal transfer from party leaders. In other words, the two pillars of the imperial party leader, nominating power and transfer of political money, disappeared as a result of institutional reform in 2004. Now party leaders have to develop new channels to sustain cohesive links with parliamentary members, be it via ideology, campaign assistance, or appointments.

The final problem for party leaders was a new provision on the relationship between the president (and presidential candidate) and the party organization. In 2002, in the wake of decentralizing party organizations, the NMDP introduced a new rule about the status of the president (and presidential candidate). It stated that a presidential candidate could not hold the title of party chairman, who commanded party organizations, policy formulation, and other party activities. If elected, the president was not allowed to have any official tie with the party beyond membership to the party. Other parties like GNP followed suit, introducing similar rules to separate the party organization and the president. Imperial domination of the party leader was replaced by a weakened, fluid relationship between party leader and parliamentary members due to changes in political finance, the nomination process, and organization links.

The end of the imperial party leader has brought about dramatic changes to the party-government relationship, and in particular to governing efficiency. As the president no longer possesses imperial domination over parliamentary members, he no longer expects simple compliance from governing party members. He must instead pursue politics of persuasion not just with opposition parties but also with his own party in passing his legislative agenda.

A complex and unpredictable dynamic began to rise between president Roh Moo Hyun and his governing Uri Party beginning in 2003. Parliamentary members of the Uri Party began to reveal their disagreement with and resistance to the presidential agenda for ideological and political reasons. Ideological disagreement happened publicly when President Roh Moo Hyun attempted to send South Korean troops to Iraq in late 2003 upon the request of the United States. President Roh, although not a passionate advocate for the Korea–U.S. alliance, decided to help the George W. Bush administration in Iraq, expecting U.S. help in dealing with the North Korean nuclear issue. However, even in the first year of his presidential tenure, the anti-U.S. stance of Uri Party members meant fierce resistance to troop dispatch, while the opposition GNP did not contradict the presidential decision. Uri Party MPs engaged in delaying parliamentary hearings and relevant sessions on the issue and even waged a hunger strike. It took more than half a year before President Roh could authorize 3,000 troops to Iraq with parliamentary consent after painstaking persuasion of his own party members.

A more serious ideological clash between President Roh and the governing party erupted when the president signed the Korea–U.S. Free Trade Agreement in 2007. Antiglobalism among governing MPs led them to oppose the president's agenda fiercely once again. While the governing party controlled the majority of the National Assembly,[44] they conducted a classic "politics of delay" by not having roll-call votes for the ratification bill of Korea–U.S. Free Trade Agreement. President Roh sent the ratification bill in September 2007, but the National Assembly did not have a roll call voting for the bill until his presidential tenure ended in February 2008. As a result, one major step of South Korea's globalization stalled in the hands of the governing party and one key agenda of President Roh could not be completed. The governing party-president relationship has become characterized by a variable dynamics of consent, resistance, and compromise.

The changing party-government relationship was manifested in the new trend of legislative support for the president. Unlike the U.S. president, a Korean president proposes government bills to the National

Assembly. The success rate of government bills has experienced a dramatic decline following the end of imperial party leadership. Until the 2002–2004 reform, the passage rate of government bills was remarkably high, 87% in the 13th National Assembly (1988–1992), 92% in the 14th National Assembly (1992–1996), and 82% in the 15th National Assembly (1996–2000). The figure plummeted to 51% in the 17th National Assembly (2004–2008) following the party reforms.[45] It was clear that the legislative leadership of the South Korean president had been seriously undermined.

Nevertheless, overall conditions for governing efficiency have not deteriorated significantly since the party reforms were passed. The shift to MMES has not led to proliferation of the number of parties or to a divided government thus far. Yet the new dynamics of the party-president relationship has somewhat undercut governing efficiency, even in unified government. It appears that structural factors such as party system configuration are likely to affect governing efficiency more than before. Rather, relationships among major actors, such as the dynamic relation between president and parties, account more for governing efficiency.

CONCLUSIONS: THE FUTURE OF KOREAN DEMOCRACY AND POLITICAL PARTIES

After 20 years of experiments moving toward a consolidated democracy, the prospect for South Korean democracy is cautiously optimistic rather than pessimistic. There have been regular alternations of government among competing political parties. By and large electoral competition has been fair and competitive. There is no serious concern that the nation is likely to retreat to a nondemocratic regime. The public's evaluation and commitment seem to provide a solid foundation for continuing democratic rule: more than 90 percent of the public preferred democracy in principle as the ideal form of government, even after the economic crisis in 1997.[46] In a word, normative support for democracy is unwavering, and democracy has become "the only game in town" in South Korea.

However, the public's support is not so unyielding in the empirical sense as in the normative perspective. Less than half of the public supports democracy in action. Forty-four percent of respondents have a favorable evaluation for the actual working of South Korean democracy in terms of legitimacy. With regard to efficacy of democratic government, even fewer respondents, 38%, offered a positive assessment.[47]

At the center of the rift between the normative commitment and empirical criticism of democracy lies political parties that are neither trusted nor favorably evaluated by the public. Even though the South Korean public views political parties as crucial components of stable democracy, the public's evaluation of political parties is not highly positive. An overwhelming majority, 95% of the public, believe that "we need political parties if we want democratic development."[48] Yet the majority of the public assess political parties as serving the interests of party leaders rather than those of the mass citizenry. Seventy-three percent of the respondents replied that operations of political parties were mostly undemocratic or nondemocratic in a 1993 survey. [49] In this vein, the public's attachment to political party has not been quite solid compared to other new democracies in the East and specifically Eastern Europe. In an early 1990s survey, public attachment to parties in South Korea (36%) lagged behind that of Bulgaria (70%), Hungary (52%), and Romania (67%).[50]

South Korean political parties are confronted with problems similar to those in established democracies, although they are less institutionalized and more fluid. On the one hand, political parties perform an indisputable role in organizing government and structuring choices for voters in electoral competition. They have contributed to a great extent to the Korean consolidation of electoral democracy. But as in established democracies,[51] the South Korean public does not have a high level of trust in political parties with regard to the function of interest representation. Also, various alternative organizations compete with political parties in the arena of interest articulation and aggregation. There is a huge discrepancy between institutional function and representative function.

Of course, the prospect is not totally gloomy. There are some promising changes. Most of all, party attachment among the public has steadily and irrevocably increased since the political reforms of 2002 to 2004. As Figure 9.1 shows, the number of voters not attached to any political party was as high as 60% in the early phase of South Korean democratization. Such nonattached voters declined consistently after the 2002–2004 reform period. As a result, only about 20% of the public has remained unattached to any political party as of 2008.[52] It seems fair to say that party reform for enhanced representativeness has contributed to such positive change. Another good sign is the consistently positive public attitude toward "the political." Having gone through 20 years of experimentation toward democratic consolidation, the South Korean public has not turned away from public affairs but sustains its interest in political issues as well as its willingness to participate in the political process. The massive protests in 2008 were a crucial showcase. They revealed not just the frail representative legitimacy of political parties but also the civic vibrancy to be able to insist on more representative institutions.

The future of parties and democracy in South Korea should be understood in the context of global trends. Although there has been growing divergence among new democracies over the past three decades, there emerged some convergence between old and new

Figure 9.1. The Trend of Nonattached Voters in South Korea (1999–2008).

Panel A

	non-attached
12/31/99	40.5
01/20/00	48.4
02/24/00	44.8
03/24/00	41.6
05/04/00	34.6
04/13/01	45.5
11/14/01	38.6
12/22/01	40.5
02/07/02	42.9
03/02/02	39.6
05/01/02	37.4
07/06/02	37.4
09/30/02	36.8
11/02/02	36.4
04/29/03	24.2
05/31/03	30.3
08/23/03	38.6
10/10/03	36.1
12/30/03	42.4
12/13/04	23.6
01/27/05	21.5
03/08/05	23.7
07/16/05	21.4
12/22/05	22.3
02/27/06	26.4
09/11/06	20.4
01/17/07	17.3
02/19/07	23.2
03/19/07	20.2
04/03/07	21
07/21/07	18.8
08/23/07	11.6
09/26/07	13.1
10/29/07	19.1
11/25/07	19
12/06/07	20.9
03/31/08	27.2

Figure 9.1. The Trend of Nonattached Voters in South Korea (1999–2008). (Continued)

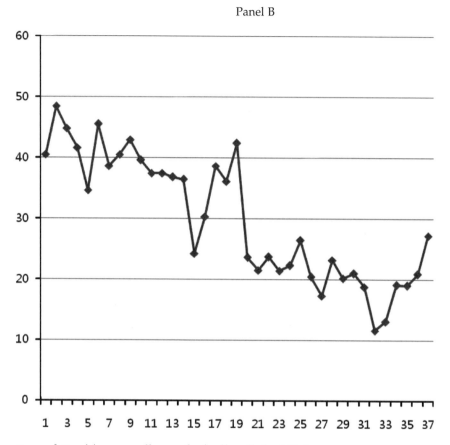

Panel B

Source: http://www.gallup.co.kr/gallupdb/public3.asp.

democracies with regard to the future of parties. South Korean parties have consolidated to some extent their institutional functions of organizing elections and government. In contrast, the representative function of political parties remains still short of being reliable, stable, and trusted, even after the significant modifications of majoritarian inclination. As in many established democracies, South Korea is now confronted with the task of filling the gap between representative and institutional functions of political parties. The future quality of South Korean democracy is largely dependent on the success of efforts made to undertake such tasks.

Notes

INTRODUCTION, POLITICAL PARTIES AND DEMOCRACY: THREE STAGES OF POWER

1. Having only indigenous authors is a unique and important characteristic of *Political Parties and Democracy* and thus well worth mentioning. As the word "indigenous" has two senses, it is perhaps also worth mentioning that here it is used in its primary sense: "living in a particular area or environment; native" to describe all authors and all co-editors, none of whom lives outside the countries he or she writes about. Authors of specific chapters occasionally use the words "indigenous" and "native" in their secondary sense, to refer to specific ethnic groups. Both usages are correct and the reader will find that the usage intended is always clear in context.

PART I: INTRODUCTION

1. Thomas Carothers, "The End of the Transition Paradigm," *Journal of Democracy 13*, no. 1 (2002): 17.

2. Anatoly Kulik and Susanna Pshizova, eds., *Political Parties in Post-Soviet Space: Russia, Belarus, Ukraine, Moldova and the Baltics* (Westport, CT: Praeger, 2005).

3. The Economist Intelligence Unit's Index of Democracy 2008. Available at: http://a330.g.akamai.net/7/330/25828/20081021185552/graphics.eiu.com/PDF/Democracy%20Index%202008.pdf

4. Congressmen Ronald Paul stated before the U.S. House of Representatives that the U.S. government, through the U.S. Agency for International Development (USAID), granted millions of dollars to the Poland-America-Ukraine Cooperation Initiative (PAUCI), which is administered by the U.S.-based Freedom House in favor of Viktor Yushchenko. Available at: http://www.house.

gov/paul/congrec/congrec2004/cr120704.htm (The data on Russia's spending in support of pro-Russian candidate Victor Yanukovych are unavailable.)

CHAPTER 1, THE STUMBLING GAIT OF PLURALIST DEMOCRACY AND POLITICAL PARTIES IN GEORGIA

1. Anthony L. H. Rhinelander, *Prince Michael Vorontsov: Viceroy to the Tsar* (Montreal: McGill-Queen's University Press, 1990); Ronald G. Suny, *The Making of the Georgian Nation* (Bloomington: Indiana University Press, 1994).

2. Donald Rayfield, *The Literature of Georgia: A History* (Oxford: Clarendon Press, 1994).

3. For a detailed description, see Stephen F. Jones, *Socialism in Georgian Colors: The European Road to Social Democracy, 1883–1917* (Cambridge: Harvard University Press, 2005).

4. Different sources give differing distribution of seats, probably reflecting certain ambiguities or changes in party membership. See, e.g., A. Mikaberidze, Historical Dictionary of Georgia, "Transcaucasian seim" (Lanham, MD: The Scarecrow Press, 2007), 631–632.

5. Firuz Kazemzadeh, *The Struggle for Transcaucasia (1917–1921)* (New York: Philosophical Library, 1951); Suny, *The Making of the Georgian Nation*; Zurab Avalov (Avalishvili), *Independence of Georgia in International Politics: 1918–1921* (London: Headley Brothers, 1940); Karl Kautsky, *Georgia: A Social-Democratic Peasant Republic—Impressions and Observations* (London: International Bookshops Limited, 1921).

6. Stephen F. Jones, "The Establishment of Soviet Power in Transcaucasia: The Case of Georgia 1921–1928," *Soviet Studies* 40 (1988): 616–639; David M. Lang, *The Modern History of Soviet Georgia* (London: Weidenfeld and Nicolson, 1962); Ronald G. Suny, *The Making of the Georgian Nation* (Bloomington: Indiana University Press, 1988).

7. Robert Conquest, *The Nation Killers: The Soviet Deportation of Nationalities* (London: Macmillan, 1970); T. Trier and A. Khanzhin, eds., *Between Integration and Resettlement: The Meskhetian Turks* (Flensburg: European Centre for Minority Issues, 2007).

8. Charles H. Fairbanks, Jr., "Clientelism and Higher Politics in Georgia, 1949–1953," in *Transcaucasia, Nationalism and the Social Change: Essays in the History of Armenia Azerbaijan, and Georgia*, ed. Ronald G. Suny (Ann Arbor: University of Michigan, 1983), 339–370.

9. Jonathan Aves, "The Rise and Fall of the Georgian Nationalist Movement, 1987–1991," in *The Road to Post-Communism: Independent Political Movements in the Soviet Union 1985–1991*, ed. G. A. Hosking, J. Aves, and P. J. S. Rucam (London: Pinter, 1992), 157–179; J. Aves, *Path to National Independence in Georgia 1987–1990* (London: School of Slavonic and East European Studies, 1991); Ronald Grigor Suny, "Incomplete Revolution: National Movements and the Collapse of the Soviet Empire," *New Left Review* 189 (1991): 111–126; Jürgen Gerber, *Georgien: Nationale Opposition und Kommunistische Herrschaft Seit, 1956* (Nomos: Baden-Baden, 1997); S. F. Jones, *A Failed Democratic Transition: Nations and Politics in the Soviet Successor States* (Cambridge: 1993), 288–310.

10. Jonathan Aves, "Opposition Political Organizations in Georgia," *Slovo: A Journal of Contemporary Soviet and East European Affairs* 3 (1990).

11. For Gamsakhurdia's version of the events see Zviad Gamsakhurdia, "The Nomenklatura Revanche in Georgia," *Soviet Analyst* 21 (1993), 9–10. available at: http://bpg.sytes.net/shavlego/zg_1d.html

12. Lincoln Allson et al., "The Georgian Election of 1992," *Electoral Studies* 12 (1993), 1–6; Lincoln Allison, *Parliamentary Elections in Georgia, 11 October 1992: Regulations and Political Parties* (Tbilisi: CIPDD, 1992); Lynn Nelson and Paata Amonashvili, "Voting and Political Attitudes in Soviet Georgia," *Soviet Studies* 44 (1992): 687–697.

13. For the review of events following Shevardnadze's ascent to power, see Jonathan Aves, *Georgia: From Chaos to Stability* (London: RIIA, 1996).

14. Lincoln Allison, *Elections in Georgia: 5 November 1995* (Tbilisi: CIPDD, 1995).

15. See the critical perspective on this as viewed from Moscow: Olga Vasil'eva, *The Foreign Policy Orientation of Georgia, Stiftung Wissenschaft und Politik, Forschungsinstitut für Internationale Politik und Sicherheit* (SWP—AP 2968, July, Ebenhausen, 1996).

16. *Central and Eastern Eurobarometer: Public Opinion and the European Union (20 Countries' Survey)* 8 (Brussels: European Commission, 1998).

17. *Elections of Local Representative Councils—"Sakrebulos" in Georgia, 15 November 1998* (Tbilisi: International Society for Fair Elections, 1999).

18. Charles King, "Potemkin Democracy: Four Myths about Post-Soviet Georgia," *National Interest* (2001), 93–1004; Nana Sumbadze and G. Tarkhan-Mouravi, *Democratic Value Orientations and Political Culture in Georgia, Occasional Papers* 3 (Bratislava: NISPAcee, 2001), 3–43.

19. Jonathan Wheatley, *Georgia from National Awakening to Rose Revolution: Delayed Transition in the Former Soviet Union* (London: Ashgate, 2006). The parallel count was made by the nongovernmental organization "Fair Elections" and exit polls conducted by the Global Strategy Group.

20. Gene Sharp, *The Politics of Nonviolent Action* (Boston: Porter Sargent, 1973). See also *From Dictatorship to Democracy: A Conceptual Framework for Liberation* (Bangkok: Committee for the Restoration of Democracy in Burma, 1993).

21. David Anable, *The Role of Georgia's Media—and Western Aid—in the Rose Revolution* (Cambridge: Joan Shorenstein Center, Harvard University, 2006); Jaba Devdariani, "Georgia: Rise and Fall of the Façade Democracy," *Demokratizatsiya* (2004), 79–115; Cory Welt, *Georgia's Rose Revolution: From Regime Weakness to Regime Collapse* (Washington, D.C.: CSIS, 2006); Georgi Derluguian, *Georgia's Return of the King*, CSIS Working Paper Series 22 (Washington, D.C.: 2004); I. Haindrava, "Political Processes in Post-Soviet Georgia," in *Diaspora, Oil and Roses* (Berlin: Heinrich-Böll-Stiftung, 2004), 25–41; Nana Sumbadze and G. Tarkhan-Mouravi, *Public Opinion in Tbilisi: In the Aftermath of the Parliamentary Elections of November 2, 2003* 1 (Bratislava: NISPAcee News, 2004), 1–14.

22. "Saakashvili's Ajara Success: Repeatable Elsewhere in Georgia?" in *Europe Briefing* (Tbilisi: International Crisis Group, 2004).

23. Lincoln A. Mitchell, *Democracy in Georgia Since the Rose Revolution: East European Democratization* (Foreign Policy Research Institute, 2006), 669–676; James V. Wertsch, "Georgia as a Laboratory for Democracy," *Demokratizatsiya: The Journal of Post-Soviet Democratization* (2005), http://www.ca-c.org; "Georgia: Sliding towards Authoritarianism?" in *International Crisis Group, Europe Report* 189 (Brussels: International Crisis Group, 2007); Laurence Broers, *After the 'Revolution': Civil Society and the Challenges of Consolidating Democracy in Georgia* (London: University of London, 2004); Pamela Jawad, "Democratic Consolidation in Georgia after the 'Rose Revolution'?" in *PRIF Reports* 73 (Frankfurt: PRIF, 2005); Jaba Devdariani, "The Withering of the Rose?" in *Transitions Online* (Prague: 2005), http://www.tol.cz; Sozar Subari, "Speech in the Parliament of Georgia", *Civil Georgia*, September 26, 2008, http://civil.ge/eng/.

24. Svante E. Cornell, Johanna Popjanevski, and Niklas Nilsson, *Russia's War in Georgia: Causes and Implications for Georgia and the World—Central Asia-Caucasus Analyst* (SAIS, August 2008); After August 2008: *Consequences of the Russian-Georgian War* (CIPDD, 2008).

25. G. Tarkhan-Mouravi, "Political Parties in Georgia: The Delayed Formation," *Political Science Quarterly* 1 (2006): 243–267.

26. For the brief analysis of the reasons for the weakness of Georgia's party system, see Max Bader, "Fluid Party Politics and the Challenge for Democracy Assistance in Georgia," *Caucasian Review of International Affairs* 2 (2008), 1–10.

27. Thomas Carothers, "The End of the Transition Paradigm," *Journal of Democracy* 13 (2002): 5–21; also Thomas Carothers, *Confronting the Weakest Link: Aiding Political Parties in New Democracies* (Washington, D.C.: Carnegie Endowment for International Peace, 2006).

CHAPTER 2, POLITICAL PARTIES AND DEMOCRATIZATION OF THE REPUBLIC OF MOLDOVA

1. Vladimir Pastii, Mihaela Miroiu, and Cornel Codita, "Romania—Real State of Things," in *Printing Company NEMIRA* 1 (1996): 23.

2. Dmitrii Furman, "I Nevozmozhnoe Vozmozhno: Pochemu Rossiya ne Kazahstan," Nezavisimaya Gazeta, May 10, 2007, available at: http://www.ng.ru/ideas/2007-10-05/10_nevozmozhnoe.html.

3. Jeannette Goehring, ed., *Nations in Transit 2007: Democratization from Central Europe to Eurasia* (Sydney: Freedom House).

4. Hans Kelsen, "La Democratie," *Economica* 31 (1988).

5. According to the official data, the number of Moldova emigrants varies from 500,000 and 600,000, while the unofficial data estimates that 1 million Moldovan citizens are living and working abroad.

6. Institute for Public Policy, "Barometer of Public Opinion," *Republic of Moldova* (2008).

7. Bessarabia (*Basarabia*) is a historical term for the geographic entity in Eastern Europe bounded by the Dniester River on the east and the Prut River on the west. This was the name by which the Russian Empire designated the eastern part of the principality of Moldova, ceded by the Ottoman Empire (to which Moldavia was a vassal) to Russia in the aftermath of the Russo-Turkish War (1806–1812).

8. Remark made by political researcher Oleg Serebrian during a preelection for participants in the "School of Young Political Leaders," May 15, 2008.

9. According to the PCRM Electral Platform in the 2001 parliamentary elections.

10. R. Gunther and L. Diamond, "Species of Political Parties: A New Typology," *Party Politics* 9 (2003): 167–199.

11. The ADR consisted of four parties: Christian Democratic People's Party (PPCD), Party of Democratic Forces (PFD), Party of Rebirth and Conciliation of Moldova (PRCM), and the Bloc for a Democratic and Prosperous Moldova (BMDP).

12. Television interview with PPCD Chairman Iurie Rosca aired in April 1998.

13. In the spring of 2005 the political compromise was reached as a result of the negotiations held between communist leaders with the leaders of Christian-Democratic Peoples' Party, Democratic Party, and Social-Liberal Party. Analyst

Vladimir Socor claimed in the *Jamestown Eurasia Daily Monitor* that "former U.S. Congressman John Conlan was the indispensable facilitator in negotiations and document drafting among the political leaders and factions in Chisinau over a two-week period." Christian-Democrat leader Iurie Rosca confirmed that when explaining his support to Vladimir Voronin, "We have consulted our foreign partners. I have personally discussed with my friends in Bucharest, Tbilisi, Kiev, Washington and Brussels. I weighted the short time Moldova has to implement Action Plan Moldova–EU. When I have to take a tough political decision I do the following: I carefully consider what my enemy wants to achieve and do the opposite. In the last month I have noted several times that political foes of Moldova want to thwart Voronin's re-election. Simple logical reasoning, personal responsibility and state interests have led me to the conclusion to endorse Voronin."

14. Georges Lavau, *Partis Politique et Rèalitès Sociales* (Paris: Armand Colin, 1953).

15. Article 1 of the Law of the Republic of Moldova 718–XII of September 17, 1991, on political parties and other sociopolitical organizations.

CHAPTER 3, ARE THE PARTIES OF THE RUSSIAN "SOVEREIGN DEMOCRACY" SUSTAINING DEMOCRATIC GOVERNANCE?

1. Elmer E. Schattschneider, *Party Government: American Government in Action* (New York: Rinehart, 1942).

2. Address to the Federal Assembly of the Russian Federation, 2000. Available at: http://www.kremlin.ru/appears/2000/07/08/0000_type63372type63374 type82634_28782.shtml

3. Freedom House, NIT 2008 Overview Essay: Petro-Authoritarianism and Eurasia's New Divides. Available at: http://www.freedomhouse.hu/images/ fdh_galleries/NIT2008/NT-Overview%20Essay%20-final.pdf

4. The chapter develops ideas presented by the author in Anatoly Kulick and Susanna Pshizova, ed., "Political Parties in Post-Soviet Russia: an Agent of Democratic Transition?" in *Political Parties in Post-Soviet Space: Russia, Belarus, Moldova and the Baltics* (Westport, Conn.: Praeger, 2005), and Kay Lawson and Peter Merkl, eds., "Russia's Political Parties: Deep in the Shadow of the President," in *When Parties Prosper: The Uses of Electoral Success* (Boulder, Colo.: Lynne Rienner, 2007).

5. Peter Mair, "Political Parties and Democracy: What Sort of Future?" Available at: http://www.ics.ul.pt/ceapp/conferencias/fulbright/18PMair.pdf

6. Thomas Carothers, "The End of the Transition Paradigm," *Journal of Democracy* 13 (2002), 5–21.

7. The Economist Intelligence Unit's index of democracy, 2007. Available at: http://www.economist.com/media/pdf/Democracy_Index_2007_v3.pdf

8. Elmer E. Schattschneider, "In Defense of Political Parties," in *American Party System*, ed. John R. Owens (New York: Macmillan, 1965), 34.

9. Seymour M. Lipset, "The Indispensability of Political Parties," *Journal of Democracy* 11 (2000), 49–55.

10. Adam Przeworski, *Democracy and Market: Political and Economic Reforms in Eastern Europe and Latin America* (New York: Cambridge University Press, 1991).

11. A. V. Ivanchenko and A. E. Lyubarev, *Rossiiskie vybory ot perestoiki do suverennoi demokratii* [Russian Elections from Perestroika to Sovereign Democracy] (Moscow: Aspect Press, 2007), 68.

12. The Constitution of the Russian Federation, Chapter 1, Article 13.

13. The prominent Russian historian Academician Yuryi Pivovarov noticed its resemblance with the "Main Laws" of the Russian Empire adopted in 1906 as a means to save the political regime threatened by the Revolution of 1905. Actually, the then ruling elite was never both ready and willing to enact and observe the "Main Laws."

14. As interpreted by the chairman of the Constitutional Court Marat Baglai, the president has "a broad right to act at his discretion, proceeding not only from letter, but also from spirit of the Constitution and laws, correcting a legal deficiency and responding to situations that are not anticipated by the Constitution. . . . President must act decisively, drawing from own understanding of his duties of a guarantor of the Constitution." Cited from Victor Sheinis, "Konstitucionnyi Process na Covremennom Etape," in *Kuda Idet Rossiya?* ed. Tatyana Zaslavskaya (Moscow: Delo, 1997), 116. Worthy of mention also is that one of the main goals of the U.S. Constitution adopted in 1787 was to ensure that all government power does not fall into the hands of a single person or group of people, and the "spirit and letter" of the Constitution is interpreted by the Supreme Court.

15. The Russian constitution defines *government* as follows: "The Government of the Russian Federation shall consist of the Chairman of the Government of the Russian Federation, deputy chairmen of the Government of the Russian Federation, and federal ministers." Article 110, Section 2.

16. Vladimir Rimsky, "Nuzhny li Rossii politicheskie partii?," in *Parlamentarizm i mnogopartijnost' v sovremennoi Rossii* ["Does Russia Need Political Parties?" in *Parliamentarism and Multiparty System in Contemporary Russia*], ed. Vladimir Lysenko (Moscow: IPI, 2000), 151–152.

17. Ivan Vandenko, "My govorim 'deputat'—podrazumevaem 'broker'," *Izvestiya* (May 30, 1997).

18. In this "Russian" context, *oligarchy* means big business of dubious origin and reputation.

19. *Parlamentarizm i mnogopartijnost' v sovremennoi Rossii*, 39.

20. Ibid., 65.

21. Tatyana Zaslavskaya, " Social'naya struktura Rossii: glavnye napravleniya peremen," in *Kuda Idet Rossiya?*, ed. Tatyana Zaslavskaya (Moscow: Delo, 1997), 168–175.

22. *Rossiya v izbiratel'nom cikle 1999–2000 gg*, ed. Michael MacFoll, Nikolai. Petrov, and Andrei Ryabov (Moscow: Gendal'f, 2000), 611.

23. One of the main campaign managers of OVR, Sergey Yastrzhembskii, accused the Kremlin of offering $700,000 to one of the principal nominees for leaving the OVR list two weeks before the ballot. See document available at: http://www.polit.ru/documents/149401.html. Worthy of attention is also that later on Putin appointed him to the presidential aide on Chechnya.

24. Vladimir Sogrin, *Politicheskaya Istoriya Sovremennoi Rossii, 1985–1994* [Political History of Contemporary Russia, 1985–1994] (Moscow: Progress-Akademia, 2001), 239

25. Lilia Shevtsova, "Dilemi Postkommunisticheskogo obshestva" [Dilemmas of the Postcommunist Society], *Polis* 5 (1996): 80–92.

26. Ol'ga Kryshtanovskaya, "Rezhim Putina—liberal'naya militokratiya?" *Pro et Contra* (Autumn 2002): 158–180.

27. Address to the Federal Assembly of the Russian Federation, 2000.

28. Robert A. Dahl, *Polyarchy: Participation and Opposition* (New Haven, Conn.: Yale University Press, 1971).

29. Transcript of meeting with participants in the third meeting of the Valdai Discussion Club, September 9, 2006. Available at: http://www.kremlin.ru/eng/text/speeches/2006/09/09/1209_type82917type84779_111165.shtml

30. Putin presented repeatedly his vision of the Russian politics of the West at the meeting of the Valdai Discussion Club. He expressed slashing criticism of this politics at the 43rd Munich Conference on Security Policy, February 10, 2007. Available at: http://www.securityconference.de/archive/konferenzen/rede.php?menu_2007=&menu_konferenzen=&sprache=en&id=179&

31. Igor' Pylaev, "ZAO "ROSSIYa". Kto Chem Upravlyaet, Tot Tem I Vladeet," *Politicheskii zhurnal* 3 (2006). Available at: http://www.politjournal.ru/index.php?action=Articles&dirid=67&tek=4947&issue=141

32. Administrative resources began to play a dominant role in elections already in the late 1990s. See Ivanchenko and Lyubarev, *Rossiiskie vybory ot perestoiki do suverennoi demokratii*, 144.

33. A judicial comment on the law identifies numerous abuses of constitutional rights of citizens. See Valentina Lapaeva, "K prinyatiyu zakona o partiyah," in Aktual'naya pravovaya informaciya. Available at: http://www.lawmix.ru/comm.php?id=5494

34. Federal Law "On Political Parties," adopted by the State Duma on June 21, 2001. Available at: http://www.cikrf.ru/eng/law/fz95_en_110701.jsp

35. Ivanchenko and Lyubarev, *Rossiiskie vybory ot perestoiki do suverennoi demokratii*, 154–156.

36. Address to the Federal Assembly of the Russian Federation, 2003. Available at: http://www.kremlin.ru/eng/speeches/2003/05/16/0000_type70029type82912_44692.shtml

37. Official site of United Russia. Available at: http://www.edinros.ru/pressl.php?first=1023436800&last=1025703600&did=54

38. *Nezavisimaya gazeta* (March 25, 2002).

39. Ivanchenko and Lyubarev, *Rossiiskie vybory ot perestoiki do suverennoi demokratii*, 171.

40. Worldwide Press Freedom Index 2007. Available at: http://www.rsf.org/article.php3?id_article=24025

41. Address to the Federal Assembly of the Russian Federation, 2003. Available at: http://www.kremlin.ru/eng/speeches/2003/05/16/0000_type70029type82912_44692.shtml

42. Having examined the law, experts came to the conclusion that it might be rightfully titled "The Law on Non-Admission of the Referendum of Russian Federation." Ivanchenko and Lyubarev, *Rossiiskie vybory ot perestoiki do suverennoi demokratii*, 195, 199.

43. Federal Law No. 168–FZ, December 20, 2004, on amendment in the law on political parties. Available at: http://www.rg.ru/2004/12/24/partii.html

44. Russian Public Opinion Research Center Publication, June 27, 2005. Available at: http://wciom.ru/novosti/publikacii-v-smi/publikacija/single/1431.html

45. Irina Nagornyh, "Edinaya Rossiya: Otchitalas' o Partizacii Vlasti," *Kommersant* (December 23, 2005). Available at: http://www.kommersant.ru/search.aspx?mode=1&pid=1&query=&date=20051223

46. *Skol'ko partii nuzhno Rossii?* VCIOM Press Release No. 1056, September 26, 2008. Available at: http://wciom.ru/arkhiv/tematicheskii-arkhiv/item/single/10746.html?no_cache=1&cHash=e4d43fbcf3&print=1

47. *Altapress* (May 30, 2007). Available at: http://www.altapress.ru/12345

48. Still in April 2006 Boris Grizlov declared that United Russia considered unacceptable any constitutional change, referring to the view of Putin. However, on November 11, 2008 the new president introduced the bill to amend the Constitution, and United Russia adopted it in the third reading.

49. The electoral result of the left party (Ivan Rybkin Bloc) was very poor, with only 1.1 percent of the votes in the PR part, compared to 22.3 percent acquired by CPRF, the then leader of contestation. Russia Votes, available at: http://www.russiavotes.org/duma/duma_elections_93-03.php?S776173303132=801d9cff98c7684e3396224b8f88ab5a

50. "Surkov: Obshestvu Nuzhna 'Vtoraya Noga.'" August 16, 2006. Available at: http://www.dni.ru/news/polit/2006/8/16/88788.html

51. "Parties: 'Fair Russia.'" Available at: http://duma.lenta.ru/parties/spavros/

52. Ivanchenko and Lyubarev, *Rossiiskie vybory ot perestoiki do suverennoi demokratii*, 220.

53. "Mass Media: Preferable Channels of Information, Poll," August 2, 2007, database of the Public Opinion Foundation, available at: http://bd.fom.ru/report/cat/smi/smi_rei/d073121&

54. Database of the Public Opinion Foundation, Indicators of Confidence, May 10, 2007. Available at: http://bd.fom.ru/report/cat/power/pow_rei/d071901#Abs6

55. Freedom House. NIT 2008 Overview Essay: Petro-Authoritarianism and Eurasia's New Divides. Available at: http://www.freedomhouse.hu/images/fdh_galleries/NIT2008/NT-Overview%20Essay%20-final.pdf

56. Yurii Korguniuk, "Zakat vtoroi partiinoi sistemy," *Politeia* 2 (2008).

57. Ol'ga Kryshtanovskaya. "Transformaciya staroi nomenklatury v novuyu rossiiskuyu elitu," *ONS* 1 (1995): 65.

58. Thomas Carothers, "The End of the Transition Paradigm," *Journal of Democracy* 13 (2002): 17.

59. Schattschneider, *Party Government*, 1.

60. This goes contrary to the Constitution of RF that stipulates that "No ideology shall be proclaimed as state ideology or as obligatory," in Article 13, Clause 2.

61. Vyacheslav Surkov, "Russkaya politicheskaya kul'tura. Vzglyad iz utopii," available at the Web site of United Russia: http://www.edinros.ru/news.html?id=121456

62. Lipset, *The Indispensability of Political Parties*, 49.

63. This clause of the law contradicts the RF Constitution that prohibits "all forms of limitations of human rights on social, racial, national, language, or religious grounds." S. M. Lipset and S. Rokkan in their seminal volume also named *workers versus owners* as a form of social division. European mass labor parties representing *workers* originate from powerful trade union movements. In Russia, trade unions have degenerated during the Soviet period and

have little impact on politics, whereas labor legislation actually prohibits strike actions that could attract attention of politicians to *workers-owners* relations. When the Union of Manufacturers and Entrepreneurs has access to different power structures and high-ranking officials from the presidential administration and federal government are delegated to boards of big corporations to link them with power, *workers* have no efficient institution to represent their interests in politics.

64. Political Parties in the Life of Russia, Poll August 2, 2007, "Public Opinion" Foundation, April 5, 2007. Available at: http://bd.fom.ru/report/cat/polit/pol_par/d071424 (according to poll data of "Public Opinion" Foundation from March 31–April 1, 2007).

65. Ibid.

66. "Kolichestvo chinovnikov v Rossii postoyanno uvelichivaetsya," *Malyi biznes Moskvy*, April 30, 2008, 155–185. Available at: http://www.mbm.ru/newsitem.asp?id=64724; http://www.newsru.com/russia/20aug2008/burokraty.html

67. "Usherb ot korrupcii v RF dostigaet 40 mlrd rublei," October 30, 2008. Available at: http://www.bfm.ru/news/2008/10/30/s-korrupciej-70-rossijan-stalkivajutsja.html

68. Review of Andrei's Pionkovsky's *Another Look into Putin's Soul by the Honorable Rodric Braithwaite*, April 1, 2007, Hoover Institute. Available at: http://www.hudson.org/index.cfm?fuseaction=publication_details&id=4852

69. Governance Matters 2008, Worldwide Governance Indicators, 1996–2007. Available at: http://info.worldbank.org/governance/wgi/sc_chart.asp

70. Nataliya Rimashevskaya, "Nanaiskaya bor'ba s bednost'yu," *Rossiiskaya Federaciya Segodnya* 3 (2008). Available at: http://www.russia-today.ru/2008/no_03/03_continuation.htm

71. Russian Public Opinion, 2007, Levada Center, 2008. Available at: http://www.levada.ru/eng/

72. Human Development Indices. Available at: http://hdr.undp.org/en/media/HDI_2008_EN_Tables.pdf

73. Opening address at a meeting of the State Council Presidium titled "On the Implementation of a Strategy for the Development of the Information Society in the Russian Federation," July 17, 2008. Available at: http://www.kremlin.ru/eng/speeches/2008/07/17/2220_type82912type82913_204259.shtml

74. Opening address at the meeting with the Governing Board of the Chamber of Commerce and Industry, November 11, 2008. Available at: http://www.kremlin.ru/appears/2008/11/11/1750_type63376type82634_209038.shtml

75. The World Competitiveness Scoreboard 2008—IMD. Available at: http://www.scribd.com/doc/3016393/The-World-Competitiveness-Scoreboard-2008-IMD

76. Oksana Gaman-Golutvina, "Menyayushayasya rol' gosudarstva v kontekste reform gosudarstvennogo upravleniya: otechestvennyi i zarubezhnyi opyt," *Polis* 4 (2007): 31.

77. Mihail Vorob'ev, "Prosto demokratiya," *Vremya novostei* (January 29, 2007). Available at: http://vff-s.narod.ru/gov/pr/opr28.html#27

78. Russian Public Opinion—2007, Levada Center, 2008.

79. Mikhail Afanes'ev. Available at: http://www.gorby.ru/rubrs.asp?rubr_id=725

80. Yurii Pivovarov, "Mezhdu kazachestvom i knutom (K stoletiyu russkoi konstitucii i russkogo parlamenta)," *Polis* 2 (2006).

CHAPTER 4, POLITICAL PARTIES IN UKRAINE: LEARNING DEMOCRATIC ACCOUNTABILITY?

1. Philippe C. Schmitter and Terry Lynn Karl, "What Democracy Is . . . and Is Not," *Journal of Democracy* 2 (1991): 76. In a later article, published in 2004, Philippe C. Schmitter has somewhat modified his and Karl's original definition of democracy. See Schmitter, "The Ambiguous Virtues of Accountability," *Journal of Democracy* 15 (2004): 47–60.

2. Philippe C. Schmitter, "The Quality of Democracy: The Ambiguous Virtues of Accountability," European University Institute, 2003.

3. For a definition of an electoral democracy see *Freedom in the World*, available on the Web site of Freedom House: www.freedomhouse.org/template.cfm?page=35&year=2006

4. For a detailed discussion of the criteria of free and fair elections see Guy S. Goodwin-Gill, *Free and Fair Elections* (Geneva: Inter-Parliamentary Union, 2006).

5. Joseph Schumpeter, *Capitalism, Socialism, and Democracy* (London: Allen and Unwin, 1976), 269.

6. European Parliament Resolution on the Results of the Ukrainian Elections, January 13, 2005, available on the Web site of the Mission of Ukraine to European Communities: www.ukraine-eu.mfa.gov.ua/eu/en/publication/content/1996.htm

7. Until 2006, Ukraine was considered a "partly free" country according to the Freedom House ratings of the freedom in the world. Beginning in 2006, Freedom House regarded Ukraine as a "free state." See the Web site of Freedom House: www.freedomhouse.org/template.cfm?page=15

8. See Sarah Birch, "Single-Member District Electoral Systems and Democratic Transition," *Electoral Studies* 24 (2005): 281–301.

9. For a discussion of the antiparty nature of the 1993 Law on Elections of People's Deputies of Ukraine, see Andrey Meleshevych, *Party Systems in Post-Soviet Countries: A Comparative Study of Political Institutionalization in the Baltic States, Russia, and Ukraine* (New York: Palgrave Macmillan, 2007), 170–177.

10. Matthew Soberg Shugart and John M. Carey, *Presidents and Assemblies* (Cambridge: Cambridge University Press, 1992), 24.

11. Juan J. Linz, "Presidential or Parliamentary Democracy: Does It Make a Difference?" in *The Failure of Presidential Democracy: Comparative Perspectives*, ed. Juan J. Linz and Arturo Valenzuela (Baltimore: Johns Hopkins University Press, 1994), 60.

12. List of Political Parties of Ukraine, available on the Web site of the Ministry of Justice of Ukraine: www.minjust.gov.ua/0/499

13. According to Article 10 of the 2004 Law on Elections of People's Deputies of Ukraine, only those political parties that have been officially registered at least one year before an election are allowed to participate in this contest.

14. Serhii Rakhmanin and Yulia Mostovaya, "Ukrainian Political Parties, Part VI: The Socialist Party of Ukraine," *Zerkalo Nedeli*, March 8–15, 2002, Internet edition, available at: www.mw.ua/1000/1550/34078/

15. Ibid.

16. Olexa Golobutsky and Vitaly Kulyk. "Partiyno-Politychnyi Spectr Suchasnoi Ukrainy," in *Politychni Partii Ukrainy*, ed. Valentyn Yakushyk (Kyiv: Kobza, 1996), 44.

17. Vitaliy Bala, Olexa Golobutsky, and Valentyn Yakushyk, *Politychni Partii Ukrainy, Sotsialistychna Partiya Ukrainy, Nayavni Resursy, Problemy, Perspectyvy* (Kyiv: Agency for Modeling Situations, 2005), 14.

18. For more on the origin and history of Rukh see Oleksa Haran', *Ubyty Drakona: Z Istorii Rukhu ta Novykh Partiy Ukrainy* (Kyiv: Lybid', 1993); Andrew Wilson, *Ukrainian Nationalism in the 1990s: A Minority Faith* (Cambridge: Cambridge University Press, 1997).

19. In the 2006 parliamentary elections, the UPP ran separately from the Our Ukraine electoral coalition as the Kostenko and Plusch Electoral Bloc obtaining 1.87% of the vote and failing to gain representation in the Rada.

20. Rukh's Program, available on the Web site of the People's Movement of Ukraine (Rukh): www.nru.org.ua/en/program/

21. Angelo Panebianco, *Political Parties: Organization and Power* (Cambridge: Cambridge University Press, 1988), 50–51.

22. Vitaliy Bala, Olexa Golobutsky, and Valentyn Yakushyk, *Politychni Partii Ukrainy, Partiya Regioniv, Nayavni Resursy, Problemy, Perspectyvy* (Kyiv: Agency for Modeling Situations, 2005), 7.

23. Ibid., 8.

24. Volodymyr Ar'ev, "Sudymosti Yanukovycha," *Ukrains'ka Pravda*, October 15, 2004, Internet edition, available at: http://pravda.com.ua/news/2004/10/15/12679.htm. See also Yulia Mostovaya, "Igry v Yanukovicha," *Zerkalo Nedeli* (November 16–22, 2002).

25. See *Our History* and *Party Program*, available on the Web site of the Party of Regions: www.partyofregions.org.ua/meet/history/ and www.partyofregions.org.ua/meet/program/

26. European Democrat Group: Aims and Statute of the Group, available on the Web site of the European Democrat Group, PACE: http://assembly.coe.int/ASP/AssemblyList/Annuaire_02W_Groups.asp?GroupID=3 and http://assembly.coe.int/ASP/AssemblyList/Annuaire_02W_Groups.asp?GroupID=1.

27. Panebianco, *Political Parties*, 145.

28. In the 2006 elections, BYuT consisted of Batkivshchyna and USDP. In 2007, the Party Reform and Order joined BYuT.

29. Viktor Chyvokunya, "Tymoshenko Changes Orientation," *Ukrains'ka Pravda*, August 7, 2007, Internet edition, available at: www.pravda.com.ua/news/2007/8/7/62363.htm

30. Ibid.

31. History of the People's Party, available on the Web site of the People's Party: narodna.org.ua/about/

32. "People's Party Intends to Become the Center of Left Forces," *Glavred*, October 24, 2007, Internet edition, available at: ua.glavred.info/archive/2007/10/24/103803-6.html

33. Meleshevych, *Party Systems in Post-Soviet Countries*, 195. For a detailed discussion of this definition of parties of power, their origin, transformation, and impact on the party system institutionalization see pages 193–204.

34. Andrew Wilson and Valentyn Yakushyk, "Politychni Organizatsii v Ukraini: Deyaki Problemy Stanovlennya i Rozvytku," *Suchasnist* 5 (1992): 164.

35. John H. Aldrich, *Why Parties? The Origin and Transformation of Political Parties in America* (Ann Arbor: University of Michigan Press, 1995), 24.

36. Kimitaka Matsuzato, "Elites and the Party System of Zakarpattya Oblast: Relations among Levels of Party Systems in Ukraine," *Europe-Asia Studies* 54 (2002): 1269.

37. Madalena Resende and Hendrik Kraetzschmar, "Parties of Power as Roadblocks to Democracy: The Cases of Ukraine and Egypt," in *Democratisation in the European Neighbourhood*, ed. Michael Emerson (Brussels: Centre for European Policy Studies, 2006), 156.

38. Richard S. Katz, "Party Government and Its Alternatives," in *Future of Party Governments—European and American Experiences*, ed. Richard S. Katz (Berlin: Walter de Gruyter, 1987), 7.

39. Timothy J. Colton and Cindy Skach, "The Russian Predicament," *Journal of Democracy* 16 (2005): 117.

40. Kathryn Stoner-Weiss, "Russia: Authoritarianism without Authority," *Journal of Democracy*, 17 (2005): 114.

41. See Public Opinion Poll "Do You Trust Political Parties? (Dynamics, 2001–2008)," available on the Web site of the Razumkov Center: www.uceps.org/poll.php?poll_id=82

42. See Public Opinion Poll "Does Ukraine Move to the Right or Wrong Direction? (Dynamics, 2004–2008)," available on the Web site of the Razumkov Center: www.uceps.org/poll.php?poll_id=66

43. For a description of the Laakso and Taagepera effective number of political parties see Markku Laakso and Rein Taagepera, "The Effective Number of Parties: A Measure with Application to Western Europe," *Comparative Political Studies* 12, no. 1 (1979): 3–27; and Rein Taagepera and Matthew Soberg Shugart, *Seats and Votes: The Effect and Determinants of Electoral Systems* (New Haven, Conn.: Yale University Press, 1989). For a discussion of the effective number of political parties in democratic nations see Taagepera and Shugart, *Seats and Votes*.

44. De facto the Electoral Coalition Our Ukraine-People's Self-Defense admitted six new member parties on the eve of the 2007 contest. Since People's Self-Defense has been registered by the Ministry of Justice less than a year before the elections, de jure it was not able to take part in the electoral race. However, a number of leading members of this organization, including Yuriy Lutsenko, who occupied the top spot on the coalitional electoral list, took part in the elections as nonaffiliated candidates.

45. See, for example, "Ekspert: Dobkin i Kernes dlya Yanukovicha—eto kak Monika Levinski dlya Klintona," *Agenstvo Televideniya Novosti*, June 6, 2008, Available at: atn.kharkov.ru/newsread.php?id=23619; Nikolay Poddubnyi, "Partiya Regionov Boitsya Poteryat Khar'kov," BBC, September 27, 2007, available at: news.bbc.co.uk/hi/russian/international/newsid_7016000/7016282.stm; "Dobkin, Mikhail: Mayor of Kharkov," *Lentapedia*, April 2, 2008, available at: lenta.ru/lib/14188177/

46. Andrew Wilson and Sarah Birch, "Political Parties in Ukraine: Virtual and Representational," in *Party Politics in New Democracies*, ed. Paul Webb and Stephen White (Oxford: Oxford University Press, 2007), 54.

PART II: INTRODUCTION

1. Samuel P. Huntington, *The Third Wave: Democratization in the Late Twentieth Century* (Norman: University of Oklahoma Press, 1991), 25.

2. One-party domination was common among nondemocratic states. In Malaysia, the UMNO has been politically dominant since 1957; in Singapore, the PAP ruled since 1959; in Indonesia, Golkar's power was seldom threatened after 1971 until in the 1990s; in Taiwan it was the KMT, and in China, the CCP. Also see T. J. Pempel, ed., *Uncommon Democracies* (Ithaca: Cornell University Press, 2000), especially Takashi Inoguchi, "The Political Economy of Conservative Resurgence under Recession," 189–225.

3. Harunhiro Fukui, *Political Parties of Asia and the Pacific* (Westport, Conn.: Greenwood Press, 1985).

4. Wolfgang Sachsenroder and Ulrike E. Frings, eds., *Political Party and Democratic Development in East and Southeast Asia: Volume I: Southeast Asia; Volume II: East Asia* (London: Ashgate Publishers, 1998). This work was based on two international workshops held in Singapore and Malaysia.

5. Russell J. Dalton, Doh Chull Shin, and Yun-Han Chu, eds., *Party Politics in East Asia: Citizens, Elections, and Democratic Development* (Boulder, Colo.: Lynne Rienner, 2008).

6. P. Whitaker, "Concept of Guided Democracy in Southeast Asia," *Political Studies* 1 (1967): 144–145.

7. Y. M. Kim, "Asian-Style Democracy: A Critique from East Asia," *Asian Survey* 12 (1997): 1119–1134. Also see T. Inoguchi, "Asian-Style Democracy?," in *The Changing Nature of Democracy*, ed. T. Inoguchi, Edward Newman, and John Keane (New York: United Nations University Press), 173–183.

8. Benjamin Reilly, "Democratization and Electoral Reform in the Asia-Pacific Region—Is There an "Asian Model" of Democracy?," in *Comparative Political Studies* 40 (November 2007): 1350–1371; "Electoral Systems and Party Systems in East Asia," *Journal of East Asian Studies* 2 (2007): 185–202. Also see M. Mietzner, "Between Consolation and Crisis: Elections and Democracy in Five Nations in Southeast Asia," in *Bijdragen Tot De Taal-Land-En Volkenkunde* 2–3 (2008): 335–337.

9. Hans Stockton, "Political Parties, Party Systems, and Democracy in East Asia: Lessons from Latin America," *Comparative Political Studies* 1 (2001): 94–119.

10. A. Ufen, "Political Party and Party System Institutionalization in Southeast Asia: Lessons for Democratic Consolidation," *Pacific Review* 3 (2008): 327–350.

11. Baogang He, "China," in *Political Party and Democratic Development in East and Southeast Asia*, ed. Wolfgang Sachsenroder and Ulrike E. Frings (London: Ashgate Publishers, 1998), 37.

12. He, "China's Step toward Democratization," 1. By contrast, Race Mathews reveals the national membership of the Australian Labor Party has plummeted to about 50,000 now from about 370,000 immediately after World War II. Paul Austin "Faction-Hit ALP 'Faces Extinction'," *The Age* (January 26, 2009).

13. Tomohito Shinoda, "Japan," in *Political Party and Democratic Development in East and Southeast Asia*, ed. Sachsenroder and Frings, 88.

14. Ibid., 91–92.

15. Ibid., 93.

16. Yong-Ho Kim, "Korea," in *Political Party and Democratic Development in East and Southeast Asia*, ed. Sachsenroder and Frings, 138.

17. Steven I. Wilkinson, *Votes and Violence: Electoral Competition and Ethnic Riots in India* (Cambridge: Cambridge University Press, 2006), 205.

18. Benjamin Reilly, *Democracy and Diversity: Political Engineering in the Asia Pacific* (Oxford: Oxford University Press, 2006), 138.

19. Shinoda, "Japan," ibid., 91–92.

20. Shinoda, "Japan," ibid., 93.

21. Kanchan Chandra, *Why Ethnic Parties Succeed: Patronage and Ethnic Head Counts in India* (Cambridge: Cambridge University Press, 2004), 13–14.

22. Kim, "Korea," 231.

23. Baogang He, Brian Galligan, and Takishi Inoguchi, "Preface," in *Federalism in Asia* (Cheltenham and Northampton: Edward Elgar, 2007), xvii.

24. Ibid., xviii.

25. Ibid., xiv.

26. Ibid., xv.

27. See Takashi Inoguchi, "Federal Traditions and Quasi-Federalism in Japan," in *Federalism in Asia*, ed. He, Galligan, and Inoguchi (Cheltenham U.K.; Northampton, MA, U.S.A.: Edward Elgar, 2007), 266–267.

CHAPTER 5, CHINA'S STEP TOWARD DEMOCRATIZATION: INTRAPARTY DEMOCRACY

1. David Shambaugh, *China's Communist Party: Atrophy and Adaptation* (Washington, D.C.: Woodrow Wilson Center Press, 2008), 138.

2. Zhonggong Zhongyang Zuzhi Bu Dangjian Yanjiusuo Ketizu [The Central Institute for Party-building at the Central Organization Department of CPC Central Committee], ed., *Guowai Zhengdang Zhuanti Yanjiu Baogao* [*Foreign Political Party Research Paper, Vol.1*] (Dangjian: Duwu Chuban She, 2007).

3. Xiao Chaoran, ed., *Zhongguo zhengzhi fazhan yu duodang hezuo zhidu* [*China's Political Development and the System of Multi-Party Co-operation*] (Beijing: Beijing University Press, 1991).

4. Major democratic parties are China's Association for Promoting Democracy, China's Democratic League, September Third Study Society, China's National Construction Association, Chinese Peasants' and Workers' Democratic Party, Guomindang Revolutionary Committee, Taiwan's Democratic Autonomy League, and Zhigong dang.

5. Bruce J. Dickson, "Threats to Party Supremacy," *Journal of Democracy* 14 (2003): 14. He also made this point in his earlier work. "Democratizing reforms are unlikely to come under the sponsorship of the CCP; instead, they are likely to come at its expense." See Bruce J. Dickson, *Democratization in China and Taiwan: The Adaptability of Leninist Parties* (Oxford: Clarendon Press, 1997), 253.

6. Kim Jae Cheol, "Party Reform in Post-Mao China: Re-Conceptualization of Party's Leading Roles," PhD dissertation, University of Washington, 1993.

7. Zheng Changzhong, Zhongguo Gongchandang Dangnei Minzhu Zhidu Chuangxin [*Chinese Communist Party's Innovation in Inner-party Democratic System*] (Tianjin: Renmin Chuban She, 2005).

8. Gang Lin, "Ideology and Political Institutions for a New Era," in *China after Jiang*, ed. Gang Li and Xiaobo Hu (Stanford, Calif.: Stanford University Press, 2003), 60.

9. Ibid., 64.

10. Yu Guangyuan, *1978: Wo Qinli de Naci Lishi Da Zhuanzhe* [*1978: A Historical Turning Point I Witnessed*] (Beijing: Zhongyang Bianyi Chuban She [Central Compilation and Translation Press], 2008).

11. Zhang Xiangni et al. *Gongchandang zhizheng fangshi tantao* [*An Investigation of the Arts of Rule of the Chinese Communist Party*] (Kaifeng: Henan University Press, 1989), 49–50.

12. Zhang Weiping, ed., *A New Work Manual for Party Affairs* (Beijing: Zhongguo yanshi chubanshe, 1995), 1673.

13. Yawei Liu, "Guest Editor's Introduction," *Chinese Law and Government* 34 (2001): 20.

14. Cai Jainwu, Yu Liedong, and Tang Xiafu, "A Comparative Study and Analysis on the Status of the 5th Round Village Elections in Jiangxi Province," paper presented at National Conference on Village Self-governance, organized by EU-China Training Program on Village Governance, Beijing, China, 2005.

15. *Yangzhou Daily*, December 20, 2004.

16. *Xiangzhen Luntan* 5, 2005, 12.

17. Fenghuang television news, September 25, 2005.

18. *Minzheng Luntan* 5, 1999, 42.

19. *Huaxi dushibao*, December 9, 2003.

20. Suzanne Ogden, *China's Unresolved Issues* (Upper Saddle River, N.J.: Prentice-Hall Limited, 1992), 239–240.

21. "Beijing," October 16, 1992, Reuter's.

22. For a detailed discussion on the party congress, see Gang Lin, "Leadership Transition, Intra-Party Democracy, and Institution Building in China," *Asian Survey* 44 (2004), 267–272.

23. *Beijing Times*, July 17, 2008, A06.

24. *Nanfang renbao*, July 14, 2008, A02.

25. Available at: www.stnn.cc, August 20, 2008.

26. *Beijing Times*, July 15, 2008, A16.

27. Gang Lin, "Leadership Transition," 275.

28. A residential community usually has 1,000 households or more. Each has a general branch of the Chinese Communist Party with more than 200 members. Each general branch of the party has subdivisions, going down to subbranches in each residential building.

29. See the special issue of *Journal of Democracy* 14 (January 2003).

30. Qinglian He, "A Volcanic Stability," *Journal of Democracy* 14 (2003): 66–72.

31. Bruce Dickson, "Whom Does the Party Represent? From 'Three Revolutionary Classes' to 'Three Representatives,'" *American Asian Review* 21 (2003): 5–6.

32. See John P. Burns, "Strengthening Central CCP Control of Leadership Selection: The 1990s Nomenklatura," *China Quarterly* 138 (1994): 474–480; "The Relevance of the Nomenklatura System to the Chinese Communist Party in a New Era," paper presented at International Conference on the Chinese Communist Party in a New Era: Renewal and Reform, East Asian Institute, Singapore, December 9–10, 2003.

33. "Sulian jubian zhihou zhongguo de xianshi yingdui yu zhanlue xuanzhe" ["China's Realistic Countermeasures and Strategic Choices after the Dramatic Changes in the Soviet Union"], an internal document printed and circulated by Zhongguo Qingnian Baoshe in September 1991.

34. For a discussion on the system, see Baogang He, "The Chinese Communist Party and Party System in China," in Wolfgang Sachsenroder, ed., *Political Party and Democratic Development in East and Southeast Asia: Volume II: East Asia* (London: Ashgate Publishers, 1998), 36–87.

35. I have elsewhere discussed China's search for the mixed regime, see Baogang He, "The Theory and Practice of Chinese Grassroots Governance: Five Models," *Japanese Journal of Political Science* 4 (2003): 293–314.

CHAPTER 6, POLITICAL PARTIES AND DEMOCRACY IN INDIA

1. Ashutosh Varshney, "Why Democracy Survives," *Journal of Democracy* 9 (1998): 36–50.

2. Emergency rule is provided for in a provision under Article 352 of the Constitution where, in a situation of a grave threat to national security due to external aggression or armed rebellion, the federal government is empowered to give directions to the States, and impose duties on or confer powers to officers of the federal government even if the matter is not one on the federal list, and likewise parliament can legislate on subjects in the States list. Basically, it is a suspension of the normal democratic process that has been used only once, in 1975–77 (a period commonly referred to as The Emergency).

3. Specifically, we focus on the period after the last general elections in 2004. We will cover the past only to the extent that the historical background is necessary for the reader. Even then we will emphasize recent, that is, post-1989, minority governments and coalition politics, but will not do a detailed recapitulation of political developments and trends. For detailed analyses of India's parties and party system, see M. V. Rajeev Gowda and E. Sridharan, "Parties and the Party System, 1947–2006," in *The State of India's Democracy*, ed. Sumit Ganguly, Larry Diamond, and Marc Plattner (Baltimore: Johns Hopkins University Press, 2007), 19–21; and E. Sridharan and Ashutosh Varshney, "Toward Moderate Pluralism: Political Parties in India," in *Political Parties and Democracy*, ed. Larry Diamond and Richard Gunther (Baltimore: Johns Hopkins University Press, 2001), 206–237.

4. Larry Diamond and Richard Gunther, "Introduction," in *Political Parties and Democracy*, ed. Diamond and Gunther, xviii.

5. Philippe Schmitter, "Parties Are Not What They Once Were," in *Political Parties and Democracy*, ed. Diamond and Gunther, 71–89.

6. Thomas Carothers, *Confronting the Weakest Link: Aiding Political Parties in New Democracies* (Washington, D.C.: Carnegie Endowment for International Peace, 2006).

7. Larry Diamond, Juan J. Linz and Seymour Martin Lipset, eds., *Politics in Developing Countries: Comparing Experiences with Democracy* (Boulder, CO: Lynne Rienner, 1995), 35–36.

8. Kay Lawson, ed., *Political Parties and Linkage: A Comparative Perspective* (New Haven, Conn.: Yale University Press, 1980).

9. Larry Diamond and Marc Plattner, "Introduction," in *Nationalism, Ethnic Conflict and Democracy*, ed. Larry Diamond and Marc Plattner (Baltimore: Johns Hopkins University Press, 1994), ix–xxx.

10. Arend Lijphart, *Democracies: Patterns of Majoritarian and Consensus Government in Twenty-One Countries* (New Haven, Conn.: Yale University Press, 1984).

11. See Diamond and Plattner, *Nationalism, Ethnic Conflict and Democracy*, xxvi, summarizing Horowitz's five functions.

12. Donald Horowitz, "Electoral Systems: A Primer for Decision-makers," *Journal of Democracy* 14 (2003): 118–119.

13. Benjamin Reilly, "Democratization and Electoral Reform in the Asia-Pacific Region: Is There an Asian Model of Democracy?" *Comparative Political Studies* 40 (2007): 1350–1371; Benjamin Reilly, "Political Engineering in the Asia-Pacific," *Journal of Democracy* 18 (2007): 63–64.

14. Juan Linz, Alfred Stepan, and Yogendra Yadav, "'Nation State' or 'State Nation': India in Comparative Perspective," in *Democracy and Diversity: India and the American Experience*, ed. K. Shankar Bajpai (New Delhi: Oxford University Press, 2007), 50–106.

15. For the eight criteria, see Larry Diamond and Leonardo Morlino, "The Quality of Democracy: An Overview," *Journal of Democracy* 15 (October 2004): 20–31.

16. In this section, we draw on our earlier work at various points, including Gowda and Sridharan, "Parties and the Party System, 1947–2006," 3–25; E. Sridharan, "The Fragmentation of the Indian Party System, 1952–1999: Seven Competing Explanations," in *Parties and Party Politics in India*, ed. Zoya Hasan (Delhi: Oxford University Press, 2002), 475–503.

17. For the Laakso-Taagepera indices of the effective number of parties see *Journal of the Indian School of Political Economy* 15 (2003): Statistical Supplement, Tables 1.1–1.13, 293–307. For 2004, the index we use is as calculated by the Centre for the Study of Developing Societies, New Delhi, and for 2009 we use our own calculation.

18. Yogendra Yadav, "Electoral Politics in the Time of Change: India's Third Electoral System, 1989–99," *Economic and Political Weekly* (Mumbai) (August 21–28, 1999): 2393–2399.

19. Rein Taagepera and Matthew Soberg Shugart, *Seats & Votes: The Effects and Determinants of Electoral Systems* (New Haven: Yale University Press, 1989), emphasize ballot structure, district magnitude, and electoral formula as the basic variables; Arend Lijphart emphasizes, in addition, a derivative variable, effective threshold of representation, and assembly size and considers the special cases of presidentialism and apparentement (linking of party lists).

20. For an account and explanation of the Duvergerian dynamic of bipolarization at the district and state levels, see Pradeep Chhibber and Geetha Murali, "Duvergerian Dynamics in Indian States," *Party Politics* 12 (2007): 5–34.

21. See Maurice Duverger, *Political Parties: Their Organization and Activity in the Modern State* (New York: Wiley, 1963) for the full argument.

22. Douglas W. Rae, *The Political Consequences of Electoral Laws* (New Haven: Yale University Press, 1971).

23. See E. Sridharan, "Duverger's Law, Its Reformulations and the Evolution of the Indian Party System," Centre for Policy Research, May 1997, and *IRIS India Working Paper* 35 (February 1997), IRIS Center, University of Maryland, for a detailed version of the argument presented below.

24. See Pradeep Chhibber and Ken Kollman, "Party Aggregation and the Number of Parties in India and the United States," *American Political Science Review* 92 (1998): 329–342; Pradeep Chhibber and Ken Kollman, *The Formation of National Party Systems: Federalism and Party Competition in Canada, Great Britain, India and the United States* (Princeton, N.J.: Princeton University Press, 2004).

25. See Sridharan, "The Fragmentation of the Indian Party System," 496–502 for a detailed account of coalition dynamics.

26. BKD/BLD, Bharatiya Lok Dal/Bharatiya Kranti Dal, farmers' parties of North India in the 1960s and 1970s.

27. For a detailed overview of state-level coalition politics in India, see Sridharan, E. (1999). "Principles, Power and Coalition Politics in India: Lessons from Theory, Comparison and Recent History," in D. D. Khanna and Gert W. Kueck (eds). *Principles, Power and Politics* (New Delhi: Macmillan), 270–290; Sridharan (2002); Sridharan, E. (2003). "Coalitions and Party Strategies in India's Parliamentary Federation," *Publius* 33(4):135–152. For a detailed state-wise analysis of the BJP's coalition strategies since 1989, see Sridharan, E. (2005). "Coalition Strategies and the BJP's Expansion, 1989–2004," *Commonwealth and Comparative Politics* 43(2): 194–221. For a detailed analysis of the Congress's coalition strategies and their criticality in the 2004 elections, see Sridharan, E. (2004). "Electoral Coalitions in the 2004 General Elections: Theory and Evidence," *Economic and Political Weekly* 39(51): 5418–5425.

28. Kanchan Chandra, *Why Ethnic Parties Succeed: Patronage and Ethnic Head Counts in India* (Cambridge: Cambridge University Press, 2004), 13–14.

29. For incumbency advantage in U.S. congressional elections, see G. W. Cox and J. N. Katz, "Why Did the Incumbency Advantage in U.S. House Elections Grow?," *American Journal of Political Science* 40 (1996): 478–497; S. Ansolabehere, J. Snyder, and C. Stewart, "Old Voters, New Voters, and the Personal Vote: Using Redistricting to Measure the Incumbency Advantage," *American Journal of Political Science* 44 (2000): 17–34; A. Gelman and G. King, "Estimating Incumbency Advantage without Bias," *American Journal of Political Science* 34 (1990): 1142–1164. For the incumbency disadvantage in Indian elections, see the tables in this chapter, and Yogesh Uppal, "The Disadvantaged Incumbents: Estimating Incumbency Effects in Indian State Legislatures," *Public Choice*, 138 (1–2), January 2009, 9–27.

30. Arvind Virmani, "Economic Growth, Governance and Voting Behaviour: An Application to Indian Elections," Working Paper 138, Indian Council for Research on International Economic Relations, New Delhi.

31. Philip Keefer and Stuti Khemani, "Why Do the Poor Receive Poor Services?," *Economic and Political Weekly* (February 28, 2004): 937.

32. Ibid., 938–939.

33. See Subrata Mitra and V. B. Singh, *Democracy and Social Change in India* (New Delhi: Sage, 1999), 188–209; Pradeep Chhibber, Sandeep Shastri, and Richard Sisson, "Federal Arrangements and the Provision of Public Goods in India," *Asian Survey* 44 (2004): 339–352, for evidence that public goods and basic social services matter. See Pradeep Chhibber, "Political Parties, Electoral Competition, Government Expenditures and Economic Reform," *Journal of Development Studies* 32 (1995): 74–96; Pradeep Chhibber and Irfan Nooruddin, "Do Party Systems Count? The Number of Parties and Government Performance in the Indian State," *Comparative Political Studies* 41 (2006): 152–187 for the argument about club goods.

34. Arvind Rajagopal, *Politics After Television: Religious Nationalism and the Reshaping of the Public in India* (Cambridge: Cambridge University Press, 2001).

35. Trilochan Sastry, "Electoral Reforms and Citizens' Initiatives," *Economic and Political Weekly* (Mumbai) (March 27–April 2, 2004): 1391–1397.

36. T. N. Pandey, "Tax Returns of Political Parties Can Be Made Public," *Hindu BusinessLine*, May 24, 2008, available at: http://www.thehindubusinessline.com/2008/05/24/stories/2008052450140900.htm

37. Sanjay Kumar, "Reforming Indian Electoral Process," *Economic and Political Weekly* (Mumbai) (August 24–30, 2002): 3489–3491.

38. Juan Linz, Alfred Stepan, and Yogendra Yadav, "'Nation State' or 'State Nation': India in Comparative Perspective," in *Democracy and Diversity: India and the American Experience*, ed. K. Shankar Bajpai (New Delhi: Oxford University Press, 2007), 50–106.

39. Arend Lijphart, "The Puzzle of Indian Democracy," *American Political Science Review* 90 (June 1996): 258–268.

40. Atul Kohli, ed., *The Success of India's Democracy* (Cambridge: Cambridge University Press, 2001), 19.

41. Lloyd Rudolph and Susanne Rudolph, *In Pursuit of Lakshmi: The Political Economy of the Indian State* (Chicago: University of Chicago Press, 1987), particularly 19–59.

42. For clientelism, see Vir Chopra, *Marginal Players in Marginal Assemblies: The Indian MLA* (New Delhi: Orient Longman, 1996); Sridharan and Varshney, "Toward Moderate Pluralism," 206–237; Kanchan Chandra, *Why Ethnic Parties Succeed: Patronage and Ethnic Head Counts in India* (Cambridge: Cambridge University Press, 2004); Gowda and Sridharan, "Parties and the Party System, 1947–2006."

43. Chandra, *Why Ethnic Parties Succeed*, 13–14.

44. For the figures in this paragraph see Election Commission of India, *Statistical Report on General Elections, 2004, to the 14th Lok Sabha*, Vol. I.

45. This draws heavily on a section in M. V. Rajeev Gowda and E. Sridharan, "Parties and the Party System, 1947–2006," in Ganguly, Diamond, and Plattner, eds., *The State of India's Democracy*, 19–21.

46. Lawson, *Political Parties and Linkage*.

47. In contrast, in the United States, incumbency advantages "scare" challengers from taking on incumbents. See Gary C. Jacobson, "Running Scared: Elections and Congressional Politics in the 1980s," in *Congress: Structure and Policy*, ed. Mathew D. McCubbins and Terry Sullivan (New York: Cambridge University Press, 1987).

CHAPTER 7, FLEDGLING TWO-PARTY DEMOCRACY IN JAPAN: NO STRONG PARTISANS AND A FRAGMENTED STATE BUREAUCRACY

1. Robert A. Scalapino, *Politics of Development: Perspective on Twentieth-Century Asia* (Cambridge: Harvard University Press, 1998).

2. T. J. Pempel, ed., *Uncommon Democracies: The One-Party Dominant Regimes* (Ithaca, N.Y.: Cornell University Press, 1990).

3. Takashi Inoguchi, "Parliamentary Opposition Under (Post-) One Party Rule in Japan," *Journal of Legislative Studies* 14 (2008): 113–132.

4. Takashi Inoguchi, "Japanese Contemporary Politics," in *A New Japan for the Twenty-First Century: An Inside Overview of Current Fundamental Changes and Problems*, ed. Rien Segers (London: Routledge, 2008), 67–86.

5. Takashi Inoguchi, "The Ghost of Absolutism or Lack Thereof," lecture at the Anglo-Japanese Foundation and the Nissan Institute of Japanese Studies, London and Oxford, England, November, 2007.

6. Ronald Toby, *State and Diplomacy in the Tokugawa Bakufu* (Princeton, N.J.: Princeton University Press, 1984).

7. Takashi Inoguchi, "The Pragmatic Evolution of Japanese Democratic Politics," in *Democracy in Asia*, ed. Michelle Schmiegelow (New York: St. Martin's Press, 1997), 217–232; Eiko Ikegami, *The Taming of the Samurai: Honorific Individualism and the Making of Modern Japan* (Cambridge: Harvard University Press, 1997).

8. Mark Ravina, *Land and Lordship in Early Modern Japan* (Stanford, Calif.: Stanford University Press, 1999).

9. Donald Keene, *Emperor of Japan: Meiji and His World, 1852–1912* (New York: Columbia University Press, 2005).

10. Richard Sims, *Japanese Political History since the Meiji Restoration, 1868–2000* (New York: Palgrave Macmillan, 2001).

11. Takashi Mikuriya, *Meiji Kokka Keisei to Chiho Keiei* [*The Formation of the Meiji State and the Management of Localities*] (Tokyo: University of Tokyo Press, 1980).

12. Robert Spaulding, *Imperial Japan's Higher Civil Service Examination* (Princeton, N.J.: Princeton University Press, 1967).

13. Takashi Inoguchi, *Japanese Politics: An Introduction* (Melbourne: Trans Pacific Press, 2005); Takashi Inoguchi, "Can the LDP Survive Globalization?," *Education about Asia* 12 (2007): 45–49.

14. Takashi Inoguchi, "Federal Traditions and Quasi-Federalism in Japan," in *Federalism in Asia*, ed. Baogang He, Bian Galligan, and Takashi Inoguchi (London: Edward Elgar, 2007), 266–289.

15. Takenori Inoki, *Senkanki Nihon No Shakai Shudan to Network Democracy to Chukan Dantai* [*Social Groups and Networks during the Inter-War Period: Democracy and Intermediate Level Social Organizations*] (Tokyo: NTT Shuppan, 2008).

16. Taichiro Mitani, *Nihon Seito Seiji No Keisei* [*The Formation of Japanese Party Politics*] (Tokyo: University of Tokyo Press, 1967); Peter Duus, *The Cambridge History of Japan* (Cambridge: Cambridge University Press, 1968).

17. Shinichi Kitaoka, *Seito seiji no saisei* [*The Rebirth of Party Politics*] (Tokyo: Chuo Koronsha, 1995).

18. Junji Banno, *Democracy in Prewar Japan, 1871–1937* (London: Routledge, 2001).

19. Jack Snyder, *From Voting to Violence: Democratization and Nationalist Conflict* (New York: Columbia University Press, 2000).

20. Robert Scalapino and Junnosuke Masumi, *Parties and Politics in Contemporary Japan* (Berkeley: University of California Press, 1962); Andrew Gordon, *Postwar Japan as History* (Cambridge, Mass.: Harvard University Press, 1993).

21. Constitutionally, females are made legally equal to males in all respects. Even the family law prescribes gender equality. Yet practice may be somewhat behind. Also employment statistics inform us that gender equality remains to be substantially improved.

22. Scalapino and Masumi, *Party Politics.*

23. Chalmers Johnson, *MITI and the Economic Miracle* (Stanford, Calif.: Stanford University Press, 1982); Harumi Hori, *The Changing Political System and the Ministry of Finance* (London: Routledge, 2005).

24. Inoguchi Takashi, *Gendai Nihon Seiji Keizai No Kozu* [*The Contemporary Japanese Political Economy*] (Tokyo: Toyo Keizai Shimposha, 1985); Inoguchi, *Japanese Politics*.

25. Inoguchi Takashi and Tomoaki Iwai, *Zoku Giin No Kenkyu* [*A Study of Legislative Tribes*] (Tokyo: Nihon Keizai Shimbunsha, 1987).

26. Inoguchi, "Parliamentary Opposition Under (Post-) One Party Rule in Japan."

27. Steven R. Reed, "Evaluating Political Reform in Japan: A Midterm Report," *Japanese Journal of Political Science* 3 (2002): 243–263.

28. Takashi Inoguchi, "The Personalization of Politics and Junichiro Koizumi," in *Political Leadership, Parties and Citizens: The Personalization of Leadership,* ed. Jean Blondel and Jean-Louis Thiebault with Katarzyna Czernicka, Takashi Inoguchi, Ukrist Pathmanand and Fulvio Venturino (London: Routledge, 2009), 209–228.

29. Steven R. Reed, *Japanese Electoral Politics* (London: Routledge, 2003).

30. Takashi Inoguchi, "Globalization and Cultural Nationalism," in *The Cambridge Companion to Modern Japanese Culture,* ed. Yoshio Sugimoto (Cambridge: Cambridge University Press, 2009), 336–351.

31. Murakami Yasusuke, "The Age of New Middle Mass Politics: The Case of Japan," *Journal of Japanese Studies* 8 (1982): 29–72.

32. Personal communication with Governor Ikuo Kabashima of Kumamoto Prefecture, April 2008.

33. Samuel Popkin and Ikuo Kabashima, eds., Special issue on mass media and politics, *Japanese Journal of Political Science* 8 (2007).

34. Jean Blondel and Jean-Louis Thiebault with Katarzyna Czernicka, Takashi Inoguchi, Ukrist Pathmanand, and Fulvio Venturino, eds., *Political Leadership, Parties and Citizens: The Personalization of Leadership* (London: Routledge, 2009).

35. Jean-Marie Guéhenno, *La fin de la Démocratie* [*End of Democracy*] (Paris: Flammarion, 1993).

36. Russell A. Dalton, *Parties without Partisans* (Oxford: Oxford University Press, 2002).

37. Blondel and Thiebault, *Personalization of Politics.*

CHAPTER 8, THE POLITICS OF ETHNICITY: AUTHORITARIAN-ISM, DEVELOPMENT, AND SOCIAL CHANGE IN MALAYSIA

1. For a discussion on the impact of the *reformasi* on the political system, see Meredith L. Weiss, "The 1999 Malaysian General Elections: Issues, Insults and Irregularities," *Asian Survey* 40 (May–June 2000); John Hilley, *Malaysia: Mahathirism, Hegemony and the New Opposition* (London: Zed, 2001); Khoo Boo Teik, *Beyond Mahathir: Malaysian Politics and Its Discontents* (London: Zed, 2003); Edmund Terence Gomez, ed., *The State of Malaysia: Ethnicity, Equity and Reform* (London: Routledge Curzon, 2004), 413–435.

2. The 13 states are Perak, Selangor, Negeri Sembilan, Pahang, Johor, Kelantan, Terengganu, Kedah, Perlis, Penang, Malacca, Sabah, and Sarawak. Singapore, along with the states of Sabah and Sarawak, located across the South China Sea from the peninsula on the island of Borneo, became part of Malaya in 1963, and the country was renamed Malaysia. Singapore left the Malaysian federation in 1965. Although historical events, such as the secession of Singapore,

would suggest that federalism in Malaysia was introduced to take into account various ethnic or communal considerations, the impact of ethnicity traverses state boundaries. Even the Chinese, for instance, are too widely disseminated (except in Singapore, which eventually seceded from Malaysia) to be considered for federal treatment. See B. H. Shafruddin, *The Federal Factor in the Government and Politics of Peninsular Malaysia* (Singapore: Oxford University Press, 1987) for details on Malaysian federalism.

3. *Bumiputera*, which means sons of the soil, is the term used in reference to ethnic Malays and other indigenous peoples.

4. Although there are a large number of indigenous communities in Sabah and Sarawak, most of them, however, are not ethnic Malays.

5. Mohammed Suffian, H. P. Lee, and F. A. Trindada, *The Constitution of Malaysia and Its Development* (Oxford: Oxford University Press, 1979); H. P. Lee, *Constitutional Conflicts in Contemporary Malaysia* (Kuala Lumpur: Oxford University Press, 1995).

6. James J. Puthucheary, *Ownership and Control in the Malayan Economy* (Singapore: Eastern Universities Press, 1960).

7. John Funston, *Malay Politics in Malaysia: A Study of the United Malays National Organisation and Party Islam* (Kuala Lumpur: Heinemann Educational Books, 1980).

8. For an account of the Malayan Union controversy, see William Roff, *The Origins of Malay Nationalism* (Kuala Lumpur: University of Malaya Press, 1967) and Khong Kim Hoong, *Merdeka! British Rule and the Struggle for Independence in Malaya, 1945–1957* (Kuala Lumpur: INSAN, 1984).

9. Heng Pek Koon, *Chinese Politics in Malaysia: A History of the Malaysian Chinese Association* (Singapore: Oxford University Press, 1988), 57.

10. Arasaratnam Sinnappah, *Indians in Malaysia and Singapore* (Kuala Lumpur: Oxford University Press, 1980); Michael Stenson, *Class, Race and Colonialism in West Malaysia: The Indian Case* (Queensland: University of Queensland Press, 1980).

11. S. Sothi Rachagan, *Law and the Electoral Process in Malaysia* (Kuala Lumpur: University of Malaya Press, 1993), 112.

12. David Brown, *The State and Ethnic Politics in Southeast Asia* (London: Routledge, 1994), 206–257.

13. Hua Wu Yin, *Class and Communalism in Malaysia: Politics in a Dependent Capitalist State* (London: Zed, 1983).

14. For accounts of the May 1969 incident and the political maneuverings that culminated in the creation of the Barisan Nasional, see Karl von Vorys, *Democracy without Consensus: Communalism and Political Stability in Malaysia* (Princeton, N.J.: Princeton University Press, 1975); Gordon Means, *Malaysian Politics* (London: Hodder and Stoughton, 1976); Diane K. Mauzy, *Barisan Nasional: Coalition Government in Malaysia* (Kuala Lumpur: Marican and Sons, 1983).

15. This division between the Chinese-based Gerakan and MCA has had limited repercussions on the Barisan Nasional since the seats they contest are in predominantly Chinese-majority constituencies, which, in most instances, the ruling coalition can afford to lose. Furthermore, the combined number of seats contested by the Gerakan and MCA is usually considerably less than one-third of the total number of seats contested by the Barisan Nasional. The victories secured by the Gerakan and MCA in most constituencies they contest during

state and federal elections are also attributed to the Malay support that UMNO had managed to secure for their candidates.

16. Means, *Malaysian Politics*, 299–305.

17. Quoted in Means, *Malaysian Politics*, 393–394.

18. For an in-depth history of PAS, see Farish A. Noor, *Islam Embedded: The Historical Development of the Pan-Malaysian Islamic Party PAS (1951–2003)*, Volumes 1 and 2 (Kuala Lumpur: Malaysian Sociological Research Institute, 2004). See also Edmund Terence Gomez, ed., *Politics in Malaysia: The Malay Dimension* (London: Routledge, 2007) for a study of PAS's electoral performance since the 1990s.

19. See Roff, *Origins of Malay Nationalism*; Funston, *Malay Politics in Malaysia*; and Khong, *Merdeka!* for an account of these important changes in the orientation of PAS.

20. Khong Kim Hoong, *Malaysia's General Election 1990: Continuity, Change, and Ethnic Politics* (Singapore: Institute of Southeast Asian Studies, 1991).

21. An incisive account of this leadership struggle between Mahathir and Razaleigh is provided by A. B. Shamsul, *The Battle Royal: The UMNO Elections of 1987* (Southeast Asian Affairs, Singapore: Institute of Southeast Asian Studies, 1988).

22. Although PAS retained control of Kelantan in the 1995 general election and obtained a marginal increase in its support in Terengganu and Kedah, its partner, Semangat, which had fared miserably in this electoral contest, ceased operations and its members returned to UMNO.

23. For PAS's views on democracy, see James Jesudason, "The Syncretic State and the Structuring of Oppositional Politics in Malaysia," in *Political Oppositions in Industrialising Asia*, ed. Garry Rodan (London: Routledge, 1996), 126–160.

24. Funston, *Malay Politics in Malaysia*; Edmund Terence Gomez, *The 1995 Malaysian General Election: A Report and Commentary* (Singapore: Institute of Southeast Asian Studies, 1996).

25. For an in-depth analysis of the *reformasi* and its failure to bring about a change of regime or major structural reforms, see Gomez, *The State of Malaysia*; Gomez, *Politics in Malaysia*.

26. PRM, then under the leadership of Syed Husin Ali, was formerly known as Parti Sosialis Rakyat Malaysia (Malaysian People's Socialist Party [PSRM]). Inaugurated in 1955 as Parti Rakyat, it had never been able to garner much electoral support.

27. See, for example, Diane K. Mauzy, "The 1982 General Elections in Malaysia: A Mandate for Change?," *Asian Survey* 23 (1983): 497–517; Khong, *Malaysia's General Election 1990*; Edmund Terence Gomez, "Electoral Funding of General, State and Party Elections in Malaysia," *Journal of Contemporary Asia* 26 (1996): 81–99.

28. Edmund Terence Gomez, *Political Business: Corporate Involvement of Malaysian Political Parties* (Cairns: James Cook University, 1994); Edmund Terence Gomez, *Chinese Business in Malaysia: Accumulation, Ascendance, Accommodation* (Honolulu: University of Hawaii Press, 1999).

29. Khong, *Malaysia's General Election 1990*; Gomez, "Electoral Funding"; Gomez, *The 1995 Malaysian General Election*.

30. See, for example, Gomez, "Electoral Funding."

31. Harold Crouch, "Authoritarian Trends, the UMNO Split and the Limits to State Power," in *Fragmented Vision: Culture and Politics in Contemporary Malaysia*,

ed. Joel S. Kahn and Francis Loh Kok Wah (Sydney: Allen and Unwin for Asian Studies Association of Australia, 1992).

32. For details on UMNO's abuse of affirmative action in a manner that serves the interests of party members, see Edmund Terence Gomez and K. S. Jomo, *Malaysia's Political Economy: Politics, Patronage and Profits* (Cambridge: Cambridge University Press, 1997).

33. Gordon Means, *Malaysian Politics: The Second Generation* (Singapore: Oxford University Press, 1991); Zakaria Haji Ahmad, "Malaysia: Quasi-Democracy in a Divided Society," in *Democracy in Developing Countries*, Volume Three: *Asia*, ed. Larry Diamond, Juan J. Linz, and Seymour Martin Lipset (Boulder, Colo.: Lynne Rienner, 1989); Diane Mauzy, "Malaysia: Malay Political Hegemony and 'Coercive Consociationalism,'" in *The Politics of Ethnic Conflict Regulation*, ed. John McGarry and Brendan O'Leary (London: Routledge, 1993), 106–127; Stephen Chee, "Consociational Political Leadership and Conflict Regulation in Malaysia," in *Leadership and Security in Southeast Asia: Institutional Aspects*, ed. Stephen Chee (Singapore: Institute of Southeast Asian Studies, 1991), 53–86; William Case, "Semi-Democracy in Malaysia: Withstanding the Pressures for Regime Change," *Pacific Affairs* 66 (1993), 183–206.

34. Mauzy, "Malaysia," 110–111

35. Chee, "Consociational Political Leadership."

36. John McGarry and Brendan O'Leary, eds., *The Politics of Ethnic Conflict Regulation* (Routledge: London, 1993), 39–40.

37. *Business Times*, March 24, 1995.

38. For discussions on the outcome of affirmative action, see Just Faaland, J. R. Parkinson, and Rais Saniman, *Growth and Ethnic Inequality: Malaysia's New Economic Policy* (Kuala Lumpur: Dewan Bahasa and Pustaka, 1990). See also Gomez and Jomo, *Malaysia's Political Economy*; and Gomez, *Chinese Business in Malaysia*.

39. For an insightful analysis of the rise of the Malay middle class, see Abdul Rahman Embong, *State-Led Modernization and the New Middle Class in Malaysia* (New York: Palgrave, 2002).

40. Crouch, "Authoritarian Trends."

41. Case, "Semi-Democracy in Malaysia."

42. Zakaria, "Malaysia."

43. Crouch, "Authoritarian Trends," p. 21.

44. Other repressive legislation consistently used to silence dissent include the Official Secrets Act (OSA), to help prevent disclosure of government misconduct, the Publication and Printing Presses Act, to check media freedom, and the University and University Colleges Act (UUCA), to curb the political activities of undergraduates.

45. K. Das and Salleh Abas, *May Day for Justice* (Kuala Lumpur: Magnus Books, 1989).

46. Lee, *Constitutional Conflicts*.

47. See, in particular, Samuel P. Huntington, *Political Order in Changing Societies* (New Haven, Conn.: Yale University Press, 1968) and Samuel P. Huntington, *The Third Wave: Democratization in the Late Twentieth Century* (Norman: University of Oklahoma Press, 1991).

48. Edmund Terence Gomez, ed., *Political Business in East Asia* (London: Routledge 2002).

49. Richard Robison, Kevin Hewison, and Garry Rodan, "Political Power in Industrialising Capitalist Societies: Theoretical Approaches," in *Southeast Asia in the 1990s: Authoritarianism, Democracy and Capitalism*, ed. Kevin Hewison, Richard Robison, and Garry Rodan (Sydney: Allen and Unwin, 1993), 9–38.

50. Daniel A. Bell and Kanishka Jayasuriya, "Understanding Illiberal Democracy: A Framework," in *Towards Illiberal Democracy in Pacific Asia*, ed. Daniel A. Bell et al. (London: Macmillan, 1995), 13.

51. Francis Loh Kok Wah, "Towards a New Politics of Fragmentation and Contestation," in *New Politics in Malaysia*, ed. Francis Loh Kok Wah and Johan Saravanamuttu (Singapore: Institute of Southeast Asian Studies, 2003), 253–282.

52. See, for example, Gomez, *The State of Malaysia*.

53. See Gomez and Jomo, *Malaysia's Political Economy*, for a discussion on this issue.

54. Chandra Muzaffar, *Protector?: An Analysis of the Concept and Practice of Loyalty in Leader-Led Relationships within Malay Society* (Penang: Aliran, 1979).

55. Gomez, "Electoral Funding."

56. See Mahathir's speech titled "The New Malay Dilemma," delivered at the Harvard Club of Malaysia dinner on July 27, 2002.

57. These seven firms were Telekom Malaysia, Malayan Banking, Tenaga Nasional, Petronas Gas, Malaysian International Shipping Corporation (MISC), Sime Darby, and Commerce Asset-Holding.

58. These three firms were Resorts World and Genting (both of the same group owned by Lim Goh Tong) and YTL Corporation (owned by the Yeoh family). See Gomez, *Chinese Business in Malaysia* for an in-depth study of the largest Chinese-owned enterprises in Malaysia.

59. However, none of the top 10 was owned by a foreign enterprise. This was an indication of the government's success in protecting the domestic economy, specifically the banking sector, from coming under the control of foreign enterprises.

60. See Hwang In-Won, *Personalized Politics: The Malaysian State under Mahathir* (Singapore: Institute of Southeast Asian Studies, 2003). See also Hilley, "Malaysia"; Khoo, *Beyond Mahathir*; Gomez, *The State of Malaysia*.

CHAPTER 9, POLITICAL PARTIES AND DEMOCRACY IN SOUTH KOREA

1. Robert Dahl, *Polyarchy: Participation and Opposition* (New Haven, Conn.: Yale University Press, 1971).

2. Arend Lijphart, *Patterns of Democracy: Government Forms and Performance in Thirty-Six Countries.* (New Haven, Conn.: Yale Unviersity Press, 1999).

3. Larry Diamond, "Three Paradoxes of Democracy," in *The Global Resurgence of Democracy*, ed. Larry Diamond and Marc Plattner (Baltimore: Johns Hopkins University Press, 1993), 100.

4. Juan Linz and Alfred Stepan, *Problems of Democratic Transition and Consolidation* (Baltimore: Johns Hopkins University Press, 1996).

5. Diamond, *The Global Resurgence of Democracy*, 100.

6. Party-list seats were allocated by the district voting results. For more about initial choice of electoral system, see David Brady and Jongryn Mo, "Electoral

Systems and Institutional Choice: A Case Study of the 1988 Korean Elections," *Comparative Political Studies* 24 (1992): 405–429.

7. Jae-Han Kim and Arendt Lijphart, "Hapeuijewa Hankukeui Kwonruk-kujo" ["Consensual Democracy and Korean Government"], *Korean Political Science Review* 31 (1997): 99–120 (in Korean).

8. There were several studies that explored the relationship between the mode of democratic transition and institutional choice. For instance, Geddes found, examining several cases in postcommunist countries in central and Eastern Europe, that when old regime elites exerted strong influence on the transition negotiation, there was a high likelihood for the choice of a majoritarian electoral system. Barbara Geddes, "Initiation of New Democratic Institutions in Eastern Europe and Latin America," in *Institutional Design in New Democracies: Eastern Europe and Latin America,* ed. Arendt Lijphart and Carlos Waisman (Boulder, Colo.: Westview, 1996).

9. For more about the South Korean transition to democracy, see Jung-Kwan Cho, "From Authoritarianism to Consolidated Democracy in South Korea," PhD dissertation, Yale University, 2000; Hyug Baeg Im, "Politics of Transition: Democratic Transition from Authoritarian Rule in South Korea," PhD dissertation, University of Chicago, 1989.

10. There were few challengers to the cartel party system in democratic South Korea. For instance, Chung Joo-Young, the chairman of Hyundai conglomerate, organized a new party for his own bid for presidential election in 1992. While the party obtained 31 seats in the 1992 parliamentary election, it was suddenly dissolved after Chung retired from politics following his loss in the 1992 presidential election.

11. Only 20% of respondents had "trust" in the National Assembly in a 2003 survey. In stark contrast, the Supreme Court and civic organizations sustain decent levels of trust from the public. Seventy percent of respondents revealed that they had trust in the Supreme Court and 80% in civic organizations. Byung-Jin Park, "Shilewa Sede" ["Trust and Generation"], SKKU-SERI paper series, Seoul, 2006.

12. Due to the nonconcurrent electoral cycle, there was a presidential election in 2002 and a parliamentary election in 2002. As a result, party reform and electoral reform were mainly pursued over the 2002–2004 period.

13. Traditionally, South Korean politics was more often characterized by factional rivalry and personal loyalty and subordination than by stable institutions and organizations. See Gregory Henderson, *Korea: The Politics of Vortex* (Cambridge: Harvard University Press, 1968), 274–289.

14. NMDP, White Paper of Special Commission for Party Development and Innovation, Seoul, 2002. Nomination rules for legislative candidates were further modified before the 2008 parliamentary election.

15. The other prominent democratization leader, Kim Young Sam, had already retired from politics after completing his five-year term as president in 1998.

16. NOSAMO means coalition of people who love Roh Moo Hyun in Korean.

17. For more about the 2002 election and abrupt rise of Roh, see Hoon Jaung, "President Roh Moo Hyun and the Rise of New Politics in South Korea," in *Asian Update Series* (New York: Asia Society, 2003). In fact, the method to nominate legislative candidates was found to influence candidates' electoral

competitiveness. When a candidate was selected through primaries, the candidate was likely to garner more support than candidates from nonprimary selection in Korean election. Yong-Joo Chun, "Hwobo Gochon gwajongeui Minjuhwawa Jongchijok Gyolkwae Daehan Yongu" ["Decentralizing Candida Nomination Process and Their Impacts"], *Korean Political Science Review* 39 (2005) (in Korean), 217–338.

18. The South Korean electoral system has maintained a nonconcurrent electoral cycle between presidential and parliamentary election. The president has a five-year tenure while parliamentary members have a four-year term. As such, there were presidential elections in 2002 and 2007, and parliamentary elections were held in 2004 and 2008.

19. Compared to presidential candidate nomination, reforming parliamentary candidate nomination was somewhat lagging behind. Whereas Uri Party selected one-third of its parliamentary candidates by newly introduced primaries, GNP nominated only 15 candidates through primaries.

20. Korean Association of Party Studies and Joong-Ang Ilbo have conducted a survey on the ideological dispositions of MPs in 2002 and 2004. The survey asked all parliamentary members their position on 10 key policy issues ranging from foreign policy issues to environmental and social policy issues. Then the survey applied the same questionnaire to the voters. The survey was conducted again right after the 2008 parliamentary election.

21. Since the 1987 transition, minor modifications were made in terms of list seat allocation method and share of seats between list and nominal tiers. Initially, the party that obtained the most seats in the nominal tier had half the list seats, for the sake of ensuring a majority. (In fact, such a majority did not occur until 2004.) The rest of the list seats were allocated on the basis of the party's share of nominal tier seats, not votes. In 1996, list seat allocation was altered to be based on each party's share of votes in the nominal tier.

22. According to Shugart and Wattenberg's study, 15 nations newly adopted or changed extant electoral systems into mixed member electoral systems during the 1980s and the 1990s. In their classification, nine countries belong to a type that does not have linkages in seat allocation and voting in the two tiers. Matthew Shugart and Martin Wattenberg, *Mixed Member Electoral Systems: The Best of Both Worlds?* (Oxford: Oxford University Press, 2001), 11–16.

23. Constitutional Court Decision Number 2000.91.112.134.

24. The old electoral system allocates list seats based on each party's share in district voting.

25. In fact, the special commission recommended that the list seats should be increased up to 100, a third of the total number of parliamentary seats. Yet the National Assembly has augmented the list seats only up to 56, while not reducing the share of districts seats.

26. Among various attempts to measure the congruence between voters' choice and their representation at party system, Rose's index has been widely used. It measures proportionality by adding the difference between vote share and seat share of each party, and dividing by two and subtracting it from 100. Richard Rose, "Electoral System: A Question of Degree or of Principle?," in *Choosing Electoral Systems: Issues and Alternatives*, ed. Arend Lijphart and Bernard Grofman (New York: Praeger, 1984), 73–81.

27. Yusun Kim, "Hankook Nodongjohap Yongu" ["A Study on the Korean Labor Organization"], *Policy Paper Series* (Seoul: Korean Institute for Labor and Society, 2007), 2–12 (in Korean). The organization rate of Korean workers has declined steadily down to 10.5% in 2005. The two umbrella labor organizations comprised about 1.3 million workers in 2005.

28. Since Duverger's seminal work, there has been a wide and extended debate about this logic of voting in plurality electoral system. Maurice Duverger, *Political Parties* (New York: Wiley, 1954).

29. The rationale for split voting ranges from coalition insurance to balancing strategy and voters' sense of effectiveness. Chan Wook Park, "17 Dae Chongsoneso Epyo Byungripjewa Yukwonjaeui Bunhal Toopyo" ["Mixed Member Electoral System and Split-Ticket Voting in the 17th Parliamentary Election"], *Hankuk Jeongchi Yongu* [*Korean Political Studies*] 13 (2004): 39–86 (in Korean). For the case of Japan, see Masaru Kohno, "Voter Turnout and Strategic Ticket-Splitting under Japan's New Electoral Rules," *Asian Survey* 37 (1997): 429–440.

30. The 2002 local election was the first in which the new MMES was introduced.

31. For more about this survey and analysis, see Park, "17 Dae Chongsoneso Epyo Byungripjewa Yukwonjaeui Bunhal Toopyo."

32. Initially, the Uri Party obtained a majority of legislative seats in the 2004 election. Yet, splits from the party forced the Uri Party to lose its majority control. Going through a series of mergers and splits, the successor party to Uri Party regained the legislative majority in 2007.

33. Disaffected by the party nomination process in 2008, approximately 20 parliamentary members of GNP split away from the GNP. Since they were members of Park Keun Hye faction of GNP, they named the new party after their leader, Park.

34. Giovanni Sartori, *Parties and Party Systems: A Framework for Analysis* (New York: Cambridge University Press, 1976), 131–142.

35. Bernard Grofman and Arend Lijphart, eds., *Electoral Laws and Their Political Consequences* (New York: Agathon Press, 1986).

36. Laakso and Taagepera developed a widely used formula to calculate the number of parties in a political system. The effective number of parties is obtained by squaring each party's share of seats, adding all of these squares, and dividing 1.00 by this number. Maarkku Laakso and Rein Taagepera, "Effective Number of Parties: A Measure with Application to West Europe," *Comparative Political Studies* 12 (1979): 3–27.

37. Scott Mainwaring, "Presidentialism, Multipartism, and Democracy: The Difficult Combination," *Comparative Political Studies* 26 (1993): 213.

38. Scott Mainwaring and Matthew Shugart, "Conclusion: Presidentialism and the Party System," in *Presidentialism and Democracy in Latin America*, ed. Mainwaring and Shugart (New York: Cambridge University Press, 1997), 394–439.

39. Although presidential parties have never received a majority in parliamentary elections, governing parties obtained a legislative majority occasionally by postelection mergers or by independents joining presidential parties.

40. David Mayhew and others have engaged in extensive debates about governing efficiency of divided and unified government in the United States. David Mayhew, *Divided We Govern: Party Control, Lawmaking and Investigation, 1946–1990*

(New Haven, Conn.: Yale University Press, 1991) and Peter Galderisi, ed., *Divided Government: Change, Uncertainty, and the Constitutional Order* (Lanham, Md.: Rowman and Littlefield, 1996).

41. One may argue that both 2004 and 2008 parliamentary elections were held during a honeymoon period for the incumbent presidents. However, it should be noted that former president Roh Tae Woo's party did not win legislative majority in his honeymoon period, but rather four months after his presidential election in 1988.

42. Political Finance Law, Article 31.

43. Before 2002–2004 reform, it was a regular pattern that leaders of big conglomerates were prosecuted for violating contribution limits and related regulations at the end of each electoral cycle.

44. President Roh's Uri Party, which obtained a legislative majority in 2004 election, went through mergers and splits several times and then eventually recovered legislative majority in 2007.

45. I excluded the legislative data in the 16th National Assembly (2000–2004) as it covered both before and after 2002–2004 reform periods. For the passing rate of government bills and parliamentary member bills see "Legislative Information Data of the National Assembly," available at: http://likms.assembly.go.kr/bill/jsp/main.jsp.

46. Korean Democracy Barometer, 2001. Quoted from Doh Chull Shin, "Mass Politics, Public Opinion, and Democracy in Korea," in *Korea's Democratization*, ed. Samuel Kim (New York: Cambridge University Press, 2003), 52.

47. Shin, "Mass Politics, Public Opinion, and Democracy in Korea," 70.

48. Doh Chull Shin, *Mass Politics and Culture in Democratizing Korea* (New York: Cambridge University Press, 1999), 189.

49. Ibid., 181–182.

50. Ibid., 190.

51. Stefano Bartolini and Peter Mair, "Challenges to Contemporary Political Parties," in *Political Parties and Democracy*, ed. Larry Diamond and Richard Gunther (Baltimore: Johns Hopkins University, 2001), 332–336.

52. In a comprehensive comparative study, the level of party attachment in South Korea was ranked as mediocre. The relevant data from CSES (Comparative Study of Electoral System) module 2 (2001–2006) shows that Korean party attachment was around 1.0 out of 2.0 scale. It was somewhat lower than those of Japan but higher than those of Taiwan, Hong Kong, and Philippines. For more about the party attachment and political participation, see Yun-Han Chu and Min-Hua Huang, "Partisanship and Citizen Politics in East Asia," *Journal of East Asian Studies* 7 (2007): 295–321.

Contributors

GENERAL EDITOR

KAY LAWSON is Professor Emerita of political science at San Francisco State University. She was a visiting professor at the University of Paris, Sorbonne, 1992–2000, and coeditor of the *International Political Science Review*, 2000–2009. She is general editor of two series: "Political Parties in Context" (Praeger) and "Perspectives in Comparative Politics" (Palgrave). She is the author of numerous books and articles on political parties including *The Comparative Study of Political Parties* (1976) and editor of many others including *Political Parties and Linkage* (1980), *When Parties Fail* (1988), and *When Parties Prosper* (2007), the last two with Peter Merkl. Her textbook, *The Human Polity: A Comparative Introduction to Political Science*, is now in its fifth edition. In 2003 she received the Samuel J. Eldersfeld Career Achievement award of the section on Political Organizations and Parties of the American Political Science Association.

VOLUME I: THE AMERICAS

JAMES BICKERTON is professor of political science at Saint Francis Xavier University in Nova Scotia, Canada. Recent publications include coeditorship of *Canadian Politics*, 5th ed. (2009), coauthorship of "Regions" in Danielle Caramani, ed., *Comparative Politics* (2008), and *Freedom, Equality, Community: The Political Philosophy of Six Influential*

Canadians (2006). His research interests include federalism, nationalism, and regionalism, as well as Canadian party and electoral politics.

DIANA DWYRE is professor of political science at California State University, Chico. She is coauthor with Victoria Farrar-Myers of *Legislative Labyrinth: Congress and Campaign Finance Reform* (2001) and *Limits and Loopholes: The Quest for Money, Free Speech and Fair Elections* (2008), as well as author of many journal articles and book chapters on political parties and political finance. She was the William Steiger American Political Science Association Congressional Fellow in 1998 and the Australian National University Fulbright Distinguished Chair in American Political Science in 2009–2010.

ALFREDO JOIGNANT is professor and researcher of the Instituto de Políticas Públicas Expansiva UDP, Diego Portales University in Chile, and past president of the Chilean Political Science Association (1998–2000). He is the author of several articles on political parties, political competence, and political socialization in the *Revue française de science politique*. His work currently focuses on the political sociology of elites and the politics of memory.

JORGE LANZARO is professor at the Instituto de Ciencia Política, Universidad de la República (Uruguay), of which he was founder and director. Among his latest publications: "A Social Democratic Government in Latin America," in Steven Levitsky and Kenneth Roberts, eds., *Latin America's Left Turn* (Cambridge University Press, forthcoming); "Uruguayan Parties: Transition within Transition," in Kay Lawson and Peter Merkl, eds., *When Political Parties Prosper*; "La 'tercera ola' de las izquierdas en América Latina," in *Las izquierdas latinoamericanas* (Madrid: Pablo Iglesias); and *Tipos de Presidencialismo y Coaliciones Políticas en América Latina* (Buenos Aires: Clacso).

FERNANDO MAYORGA is professor and director of CESU-UMSS, Saint Simon University in Cochabamba, Bolivia. He is the author of *Encrucijadas. Essays about Democracy and State Reform in Bolivia* (Gente Común 2007) and *The Antiglobalization Movement in Bolivia* (Plural/ UNRISD 2008) as well as multiple book chapters and articles about neo-populism, parties, and political discourse.

ANA MARÍA MUSTAPIC is an associate professor in the Department of Political Science and International Studies of the Torcuato Di Tella University in Buenos Aires. Her primary areas of research include Congress, political parties, and electoral systems. She has served as a consultant for the OAS, the UNDP, and the IDB on political reform. She is currently finishing a book on the micro foundations of party politics in Argentina.

JAIRO NICOLAU is professor in the Department of Political Science, Instituto Universitário de Pesquisas do Rio de Janeiro (IUPERJ), Brazil. He is author of *História do Voto no Brasil* (2002) and *Sistemas Eleitorais* (2004), and multiple book chapters and articles on political parties, electoral systems, and elections.

ESPERANZA PALMA is professor in the Department of Social Sciences, Universidad Autónoma Metropolitana-Cuajimalpa, in Mexico City. She is the author of *Las bases políticas de la alternancia en México: un estudio del PAN y el PRD durante la democratización* (México, UAM-A 2004) and author of multiple book chapters and articles on political parties during transitional processes in Latin America, particularly in Mexico, the so-called crisis of parties, and the perspectives of consolidation of the leftist parties in Mexico.

MARTIN TANAKA is Peruvian and took his PhD in political science from FLACSO Mexico. He is currently a senior researcher at the Institute of Peruvian Studies (IEP) and professor at the Catholic University of Peru. He is the author of numerous books, book chapters, and articles on political parties, democracy, and social movements, in Peru and in Latin America; published by the IEP, Cambridge and Stanford University Presses, Brookings Institution Press, and the University of London, among many others.

VOLUME II: EUROPE

ATTILA ÁGH is a professor of political science at the Budapest Corvinus University and director of the research center Together for Europe at the Hungarian Academy of Sciences. He has published books in the United Kingdom on the democratization of the east-central European region and has recently edited a series of books in English on the new member states of the European Union, focusing on governments, parties, and organized interests.

ELIN HAUGSGJERD ALLERN is postdoctoral fellow of political science at the University of Oslo, Norway. Her research interests include party organizational change, the relationship between parties and interest groups, and multilevel government and political parties. Her work has appeared in several edited volumes and journals, including *West European Politics* and *European Journal of Political Research*, as well as her book, *Political Parties and Interest Groups in Norway* (ECPR Press 2010).

JØRGEN ELKLIT is professor of political science at Aarhus University in Denmark. His main professional interests are local and national politics and elections in Denmark and elections and democratization in new democracies. His latest book is *Nye kommunalvalg? Kontinuitet og forandring ved valget i 2005* (New local elections? Continuity and change in the 2005 elections) (2007, coedited with Roger Buch).

CHRISTIAN ELMELUND-PRÆSTEKÆR is an assistant professor at the Department of Political Science, University of Southern Denmark. His most recent book is on negative campaigning in Danish elections (*Kammertoner og Unoder i valgkamp*, University Press of Southern Denmark 2009). He has published several articles on political communication, negative campaigning, agenda-setting, and party organization.

JUERGEN FALTER is professor of political science at the University of Mainz (Germany) and was president of the German Association of Political Science (2000–2003). He has published about 25 books and monographs, and over 200 articles on voting behavior, the Nazi electorate, political extremism, political attitudes, and methodological problems of the social sciences.

PIERO IGNAZI is professor of comparative politics at the faculty of political science of the University of Bologna, Bologna, Italy. His recent publications include *Political Parties and Political Systems: The Concept of Linkage Revisited* (Praeger 2005, coedited with A. Rommele and D. Farrell), *Extreme Right Parties in Western Europe* (Oxford University Press 2006), and *Partiti politici in Italia* (Il Mulino 2008).

ULRIK KJAER is professor of political science, University of Southern Denmark. His most recent book is on local political leadership (*Lokalt politisk lederskab*, with Rikke Berg, University Press of Southern Denmark 2007). He has published several articles and book chapters on political recruitment, elections, parliamentarians, local governments, and local party systems.

HIERONIM KUBIAK is professor of sociology at the Jagiellonian University and Andrzej Frycz Modrzewski Cracow University, Poland. Among his recent publications are: *Democracy and the Individual Will* (1997); *Parties, Party Systems and Cleavages in Poland: 1918–1989* (1999); *Reformers in PUWP* (2000); *Poland's Democratic Left Alliance: Beyond Post-communist Succession* (2007); and *On the Threshold of the Post-Westphalia Era. A Theory of Nation* (2007).

LAURA MORALES is a research fellow at the Institute for Social Change of the University of Manchester. Her interests lie in the areas of political behavior, social capital, and political parties. She is the author of *Joining Political Organisations* (ECPR Press 2009) and of many book chapters and articles, among which is "European Integration and Spanish Parties: Elite Empowerment amidst Limited Adaptation" (with L. Ramiro), in Thomas Poguntke et al., eds., *The Europeanization of National Political Parties: Power and Organizational Adaptation* (London: Routledge 2007).

MIROSLAV NOVAK is the first professor of political science at the Charles University and rector of the CEVRO Institute, both in Prague. He has published regularly in French and in Czech, including *Systemy politickych stran* (Political Party Systems, 1997). He is—among other appointments—a member of the editorial boards of *La Revue internationale de politique compare, La Revue d'etudes politiques et constitutionelles esteuropeennes,* and *l'Annuaire francais des relations internationals.*

LUIS RAMIRO is associate professor of political science at the University of Murcia, Spain. He is the author of many book chapters and articles on political parties, including "Euroscepticism and Political Parties in Spain" (with I. Llamazares and M. Gmez-Reino), in P. Taggart and A. Szcerbiak, eds., *Opposing Europe? The Comparative Party Politics of Euroscepticism* (Oxford University Press 2008) and "European Integration and Spanish Parties: Elite Empowerment amidst Limited Adaptation" (with L. Morales), in T. Poguntke et al., eds., *The Europeanization of National Political Parties: Power and Organizational Adaptation* (Routledge 2007).

NICOLAS SAUGER is senior research fellow at Sciences Po (Paris) and associate professor at the Ecole Polytechnique, France. He has coedited the special issue "France's Fifth Republic at Fifty" of *West European Politics* 32(2) (2009) and several book chapters on political parties, institutions, and methodological issues related to survey research.

PAUL WEBB is professor of politics at the University of Sussex. His research interests focus on representative democracy, particularly party and electoral politics. He is author or editor of numerous publications, including *The Modern British Party System* (Sage 2000), *Political Parties in Advanced Industrial Societies* (Oxford University Press 2002, with David Farrell and Ian Holliday), and *Party Politics in New Democracies* (Oxford University Press 2005, with Stephen White). He is currently coeditor of the journal *Party Politics.*

VOLUME III: POST-SOVIET AND ASIAN POLITICAL PARTIES

Post-Soviet

IGOR BOTAN is the executive director of the Association for Participatory Democracy, an independent center of analysis and consultation on the decision-making, political, electoral, and socioeconomic processes in the Republic of Moldova. He is the author of many articles on electoral and party system development in Moldova and is also the political analyst for Moldovan issues at Radio Free Europe/Romanian Service and at the Intelligence Unit of *The Economist*.

ANATOLY KULIK is senior research fellow in political science at the Russian Academy of Sciences and lecturer at State University—Higher School of Economics (Moscow). He writes widely on comparative party politics, political party development in post-Soviet Russia, and e-governance. Among his recent publications are: "Russian 'Mnogopartijnost'' in the Light of Political Competition," in *Political Competition and Parties in Post-Soviet States*, edited by E. Meleshkina et al. (2009); "Russian Party System after Electoral Cycle 2007–2008: The End of the History?," in *The New Political Cycle: Agenda for Russia*, edited by O. Maliniva et al. (2008); and "To Prosper in Russia: Parties Deep in the Shadow of the President," in *When Parties Prosper: The Use of Electoral Success*, edited by Kay Lawson and Peter Merkl (2007).

ANDREY A. MELESHEVYCH is professor and dean of the School of Law, National University of Kyiv-Mohyla Academy in Ukraine. He is the author of *Party Systems in Post-Soviet Countries: A Comparative Study of Political Institutionalization in the Baltic States, Russia, and Ukraine* (2007) and multiple book chapters and articles on political parties, electoral law, and institution building in transitional countries.

GEORGE TARKHAN-MOURAVI is codirector of the Institute for Policy Studies (IPS) in Tbilisi, Georgia, and chairman of the board of directors, PASOS association of Eastern European think tanks based in Prague, Czech Republic. He has authored a number of publications on political developments and regional security in the Caucasus and the Black Sea region, interethnic relations, forced migration, human development, and democratic transition in Georgia.

Asia

BAOGANG HE received his MA from the People's University of China, Beijing, and PhD from ANU, Australia. He is chair in international studies at the School of Politics and International Studies, Deakin University, Melbourne, Australia, and author of four books, three edited books, and numerous refereed articles. His current research interests include deliberative democracy, Chinese democratization, and Chinese politics.

EDMUND TERENCE GOMEZ is an associate professor of political economy at the Faculty of Economics and Administration, University of Malaya, and recently (2005–2008) served as research coordinator at the United Nations Research Institute for Social Development (UNRISD) in Geneva. His many books include *Malaysia's Political Economy: Politics, Patronage and Profits* (1997), *The State of Malaysia: Ethnicity, Equity and Reform* (2004), *Politics in Malaysia: The Malay Dimension* (2007), and *The State, Development and Identity in Multi-ethnic Countries: Ethnicity, Equity and the Nation* (2008).

M. V. RAJEEV GOWDA is professor of economics and social sciences at the Indian Institute of Management Bangalore. He coedited *Judgments, Decisions, and Public Policy* (2002). He is also active in Indian politics. He has authored book chapters and articles on Indian political parties and also on e-democracy.

TAKASHI INOGUCHI is president of the University of Niigata Prefecture, professor emeritus of University of Tokyo, executive editor of the Japanese *Journal of Political Science*, and director of the AsiaBarometer project. He has published 80 books and numerous journal articles on Japan and international affairs. His current interests include political party systems, political cultures, and cross-national comparisons of norms and values through surveys. He is the coeditor of *Globalization, the State and Public Opinion* (with Ian Marsh, 2008) and "Demographic Change and Asian Dynamics: Social and Political Implications," *Asian Economic Policy Review* (June 2009).

HOON JAUNG is professor of political science at Chung-Ang University in Seoul, Korea. He is the author of *President Roh Moo Hyun and New Politics in South Korea* (2003) and numerous articles on party politics and democratization issues of Korea. He was Reagan-Fascell Fellow at the National Endowment for Democracy (Washington, D.C.) in 2005 and now serves as editor-in-chief for *Korean Legislative Studies*.

ESWARAN SRIDHARAN is the academic director of the University of Pennsylvania Institute for the Advanced Study of India (UPIASI), New Delhi. His research interests are in comparative party systems and coalition politics, political economy of development, and international relations of South Asia. He has written or edited five books, published over 40 journal articles and book chapters, and is the editor of *India Review* (Routledge).

VOLUME IV: AFRICA AND OCEANIA

Africa

ADEKUNLE AMUWO is professor of politics at the Howard College Campus, University of KwaZulu-Natal, Durban, and has recently completed a term as executive secretary of the African Association of Political Science (2004–2009). He is a widely published pan-African scholar and activist. Two recent works are *Constructing the Democratic Developmental State in Africa: A Case Study of Nigeria, 1960–2007* (2008) and a coedited book on *Civil Society, Governance and Regional Integration in Africa* (2009).

NICOLA DE JAGER holds a DPhil in political science from the University of Pretoria and is a lecturer at the political science department of the University of Stellenbosch in South Africa. She has published in peer-reviewed research publications and has consulted locally and internationally on issues of democratization, dominant party systems, political society, and civil society with a specific focus on South African and African politics.

LEAH KIMATHI holds a BED (Hons) from Moi University and an MA in history specializing in international relations from Kenyatta University. She also holds a fellowship in international philanthropy from Johns Hopkins University. A recipient of the Claude Ake Memorial Award in 2004, she has been involved in several research works in the area of the African state and has published in the same. She is programs coordinator with Africa Peace Point, a Pan-African conflict resolution organization, and a part-time lecturer at the Catholic University of Eastern Africa in Nairobi. She is currently a conflict mediator and researcher.

WILLIAM A. LINDEKE now serves as the senior research associate for democracy and governance at the Institute for Public Policy Research (IPPR) in Windhoek, Namibia. He was professor of political science at the University of Massachusetts Lowell (retired) and professor of political studies at the University of Namibia. He has authored or coauthored several book chapters and articles on Namibian politics and on SADC issues. He is co-national investigator for Round Four of the Afrobarometer in Namibia.

ANDRÉ DU PISANI is professor of political studies and former dean of faculty at the University of Namibia (UNAM) and is the director in Namibia of the Southern African Defence and Security Management Network (SADSEM). He is the author, editor, or coeditor of several books and numerous articles on Namibian politics and security issues in the SADC region.

LUC SINDJOUN is professor and head of the political science department at University of Yaoundé II (Cameroon). He is the author of several books, chapters, and articles on comparative politics, African politics, and international relations.

HERMAN TOUO is a lecturer at the University of Ngaoundéré, Cameroon. His PhD dissertation was titled "Les dynamiques d'ancrages du pluralisme partisan au Cameroun (1990–2006): l'economie des rapports entre pouvoir et opposition." He is also interested in youth movements, especially the impact of youth mobilization on democratic governance in Cameroon. He participated as 2002–2003 fellow on Understanding Exclusion, Creating Value: African Youth in a Global Age, a project initiated by the Africa Program of the Social Science Research Council (SSRC).

Oceania

ALUMITA L. DURUTALO is a lecturer in the Division of Politics and International Affairs at the University of the South Pacific, Fiji Islands. She obtained her PhD from the Australian National University in Canberra and specializes in party and electoral politics and customary and modern political leadership in the Pacific. Her numerous journal articles and book chapters include "Fiji: Party Politics in the Post-Independent Period" (Roland Rich et al., eds.).

RAYMOND MILLER is an associate professor and chair of the Department of Politics at the University of Auckland, where he specializes in political parties, representation, electoral systems and elections, and leadership. He has collaborated on a number of election studies, including *Proportional Representation on Trial* (2002) and *Voters' Veto* (2004). Recent publications include *Party Politics in New Zealand* (2005), *New Zealand Government and Politics* (2006), and *Political Leadership in New Zealand* (2006).

GORDON LEUA NANAU is a researcher at the Solomon Islands College of Higher Education (SICHE). In 2009 he completed his PhD at the School of International Development, University of East Anglia, U.K., with a doctoral dissertation on insecure globalization in the South Pacific. His research interests are in the areas of rural development, decentralization, conflicts and peace making, globalization, and international development. His chapter on "Intervention and Nation-Building in Solomon Islands: Local Perspectives" appeared in *Interventionism and State-building in the Pacific: The Legitimacy of "Cooperative Intervention"* (eds. Greg Fry and Tarcisius Tara Kabutaulaka, Manchester University Press, 2008).

MARIAN SIMMS is professor of political studies and Head of Social Sciences at Deakin University in Melbourne, Australia. She has published numerous articles and books including "Australian and New Zealand Politics: Separate Paths but Path Dependent," *The Round Table*, 2006, and *From the Hustings to Harbour Views; Electoral Administration in New South Wales, 1856–2006* (University of NSW Press, 2006). Her next book, *Kevin07: The 2007 Australian Election*, is in press.

ISALEI SIOA is a senior lecturer in history and head of the social sciences department at the National University of Samoa. She has made contributions to the following books, *Lagaga: A Short History of Western Samoa, Tamaitai Samoa (Women of Samoa: Their Stories)*, and has published articles in the *Journal of Arts Faculty*, National University of Samoa.

VOLUME V: THE ARAB WORLD

Arab World

MOHAMED OULD MOHAMED ABDERRAHMANE MOINE is a Professor of Diplomacy in the Ecole nationale d'administration of Nouakchott University in Mauritania. From 1992 to 2008, he occupied diplomatic and governmental positions in Belgium, Canada, and South Africa. He is the author of numerous articles on the subjects of human rights protection, international relations, and democratization.

MOKHTAR BENABDALLAOUI is professor of philosophy and head of the Department of Philosophy at Hassan II University, Casablanca, and director of the Center for Studies and Research in the Humanities.

SAAD EDDIN IBRAHIM is professor of sociology at the American University in Cairo, founding chairman of the Ibn Khaldun Center for Development Studies and founder of the Arab Organization for Human Rights. He is widely known for his work on electoral fraud in Egyptian elections, work that led to his arrest and conviction and a global outpouring of support from scholars, human rights organizations, and political leaders. Recently convicted a third time, he is now in exile. During 2008–2009 he served as professor of political sociology at Indiana University and as the Shawwaf Chair Professor at the Center of Middle East Studies at Harvard University. His numerous awards and publications are listed at http://www.eicds.org.

SALAHEDDINE JOURCHI is a journalist and the vice president of the Tunisian Human Rights League in Tunis.

ABDERRAZAK MAKRI is a medical doctor and holds an M.A. in Islamic law and a post-graduate degree in Management Sciences. He is a founding member of the Movement Society of Peace (MSP) in Algeria and is currently the vice-president of the Movement and an elected member of the Parliament in Algeria. Dr. Makri is the author of several publications, including *Islam and Democracy, Towards an Effective Citizenship*, which was developed by the Center for the Study of Islam and Democracy (CSID) and Street Law, Inc., and has been used as a training manual for NGO leaders and Imams throughout the Arab world.

ANTOINE NASRI MESSARRA is professor of political science at Lebanese University and Saint Joseph University, Beirut. He is president of the Lebanese Political Science Association and program coordinator of the Lebanese Foundation for Permanent Civil Peace.

EMAD EL-DIN SHAHIN is the Henry Luce Professor of Religion, Conflict and Peacebuilding at the University of Notre Dame. He was an associate professor of political science at the American University in Cairo and visiting associate professor of the Department of Government, Harvard University, while writing for this study. His recent works include *Political Ascent: Contemporary Islamic Movements in North Africa* (1997); coeditorship of *Struggling over Democracy in the Middle East and North Africa* (2009); and coauthorship of *Islam and Democracy* (2005, in Arabic).

Neighboring States

YUNUS EMRE is a Ph.D. candidate at Bogazici University, Istanbul, and a graduate assistant at Istanbul Kultur University. His research interests are European and Turkish politics, the economic and social history of modern Turkey, and 20th-century historiography.

YAEL YISHAI is Professor Emerita of political science at the University of Haifa, Israel. She is the author of several books including *Land of Paradoxes. Interest Politics in Israel* (SUNY, 1991) and multiple articles and book chapters on interest groups, civil society, and political parties in Israel. Her current research interests are in the processes leading to "antipolitics" and its outcomes.

Index

Figures indicated by *f*. Tables indicated by *t*.